An Active Learning Approach

Business Skills

THE OPEN LEARNING FOUNDATION

An Active Learning Approach

BUSINESS SKILLS

University of Sunderland,
Open Learning Institute of Hong Kong,
Kevin Gallagher, Bob McClelland,
Christine Swales

BLACKWELL Business

Copyright © Open Learning Foundation Enterprises Ltd, 1998

First published 1998

Blackwell Publishers Ltd
108 Cowley Road
Oxford OX4 1JF
UK

Blackwell Publishers Inc
Commerce Place
350 Main Street
Malden, MA 02148
USA

British Library Cataloguing in Publication Data

A CIP catalogue record for this book is available from
the British Library

Library of Congress Cataloging-in-Publication Data

Library of Congress data has been applied for.

The ISBN for this title is 0–631–20801–1

Typeset in 10 on 12pt Times New Roman

Printed and bound in Great Britain by MPG Books Ltd, Bodmin, Cornwall

This book is printed on acid-free paper

Acknowledgements

For the Open Learning Foundation

Martin Gibson, *series editor*

Christine Swales, *copy editor*

Leslie Mapp, *Director of Programmes*

Stephen Moulds, (DSM Partnership), *Production Manager*

Tim Gutteridge, *Publishing Manager*

Rachel Spungin, *Programmes Assistant*

The Foundation would also like to thank Kathleen Farren and Lynda Kerley for their assistance in producing this text.

Copyright acknowledgements

Contents

Unit 4   Presentation and Social Interaction Skills   137

GUIDE FOR STUDENTS

What is in this workbook?

The core of the workbook is eight study units. These were written specifically for undergraduate business students by authors who are experienced in teaching such courses. The content has been revised as a result of comments from experienced Business Studies tutors who have worked through the material.

The units are particularly useful to students who may be following a course where an open learning approach is being adopted. The features which make it particularly suitable for open learning include:

- very careful sequencing of the materials so that there is a clear and logical progression

- a step-by-step approach so that you will be able to understand each new point thoroughly before proceeding to the next one

- very clear layout with relatively short sections and paragraphs

- numerous short examples which help to illustrate the ideas

- many worked examples with an emphasis on understand the methods and techniques

- lots of opportunities for you to check that you understand what you have just read

- review activities for each unit which enable you to extend and apply your knowledge as well as to test your understanding

- plenty of opportunities for you to test your progress through end-of-unit exercises.

The combination of all these factors should make it possible to develop your understanding of operations management with only limited support from tutors and traditional means such as lectures and seminars. Students on more conventional courses will also find that the workbook provides a useful supplement to other text books which they may have been recommended.

At the back of the book there is a resource section which consists of a collection of journal articles and other materials. This allows you the opportunity of wider reading but in a way which ensures that it is highly relevant to and closely integrated with the material covered in the units.

Unit structure

Unit 1 focuses on study skills and tackles such issues as organising your learning, reading and notetaking skills and preparing assignments. Unit 2 focuses on business communication and looks at theories and models of communication, barriers to communication and formal versus informal communication. Unit 3 and 4 look at the practical application of communication skills. Unit 3 focuses on effective business writing. It looks both at general writing skills and at specific tasks such as writing letters and reports. Unit 4 focuses on presentation and social interaction skills.

Units 5 to 8 focus on a range of computer skills. Unit 5 provides an introduction to Windows and Unit 6 focuses on Wordprocessing with Word 6. Unit 7 deals with Spreadsheets using Excel while Unit 8 looks at databases using Access.

Using the workbook

You will probably find it most effective to work through the units in sequence. You should begin by noting the points which the unit outlines identify as the crucial aspects of the material. This will put the contents of the units into context and guide you through them.

Each unit is interspersed with a number of activities and review activities. All of these are intended to be attempted by you as they arise and completed before you move on. The suggested solutions to each activity are given immediately following the activity. The solutions to the review activities are given at the end of the relevant unit.

The activities are intended to be a combination of a check that you are following and understanding the unit and a way of helping to make your learning a more active experience for you. By working through the activities, you can effectively divide your study time between that which is necessary for taking on new ideas and that which is necessary to reinforce those ideas. Avoid the temptation to skip through the activities quickly. They are there to assist you in developing your understanding of the material.

Typically, the activities will only take you a few minutes to deal with. By contrast, the review activities may take considerably longer to complete and may involve reading an article from the resource section and thinking about the issues raised. It is important that you discipline yourself to complete each activity, self-assessment question or exercise before you refer to the answer provided.

You should read the items in the resource section when recommended. They have been carefully chosen to aid or broaden your understanding of the subject.

There are frequent cross checks in the text to refer you back to where underpinning ideas or techniques have been presented. Do take the time to refer back to these points in order to refresh your memory and test your understanding.

Avoid rote learning

You should avoid any attempt at rote learning the material in this workbook. You should aim to understand the underlying logic in the ideas being presented by working through all the activities. Simply trying to learn the theories or remember the techniques is inappropriate and insufficient. Rather, you should attempt to understand the principles behind the theoretical ideas and models and understand the thinking behind the particular operations management techniques presented. Wherever possible look for connections between the theories and ideas explored here and those covered elsewhere in your Business Studies course.

Set aside time for your studies

At the start of the study period you will not know how long it will take to do the necessary work. It is sensible, therefore, to make a start on the work at an early stage in the study period. Try to discipline yourself to set aside particular times in the week to study, though not necessarily the same times each week. Experiment with different ways of studying the material to find the one which suits you. Try skimming each unit to get a grasp of the ideas covered before you go through it in detail. Alternatively, try reading the unit objectives and the summaries before you settle down to study the unit in depth. Try to find the most suitable time to study when your concentration is at its highest and interruptions are at a minimum. And do set aside sufficient time to complete all the activities – they are a crucial part of the learning process.

INTRODUCTION TO THE MODULE

The title of this module is *Business Skills,* and that is exactly what it covers. What skills do you need in business? You will cover anything from getting a job, writing a letter or a report, doing a presentation, wordprocessing and other computer applications. As you can see there are many different skills involved in these varied functions. Many of the skills you will cover will also benefit you in your studies. To focus on this we have also included a study skills unit that identifies and helps you with any problems you might have in returning to study again. The skills areas in this module are also fundamental to your everyday life whether you are applying for a job, writing a letter to apply for a grant or a mortgage, working out your personal finances on your computer, speaking at a special anniversary or conducting a meeting of your local music society. Whatever your career or your interests, in today's business environments you need to be able to communicate and to use a computer!

An increasing number of skills are required for the workplace, and you will be able to develop the necessary set of skills by working through this module. Business life has become increasingly varied as our environment changes and individuals are required to undertake more and more different functions. The key themes for the future are flexibility and adaptability. Throughout a normal working day, for example, a manager might answer urgent queries in the mail using a wordprocessor and fax, attend a meeting, use a spreadsheet to analyse some sales results to prepare for a presentation and a written report, send a memo to colleagues in other branches, make decisions using information given in a report, manage and direct staff, interview some candidates. Many other issues that take up a lot of the working day are concerned with communication. You will learn more about the fundamentals of communication and how to be more effective yourself.

The computing units are not designed to turn you into programmers or information technologists. They are simply designed to give you the basic techniques for effectively handling some key business software as an end user. We have focused on developing those skills in wordprocessing, spreadsheet and database use within a windows and office environment. The technology and package types now change rapidly but the concepts remain relevant and generic.

The module consists of the following units:

Unit 1: Study Skills

You will find this unit particularly useful if you are a new student as it allows you to assess your learning style and study skills and develop any new techniques you will need to be a successful student. You will cover basic reading and notetaking skills and learn how to approach assignments.

Unit 2: Business Communication

Communication is a vital element of business, and everyday, life. In this unit, you learn the basic theories and types of communication. You look at the structuring of communication within an organisation so you have the basic information to make yourself into a more effective communicator.

Unit 3: Effective Business Writing

Even in today's technological age, the ability to write well is an increasingly essential skill. In this unit, you learn some basics about writing and how to write effective business correspondence – letters, memos and faxes. Then you identify some approaches for compiling reports and how to present them professionally.

Unit 4: Presentation and Social Interaction Skills

One fundamental skill you will require in business is to be able to prepare and deliver an effective presentation whether it is in a small meeting situation or to many people in an auditorium. In this unit, you learn the basic skills of presenting. You then look at ways to get the most out of meetings, whether as a chairperson or as a participant. Again meetings are an essential feature of today's business world. You will prepare a job search file with a covering letter, a curriculum vitae and a follow-up letter. You will learn some tips about the interview process. In the final section, you learn about the culture of an organisation and how this affects the recruitment process.

Unit 5: Introduction to Computers and Windows 3.1

In business today, you will need some basic computing skills. In this unit, you learn some basics about your computer and the Windows environment.

Unit 6: Wordprocessing with Word 6

In this unit, you develop your wordprocessing skills using Word 6. You will learn the fundamentals and some more advanced techniques that will help you in presenting your correspondence and reports.

Unit 7: Spreadsheets using Excel

In this final unit, you learn the basics of spreadsheets using Excel. You will be able to present numbers and results effectively in your written reports and in your presentations.

Unit 8: Databases using Access

You learn some fundamentals about databases so you can set up and use your own. They have a variety of uses in business. Using Access will enable you to get the most from your data.

This module provides you with a foundation for some of the basic skills essential for a career in business. However, full development of these skills, and the true test of how well you have acquired them, will only come from applying them in real-life business situations.

UNIT 1
STUDY SKILLS

Introduction

Whether you left school last year or many years ago, you may find that your learning skills – reading, studying, notetaking, and assignment preparation – need to be changed or improved to cope with the demands of *Business Skills* and your other degree or diploma modules. In this unit, you will be able to assess your learning style and study skills and, if necessary, develop new techniques that you will need to be a successful student. If you are a continuing university or college student you need only skim this unit.

As an adult student studying for a qualification by different learning methods, you need to be aware of two major differences from studying at secondary school level. Firstly, you are in charge of your learning; secondly, you will find that even more demands will be placed on your time.

To complete your studies successfully, you will need study skills and techniques that are much more efficient than those that you used at school. Those of you who are returning to study after a long break may also find that you are out of practice in the study skills you *did* have. However, as a more mature learner, you have many advantages. You bring to the learning situation experience, skills, and knowledge. These factors will be a great help to you because higher education courses are *not* about memory recall, but about *understanding, thinking, evaluating,* and *applying knowledge*. Rote learning methods are inadequate and inappropriate for the module you are beginning. This module particularly is about learning through 'doing', and you will be able to develop these skills as you study and in your business life.

You may have some difficulty with the amount of reading required in some of your studies particularly as most textbooks have been written by academics and subject specialists. It is important that you become as efficient as possible in your study techniques. The first step is to assess your current skills.

In this unit we guide you in some techniques and disciplines that you will need to be a successful student. The *Assess your learning style or other skills* questionnaires that follow are for **your** information only. Try hard to be very honest with yourself. Most of us find this surprisingly difficult! You do not need to show your results to anyone.

When you come to an *Assess your learning style or other skills* questionnaire in this unit, follow these steps before progressing to the next topic:

1   Do the questionnaire. Try to be honest with yourself about what you *usually* do.

2   Follow the instructions at the end of the questionnaire.

3   For those questionnaires where you give yourself a score, use your score to decide how much time and effort you need to spend on the topic that follows.

Remember that you are in charge of your learning. The skills you will acquire in being an effective student will also be invaluable to you in your business life.

Objectives

By the end of this unit, you will be able to:

● determine your preferred learning style

● assess how organised you are for studying

● assess how efficiently you use texts

● assess your notetaking skills

● identify the importance and use of a bibliography

● identify approaches to undertaking university or college assignment work.

1.1 Approaches to learning

'There has been a recent upsurge of interest in student learning styles. Much of this has been concerned with the need to understand the different ways students learn and the strategies that can be devised both to suit individual needs and to improve the effectiveness of student learning generally.

Learning styles are best understood as the characteristics which a student brings to studying and learning situations. These characteristics have evolved over time as a result of both the individual's experiences and personality.'

(Lashley, 1995)

Pask (1976) has showed that many students adopt one of two approaches to learning, when faced with new problems. He termed these **holistic** and **serialist** approaches. Using a holistic approach, an individual tends to overview the situation, attempting to gain a broad outline of the problem before fitting in the details later. The serialist uses the opposite approach, coming to terms first with the details, then building up a complete picture through a step-by-step approach.

Kolb (1984) developed a model for understanding how students effectively learn from experience (**experiential model**). Kolb sees effective experiential learning as resulting from students following a four-stage learning cycle of *feeling, watching, thinking* and *doing*.

● **Feeling** (concrete experience) – learning through the feelings developed when undergoing specific experiences. The learning task relies more on intuition than logic, as it takes place by being immersed in a problem.

- **Watching** (reflective observation) – this involves careful consideration of previous experience, or watching, listening and careful reflection before taking action.

- **Thinking** (abstract conceptualisation) – involves analysis of the problem and the application of reflections so as to develop theories for the future. This process will often depend on logical thought and the development and testing of hypotheses.

- **Doing** (active experimentation) – learning at this stage involves the application of thoughts and ideas. It involves learning through trial and error, developing and amending theories to suit the situation.

Most people have a 'preferred learning style' which implies a tendency to emphasise one of these stages. A knowledge of your own preferred learning style will help you to arrange your studies to best effect, or to achieve a more balanced learning style.

Many writers support the Kolb model and a number including Lashley (1995), have suggested that there are two broad strategies which students adopt when undergoing learning:

- **surface learning** which is associated with an instrumental approach to learning, where the student views learning as a chore to be undertaken in pursuit of some desired goal; and

- **deep approach** to learning is used by students who seek to make sense of what they learn. These students actively follow up learning by setting new information against what they (the students) know already.

ACTIVITY 1

Read the introduction of Resource Item 1.1 and undertake the learning styles questionnaire. This item is part of a chapter taken from Lashley (1995) *Improving Study Skills*. Attempt the questionnaire and self assessment, you can read the rest of the item at the end of this unit. This questionnaire should take no longer than 30–35 minutes to complete and assess and will give you a valuable insight into your own learning preferences.

1.2 Organising yourself for study

You now undertake an *Assess your skills* questionnaire to examine how well organised you are for study. You focus on the most important organisational skills you will need to be a successful student.

ACTIVITY 2

Assess how organised you are for studying.

Answer the following questions:

Where to study

1 Do you have a specific place (desk, table, etc.) where you can study?

2 Will you be able to avoid distractions (TV, phone, family) when you are studying?

3 Do your family and friends understand your need for regular, uninterrupted study time?

4 If you will be studying at work, can you reduce the number of interruptions you will have?

When to study

5 Do you have the appropriate numbers of hours per week available for the modules you are studying?

6 Will you have enough time left after work, study and family commitments to get some exercise and have some relaxation?

If you have answered 'no' to any question, read the relevant part of section 1.2.

WHERE TO STUDY

You may not have an ideal place where you live or work in which to study – very few people do. Nevertheless, there are a few things you can do to improve the situation:

- Whenever you study, try to study in the same place. After a while, this will help you to get started quickly.

- You will need a table or desk, a chair (preferably not an armchair), and a good light. You will also need a place to keep your books and study materials. Try to keep your study area equipped with paper, pens, etc. so that you do not waste valuable study time looking for supplies. Perhaps you are lucky enough to have your own computer.

- Get rid of anything from your study area that might distract you. At home, such things as magazines, CD players, photo albums, etc. are hard to resist when you are tired but you still have to study. If you are studying at work, try to clear your desk of other tasks.

- If it is impossible for you to study effectively where you live, investigate the university or college library or resource centre, your local library or your workplace (after colleagues have gone home) as possible study venues.

- If you are studying at home, try to get away from other family members and distractions such as the telephone and the television set. At work, tell your work colleagues about your study programme and ask them to interrupt you as little as possible.

WHEN TO STUDY

Time, or a lack of it, is likely to be your greatest problem. As an adult student, you will probably have work, family, and study commitments all competing for your time. It is difficult, particularly when you start, to keep everything balanced. However, most students find that things improve after their first semester. You need to find the balance and way of studying that suits you. Everyone is different, so although we can make some suggestions, they may not be helpful to you. You will need to experiment and work out what is best for you.

- You need at least 10 hours a week to study, read, and do exercises and assignments for a module such as this. Look carefully at how you usually spend your time each week. You may find that you have to give up something you enjoy to make enough time.

- If you are returning to study, remember that it can be a very difficult time for your family and friends as well as for you. Face this first by discussing with them any necessary changes in your lifestyle and any re-allocation of duties and responsibilities. You will need to be clear about the times you need to be left undisturbed.

- Make use of any spare time you have. For example, if you are a regular traveller by train, bus or ferry, you may be able to use this time for short sections of reading or revision. Time spent waiting for appointments can also be used in this way.

- You should leave some time for exercise and leisure activities. It is important not to let your studies affect your health. If you spend all your time working and studying, then you, your family, and your studies will suffer.

HINTS ON PLANNING YOUR STUDY

- At the beginning of each module, plan the study sessions you think you will need to get the work done.

- On the same day each week, make a detailed study plan for the week ahead. Try to be very specific about:
    - **when** you will study
    - **how long** you will study for
    - **what** you will study in each session.

Try to get into the habit of studying six days a week. If possible, give yourself a day off. This will prevent you from feeling overwhelmed by study and will help you to work more efficiently on the other days. On the other hand, try not to be away from your studies for more than one day if you can, as it will take longer to get started again. Everyone has their own particular way of studying; there are no hard and fast rules about how and when you should put in the hours. With this module particularly the quickest and most effective way of learning is by applying the theory and techniques in a real situation.

SUGGESTED PROCEDURE FOR A STUDY SESSION

- Work out your study goals for the session. They might be:
    - completing a section in a unit, together with activities and readings
    - taking notes for an assignment
    - drafting an assignment
    - completing an assignment
    - revising units to prepare for an examination.
- In this module, the units are designed to assist you in this planning. You will find the work divided into sections that allow you to begin and break off your study at many different points.
- Review what you did in your last session.
- If possible, do the activities as you come to them. This will not always be possible because some activities require you to do surveys or observe behaviour. Activities are located in each unit to help you turn theory into practical applications.
- Take a 5–10 minute break every hour, especially if you are studying for a few hours at a stretch.
- End each session by reviewing what you have achieved in the session. Did you achieve what you set out to do? If not, what do you plan to do about it? Jot down the starting point for your next session.

Make a reminder list of things you must do in order to get yourself organised.

1.3 Reading skills

The following questionnaire allows you to assess your reading skills and associated techniques. You can then determine if they are efficient enough for your future studies. However, you will probably feel that, no matter how much time you spend reading, it is not enough. You will need to:

- be selective in what and how much you read.
- be organised so that you can retrieve what you have studied for use at a later date.

ACTIVITY 3

Assess your textbook reading skills

Instructions

Read each question carefully. Circle one of the letters after the question, according to the following:

A = You almost ALWAYS do what the question asks

S = You SOMETIMES do what the question asks

N = You almost NEVER do what the question asks

Questions:

1 Do you read the preface, foreword, and introduction of your prescribed textbooks?   **A   S   N**

2 At the beginning of a module, do you preview your prescribed texts by skimming the table of contents and analysing the format of the book?
                                                                      A   S   N

3 Do you know when and where your textbook was published?
                                                                      A   S   N

4 Do you have a specific purpose in mind each time you read your text?
                                                                      A   S   N

5 Do you ask yourself questions about what you already know *before* reading each topic?   **A   S   N**

6 Do you vary your *speed* of reading according to your *purpose* for reading?
                                                                      A   S   N

7 Do you read the summaries in your text *first?*   **A   S   N**

8 Do you make thorough use of the illustrations, graphs, tables, and other visual aids in your text?   **A   S   N**

9 Do you use the index to find *specific* ideas, information, names, etc.?

                                                      A   **S**   **N**

10 Do you mark your texts with underlining, marginal notes, etc.?

                                                      A   **S**   **N**

SCORING AND INTERPRETING:
How to score

1 Add up the number of **A, S,** and **N** answers you had.

2 Multiply the number of **A** answers by **5,** the **S** answers by **3,** and the **N** answers by **1.**

How to interpret your score

40–50   You are reasonably competent in the use of textbooks. Quickly skim the section, *Getting to know your textbooks,* then move on to the next section.

30–40   You have a fairly good idea of how to use a textbook in a way appropriate for your needs, but a few reading techniques need to be developed. Work through the section, *Getting to know your textbooks,* concentrating on ideas that are new to you.

Under 30   You really need to work on your reading techniques before you go any further with your studies. Go through the section, *Getting to know your textbooks,* point by point.

1.4 Getting to know your textbooks

PREVIEWING YOUR TEXT
We suggest you use this procedure with the main texts of *each* module you are doing. Fifteen minutes spent on getting to know your text at the *beginning* of a module can save you many hours of study.

1 Get information from the title page and the back of the title page. Find the following:

– the date of first publication

– the edition and year of edition

– the 'nationality' of the book

– the International Standard Book Number (ISBN).

Now you know how up-to-date or current your text is. Keep in mind that texts take a while to produce, so for really up-to-the-minute information you need to read journals, magazines or newspapers. Some texts however, are useful for many years. You always need to know the age of the text you are working from.

You should try to have the UK edition. This means that some of the content has been written or adapted to make it more useful to British readers.

You may have a book that is American, for example. Therefore, you must expect an American flavour even in an adapted version.

The quickest way to order a text is by quoting its ISBN number. It is also usually on the back cover.

2   Read the preface. Notice in particular any description of how the book can be used. If your text has a foreword or an introduction, you should also read this.

3   Get an overview of the whole text. Turn to the table of contents. Focus on the *structure* or *organisation* of the text and what it has to offer you. First, look at the text as a whole. Identify the sections and parts into which the text is divided.

   –   What are the headings of the main parts?

   –   Are there any appendices? Consider when these appendices may be useful.

   –   Is there a glossary or an index?

   –   Is there a resource section?

   By doing this first, you will get an overview of the textbook.

4   Narrow down to chapter or unit. Read the chapter or unit headings only. How many are there?

5   Narrow further to Chapter or Unit 1, Section 1. Turn to the first page and follow these steps:

   –   Read the main headings. You may find these on the contents page of the module and in the chapter or unit itself.

        Do not read anything else at this stage.

   –   Read the first paragraph. This forms the introduction to the section or unit.

   –   Flick through the unit, reading the subheadings and having a quick look at the diagrams and illustrations.

– If there are activities or assessment questions read one or two to discover what they are like.

– Cases. Note but do not read.

– References. Note but do not read.

– Recommended Readings. Note but do not read.

6 Turn back to the table of contents and check what you now know:

– You know what the unit or chapter is generally about; that is, you have some background knowledge to build on.

– You know how the unit or chapter is organised. This will help you to remember what you read.

– You know how long and how difficult the unit or chapter is and approximately how much time you need to allow yourself to study it.

This survey should take you no more than 15 minutes. Investing this time pays good dividends. Try it and you will find that with practice even a few minutes will give you an overall idea of the content and layout of the materials. You can review other texts and modules in your education or training programme like this. It is also a useful approach to your general reading, for example, if you are at work it is very helpful for reading long reports.

EFFICIENT READING

You should note two important general points about reading:

● You need to relate what you read to what you already know.

Reading is about *extracting meaning from print* and *bringing meaning to print*. You can only comprehend or understand what you read if you build a bridge between what you know and what is new. This is why you should think about your existing knowledge before you begin to read a new topic.

You may think that you know absolutely nothing about a topic, but this is rarely the case. For example, if you are reading about the theory of communication barriers, think of a time when you were frustrated because you could not understand an instruction someone had given you. Think about how you felt and what was causing the problem. This will help you to understand when you read about the theory of communication barriers.

● Reading is an active process.

If you just let your eye pass over the words you will achieve very little. You must know what you are looking for and why you are reading. Knowing your purpose for reading will help you to choose an appropriate speed and method of reading. It is very inefficient to read everything at the same speed and in the same way. To be an *efficient reader* you need a whole range of techniques that you can use:

- You can **scan** to find specific information.
- You can **skim** to get general ideas or background knowledge.
- You can **study read** and **take notes** as you go when you need to understand important ideas.
- You can **skip** parts of the text if the part has nothing to do with your current purpose.

Check your reading strategies. It is easy to get into the habit of reading everything in the same way. Remember that you are in charge of your learning. Your time is precious – read efficiently.

1.5 Notetaking skills

When you study, you need to take notes you can use at a later date, perhaps for assignments or for exam preparation. A questionnaire follows that will enable you to find out how efficiently you take notes. Your score will tell you how much work you need to do to improve your skills.

ACTIVITY 4

Assess your notetaking skills

Instructions:

Read each question carefully. Circle one of the letters after the question, according to the following:

A = You almost ALWAYS do what the question asks

S = You SOMETIMES do what the question asks

N = You almost NEVER do what the question asks

1   Do you keep your notes in a ring binder or on computer?

                                                       A   **S**   **N**

2   Do you keep your notes well organised and together so that you can refer to them easily when necessary?   **A**   **S**   **N**

3   When you take notes from various sources, do you keep a record of the author, title, publisher, etc.?

                                                         A   **S**   **N**

4	Do you usually take notes in your own words?		**A**	**S**	**N**
5	Do you take care to write down the author's exact words for definitions and quotations if you intend to use them later?		**A**	**S**	**N**
6	Do you keep your notes brief?		**A**	**S**	**N**
7	Do you use your own set of special abbreviations and symbols in your notes?		**A**	**S**	**N**
8	Do you highlight key words and phrases in your notes and text, for example, by using a highlighter pen or underlining?		**A**	**S**	**N**
9	Do you concentrate on noting the main points?		**A**	**S**	**N**
10	Do you look for the main sentence in a paragraph when taking notes?		**A**	**S**	**N**

SCORING AND INTERPRETING:
How to score

1   Add up the number of **A, S,** and **N** answers you had.

2   Multiply the number of **A** answers by **5,** the **S** answers by **3,** and the **N** answers by **1.**

How to interpret your score

40–50   You know quite a lot about how to take notes efficiently. Quickly skim the section, *Developing your notetaking skills,* then move on to the next topic.

30–40   You have some good notetaking strategies, but you need to develop others before you continue. Work through the section, *Developing your notetaking skills,* concentrating on ideas that are new to you.

Under 30   You need to work on your notetaking skills before you go any further with your studies. Go through the section, *Developing your notetaking skills,* point by point.

DEVELOPING YOUR NOTETAKING SKILLS
As a student, you must develop the ability to extract all the information you need from your texts, and from any additional reading you do. You need to be able to organise, study, understand, and retrieve this information.

One of the greatest aids to doing all this is to take good notes while you read. Taking your own notes requires you to pull together all the main points in an organised way. Making clear notes will help you to understand and remember the material.

There are two main ways of doing this. You should aim to use *both* methods together.

1   In your texts and workbooks, you can:

   –   Underline key points and number supporting points.

   –   Highlight key sentences with a highlighter pen.

   –   Write questions in the margin.

   –   Draw a line down the margin to mark more than one line of important text.

   –   Highlight key structure words, for example, *first, second: not only . . . but also.*

2   On notepaper or index cards, you can:

   –   Write down the author's main thoughts and supporting detail in your own words.

   –   Copy out word for word quotable quotes and definitions that you may need to use or learn.

   –   Draw diagrams which show the material's organisation and line of argument.

   –   Note bibliographical information of the source you are using. (See *Noting bibliographical information.*)

ORGANISING YOUR NOTES

Once you have written your notes, you must make sure you organise them so that they are easy for you to find and use.

You can use a ring binder, inserting your notes, summaries, and answers to activities. Or you can use index cards with appropriate storage. If you are using a computer to compile your module notes, you still need to be organised so you can retrieve information later.

NOTING BIBLIOGRAPHICAL INFORMATION

You must make a habit of noting the details of any book from which you are taking notes. This is sometimes referred to as a **working bibliography**. There are two good reasons for doing this. First, you may want to refer to the book again, and you will be able to find it much more easily if you have kept accurate bibliographical details. Second, if you are using your notes in the preparation of an assignment, you will need the details for your footnotes and references and you will need to make sure that you do not plagiarise.

If you are using index cards for your notes, put bibliographical information on one side and notes on the other. This allows you to sort references into alphabetical order easily when you are compiling a bibliography or set of references. Alternatively, as your computer skills develop, you may wish to commit your bibliographies to files, on a wordprocessor or a database. You will have more help with use of technology in later units in this module. Many CD ROM and World Wide Web (WWW) search facilities now exist which allow you to save reference material and abstracts from databases for example. However, be very careful of plagiarism if you use any of this material in your assignments.

You need to include the key idea, the author, date, title of book, city and publisher and page numbers if it is a book reference, and the title of the article, the journal, volume and issue numbers if it is an article. Also add in a reminder to yourself of where you located your reference, in a book you own, or borrowed from the library, for example.

EXAMPLE OF A WORKING BIBLIOGRAPHY:

> **Format of business letters**
>
> Morgan, D H (1990) *Effective Business Letters*
>
> London: Pitman
>
> pages 45–65   (borrowed from David)

> **Format of business letters**
>
> Morgan, D H (1994) 'Writing for success',
>
> *Journal of Business Studies,* vol. 3, issue (4), pp. 23–27
>
> (College library)

Practise by noting the bibliographical details for any modules you are currently studying. Depending on your computer skills, you may wish to construct a bibliographic database on computer, initially, or at a later stage. See Unit 7 for help on this.

PLAGIARISM
This section is important. Please read it carefully.

Plagiarism is copying or imitating the language, ideas, thoughts, or writings of someone else and pretending that the work is your own. Lecturers and tutors find plagiarism easy to identify, either because they know the text or because of a difference in writing style. **Plagiarism is theft** of another's work and is taken very seriously in academic circles. Check with your institution on what official action it will take in cases of plagiarism. But in any event, **don't**. Plagiarising inadvertently is not an excuse. You must make sure that your notetaking and any copying of materials from your texts or reference works is properly identified as you do it, so that when you come back to the material for an assignment, you know whose material and ideas you are working with. You may forget and think they are yours!

Plagiarism is something you need to remember throughout your academic and business life. In business, if you try to pass off someone else's ideas as your own in a report, for example, it may have serious legal implications.

1.6 Preparing assignments

Here we give you a few ideas on how to prepare and present assignments. Hopefully, you will find this information useful for all modules with assignments. We suggest you skim this section in order to know what it contains. You should return to it and use it as a guide when you begin your first assignment.

PREPARATION
1   Check that you know all the following about the assignment:

- what the question means
- what the assignment requires you to do
- how many marks it is worth
- when it is due
- how long it should be
- how it will be assessed
- what your mark means.

What the question means
The following list contains the typical words you find in assignment questions. The explanation of their meaning will usually give you some ideas on how to structure your assignment.

Analyse	Means to find the *main ideas* and show *how they are related* and why they are important.
Comment on	Means to *discuss, criticise,* or *explain* its meaning as completely as possible.
Compare	Means to show both the *similarities* and *differences.*
Criticise	Means to give your judgement or reasoned *opinion* of something, showing its *good and bad* points. It is not necessary to attack it. Throughout your period of study you will need to refine your critical and evaluative skills. This will mean identifying good writing, balanced non-bias views and misleading unsupported comments.
Define	Means to give the *formal meaning* by distinguishing it from related terms. This is often a matter of giving a memorised definition.
Describe	Means to write a detailed account or verbal picture in a *logical sequence* or story form.
Diagram	Means to make a *graph, chart,* or *drawing.* Make sure you *label* it and add a *brief* explanation if it is needed.
Discuss	Means to describe, giving the *details* and explaining the *arguments for* and *against* it.
Enumerate	Means to list. *Name* and *list* the main ideas one by one. Number them.
Evaluate	Means to give your opinion or some *expert's opinion* of the truth or *importance* of the concept. You should outline any *advantages* and *disadvantages.*
Illustrate	Means to explain or make it clear by *concrete examples, comparisons,* or *analogies.*
Interpret	Means to give the *meaning,* using *examples* and *personal comments* to make it clear.
Justify	Means to give a statement of *why you think it is so.* Give *reasons* for your statement or conclusion.
List	Means to produce a *numbered list* of words, sentences, or comments. It means the same as *enumerate.*

Outline	Means to give a general summary. It should contain a *series of* main ideas supported by secondary ideas. *Omit minor details.* Show the organisation of the ideas.
Prove	Means to show by *argument* or *logic* that it is true. In mathematics and physics, the word 'prove' has a very specific meaning.
Relate	Means to show the *connections* between things, telling how one *causes* or is *like* another.
Review	Means to give a *survey* or *summary* in which you look at the *important parts* and *criticise* where needed.
State	Means to describe the *main points* in precise terms. Be *formal.* Use brief, clear sentences. *Omit details* and *examples.*
Summarise	Means to give a *brief,* condensed account of the *main ideas. Omit details* and *examples.*
Trace	Means to follow the *progress* or *history* of the subject.

(Study Skills Program – Student Counselling Service, Monash University)

What the assignment requires you to do

To gain marks for assignments, you must answer the questions asked. If the assignment question has parts, do each part. Showing your tutor that you have done the reading is not enough to gain marks. You must apply your knowledge by answering the specific question.

How many marks it is worth

This is a useful guide to how much effort you should put into your assignment. Make sure you do not spend the same amount of time, for example, on assignments worth 10% or 20% of the total module mark. You can find out the assignment weighting, that is, what percentage of the total module marks it is worth, by referring to your tutor or module information.

When is it due

You should find out the due date as soon as you can and allot time for preparation in your study schedule. Submission of late work can send out the wrong signals, such as an inability to organise yourself or meet deadlines and lack of discipline. More seriously, it may mean that the work could automatically be failed.

How long should it be

Your assignment question will give you a suggested number of words for each assignment. This word count gives you an idea of the amount of detail the tutor expects in your assignment. This is only a rough guide. No one will count the words, but your tutor will know if it is too long or too short by your treatment of the content.

The next full A4 page of writing you do, count up the words. This will give you an idea of how many words you write or type to a page. You can then judge easily how many pages your assignment should be. If you are using a computer or wordprocessor, find out if it has a word count facility. Remember also to always use a spell check.

How will it be assessed

You should find a guide to how each assignment is assessed in the module outline. Read this carefully before you begin each assignment to guide you on distributing your effort.

What your mark means

Assignments will be marked using your university's or college's marking scale. This may mean, for example, that 40% is a Pass. This will mean that your scores for assignments may seem lower than you are accustomed to.

2   Read, taking notes, as suggested in *Notetaking skills*. Make sure you note bibliographical details as you go, as you will probably need to return to some of your references.

3   Begin writing! You can adopt one of two approaches here.

From a plan

Using your notes, work out an outline or plan for your assignment. Your outline should be detailed and contain an introduction, body, and conclusion if the assignment is in essay or discussion form. Turn the points in your plan into a draft.

From a draft

The second approach is to begin writing a rough draft without any attention to organisation at this stage. Then sit down and look at what you have written and work out the most effective way of organising it.

Whichever approach you begin with, the final product must:

● answer the question

● be arranged clearly and logically

● should be edited, proof read and spell-checked to ensure that the English is simple, clear, and correct.

In Unit 3 we discuss writing techniques in detail. These will help not only in the report writing approach that we outline but also in writing your assignments. This unit will help you with the overall structure and in the detailed paragraph and sentence structure.

PRESENTATION

Your university or college *Student Handbook* or guides from your tutor should provide you with details on layout and presentation of your assignments. Note also some of the comments we make about report writing in Unit 3, these will help you here too. Make sure also that you get the most from your wordprocessing package, if you are using a computer, so you can use the same basic format for each assignment. See Unit 6 for more help on this. Don't forget to file your assignment too on computer. You will need to submit a hard copy for marking. Many lecturers will not accept an assignment unless it is typed, so make sure you check this first.

ACKNOWLEDGING YOUR SOURCES OF INFORMATION

Whenever you use a quotation, an idea, or a thought that belongs to someone else, you need to acknowledge the source. When marking your assignments, your tutor needs to know the source of your references in case he or she wants to check the context and to check that you are not plagiarising. There are many ways of acknowledging sources; however, the method we recommend is the author-date system. This system has two parts:

- in-text references
- a bibliography at the end of your assignment.

In-text references

In the text, when you quote from, or refer to, a source, you need only write the surname of the author, the date of the publication, and the page number(s) in parentheses:

Your posture – the way you stand or sit – is the first major influence on the initial impression you make. (Munter, 1991, p. 259)

According to Jones (1996, p. 27)

Richardson (1994, p. 74)

Notice that, in the last two examples, the author's name can be omitted from the parentheses to avoid needless repetition.

Bibliography

This is a complete list of references at the end of your assignment or essay. The minimum information needed is: author's name, date of publication, title of article or book, journal details with volume and issue number for an article, and place of publication and publisher details for a book.

With the author-date system, list your references in alphabetical order according to the author's surname. You do not need to show the page numbers you actually consulted in a book, but you do for a journal article.

Knapp, M L (1989) 'Writing for success', *Journal of Business,* vol. 23, issue (4), 34-38.

Rosenblatt S B, Cheatham T R and J T Watt (1992) *Communication in Business* 2nd edition, Englewood Cliffs, NJ: Prentice Hall.

There are many acceptable ways of documenting your references. We suggest that you check for each module you are doing to see if a special format is required. The most important thing to remember is that you must acknowledge the work of others. If you do not, you are guilty of plagiarism.

Remember to refer to this section when you are ready to do your first assignment.

ACTIVITY 5

Consider another module that you are studying as well as *Business Skills*. Note any references and recommended readings that you have been given by your tutor or included in the module materials. Construct a bibliography as a database, wordprocessed file or card index using this information. You may like to repeat this activity when you have studied Unit 8 on databases.

REVIEW ACTIVITY 1

Read the remainder of Resource Item 1.1 from the book by Lashley (1995).

Consider your preferred learning style that you determined in Activity 1. This will undoubtedly change through your years of study and you may wish to reassess yourself periodically. How do you think your preferred style relates to the concepts of deep and surface learning?

Unit Summary

In this unit, you have undertaken a series of self-assessments which have enabled you to identify your preferred learning style, determine how well organised you are for study, undertake an examination of how efficient you are at using texts and make an assessment of your notetaking skills.

In addition to these assessments you have explored the use of bibliographies and approaches to undertaking assignments. Remember the penalties for intended or inadvertent plagiarism. It's not worth it!

References

Bentley, M (1991) *Mary Munter's Business Communication: Strategy and Skill,* Prentice Hall, Singapore

Gibbs, G (1992) *Improving the Quality of Student Learning,* Technical and Educational Services, London

Honey, P and Mumford, A (1986) *Manual of Learning Styles,* BBC Books, London

Lashley, C (1995) *Improving Study Skills: a Competence Approach,* Cassell, London

Kolb, D A (1984) *Experimental Learning,* Prentice Hall, Englewood Cliffs, NewJersey

Pask, G (1976) 'Styles and Strategies of Learning', *British Journal of Educational Psychology,* 46, 128–148

Answer to Review Activity 1

One of the major influences on an individual's approach to study is his or her learning style. The learning styles we all exhibit take contributions from **abstract conceptualisation** (thinking), **concrete experience** (feeling), **active experimentation** (doing) and **reflective observation** (watching). There is obviously an ability to lean more towards deep learning based on the degree to which we exhibit one or more of these styles. Lashley identifies the four learning styles as **theorists** who learn through intellectual analysis; **pragmatists** who learn through practical experiences; **activists** who learn through active experiences; and **reflectors** who learn through observation. These are based on Honey and Mumford's learning cycle of experiencing, reviewing, concluding and planning.

It is probably the case that there are many psychological, social and personal factors that influence our approaches to study which extend beyond the context of this unit. When these are coupled with the fact that the styles can be modified, adapted and changed, the processes by which we could possibly approach study become extremely complex.

UNIT 2
BUSINESS COMMUNICATION

Introduction

Communication is essential in all business. It is important at all levels and in all areas of organisations what ever they do and where ever they are. In this unit, we look at some basic communication theory that you need to understand to help you communicate more effectively. This will lead you on to Units 3 and 4 when we cover written and spoken communication. Communication is a complex subject as we, as human beings, are complex, our work tasks are complex and our world is becoming increasingly more complex.

Communication skill is an enabling factor that allows us to perform the work of the organisation. It is essential for business success and as an individual, you need to be an effective communicator for your future career.

We look at some communication models and some effects on and barriers to the communication process. It is obviously important for us to understand how these might arise, if we want to improve organisational effectiveness and efficiency. We also consider how organisational structure affects the flow of information required for co-ordination, decision-making and awareness.

The term **communication** covers a vast field of study. There are many books you can consult on specific skills such as report writing, presentations, interviews, and body language. Our aim here is to cover basic concepts which will help you in the world of communication at work.

Objectives

By the end of this unit, you will be able to:

- explain what organisational communication means and its importance in management
- identify types and examples of verbal and non-verbal communication
- understand the basic features of some models of communication
- analyse barriers to communication
- explain how communication occurs within formal organisation structures
- explain the role of communication in decision-making and its relation to centralised and decentralised systems
- discuss the advantages of both formal and informal communication networks in the organisation.

SECTION 1

Communication: Some Theories and Models

Introduction

We must first look at what communication is. What is its purpose? Why is it so important? We investigate some different types of communication including verbal and non-verbal. We use some basic models of communication and see what the problems are with delivering and receiving our message.

1.1 What is communication?

The field of communication covers a wide range of activities and the act of communication includes a number of processes. So how do we define this all-pervasive factor in our lives? How do you communicate? Your answers to this question are probably diverse and un-focussed. We use the case study, *Shopquick Supermarket Chain,* to focus our ideas. Read through it and then answer the questions which follow in the activities throughout the section. Throughout this module, we use case studies so you can try to envisage a situation close to real-life. This gives you the opportunity to apply your knowledge in a practical way and also makes abstract concepts easier to understand. You will find this approach throughout your business studies so you need to become familiar with it.

CASE STUDY

Shopquick Supermarket Chain

Shopquick (UK) Ltd is a major supermarket chain with stores in England and Scotland. It is one of the newer supermarkets which have the policy of discount, no-frills shopping. Its stores compare in size with those of the competition: Food Giant, Aldi and Kwiksave.

Recruitment and training

Reginald Homeworthy is the general manager of the new Sunderland outlet. A man in his late forties and having worked his way 'up through the ranks' he was personally involved in recruiting all of the store's staff – 22 in total. Staff are expected to be able to function in any area of the store, from shelf stacking to checking out shopping at the tills and they have all been specially trained

shelf stacking to checking out shopping at the tills and they have all been specially trained in store by the company's training manager. Later recruits are given careful guidance by one of the two supervisors. Reginald also has a deputy manager, Sheila, to assist him. Sheila has a degree in French and marketing and this is her first job since graduating, although she did spend 6 months of her placement year with Shopquick at one of its London sites.

Store layout

As in many modern stores, the arrangement of items in the store, as well as storage, check-out and access details is well planned. Reginald was insistent that the store had its own bakery –'The smell, it makes customers think of the bread their Granny used to bake' – and has been closely involved with getting the lighting levels right. This is intensely bright in the cold storage areas, and nicely mellow in the bread and cakes section. He has quotas to meet for the company's own brand products so he has had to think of where to position these.

Like all modern supermarkets all of the products have a bar code and the check-outs act as EPOS (electronic point of sale) which means that Reginald knows how well particular lines are selling and what the stock levels are and is prompted by the computer for re-order quantities.

Competition is fierce and Shopquick runs a lean operation which means using the fewest personnel possible. Check-outs are only fully staffed at peak times.

Staff – attitudes and perceptions

Sandra and Barbara were recruited as 'operative staff' from the closely-knit local housing estate. Sandra is in her late teens and still living at home whilst Barbara is a single parent with a two-year-old son, Wayne. They were asked to give their views on various aspects of their jobs. Whilst they are grateful to have a job, they both think that their take-home wage is inadequate. Barbara concedes that if it was not for her mother looking after Wayne, she would not be working at all.

'It's OK, I suppose,' says Sandra guardedly, 'although Mr Homeworthy can be a bit strict at times. I prefer it when Sheila is in charge – she lets the supervisors decide in which order to do jobs, as long as things get done. Whereas, for instance, Mr Homeworthy gives us a print-out from his computer and highlights the stock replacements for us.'

Barbara has different views 'I'm not really bothered about that,' she says, 'but it would be nice if I could be allowed to leave early on Tuesday nights to pick Wayne up – it's my Mum's crafts night and she really likes to go out.'

They both agree that the physical working conditions can be tough. 'Have you seen the size of some of the pallets we're expected to pull around – massive! They're designed for gorillas, not us!' complains Sandra. 'And the rest breaks – half an hour for lunch – if you can get it. Last week both Dawn and Sarah were down with the 'flu and we both had to cover for the whole week; we hardly got a lunch break between us! At this rate we'll be on sick leave too.'

And then there's the issue of smoking, or rather lack of it. Both women readily admit to being nicotine addicts and yet there is a strict no-smoking policy within the store and the rest rooms. As Barbara explains, 'Mr Homeworthy has said that he will sack anyone caught smoking on the premises. By break time we're desperate and used to go in the toilets but now Mr Homeworthy has installed smoke alarms there and so we have to go outside to the car park. Someone told me that he was even thinking of making us change out of our uniform if we needed a smoke but I suppose he realised we'd probably be late getting back so he didn't go ahead with that one.'

Both women have had worse bosses. Reginald is courteous, always greeting his staff with a friendly 'Good morning'. But he doesn't really appear to appreciate their problems, nor is there any mechanism by which he may be made aware of them. In his eyes, 'an efficient store is a happy store', as he so often tells his staff.

'I do enjoy working here, for all that,' says Sandra. Barbara agrees, 'Yes, I know that the money's just as poor as most places around here, but a job's what you make it, isn't it? I mean, at least we can have a good gossip with the other girls. If any of us has a problem we can talk about it here. And old Reggie – he may think he can make us work our socks off but he doesn't have a clue really. We do enough to keep him happy most of the time, although he can't expect miracles for the money he pays us!'

ACTIVITY 1

Can you identify some ways that Reginald communicates with his staff, either on a social level or as the general manager of the store. You can see some in the case study, others you will need to imagine.

You might have included any of the following:
- speech – Good morning!
- gestures (fist shaking, thumbs-up sign)
- facial expressions (smiling, frowning, quizzical, etc)
- grunts, groans, sighs
- silence
- written words
- pictures, diagrams, graphs.

All of these carry some form of message. You might have gone further and included some of the following:

- the way he dresses
- his manner, posture, behaviour, for example, obsequious, domineering
- use of status symbols such as a title or salary, large office or car.

You might have interpreted 'ways' of communication in a different sense and included:

- telephone
- letters
- fax
- memos
- minutes
- meetings
- briefings
- appraisals
- interviews
- electronic data interchange
- computer print-outs.

These are ways in which communication is manifested or expressed. In other words, they are the means by which we communicate. They are not in themselves communication. Computer print-outs, graphs and even language are only tools to enable the process of communication to take place.

Is the passage of speech from one person to another communication? John, Shopquick's office accountant shouts across the room to Jim, the transport manager: 'It's important that we use an accurate rate of depreciation on the new articulated lorries. Do you think it would be more accurate to use a straight-line or a decreasing balance method?'. Communication may or not have taken place in this case. Has Jim, the intended recipient of the information, heard the words spoken? He may be listening to someone else. Have these words been interpreted and meaning given to them? Jim might not have the same background and technical knowledge about accounting terms.

So what is communication? We now consider a few definitions. The first one is the most succinct: 'the exchange of information and the transmission of meaning' (Katz & Kahn, 1966).

Other definitions consider the exchange of information or a process during which symbols are formed and passed between people. For example, communication can be defined as 'sorting, selecting, forming, and transmitting symbols between people to create meaning' (Rasberry & Lemoine, 1986). Words are an example of symbols; meaning does not reside in the words themselves but in the meaning which we, as the recipients, can give them.

The ways in which an organisation communicates to other organisations and the ways in which members communicate to each other is at the heart of what the organisation is, in other words, its culture. These factors lead us towards a definition of communication: 'Organisational communication is an evolutionary, culturally dependent process of sharing information and creating relationships in environments designed for manageable, goal orientated behaviour.' (Fisher, 1993) We look at the significance of culture in Unit 4.

1.2 Purposes of organisational communication

Organisational communication has three main aims or purposes that are interrelated as shown in Figure 1.

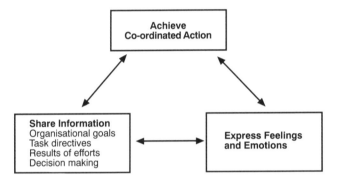

Figure 1: Three purposes of organisational communication
Source: Moorhead & Griffin, 1995

- The first, **achieving co-ordination,** is often considered to be the primary objective; this accords with general concepts of administration and control.

- Clearly, the second, **sharing of information** is closely linked to this need for co-ordination and is linked to strategy and feedback on plans and directives.

- The third objective is not directly linked to either of the other two. If, for example, we feel that something is important, then we need to **communicate that feeling**. If that feeling is concerned with a particular directive or linked to co-ordination then it will, of course, reinforce the message. Other examples might include management wanting to convey its excitement about the launch of a new product or, conversely, its disappointment at losing a major contract.

1.3 Communication and leadership

Managers have a leading role to play in the organisation and in the co-ordination, leading, controlling and planning of work. We can look at the importance of communication by analysing its application within the management situation.

Consider leadership. John Adair, a British leadership 'guru', talks about leadership in terms of achieving the common task, building the team and meeting the needs of individuals. As he says: 'To lead at all requires communication; to lead well requires that a leader communicates effectively' (Adair, 1989).

ACTIVITY 2

At Shopquick, Reginald has been sent by senior management on a week's executive training course in the USA, leaving Sheila to run the supermarket in his absence. No sooner has Reginald's plane taken off when a message from an outside sales representative reaches Sheila that their arch supermarket rival 'Savings-U-Like' has negotiated the lease of a factory unit adjacent to Shopquick and is planning to immediately develop it, already announcing that it will open within the month.

Sheila phones Head Office with the information and faxes the details that she has. Head Office thanks her and vaguely instructs her to 'take appropriate action'. Sheila decides that she needs to act on two fronts. Firstly, to reassure staff that they are not under immediate threat of redundancy as Head Office will support the store and that plans for handling the situation will be given by Reginald upon his return. Secondly, in the meantime, she wants all of the views of the staff in their various departments about how they can improve the service and image of the store.

What do you think might be the main problems facing Sheila in carrying out her two strategies? How might Sheila communicate with her staff to help overcome these problems?

Clearly, Shopquick staff may feel anxious and despondent. They fear that Shopquick may be forced to cut down on staff to remain competitive or even that Head Office may be forced to close the store. Staff may not believe that Head Office will support the store if it becomes unprofitable. Staff may not believe that Sheila carries any authority and not respond to her wish to pool ideas.

As a leader, Sheila's style of communication will need to be adjusted to meet the needs of this particular situation. The ways in which she communicates with her staff will be vital if she is to achieve her stated aims and she will need to spend a lot of time on it. She has had some success with her participative style of leadership and she may wish to capitalise on this.

A good sequence of communication might be to talk firstly to the supervisors to gain their support, and later to all staff. With both audiences, she needs to prove the credibility of herself and the organisation.

Her message needs to be:

- clear

- strong

- conveyed with energy.

She must lead by example and convey this by appearing:

- confident

- determined

- in control.

We should remember the definition of a leader. A leader is someone whom others follow. Also, we may hear but we don't listen. And, although effective communication means that we understand the meaning (we don't have to agree with the message), if we don't listen, how can we follow?

1.4 Verbal and non-verbal communication

In Activity 1, we noted that we can convey meaning not only by words, **verbal** methods, but in other ways which we classify as **non-verbal**.

Some writers also classify the written and oral use of words as separate categories. Figure 2 gives this kind of framework.

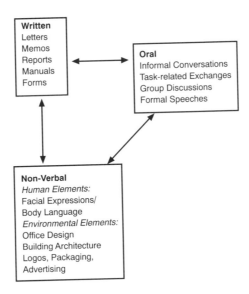

Figure 2: Verbal and non-verbal communication
Source: Moorhead & Griffin, 1995, p. 353

We have already mentioned some of these terms. An example of the environmental elements in Figure 2, might be a managing director's office featuring a large, imposing desk and leather chair to signify the power of the occupant. In Units 3 and

4, we look at various aspects of written and oral communication, and how you can be more effective as a communicator in these. In our discussion of culture, particularly, you will become more aware of some of the non-verbal aspects and how to read them and how to best present yourself. All the categories of communication identified in Figure 2 offer a rich field of study and writers have devoted entire works to areas such as 'body language'.

Body language is the way we communicate through our bodies. We can do this in many different ways. Manning and Curtis (1988) provide the following guidelines:

- **Facial expressions**

  Perhaps the most informative area of our bodies. We might exchange meaning by: smiling, frowning, grinning, blushing, looking worried, anxious, smug, puzzled, satisfied, sly, angry, friendly, tired, energetic, etc.

- **Eye contact**

  This can convey the fact that we seem steady or shifty, interested or dull.

- **Head movement**

  Nods of the head to signify acceptance or encouragement to the other person to continue.

  Shakes of the head to signify non-acceptance.

- **Hand and arm gestures**

  Pointing, beckoning, stopping.

  Folded arms, for instance in a defensive posture.

  Arms uplifted outward, conveying puzzlement or disbelief.

  Hand to mouth whilst talking – can indicate lying!

- **Body posture**

  Fidgeting – nervousness or boredom.

  Hands-on-hips – arrogance or confrontation.

  Slouching – indifference, apathy or depression.

  Shrugging shoulders – uncertainty or disbelief.

- **Dress**

  Business suits – conveying a formal, serious approach to work.

  Casual – informality of the event, for example, a weekend residential course, also denotes the prevailing culture within the organisation, for example, film studio.

Remember these guidelines when you are in an interview or doing a presentation! Non-verbal communication has clearly many dimensions. Even in verbal communication there is often a non-verbal element. As the saying goes 'It's not what you say, it's the way that you say it'. The manner in which we say something will affect the message – this is all part of the discipline of paralinguistics. However, care needs to be taken in interpreting non-verbal communication. Some body language differs markedly between different national cultures or even organisational cultures. Interpreting non-verbal clues from a stranger may be more difficult than with someone whose habitual behaviour you know well. And remember that a skilled communicator will be able to project a desired image by controlling their non-verbal clues.

You can alter your message by the way in which you speak by:

- timing
- emotional tone, inflection
- speech errors, such as umm and err
- national or regional accents
- choice of words, sentence structure
- verbal 'tics', for example, repeated use of 'you know'
- stressing particular words.

Note these seven categories when you are rehearsing your presentation in Unit 4 and next time you want to get your message over in a meeting.

1.5 Five models of communication

To analyse communication more fully in the work situation, it is extremely useful to use models. These models give a simplified view of a complex situation. They enable us to make sense of what is going on. We can use them for further analysis as they provide common terminology and concepts.

Fisher (1993) provides an overview of five well-known models:

- one-way
- interaction
- two-person relationship
- communication-in-context
- strategic model: organisation-environment transaction.

ONE-WAY MODEL

In the one-way model of communication, the sender sends a message to a passive receiver, as depicted in Figure 3. It is the simplest model.

Figure 3: One-way model of communication

Many types of oral communication – speeches, lectures, courtroom arguments, presentations, TV commercials – are often one-way.

Requirements for effectiveness

True one-way communication does not allow for any feedback from the receiver and so the single most important factor for effectiveness is the sender's knowledge of the audience or 'receiver'. In particular, you need to know:

- existing technical knowledge and interests
- likely appeal of the presentation and its approach
- relevance of your topic.

You need to 'put yourself in the audience's shoes' and you need to get it right first time because the audience cannot obtain further clarification.

The next most important factors to communicate successfully are:

- structure and language of the talk
- your delivery of it.

The talk needs to be set up to keep the audience with you. This will mean that you need to:

- tell people where the talk will go
- provide signposts so that they know which stage you have reached
- summarise to indicate the completion of sections and remind the audience of key points covered so far.

You will, of course, need to keep their interest, or else they will simply not listen!

Written one-way

Messages do not have to be delivered orally. Written directives, for instance, and material given in books, journals, magazines, etc is one-way. Again, all of the points given above, structure etc, would apply with regard to the receiver or reader, although there would be a difference in technique. Oral presentations would be short and biased towards impact and key facts; books can be very much longer and go into a lot more depth.

Advantages of one-way communication

One-way communication is widely used and has the following advantages:

- fast and efficient delivery of the message
- easily recorded; this may be done in advance of delivery.

Senders often think that one-way communication is:

- more logical, although, the sender's logic may differ from the receiver's
- it is 'messy' – it doesn't allow for 'distractions' such as the sender not keeping to the topic.

Senders may also favour it if they are short of time, and if there are any controversial issues they do not wish to discuss!

Disadvantages of one-way communication

The major disadvantage with strictly one-way communication is the lack of feedback. This means that mis-judging or not knowing the knowledge, interest, expectations or motivation of the audience can be a problem as the sender does not know whether or not the message has been received.

Poor structure and delivery also mean failure. It is easy to lose the interest of an audience through monotonous delivery, or to antagonise a reader by a pompous, patronising or peremptory tone in a written communication. A report or lecture which is confusingly ordered and not clearly signposted will equally fail to communicate. Remember this when we look at writing a report and preparing an oral presentation in Units 3 and 4.

INTERACTION MODEL

This model assumes that two-way communication is taking place. Even in many so-called 'one-way' situations, the speaker will be looking for signs from the audience. Do they look bored, excited, puzzled, for example? The skilful presenter will alter the talk as he or she proceeds. Two-way communication is happening as the receiver is responding by body language. The speaker might even stop the talk and invite questions if he or she sees a lot of puzzled frowns; he or she has then entered into two-way communication much more fully. Look now at the model in Figure 4.

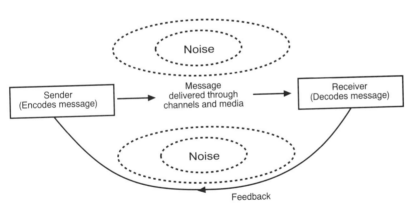

Figure 4: The interaction model

Recall that communication concerns 'the exchange of information and the transmission of meaning'. Another person cannot know what we are thinking, so we need to use some form of symbols, such as language, to form a message. The process by which the sender achieves this is called **encoding**.

Channels and media

The message is sent via one or more **channels** or cues. In face-to-face conversation, for instance, we might typically use the five sensory channels of:

- sight
- sound
- touch
- smell
- taste.

Fisher (1993) defines channels in the broad sense as 'the means by which senders convey messages: oral; written; and non-verbal'. Often a message carries more force if it is repeated or delivered through more than one channel. Thus a face-to-face conversation is likely to be more effective than a telephone conversation because in addition to using sound, you can use sight, for instance, facial expressions, and touch.

We could use various **media** to assist us. Fisher defines media as 'the various tools or vehicles of communication'. A talk could make use of a microphone or a television programme. A written message might be given on a letter, a fax or electronic mail (e-mail). Note also that the medium itself can have an impact upon the effectiveness of the message; for instance, a fax carries more urgency than a letter. Figure 5 suggests the most effective media and channels for various types of communication.

Media	Characteristics		Best for Communications that are:
	Feedback	Cues and Channels	
Face-to-face	Immediate	Audio and Visual	Ambiguous, emotional divergent in background
Telephone	Rapid	Audio	
Addressed documents	Slow	Limited Visual	Clear, rational, similar in background
Unaddressed documents	Slowest	Limited Visual	

Figure 5: Effective use of media and channels
Source: Adapted from Daft and Weick, 1984

We might also speak of sending messages via certain channels in the organisation, by this we mean via certain departments or individuals. In this sense, a channel is the conduit along which the message travels. Note, channels and media are closely linked. Some writers use the terms interchangeably. Although we have differentiated these terms you may see them in the literature in either context.

Feedback is the process by which the receiver responds to the message. As we mentioned earlier, this can be oral, verbal or non-verbal. Feedback is an extremely important feature of communication.

Noise is anything which diminishes the impact of the message. It can be physical, for example, loud traffic, or it can be defined in other ways, for example, boredom, pre-occupation with something else, or anger. We consider other types of noise when we look at barriers to communication.

ACTIVITY 3

What channel and media would you use to:

1 Inform a prospective employee that he or she had been successful in a job interview? Why would you use this method(s)?

2 Inform a member of staff that you were making him or her redundant because of work shortage? Why would you use this method(s)?

---

1 You would inform this person by written letter, because of its:

- formality
- record purposes
- details of start date, salary, etc. can be attached.

2 You would inform this person by one-to-one conversation, privately, and follow-up later with an official letter, because:

- it shows that you think it is important
- it offers a forum for feedback from the receiver, no matter how unpleasant the message is
- it gives you the opportunity to offer further advice or consolation
- the letter is brief and is there for your records after you have discussed the matter.

As in many aspects of business, actual practice will vary from organisation to organisation. So, for example, some organisations may choose to make an initial verbal offer of employment straight after the interview process. This would then be followed up with written formal confirmation including details of salary.

TWO-PERSON RELATIONSHIP MODEL

This model states that how we view ourselves and the other party and how we behave are all affected by how the other party views him or herself and us and how he or she behaves. This may sound complicated but an example will illustrate.

People tend to act in ways which reinforce their own self-perceptions. A manager (male) may thus act differently towards subordinates than towards colleagues because of his perceptions that they expect different kinds of behaviour from him. His behaviour, and communication, with subordinates is affected by his perception that they expect an authoritative approach from him. He, therefore, adopts the role of leader that he feels is expected. Equally, the subordinates see him as leader and take on the expected role of subordinates to him. With peer colleagues, who expect a more friendly style of communication and behaviour, he adopts an approach that reflects their perceived equality of status.

This communication model, with each person adapting the perceived roles and status relationship of the situation, can be carried into any inter-personal relationship. Remember this concept particularly when we discuss how to get the most out of meetings and also your own behaviour in an interview situation in Unit 4.

COMMUNICATION-IN-CONTEXT MODEL

This model incorporates elements of all of the previous models and then considers the organisational context in which communication takes place (Figure 6). Communication is shaped by other important factors as well as the individuals directly involved. These include:

- **task characteristics** – is the task complex or straightforward?

- **group characteristics** – how big is the group, what sort of people are in it, what are their relationships to each other?

- **organisation structure and culture** – how is work allocated, tasks carried out, what are the values of the organisation?

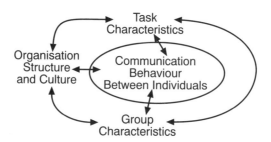

Figure 6: Communication-in-context model
Source: Fisher, 1993, p. 14

You should remember this model in our discussions in Unit 4 on meetings and interview situations. And note also the concept of organisational culture that we also review in Unit 4. For practical purposes, the model highlights the important skills required in 'reading' the context (tast, group and organisational context) and adjusting communication style, choice of channel and so on, to suit the circumstances.

ORGANISATION-ENVIRONMENT TRANSACTION MODEL

This model is even wider based than the communication-in-context model. It is a strategic model which takes into account the wider context in which organisations operate and the environment they communicate in. Thus many organisations are now keen to promote a 'green' image to their customers and also to other competitors, pressure groups and local government. Again remember this in our discussions in Unit 4.

1.6 Perspectives of communication

We have analysed communication in terms of models, going from the simple one-way model to the more complex strategic model. Which model is the right one to use? It is possible to use one, several or all of the models to analyse a particular situation.

The models we use and the emphasis we place upon them is governed by our perspective, in other words, the way in which we view the situation. Consider the case in which a manager asks a worker to work the next weekend and the worker refuses.

- From one perspective, we could look at how the manager asked. Was the question verbal or written? Our concern is clearly the medium and channel of communication.

- From another perspective, we could look at the communication processes in terms of what perceived importance the manager gave to the message (perhaps it was very important); his perception of the worker (he must want the work); and the perceptions of the worker (it was not so important and he didn't want to work).

- From another perspective, we could look at the message in terms of the culture of the organisation – 'people never work on Sundays here'.

REVIEW ACTIVITY 1

Read the case study, *Helenne,* and answer the questions that follow.

Helenne

Gordon McGreal is the marketing manager for Godiva Beauty Products Ltd. In the past, Godiva has concentrated its product range on moisturising lotions and creams under the Dermiplex label designed to 'rejuvenate sagging and tired skin'. The company has enjoyed a degree of success with these but has recently been the subject of scrutiny from animal rights activists after a local newspaper revealed that the Dermiplex range had been initially tested on animals.

Now Gordon has decided that the future for Godiva Beauty Products lies in products which are made from natural ingredients and not tested on animals. He has thought of a name for the new product range – *Helenne* – which will feature a soap, facial scrub, and shampoo.

Of course, he is aware that this is no longer a totally unexploited niche market (Body Shop, in particular, is already well known) and is aware that he will have a tough fight on his hands to convince his own company to agree to his plans. However, he is convinced that this is the direction for the company to take. He is tired of those in the company's management who are afraid to change and feels passionately that the time to get into the natural market is 'now or never'. In fact, he feels so strongly that he is prepared to resign if the board turns him down and he has another job lined up anyway.

He feels that his role as marketing manager means that he must be the catalyst for new products; this is a view shared by the majority of senior managers and directors. He tries to communicate an appropriate self-image by always appearing energetic and wearing designer suits and trendy ties.

Gordon had gained approval from Mr Dermot, the managing director, to give a presentation of his ideas at the next monthly board meeting. Approval had not been easy to obtain as Mr Dermot was a busy man. Gordon had made an appointment to speak to him but, as usual, Mr Dermot had been behind schedule and was busy putting various papers into his briefcase prior to leaving for the airport when Gordon was summoned in by the secretary. Gordon had tried to quickly explain the whole business of *Helenne*. Mr Dermot, now searching for something in his desk, had scarcely looked up, only acknowledging Gordon's idea with the occasional grunt. Wanting to complete his packing, Mr Dermot had muttered 'Yes, McGreal, put it on the agenda. See Norma on the way out. See you at the meeting'.

Gordon had seen Norma (Mr Dermot's secretary) and had also persuaded her to include his paper, *Natural products: the way forward?* to accompany his presentation which was the second item on the meeting agenda. This paper firstly showed how profits appeared to have stagnated at a moderate level, and secondly introduced the field of natural beauty products for future product portfolio consideration. All board members had now received this information and with the monthly meeting only a week away, Gordon was already receiving nods of approval and equally threats of opposition. The production director, Alec Smallfield, in particular pointed out to Gordon over the telephone that neither his staff nor his factory were set up to manufacture the proposed range.

If his strategy receives company backing, Gordon will have to sell the idea to major stores and pharmacies as the company does not have its own sales outlets. However, final approval will only come from the customer!

It will be important to launch the *Helenne* range at the most auspicious time. Gordon has decided that an ideal launch date would be immediately after a nationally publicised day of action, *Animals have feelings too!*, by animal rights activists. It will, therefore, be essential to have the first of the product range available and in the stores by this date and to have all of the publicity sorted out well in advance.

1 How are the three purposes of organisational communication illustrated in the case study?

2 Describe the following communication models and comment on features in the above scenario which relate to each:

- one-way

- interaction

- two-person relationship

- communication-in-context

- organisation-environment transaction.

3 What media and channels:

- Has Gordon McGreal used to communicate with senior management?

- Would you use if you were Alec Smallfield, production director, assuming the following situation: Gordon's proposals have been accepted and you have to tell your staff that there will be big changes ahead for everyone but that their co-operation will be vital for the organisation's success?

Why would you use these particular media and channels?

Summary

In this section, you have been introduced to communication as a means of exchange of information and transmission of meaning, and have discussed its specific meaning within an organisational context. You have examined its purpose and importance in organisations. There are different types of verbal and non-verbal communication; messages are constantly being conveyed non-verbally and informally. You have identified the basic features of five models of communication.

SECTION 2

Barriers to Communication

Introduction

In this section, we look at barriers to organisational communication. These exist in many shapes and forms and are potentially present in all communication and in all models. Barriers range from the obvious, for example, language differences, to the more subtle, for example, difference in perceptions. Understanding how these barriers can arise is essential, if we want to improve our communication skills.

2.1 Barriers to communication

All of the models of communication are concerned to a greater or lesser extent with barriers. These can be physical, psychological, or cultural:

Physical barriers
- Message ambiguity
- Physical noise, for example, the background noise of traffic, or television, or loud music
- Distance, for example, sometimes it is better to meet in person
- Language
- Jargon
- Lack of interest by receiver
- Mismatch of knowledge, for example, receiver might not have the relevant technical background
- Distortion of the message
- Lack of time
- Number of times that the message is passed from one to another
- Information 'gatekeepers'

Psychological barriers
- Difference in perceptions
- Emotions – happiness, anger, sadness
- Fear, anxiety
- Mistrust

Cultural barriers

- Differences in values of sender and receiver
- Status
- Deliberate by-passing
- Assumptions, jumping to conclusions
- Expectations
- First impressions
- Stereotyping
- Polarisation
- Tendency to evaluate too early and not really listen

2.2 Message ambiguity

Consider the following statement in a pharmacy window:

We dispense with accuracy

At first glance, this is a perfectly sound statement. We assume that the pharmacy is accurate in dispensing drugs and medicines. We could, however, interpret the statement as meaning that the pharmacy does not use (i.e. dispenses with) accuracy!

The following statement was drafted as part of a university regulation: *'The student will fail and must repeat the subject if he/she fails to produce any work with regard to the three assessments'*.

This statement caused much confusion at an examinations board. Did the statement mean that the student:

- failed and had to repeat the subject if there was non-submission of any one assessment? (that is, failure to submit one or more), or
- failed and had to repeat the subject if there was no evidence whatsoever of submission? (that is, failure to submit all three assessments).

Note your choice of words and sentence structure in written and oral communication.

2.3 Language

We could argue that the cause of the ambiguity illustrated above was the language used, specifically the word 'any'. Here, the word has been used too loosely. As we mentioned earlier, meaning does not lie in the words themselves but in the meaning that we give them. Of course, it takes time to learn all of the symbols in a language and some of us might have a larger vocabulary than others. Language may be a barrier between people of different nationalities in a multi-national company, for instance, and even between different cultures.

In organisations, the use of jargon – words which only have meaning within the organisation or department or profession – can cause barriers. Sometimes, this might be done deliberately to either exclude others or to foster a sense of mystery and difficulty. Information technology specialists, lawyers and accountants are examples.

2.4 Distortion

A message does not have to be ambiguous to cause problems. The problem might be that the encoding process hasn't been very good and what the sender communicates isn't quite what was intended.

ACTIVITY 4

Consider the following examples of ambiguity, language problems and distortion and comment upon them and identify the type of barrier:

1 Nothing is better than this product.

2 This ice-cream is really wicked!

3 I found it very educational.

4 This job requires a part-time man.

5 That's not very pc.

1   Ambiguous – does it mean that the product is the best or that anything is preferable to it?

2   A language problem – a child telling the merits of a new ice-cream, but it could be ambiguous if taken out of context.

3   It could be used in a sarcastic, intentionally ambiguous way – It taught me a lesson! I'll know next time not to do that!

4   Distortion – what the sender meant was for a man to take up the position on a part-time basis, not for the person to be a man part-time.

5   Language – use of jargon, pc means politically correct.

2.5 Physical noise and distance

Clearly physical noise can be a barrier. Distance can compound the problem. People have recognised this. For instance, construction sites can be noisy places. To make themselves understood, engineers often use a series of hand signals to the surveyor working with them. Crane operators and banksmen on the ground directing and informing them, and taxiing aircraft and ground personnel may also use hand signals or more increasingly mobile phone or radio communication.

What is important is that the symbols have been previously agreed and are unambiguous and they will still make sense even if subject to distortion. Consider two rock climbers tied together. One climbs out of sight of the other and the wind carries all sound away. How does the second climber know that the first one is safe and that it is time to climb? If the pre-arranged signal is that one tug on the rope means 'Climb!' and two tugs means 'Don't climb, I'm not ready!' then disaster awaits if the two tug message is sent and only one tug is received. One practice is for three sharp tugs to mean 'Climb!' and no signal for anything else. Thus, even if the distorted message of one or two tugs is received, the climber will know that it is time to climb.

Distance can also be a problem, especially if people have never met before. We gain so much useful information from body language. We are also much more likely to feel a sense of commitment if we meet someone in person. It's hard to tell someone face-to-face that the order is going to be late! It is important to build a relationship with those with whom we communicate. What are their values? How do they view the situation? How important is the issue to them? If distance prevents or reduces meetings to such an extent that these relationships suffer, then we can create barriers.

2.6 Emotions – fear, anxiety, mistrust, anger

ACTIVITY 5

Imagine that you work for a small, family business, D R Giles Ltd, which employs a workforce of semi-skilled craftsmen. It is taken over by an international company, Reckitt UK, with factories all over the world and with its headquarters over 400 miles away. As yet, you have not even seen the new managing director. How would you view the new parent company? How would these views affect communication between your small organisation and the international company?

You might fear for your job security or status, be anxious about new working practices and be mistrustful in general about Reckitt's intentions. These would be common feelings. It is usual for people to have these feelings about change and the unknown. People tend to fear the worst. The effects upon communication can be dramatic. Fear and mistrust will block out organisational goals of effectiveness and efficiency from Reckitt's headquarters to the small organisation. Personal survival will take precedence. Perceptions may form of a 'them and us' type and these may be self-perpetuating as each side acts out its role.

Of course, people in D R Giles may be quite right to be fearful. However, if there is no real justification for such fears, it would be wise to break down the barriers regarding these misperceptions before they become any worse. The business needs to know that it is welcomed and needed by the larger parent company. A visit by the managing director and (truthful) reassurances would be welcomed; a statement outlining the direction the parent company is moving in and where the smaller company fits into the plan would be welcomed.

ACTIVITY 6

Imagine that you are a worker in D R Giles Ltd and you have just heard a rumour that your pay is to be reduced. You are very angry. Your manager requests that all workers attend a briefing on the new terms and conditions. The news is that the pay package will be restructured; whereas previously you were paid on an hourly basis (including overtime) you will now be paid a basic salary plus performance-related bonuses. Your manager wants to explain that, although initially this would mean a cut in take-home pay because the factory is old and inefficient, as soon as the new methods and machinery are installed in line with Reckitt UK's systems, you will have an increase in your weekly take-home pay.

How do you think your anger will affect the communication process at the briefing?

It is probable that your anger will act as a barrier, initially, at least. It may influence your perception of the deal offered by Reckitt UK to the extent that you do not believe that it is better. You might be particularly vocal at the meeting and arouse the anger of the managers, so that you have a fruitless argument.

Perhaps, you are so angry that you resort to personal insults. If this happens, your argument will fail. Your ability to express yourself is diminished because of excessive emotional anger. Also, communication failure will apply in the opposite direction. You will simply not 'listen to reason' in the other person's view and any attempt to communicate with you is a waste of time.

We have seen in our discussion that emotions may be a barrier either to the reception of a message or to the ability of the sender to communicate the message effectively. A simple diagram highlights our ability to express ourselves as a function of our emotions (Figure 7).

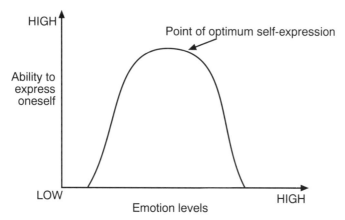

Figure 7: The relationship between emotion levels and the ability to express oneself
Source: Manning and Curtis, 1988

Note that a certain amount of emotion is a good thing. It shows that we are interested! And, a certain amount of adrenaline usually brings out the best in us as communicators. As you will see in Unit 4, an oral presentation and an interview situation require you to overcome extreme nerves.

2.7 Perceptions

Perception is always an important consideration. It applies to many situations, as we have just seen. Consider the concept of danger. Danger may be minimal, but if we perceive that some activity involves an element of danger, then our fear is very real.

ACTIVITY 7

What do you think might be the perceptions of the managers and the workers of D R Giles Ltd to the role of work in their lives? How would these perceptions raise barriers to communication?

Managers may:

- view work as a career
- not intend to stay with the company but use it as a route to a better position somewhere else
- take the view that the company buys their professional expertise
- regard additional work hours (including work at home) as part of doing their job
- assume that they do the managing and the workers do the working
- see themselves as either fitting in, or not, with the new management.

Perhaps the most relevant of these perceptions in this scenario is the last one. If a managers sees him- or her-self as the sort of person whom the new company encourages then he or she will want to stay and will seek out as much information as possible on its goals and objectives. Conversely, perhaps the manager does not or cannot work in the style of the new owners.

Workers may:

- view work as a job – just earning a livelihood
- intend to stay with the company and gradually work their way to a better paid position
- believe that they will never work again if made redundant
- view that the company buys their scheduled time with any extra being paid as overtime
- view that as a time-based commodity they are easily replaced
- view that it is their job only to follow management's instructions.

Workers will tend to be anxious and suspicious of anything that management says. The whole situation is much more likely to end in conflict.

Some of the other perceptions could act as barriers to communication. For instance, Reckitt UK might expect workers to contribute their own ideas and to accomplish their tasks even if this occasionally meant unpaid overtime. Workers' minds would not be open to these approaches.

2.8 First impressions and frozen evaluations

First impressions matter. We tend to make instant judgements when first encountering a person or a situation. The first few minutes in a job selection interview can be crucial to the potential candidate's success. Often our first impressions are superficial and subjective as we have little 'hard' information to work on. It is easy to gain a false impression under these circumstances. It is often compounded by our unwillingness to change our evaluation when presented later with conflicting evidence to our initial 'judgement'. This unwillingness to change our opinion is called a **frozen evaluation** and is recognised as a barrier to communication (see Haney, 1974).

Again, recall the danger of making assumptions. Assumptions are inferences we make – sometimes without realising! We observe one thing and then infer something from that. We assume people will be interested because they have turned up for our speech – they might have been coerced. We assume that they don't need further information because they don't ask questions, whereas they might be so confused that they don't know what to ask!

2.9 Stereotyping

There is often a strong tendency for us to want to put people into certain categories or **stereotypes** according to profession, race, or sex, for example. We have a mental picture of the characteristics of this group – how its members look and behave, and what their attitudes are.

The use of the stereotype model simplifies the process of getting to know an individual; once we have put the individual into a certain category it is easy to infer that person's characteristics.

Although stereotyping may be part of the process of discriminating against certain social groups, in another sense they make it less easy to discriminate between different members of the social group. In reality, people are not identical. Just because a person belongs to a certain profession or group does not mean that this person conforms to the stereotype.

ACTIVITY 8

What personality characteristics do you associate with an accountant?

You might include the following characteristics:

- dull
- grey
- methodical
- painstaking.

Or you might have adopted a more modern approach and think that accountants lead exciting, dynamic lives surrounded by computers and advising major corporations, then you might have listed characteristics such as:

- dynamic
- astute
- ruthless
- business-like.

This is a very different stereotype!

The danger of using any stereotype is that the person might only have some of the characteristics and not others. Indeed, the person might possess none of the characteristics! As our perceptions about the receiver of our communication will strongly affect what and how we communicate, using stereotypes can seriously impair our effectiveness in the communication process.

2.10 Polarisation

We talk about people thinking in 'black and white'. This tendency to think of something as either one thing or the other, all or nothing, is known as **polarisation**. It can be a significant barrier to communication.

Consider the statement: 'Chocolate makes you overweight because it's loaded with fats and calories'. Is this is a valid statement? Chocolate does contain a high percentage of fats and calories; this part of the statement is true. However, the first part of the statement is highly polarised; chocolate will not necessarily make you overweight if you only eat a little or if you use a lot of calories because you are very active, for example.

In organisations there are very few issues which are completely black or white, most are shades of grey. For example, a polarised management statement might be that 'unions are counter-productive to profits and efficiency in the workplace'. It is true that union activity can be counter-productive. Union members will view the company in a different light to management. However, an exploited workforce will tend to work poorly and will have long-term problems such as absenteeism, high labour turnover and even sabotage. These problems may have been avoided by dialogue between union and management. Also unions may play a positive role in training, safety and other functions.

2.11 Evaluate too early and not listen

Carl Rogers (1991) argues that one of the main barriers to communication is the tendency to evaluate, that is to approve or disapprove of what the other person is saying too early, before the person has finished communicating. Once you have made an evaluation you will then simply twist the rest of the communication to fit this evaluation. You may thus stop listening to the real arguments put forward by the sender.

We can reduce this tendency to evaluate by putting ourselves in the place of the person sending the message. What is their background? What are their hopes, aspirations, and values? How will the outcome of the situation affect them? We should try to understand the feelings of the other party.

Managers need to encourage people to talk frankly with them so that they can offer their support and get their employees to answer their own questions. 'So, Tim, you say you've had problems with the machine. Have you any ideas on how to solve them?' Managers can assist by a process of **active listening**.

We need to make a conscious effort to suspend evaluation until all angles have been covered. The danger of this, as Rogers concedes, is that our own view of the situation might be unduly influenced and we end up agreeing when we don't really want to!

REVIEW ACTIVITY 2

Re-read the *Shopquick* case study given at the beginning of the unit. Then answer the following questions.

1 Look at the section in the case study entitled *Staff – attitudes and perceptions.*

   Briefly describe the essential differences in perceptions between the staff, Sandra and Barbara, and Reginald Homeworthy towards the work situation, that is, their values and attitudes towards work.

2 Reginald receives a fax from Head Office which reads: *Stock Records: Discrepancies on confectionery items type 56. Please explain these losses.*

   Reginald immediately orders his secretary to place a poster in the works canteen which reads: 'It has come to my attention that a certain amount of pilfering has been going on in the store. May I remind you that this is a sackable offence and any one discovered partaking in such action will be instantly dismissed? Signed Mr R Homeworthy (Store Manager).

   Comment on

   (a) Reginald's interpretation of the message from Head Office

   (b) The way in which he transmits the message to his staff

   (c) What sort of barriers to future communication are likely to arise from this action?

3 In the meantime, Sheila has pointed out to Reginald that confectionery item 56 was a batch of old Easter eggs which he had ordered to be thrown out at the beginning of the month.

(a) Comment further on Head Office's message and Reginald's interpretation of it.

(b) Reginald now has irate staff to deal with. Suggest how he might communicate that a genuine error has been made.

4   Imagine that Reginald is told by Sheila that he ought to improve his human relations style. What sort of barriers do you think Sheila might have to contend with in order to get her message accepted?

5   Suppose that Reginald understands and accepts the message from Sheila about his management style. What barriers, apart from the recent confectionery fiasco, do you think he might face as he attempts to communicate to the workforce his intention to adopt a more co-operative and friendly approach. How could he overcome these barriers?

Summary

In this section, we have looked at barriers to communication. Barriers are present in many situations and have a wide range of sources. For instance, we have looked at examples where the message itself has become distorted; barriers which we put up ourselves due to our unchanging opinions of other people; and barriers which arise because of our emotions.

SECTION 3
Formal and Informal Communication

Introduction

In this section, we look at how communication occurs within formal organisation structures. We consider the role of communication in decision-making and then look at the need for communication to occur informally, as well as through formal channels. We also cover formal information sources inside and outside the organisation. The type of communication affects its execution whether it is in a written or an oral form.

3.1 Formal and informal communication

We define **formal communication** firstly as concerned with the flow of information through the authorised channels in the organisation. This definition covers **downward** and **upward** communication and also some of the **network patterns** we cover.

Secondly, we often talk of **formal** and **informal sources of information**. For example, we might say that a supervisor gave an 'informal' verbal warning (off-the-record) to an employee rather than a formal, written warning (as laid down in the rules and regulations of the organisation). This leads us to another consideration of the terminology. A **formal information source** uses the organisation's own approved media which is usually capable of retrieval, for example, a letter to a job applicant informing him or her of success at an interview. By inference, any other source is informal. For example, a request for stationery within a company might have to be made formally on the correct requisition form rather than informally over the telephone.

We can define informal communication along similar lines: **informal communication** is concerned with the flow of information outside of the authorised channels in the organisation'. This does not mean outside of the organisation. We look at **horizontal communication, network patterns** and the **grapevine** in this context.

3.2 Vertical communication

Communication in an organisation can be either vertical or horizontal. **Vertical communication** can occur either **downward** or **upward** and is usually formal. Although it may be considered informal if a subordinate communicates with his superior's boss as we see later. Vertical communication concerns the passing of commands down the line and the flow of control information up the line.

DOWNWARD COMMUNICATION

Katz and Kahn (1966) split communication down the line into five categories:

- job instructions
- job rationale – explains why a task is being performed
- information about procedures and practices
- feedback to subordinates
- indoctrination of goals – mission

Consider a typical organisation chart as in Figure 8. This chart is useful in that it lays out diagrammatically the authority and reporting relationships between people in the organisation. It is often the first thing that is given to a newcomer upon arrival. Vertical communication is typically through this hierarchy.

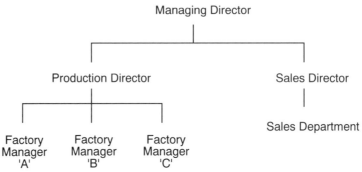

Figure 8: Typical organisation chart

Are there any drawbacks to downward communication through this hierarchy? The first thing to note is that most downward communication is one-way. Katz included feedback as one of his categories but, in reality much downward communication does not allow subordinates to respond to their managers. It assumes that all operations can be carried out by following a systematic series of rules and directives sent down through the hierarchy. In fact, as we see, when we discuss informal communication, it is almost impossible to allow for all likely happenings in the course of the working day.

The second thing to note is that there is often information loss, especially if there are many levels within the organisation, see Figure 9. Note in Figure 8 another hierarchical level might be a sales or production supervisor between the manager and the staff.

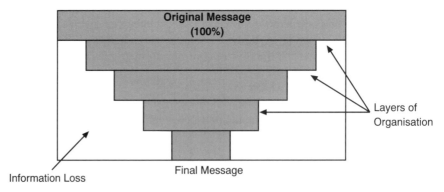

Figure 9: Downwards information loss
Source: adapted from Fisher, 1993, p. 38

UPWARD COMMUNICATION

Katz and Kahn summarise upward communication from subordinate to superior as being about:

- him- or herself, performance and problems
- others and their problems
- organisational practices and policies
- what needs to be done and how it is to be done.

ACTIVITY 9

Imagine that you are one of several sales representatives working for D R Giles Ltd, which you will recall has just been taken-over by Reckitt UK. Your immediate superior is your old boss, the sales director Mr Brown, now just a sales manager reporting to Reckitt UK's sales director, Mr Plunkitt. You are sorry that Mr Brown has been effectively demoted, because you got on well with him. The new situation looks far from certain, and you think that 'old Brownie' has been lucky to keep his job.

Can you see any barriers to your communications upward with Mr Brown? What do you think about communications between Brown and Plunkitt?

You are sympathetic towards Mr Brown and will probably confide in him to a certain extent. You might try to help by suggesting how to improve operations. Mr Brown is likely to be extremely wary of communicating with Mr Plunkitt. He will be acutely aware that the majority of information will be of the 'performance' type and used as control information. If such control information shows that either he or his section is performing badly it could threaten his job.

Additionally, Mr Brown is unlikely to think that he should be offering information other than this to Mr Plunkitt. He has, he thinks, been demoted; so why should he help? He is likely to be protective of his sales staff and will certainly be wary of discussing any of their weaknesses with Plunkitt. In any case, Mr Plunkitt is trying to establish his authority and that probably means he will adopt a telling, rather than a listening, approach.

This scenario indicates that upward communication is difficult for both superior and subordinate!

3.3 Network patterns

Information networks describe the pattern in which communication is carried out. Research carried out by Harold J Leavitt in the early 1950s provides five well-known models, for example, see Greenberg and Barron, 1993. In each of these models, communication, for our purposes, is two-way between each of the circles which represent people (see Figure 10).

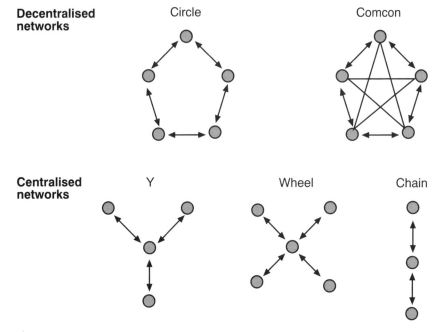

Figure 10: Centralised and de-centralised networks

The chain, Y and wheel represent centralised networks, that is, control information flows to a central point where decisions are made. These decisions are then disseminated out from this central point to the other members who are, in effect controlled from the centre. Communication is usually formal.

The circle and comcon networks are de-centralised. Communication flows between group members for the purposes of sharing information, achieving co-ordination and expressing feelings. Control is not held by any one member; members are free to make their own decisions. Communication is often informal.

CENTRALISATION VERSUS DE-CENTRALISATION

The decision to centralise or de-centralise is not simply the question 'Do we de-centralise or not?' but 'What decisions should we centralise and de-centralise?'

Advantages of centralised networks are:

● good for simple tasks

● fast

● strong leadership can be demonstrated.

Advantages of de-centralised networks are:

● better for complex tasks requiring multiple inputs from members

● involves people in decisions and gives them ownership.

For example, a division within a large company might have its budget decided centrally at corporate head office and management development might also be a centralised function but the division might be able to make decisions itself on how to spend its budget and on hiring and firing staff.

Often, in the early stages of growth within an organisation it is relatively easy for certain managers or directors to act as 'nerve centres'. Control is 'tight'. Often, in an internally competitive environment, managers will want to retain information themselves both as protection from company rivals and as a means of controlling their work situation.

However, as the organisation grows there is a tendency for the sheer volume of decision-making to increase. There will come a point at which the manager can no longer deal with his or her work in the way in which he or she did previously. At this stage, an overload situation has been reached. Various strategies can be adopted by the manager to cope:

- spending less time on decisions
- managing by exception, that is, only looking at those decisions which are noted as requiring special attention and pushing the rest through a routine system
- dealing with complaints – fire-fighting – and hoping that the other decisions will resolve themselves!

Often one or more of these strategies will have been tried before the manager reluctantly admits that the situation is still not effective and likely to get worse as the company grows. Decisions aren't being made or else they are being poorly taken.

One way to deal with this overload is to de-centralise. This has both structural and communication implications for the organisation. This empowerment of others should then free the manager for the more important tasks even though direct control is lost to a more co-ordinating role.

ACTIVITY 10

Now that D R Giles Ltd belongs to Reckitt UK it can no longer function as it used to. In particular, the flows of information and the focus of decision-making are likely to change. Several issues need to be tackled by senior management of Reckitt UK with regard to the takeover, namely:

1 collation of detailed end of month management accounts, this shows for instance, profit on individual product lines

2 summary of management accounts, this gives overall profit/loss and key financial information only

3 collation of debtors' and creditors' accounts, this shows detailed information of customers owing money and suppliers that D R Giles Ltd owes money to

4 sales 'intelligence gathering' on competitors

5 equal opportunities statistics compiled by D R Giles Ltd, for example, number of workers with disabilities, number of women managers

6 company newsletters.

Which of the above areas do you think Reckitt UK will centralise and which do you think it should de-centralise to D R Giles Ltd? Give brief reasons for your choices.

Some of the above items definitely fit one or other of the two approaches. Others are open to debate, depending upon the advantages sought. Your answers may have included:

Centralised decisions and information flow

Item 1: detailed management accounts. Unless Reckitt UK confident it might ask for this information to be sent to headquarters as well.

Item 2: summary of key financial information. Reckitt UK must have access to this information for overall control of all of its units and factories and to know at any time the overall financial health of the entire organisation.

Item 5: equal opportunities statistics. For comparison amongst factories and units and to demonstrate an organisational commitment, this information would be best dealt with centrally.

De-centralised decisions

Item 3: Probably best to deal with this information at individual units, that is, at D R Giles Ltd, as it would only overload a centralised system and is best left to the individual units to manage directly.

Centralised or de-centralised?

Item 4: Intelligence gathering. This could be de-centralised, for example, using a comcon network pattern, so that each unit feeds information to other units, allowing for rapid information flow. However, if Reckitt UK feels that it wishes to retain a tight control then it may prefer a wheel type of centralised information flow.

Item 6: Essentially is there to be one newsletter for the whole organisation or will D R Giles Ltd have its own? The advantages of an organisation-wide newsletter include learning about other factories in the group, a sense of belonging and the corporate culture. Information would flow to an editor at Head Office. The advantages of a D R Giles Ltd newsletter concern retaining identity and information would be focused within D R Giles Ltd.

3.4 Horizontal (lateral) communication

In horizontal communication, people communicate directly and informally with each other across the chain of command, rather than following the formal route through it. It involves people on the same hierarchical level. Horizontal communication is extremely important and widespread in an organisation. Its primary function is to co-ordinate work, formal activities, goals and objectives of a particular sub-unit or department. Many writers describe horizontal communication as having a formal role (Rasberry & Lemoine, 1986).

There are other purposes for horizontal communication. Katz and Kahn (1966) refer to the socio-emotional support for people in both unorganised and organised work groups. People in similar situations have a natural need to talk to and help each other.

Mintzberg (1979) discusses horizontal communication in a different light. If something cannot be achieved by formal directions from above and requires an informal approach of co-ordination to achieve, then it is part of the informal communication network. He talks of 'communicating outside the chain of formal authority'. Mintzberg gives the example of a management information systems manager engaging in such informal activity by gathering the 'real information and intelligence' from informal contacts. 'Soft' information – 'intangible and speculative' gathered from talking to these contacts – was no less useful just because it had not come through official channels and could not be quantified.

ACTIVITY 11

Suppose that you are a design engineer working on a new project. You report to the project manager. However, it soon becomes apparent that you need to talk to your counterpart, Samantha, within another division of the company to solve a technical question that you have. During your telephone conversation, Samantha tells you that she's heard a rumour that your boss is about to leave the organisation. You tend to believe her, especially as recently the operations director, the project manager's boss, has been sending instructions directly to you.

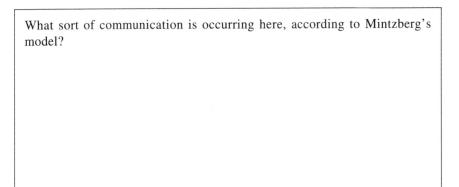

What sort of communication is occurring here, according to Mintzberg's model?

Communication with Samantha is peer-based and is informal and outside the chain of command. Communication with the operations director is an over-ride of scalar chain and is again informal. The rumour mentioned by Samantha is worth noting in that the message itself is informal. We consider rumours shortly when we look at the grapevine.

Mintzberg (1979) states: 'Most work simply cannot be done without some form of informal communication'. He goes on to explain that the reason for this is that, even in the simplest and stablest of work, there are so many variables that rules and regulations are unlikely to work on their own. What is required are people to make the system work and this requires informal communication.

COMPARISON OF INFORMATION SOURCES – FORMAL WRITTEN VERSUS INFORMAL VERBAL

Below we highlight the essential differences between formal and informal information sources. It is not a question of 'formal' being somehow 'better' than 'informal', the two are complementary. Indeed, often the best way to get a message across is to repeat it formally and informally.

Formal

- public – large potential audience
- information permanently stored and retrievable
- information relatively old
- orientation of information chosen by originator
- moderate redundancy in information
- no direct feedback to originator.

Informal

- private – restricted audience
- information typically neither permanently stored nor retrievable
- information more likely to be up to date
- information primarily user-selected

- sometimes much redundancy of information
- often considerable feedback to the originator.

ACTIVITY 12

Mr Brown has just received an internal memorandum from Mr Plunkitt. Plunkitt has been reviewing the last six months' sales figures and has expressed surprise about a dramatic dip half way through this period in the northern area. As this is your area, Mr Brown has urgently tried to contact you (you are visiting customers), by fax and car telephone and also leaving messages at the places you are likely to visit. As you spend a long time on the car telephone talking to the other sales reps, it is not until late afternoon that the message reaches you.

You explain that one of your major customers, Quickchange, tightened the tolerances (that is, it has reduced the acceptable variation in size of your product) on its product specification and word of this didn't reach you or your firm's production department. This resulted in an enormous number of rejected goods which meant issuing credit notes. You have only found this out yourself through talking in the pub the previous night with Fred, one of Quickchange's foremen. Fred was most surprised that we were not aware of the change of specification. It was common knowledge as far as he was concerned, details of the new specification had been given to everyone and had been backed up by large reminders on the notice board. A letter was sent to your company but it had been addressed to 'The Quality Department', which your company does not have, and was lying gathering dust on some shelf in the disturbances of the take-over by Reckitt UK.

You reluctantly explain to Mr Brown that the sales figures projections for the next six months for the north are wildly inaccurate, as they are far too high! What they do not show is one of your major customers, Maxisell, has altered its product range this month and is not renewing its contract. Your monthly report to Mr Brown, which is now being typed, shows this. Mr Brown sighs and wonders how he might 'massage' the figures.

What are the major shortfalls of the formal communication system? What are the benefits of the formal system?

The major shortfalls of the formal communication system are three-fold:

- Old information: because of the time it takes in the formal routes

  Quickchange's letter lying gathering dust

  Maxisell's lost contract not included in sales projections

  Your report to Mr Brown has information which can be up to one month old.

- Lack of feedback to the originator

  In this case, a response back to Quickchange on the specification change.

- Accuracy

  Old information tends to be inaccurate. Also, Mr Brown's thoughts on 'massaging' the figures indicate that the presentation can mask the true situation.

The benefits of the formal system include:

- permanent records, in this case, past sales
- written plans, in this case, profit projections can be shared with a wide audience – the sales team, senior management, accounts
- concise
- easily understood – acceptable format
- potential use as control data, for example, 'Shall we sack Brown?'

3.5 The grapevine

The term **grapevine** is often used to describe the way in which 'interesting' bits of information travel informally around an organisation, for example, what the next pay rise is going to be, who is getting promoted or sacked, whose wife is expecting a baby, if that important contract has been secured, etc.

The grapevine is an extremely fast communication channel. It does not respect hierarchies or departments with the result that within a very short space of time, many people in the organisation are aware of the message. Suppressing the grapevine only makes people more determined to promulgate it. It has often been accused of supplying erroneous information – rumours, for example. However, studies have shown that the grapevine is often highly accurate, not least because those who are part of its transmission value their reputation as providers of accurate, up-to-date information. Effective managers are often 'tuned in' to the grapevine and know how to influence the message content.

Keith Davis's work on grapevines showed four ways in which the grapevine could operate (1953).

- **Single strand** represents the 'Chinese whispers' type of chain in which information is passed one-to-one down a line, the message is liable to distortion at each stage. It is the most inaccurate because of this distortion.

- In the **gossip chain,** one person is actively on the look out for messages and then tells everyone.

- The **probability** chain starts with someone who has a message but only delivers it on an ad hoc basis, depending more or less upon whom he or she happens to be in contact with.

- The **cluster** chain is more selective; an individual will only pass on messages to a select group or cluster, one of whom might then become the message source for subsequent clusters. Sometimes different ways are used depending upon the perceived importance of the information. It is relatively accurate and the most dominant form in organisations.

We can list the advantages and disadvantages of informal communication networks:

Advantages

- Fast
- Informs a large number of people
- Often highly accurate.

Disadvantages

- Single strand prone to distortion
- Can supply rumours and incorrect information.

REVIEW ACTIVITY 3

Read the case study, *The Roving Area Representative,* and answer the questions which follow.

The Roving Area Representative

Jane Cassidy has been appointed as the sales director in a national company which packages and distributes various grades of motor oil to haulage contractors, travel operators and agricultural users. She has a university education in which she studied marketing and commerce and has worked her way up the ranks in sales since getting her first job eight years ago. Jane's sales team consists of area representatives whose job it is to visit both existing and prospective clients. The majority have risen to their current positions by 'being in the right place at the right time', for example, by taking over someone else's job after that person has left the company. They tend to have varying amounts of experience and have attended the occasional short sales course although few have any professional or academic qualifications. It appears that there are some managers who are undoubtedly good at their job but, equally, there are some who Jane would rather sack.

Sales contracts are normally negotiated annually. The market is highly competitive and so area representatives have traditionally been given some discretion, within limits prescribed by the sales director, to set contracts according to volume, price and delivery. They can receive up to 25% bonus depending upon the volume of business they generate and how this relates to agreed individual targets. Up until now, the area representatives have operated on a written call card basis. Cards are kept for each client recording details such as company name and address, key contact person(s), last date visited, type of contract, expiry date of contract, price, delivery terms, and other comments. Information from these cards is summarised and has, in the past, been sent to the sales director so that he could co-ordinate on a national basis.

Area representatives like to feel that they lead exciting working lives, although, in reality, the job can be rather lonely so they constantly chat to each other on the car telephone during the long hours of motorway driving. Cliques exist which share local sales information and gossip. These have previously excluded the sales director.

Jane feels that the reporting mechanism is far too slow for her purposes as oil prices fluctuate dramatically. Additionally, she feels that she is not always receiving the 'full picture' and that some of the area representatives are rather unprofessional. For example, they may be offering unrealistic delivery times, and offering incentives such as oil storage tanks etc. In a bid to obtain up-to-date, accurate and full information, Jane is thinking of giving area representatives portable laptop computers and developing a whole new system of working. The area representatives would take the laptops on their travels and enter the information into them each night, either at home or in their hotel room. They would have to report in at least once a week at pre-set times by downloading their laptop information via a modem to the central Head Office computer. Jane is also thinking of using the system in reverse and sending messages to each area representative via her office computer to their home computer terminal which they will be told to access upon their return. In the past, communication has proved problematic due to the roving nature of the area representatives, also she is slightly suspicious that they sometimes choose not to receive messages!

Jane has doubts about whether or not all of her representatives can be relied upon to use this new technology. She intends to provide training specifically for this but has started to think that perhaps she should introduce a programme of careful recruitment of younger, more 'professional' staff, both from outside the organisation and through careful management development of promising 'high flyers' within the organisation.

Jane is also thinking of holding monthly meetings in her office at which all of the area representatives must be present. Each manager will be asked to give a report on progress within his or her area. The format of these reports will be standardised and will include details such as the number of clients visited, the number, type and value of successful contracts serviced and those obtained, as well as any contracts lost. Previously area representatives were more or less left to their own devices and there was little monitoring of their progress. She intends to initially use the reports as the basis for determining good performance, as given by these indicators. Given that the good performers are likely to be the sort of manager she is seeking to develop she intends to involve one or two of them in future development of specific sales methods and procedures. She will ask these good performers to assist in training and selection, using their existing knowledge of the industry.

She also would wish to go further than this by then applying her own ideas with regard to efficiencies to be gained through computer routing of calls, so as to minimise unproductive time on the road between calls, and of drawing up schedules to visit existing clients, rather than waiting until their contract is almost expired. She has promised them that any useful suggestions will be looked at seriously. She also thinks that this would be a good time for area representatives to socialise with more than their immediate 'neighbour' and Jane intends meetings to be completed by 1pm so that a relaxed business lunch may be arranged. Jane is well aware of the coolness of relations between the area representatives and the previous sales director and intends to adopt a more constructive approach. She intends also to arrange a company-paid annual weekend break for managers and their partners at a 4-star hotel. Key customers will also be invited. An internal company magazine is a further idea which will be pursued and notable events covered.

And, of course, there is the issue of bonuses. This has long been a thorny problem. It is true that large bonuses have been awarded in the past but the concern has always been from those who were not awarded them that they did not reflect issues such as the number of contracts involved or the degree of competition. For example, one area representative received a large bonus whenever one particular very lucrative contract was renewed allegedly because he was friendly with his contact. The other issue is the size of the market – the potential number of clients and how geographically spread they were. Some managers complained that in some areas a 'monkey could do the work and get a bonus' whereas in other areas it was almost impossible to meet the targets. Jane is aware of this unfairness and feels that it undermines the motivation of managers in poor areas and over-rewards managers in good areas.

Of course, if the managers follow the proposed new systems, Jane is confident that they will soon be hitting targets they never thought possible, and she has plans to make this a key note in her initial meetings with them. However, she proposes to devise a points system which would weight the bonus according to the degree of difficulty of achieving targets. In theory, the bonus maximum would remain at 25% but privately she is wondering if this is the right level. Certainly, she intends to monitor the degree of difficulty allowed by her points system against the actual securing of individual contracts within her best managers' portfolios. She suspects that difficult targets which do not allow sufficient 'difficulty weighting' will restrict success because the payoff for additional work is seen not to be worthwhile. By systematically analysing targets, their difficulty weighting and actual performance achieved over the next 6 months, Jane will set the next targets.

1   How do you think Jane Cassidy might successfully use Katz and Kahn's five categories of communication down the line with her proposed system?

2   What sort of communication network(s) do you think existed amongst the area representatives before Jane took control? Why? What sort of network do you think Jane would like? Why?

3   What sort of issues do you think the area representatives might communicate about with Jane Cassidy using the proposed system? Use Katz and Kahn's four categories as a framework.

4   Jane is thinking of using standardised reports. Her initial thoughts were that the area representatives would circulate the written report in advance of the meeting and then each one would back this up with a quick verbal summary at the monthly meeting. What are the advantages of doing this?

5   Apart from the 'official' presentation of reports, are there any other advantages in communication terms, for having a monthly meeting?

6   How do you think the informal networks of the area representatives might change as a result of the new proposals?

Summary

In this section, we have considered the role of formal and informal communication and the roles of both vertical and lateral communication within the organisation. All types of communication are essential for effective and efficient operations. We introduced communication network patterns, such as the wheel and comcon, and used them to illustrate the flow of information and directives in centralised and de-centralised decision-making. We considered informal information according to messages which lie outside the chain of formal command. The advantages and disadvantages of formal written versus informal verbal communication were briefly covered. Finally, we discussed the grapevine and found that it is usually quite accurate!

Unit Summary

In this unit, we have covered basic elements of communication in organisations. You have been shown various models of communication to help and develop your understanding. In particular, you should now be able to analyse barriers to communication in the workplace and be able to suggest ways in which communication might be improved.

You have also considered the benefits and pitfalls of formal and informal communication so you should now have a more informed basis to help you decide which of these, or what sort of mix of the two, you would use in certain work situations. The issues of centralisation and de-centralisation have been analysed in relation to the flows of information and directives required for decision making.

References

Adair, J (1989) *The Effective Communicator,* Industrial Society, London

Daft, R L and Weick, K E (1984) 'Toward a model of organizations as interpretation systems', *Academy of Management Review,* 9, 284–295

Davis, K (1953) *Harvard Business Review,* Sept-Oct, 31 (5), pp. 43–49

Fisher, D (1993) *Communication in Organizations,* West Publishing Company, St Paul

Greenberg, J and Barron, R A (1993) *Behaviour in Organizations,* Allyn and Bacon, Boston

Haney, W V (1974) *Communication and Organizational Behaviour, Text and Cases,* Irwin, Homewood

Katz, D and R L Kahn, (1966) *The Social Psychology of Organizations,* John Wiley & Sons, New York

Manning, G and Curtis, K (1988) *Communication, the Miracle of Dialogue,* South Western Publishing, Cincinnati

Mintzberg, H (1979) *The Structuring of Organizations,* Prentice Hall, Englewood Cliffs, New Jersey

Moorhead, G and Griffin, R W (1995) *Organizational Behaviour,* fourth edition, Houghton Mifflin, Boston

Rasberry, R W and Lemoine, L F (1986) *Effective Managerial Communication,* Kent Publishing Company

Rogers, C R (1991) 'Barriers and gateways to communication', *Harvard Business Review,* 69, 6, 105–111

Recommended Reading

Argyle, M (1993) *Bodily Communication,* Routledge, London

Berko, R M, Wolvin, A D and Wolvin, D R (1995) *Communicating,* Houghton Mifflin, Boston

Bolton, R (1986) *People Skills,* Simon & Schuster, New York

Bonington, C (1994) 'The heights of teamwork,' *Personnel Management,* Oct, pp. 44–47

Clampitt, P G (1991) *Communicating for Managerial Effectiveness,* Sage, London

Evans, D W (1990) *People, Communication and Organisations,* second edition, Pitman, London

Fisher, D (1993) *Communication in Organizations,* West Publishing, St Paul

Francis, D (1987) *Unblocking Organizational Communication,* Gower Publishing, London

Mintzberg, H (1980) *The Nature of Managerial Work,* Harper & Row, New York

Stanton, N (1990) *Communication,* Macmillan, London

Answers to Review Activities

Review Activity 1

1   The three purposes of organisational communication are to:
- achieve co-ordinated action
- share information
- express feelings and emotions.

These are illustrated by the case study in the following ways:

Achieve co-ordinated action
The first people to persuade are the members of the board. The purpose of the monthly meeting will be to approve or to reject Gordon's ideas. If approval is granted the company will then be able to co-ordinate its planning. Even Alec Smallfield will be included in this.

Other activities to be co-ordinated will be concerned with the product launch: liaison with major stores, who will stock the product; and publicity agents. These activities will probably involve further meetings, letters, telephone conversations etc.

Share information
The first person Gordon shared his idea with was the managing director in his hurried meeting. The agenda and the paper *'Natural products: the way forward?'* was the next instance of sharing. Gordon did not have to share his ideas at this stage; however, people like to know about new developments. The information he is sharing relates directly to organisational goals and results of efforts.

Express feelings and emotions
The animal rights activists' day of action *'Animals have feelings too!'* is an obvious expression of strongly felt beliefs and emotions. Alec Smallfield's telephone conversation to Gordon was also partially to express his feelings over someone else trying to alter his entire production set-up! Gordon might also use the monthly meeting to show how he feels about the conservative policies that the company has been following for so long.

2

One-way model
Gordon's paper was written as a 'one-way' message, its intention was to raise concerns about the company's future with the board members and suggest that perhaps there was a new way forward. He would need to choose his words carefully and consider all his intended readers and their interests and knowledge about natural products.

Interaction model

The most obvious illustration of the interaction model is the planned monthly meeting. Communication is definitely two way. The board members will ask for clarification on some points and question the validity of others.

Two-person relationship model

This model considers the ways in which others expect us to behave and the ways in which we think we should behave towards them. Gordon clearly thinks it is his role to be creative and dynamic. His new proposals clearly communicate this. Equally, other managers see his role in the same light; they expect him to act and communicate in this way.

Communication-in-context model

This model takes into account the context in which communication takes place. If we consider the monthly meeting, or even communication now going on in the company subsequent to Gordon's paper, we can see that the following will impact upon the effectiveness of communication:

- The task: this is not straightforward which would mean a major change in production and sales.

- Organisation structure and culture: Alec Smallfield informs us that 'neither staff nor his factory' is set up to deal with the proposed changes.

- The change in strategic focus from synthetic to natural products would cause a change in the values of the company.

- Group characteristics: Gordon's task at convincing the board would be much easier if they were not such a bunch of old-fashioned conservative thinkers! Additionally, he has Alec Smallfield to contend with.

All of these factors shape the communication process.

Organisation-environment transaction

This is a strategic model which demonstrates the ways in which the organisation communicates with the outside world and the ways in which elements of the outside world communicate with the organisation.

By adopting and promoting *Helenne* as a natural product, the organisation would be telling existing and potential customers and interested bodies, for example, animal rights activists, that its new values were friendly to the animal environment.

It is clear that the values of people outside the organisation have permeated their way into the company's strategy.

3

Gordon has used the following media and channels:

- media: written his paper; channel: limited visual

- media: telephone to Alec Smallfield; channel: audio

- media: face-to-face initial meeting with managing director; channel: audio and visual.

Alec Smallfield has a difficult message to communicate. His staff may feel that their jobs are threatened. They will certainly not like the major changes in their daily routines.

Alec should choose media and channels which can best deal with the strong feelings his workers are likely to experience. Face-to-face communication could be via one-to-one meetings and also group discussions. He should allow for feedback and also use audio and visual aids for clarity.

He might want to reinforce these meetings with a personally addressed letter explaining the company's new proposals. This has the advantage of laying out the issues in a clear, rational format. It is easy for someone to miss a vital point in a meeting, or indeed for someone such as Alec to either forget or not emphasise a point properly. The personally addressed letter at least shows that the company thinks that the issue is important to its employees.

Review Activity 2

1   There are obvious differences in perceptions to the work situation.

Sandra and Barbara regard work as:

- not their main priority – home life takes precedence

- a means to an end – their pay packets

- a place to have a chat with friends and to share problems.

Reginald views work as:

- his main priority

- an end in itself

- a place where he can put into effect his ideas regarding efficiency.

2

(a) Reginald's interpretation of the message is incorrect. He jumps to conclusions, perhaps he has pre-conceived stereotypes of his staff as people whom he cannot trust.

(b) Reginald has fallen down very badly in this area! He has made a number of basic errors:

- using one-way communication for a very sensitive issue, allowing no further explanation or feedback
- a group setting arouses emotions amongst the staff
- tone of the message is very autocratic and condescending
- not checking on the validity of the message from Head Office.

(c) Likely barriers are:

fear

mistrust

anxiety.

He is likely to distance himself from the staff even more than he is at present.

3

(a) The message has misled Reginald, probably on two counts:
- Item 56 clearly has not registered in his mind; Easter eggs might have done
- He has read 'losses' as theft. In fact, the discrepancy is the way in which the stock was 'written off'. The word 'losses' is emotive.

(b) Reginald really is in a difficult position now. Quite apart from the new barriers of mistrust, anxiety and fear that his management style is in danger of producing, he now has the added barrier of anger. His staff are even less likely to hear what he has to say than before.

He could put up another poster to apologise but this would appear crass and distant. He needs to time his communication; perhaps allowing a cooling off period, passing word through the grapevine via Sheila that he intends to hold a meeting, in work time and at the end of their shift, to say that he has noted their comments and he can understand their anxiety. He will attempt to use this event as a way to launch a new commitment between management and the workers. Well, it's worth a try!

The other option is for him to quietly take the poster down and hope that it will 'all blow over'.

4   Sheila might have difficulty in getting Reginald to accept that his managerial style is in drastic need of change.

Barriers which Reginald might put up could include:
- Pride (yet another emotion!): He has to admit that his style of

management has weaknesses. He might also resent this suggestion coming from Sheila if he has a stereotype about her as a woman and his subordinate.

● Perceptions: Reginald might simply not perceive the problem as his! He has, in his eyes, merely pointed out (albeit a little heavy handed) what employees already know. Pilfering leads to dismissal. Although, he mistook the discrepancy to be due to pilfering that does not detract from his message which is still valid and it shows staff that he intends to run a tight and efficient store.

5   Obviously there are barriers due to the differences in perceptions and possible mismatch of knowledge, skills and interest. However, one of the major barriers will be that of credibility. Quite simply, will the staff believe that he is about to reform his ways? He might try to explain to his staff how things will be in future but they will have a tendency to evaluate him too early and not really listen to what he has to say. They might even have a frozen evaluation of him for months if not years to come and never accept the 'new' Reginald, even if he does begin to behave differently.

He needs to convince people of his genuine desire to change. Some of his staff might suspend judgement until his actions become consistent with his words. Reginald needs to repeat his message in different ways – hold meetings, briefings, manage more by walking around the store, adopt an 'open door' policy, be seen to react to staffs' comments and to give feedback. He needs to reward staff appropriately and to recruit the sort of people who will fit in with his style of management. Most of all, he needs time and patience and a genuine desire to improve communication.

Review Activity 3

1   Katz and Kahn(1966) split communication down the line into five categories:

1   job instructions

2   job rationale (explains why a task is being performed)

3   information about procedures and practices

4   feedback to subordinates

5   indoctrination of goals (mission).

● Jane is going to use computers to download information and monthly meetings to issue job instructions. Memos and telephone conversations are not mentioned, although Jane may use them on an ad hoc basis.

- One aspect of her communication to the area representatives will be to explain why she is introducing the new system and what it is she hopes it will achieve. Hopefully, there are benefits for both the company and the reps. She will need to explain why she is preferring the use of computers. Probably the rationale she will use is one of standardisation and efficiency, coupled with up-to-date information.

- As important – or more important to the sales reps! – will be her rationale for the new bonus system; why she thinks the old system is unfair and why her new points-weighted system will be better.

- She will certainly have to give information about procedures and practice. For instance, the procedures relating to the downloading of computers and the ways in which the standard report forms must be completed; procedures to be adopted at meetings.

- Feedback to subordinates is one area which has been sadly lacking in the past! Feedback will now be formally given in two ways: through the forum of the meetings; and via a modem to the area representatives' laptops.

- Indoctrination of goals. Sheila will be trying to indoctrinate her new goals and values to the sales team. She might have difficulty as inevitably there will be some resistance to change. She will try to win over the high performers in the organisation. Additionally, she could use training events, for example, the 'high flyers' programme as a means of communicating these new values. And the new 'professional' staff she will be taking in to the organisation will be put through an induction programme in which they will be immersed in these new values.

2   The communication networks which existed before Jane took control were probably of the circle or comcon type amongst the cliques. This represents de-centralised control, information sharing and decision-making are carried out among the group members.

There is a probably an element of grapevine communication, probably of the cluster type with sharing of unofficial information – gossip, rumours, etc – amongst selected members.

This system probably came about for two reasons:

- It was the natural and preferred style of the area representatives; they would have sales areas which would border, or possibly overlap, with their neighbours and they would need information regarding what contracts they were dealing with. They might even be dealing with the same client. They required information in order to up-date their knowledge and as a means of co-ordinating their efforts. It was a lonely life; they needed others in a similar situation to talk with and share their everyday problems.

- There appears to have been little control or co-ordination from the previous sales director, thus leaving little choice for any other form of communication!

It is evident that Jane wants a centralised information system, a wheel, in which control information is sent to her and she sends directives out to the sales representatives. She wants this for control purposes. She wants to have the overall picture of a very-fast moving market. She also wants accountability of staff to herself.

3   Katz and Kahn summarise upward communication from subordinate to superior as being about:

- him-or herself, performance and problems

- others and their problems

- organisational practices and policies

- what needs to be done and how it is to be done.

The area representatives will be wary of giving any information concerning themselves or others as this information identifies performance with their various contracts. In other words, they are providing control information which is likely to be used by Jane to determine bonuses, etc. It is highly likely that under-performing individuals will only want to present the minimum of information. There is, after all, the element of being watched in Jane's new system.

There is likely to be concern over the new policies, procedures and what is to be done. Thus, some of the area representatives are likely to seek advice from Jane on these issues, certainly as a preliminary measure and possibly also in an ongoing manner.

4   There are advantages in using the standardised report and also in using the verbal summary. There are also advantages in using the two together. To take each in turn:

Report provides:
- a permanent record which reaches all of the relevant people, Jane and the sales reps, and allows them to read the information in their own time and convenience
- a consistent format, hopefully, Jane will have chosen an appropriate format
- only relevant information and should be relatively quick to read.

Verbal summary
The first advantage of this method is that it allows Jane, or the others, to ask questions and to seek clarification on data presented to them. It also allows more probing questions along the lines of 'that's interesting, tell us more'. This two-way process involves those present, and this involvement is a great stimulator of ideas and a motivator of initiatives.

Reports can be dull depending upon your perception and what the sales people really want is some personal interaction. Think about the amount of time they spend on the car phone. Remember as well, that a verbally delivered summary also makes use of body language, and paralinguistics. If delivered with enthusiasm and clarity, it can be much more interesting than the report.

Together

Putting the two together reinforces the message; these monthly meetings are evidently important; the new reporting system is important. Some people will want to carefully analyse the reports; others would prefer the personal approach. Some people will be good at writing good reports; others will write poor ones, although the standard format will hopefully overcome some of these problems. Some people will deliver their message better in presentation form.

Putting the two together is likely to have a synergistic effect. The combined effect is likely to be greater than the simple benefits which could be derived from having one or other forms of communication on their own.

5   Area representatives get to know more than their immediate neighbours and Jane Cassidy.

These two factors in themselves are important to communication. Although, it is quite possible to develop some sort of understanding of another person over the telephone, it is never quite the same as meeting that person face-to-face. Again body language says much about a person. Feedback is also possible.

In this respect, the apparently informal nature of the rest of the afternoon – the lunch, for instance – is useful for icebreaking. This is also a time when more favourable impressions of people may be formed. Perhaps so-and-so isn't so bad after all – he or she seems to have the same sort of homelife as myself. This might help us to avoid the stereotype scenario or the frozen evaluation we mentioned earlier. The more comfortable we feel with someone, the more likely we are to communicate at a deeper level with them. We might discover how they see things – their perceptions – again this is extremely useful.

From a network point of view, it should increase the size, number and/or strength of the networks.

6   It is unlikely that the informal networks of the area representatives which have built up over the years will suddenly vanish. Nor is this necessarily desirable. Hopefully, the networks will carry more meaningful information and have more sense of purpose than previously. The cluster chains of the grapevine will probably still persist.

The networks grew out of a need for self-support amongst the area representatives. This need for information and group identity will persist but because it is now only one of the ways in which communication takes place, its importance as the sole provider of information is likely to decrease with the introduction of the meetings, written reports and the computer.

UNIT 3
EFFECTIVE BUSINESS WRITING

Introduction

As we saw in Unit 2, communication is of vital importance in an organisation. This communication can take many forms. In this unit, we look at the written form, and how to get the maximum benefit from your business writing whether it is a short memo, a letter or a formal report. This will also help you with all your written communication including preparing assignments in your study programme. The key to improving any written communication is practice, so you will find several writing exercises to complete. You should do these with care. They are rather different from the long case studies you met in the previous unit. However, in some of the activities you will be writing using the case study approach. The skills you will learn in this unit will also help you in everyday life – writing letters to your bank manager, or requesting information on a particular company product, or to complain about the accommodation on your dream holiday.

Objectives

By the end of this unit, you will be able to:

- use various pre-writing techniques
- perform the steps in the process writing approach to business communication
- avoid writer's block
- construct paragraphs using a topic sentence, controlling ideas and supporting sentences
- produce effective business letters and memos
- define the purpose of a report and select an appropriate format
- write an effective business report using a commonly accepted format and associated graphics
- present a report effectively.

Section 1

Introduction to Effective Business Writing

Introduction

In this section, we consider how to produce good business correspondence. You will use an approach to writing which emphasises the writing process itself. This will equip you to tackle both your business writing tasks and your university or college assignments. We first introduce you to a process often used by professional writers when working. Then we focus on the macro level of editing. We look at the big issues of the shape of the document, the arrangement of ideas and the quality of the paragraphing. Finally we deal with the micro level of editing; that is, detailed editing of sentences for aspects such as correct grammar, punctuation and word usage.

First, consider some common misconceptions about writers and writing:

- Writing is easy for some people.
- All good writers work from a plan.
- As you improve as a writer, you need to do fewer drafts.
- Good writers seldom have to edit their work.

Writing is easy for some people. Many inexperienced writers think that others find the task of writing very easy. They think others can simply sit down at a desk and produce good writing without any real effort. This is rarely the case. Interviews with authors who earn their living by writing often reveal that they have constant battles with not wanting to get started, poor attempts and non-productive periods.

In the business world, busy executives cannot afford the luxury of waiting around until they feel like doing some writing. Often there is a very tight time frame in which business correspondence has to be produced.

All good writers work from a plan. Some good writers feel comfortable with working out a detailed plan before they begin to write. Most, however, do not know in advance exactly what they are going to write. They have to go through the process of generating ideas to get started on their writing tasks.

If you work out a plan before you have explored the subject fully you might limit your writing considerably. In this unit, we discuss some alternative strategies for starting your writing tasks.

As you improve your writing, you do fewer drafts. Few people write a first draft that is good enough to become the final product. If they are able to do this, then they have usually gone through an intensive creative, organising and editing process in their heads. Even work done like this can usually be improved.

Good writers seldom have to edit their work. We make things more difficult for ourselves if we try to create and edit at the same time. Most professional writers write their first drafts without worrying about mistakes in spelling, grammar and punctuation, or in sentence and paragraph structure. They concentrate first on setting on paper *what* they really want to say. Then they go back and look at *how* to say it correctly.

You will see better results if you adopt the professional writers' approach to your writing. They go through the following steps for producing their final product:

1   prewriting

2   organising

3   drafting

4   editing

5   producing the final version

6   proofreading.

One key theme that you need to remember as you go through this process is your communication objective. There is no point in having a brilliant piece of writing if it doesn't answer the question that you wanted it to. You need to think about this objective: 'As a result of my message, the reader will be able to. . .' By identifying this objective, you will also have to identify your reader. Again, there is no point producing a brilliant piece if your intended audience cannot understand it because you haven't taken into account their background, or don't want to understand it because it is of no interest or importance to them. We look at some Audience Analysis checklists later in the unit.

1.1 The composing process

STEP 1: PREWRITING

Prewriting is about generating material or ideas. You can do this from inside your head or by going to outside sources once you have decided what information you need. In either case, prewriting techniques are useful starting points.

Imagine a situation where you are unclear about the content of your message. You have been told by your tutor or boss that your section has to produce 'something' for the university or company newsletter by tomorrow and you have to write it. You have no ideas. This would result in you staring helplessly at an empty page or an empty computer screen. It is known as writer's block.

There are a number of techniques for getting the writing process started. Two techniques which may be unfamiliar to you are freewriting and brainstorming.

Freewriting

You would probably have very limited time for a task like the one we described above.

ACTIVITY 1

Allow yourself five minutes freewriting to see if you can come up with any ideas. Just write without worrying about correct grammar, spelling, sentences, structure or anything else. If you get stuck, repeat the last words you have written until new thoughts start to come.

The following is an attempt at freewriting on the task of finding a topic for the company newsletter:

> What can I write about? Why me? me? me? I hate these tasks. Why do I have to do it? I'm too busy to be doing this. I'll have to think of something fast. What's new? new? new? staff? No — nothing interesting there. New equipment? Photocopiers? Very uninteresting. Who wants to read about photocopiers? What's interesting??? Got to be something new. What's new? Computers? Computers. Yes — new personal computers! All students/staff have been issued with laptop computers. Most have no idea what to do with them. I like the idea although I don't know how to use it. We all need training. Others are worse than me about using them. At least I try. Some seem terrified of them. Secretaries may be worried about their jobs. The general impact might be interesting. Need for training might have possibilities. Cost high. . . On Friday last, every student/officer in this department was issued with an ABC laptop computer. It is interesting to see the individual reactions to this event...

Through the process of freewriting we have generated a draft opening (the last two sentences in our freewriting) which gives us a good start for the task.

Brainstorming

You will find brainstorming most useful when you have a lot of information in your head about a topic. There are two stages:

Stage 1: Free, seemingly unrelated idea formation.

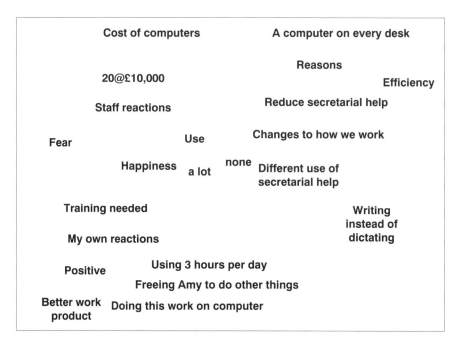

Stage 2: Looking at our Stage 1 brainstorming, we can see some ideas that might go together, and a possible plan of action:

1   What we did and why.

2   How staff/students are reacting to having computers on their desks.

3   The effect on your own work.

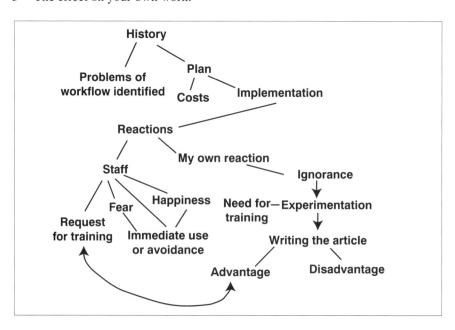

Note the links between sections; for example, 'request for training' under the heading 'staff/students' and own 'need for training'. You can use links like these for connecting sections.

(End of one paragraph)

. . . a common reaction from staff/students was to request training in the use of computers.

(Beginning of the next paragraph)

I too felt the need for training when I began to experiment. . .

This kind of sentence is one type of transition, an important concept which you will meet later in this unit.

Usually in the business environment you have a good idea of what your writing must be about. Prewriting then becomes a matter of gathering up and connecting ideas, and of finding out what other information you need to complete the task.

Freewriting and brainstorming are both very useful techniques for starting a writing task. Don't give up if they don't work for you right away. They need to be practised to become useful skills.

Points to remember

Brainstorming is an effective way to start your writing. As you become more and more confident in your written communication skills, you may find that the amount of brainstorming you do varies from task to task. When you tackle writing tasks such as reports and proposals, brainstorming is an excellent way of ensuring that you include all the important and relevant points for your reader.

STEP 2: ORGANISING

After you have generated your ideas, you need to organise them to make it easy for your reader to follow your line of thought. The ideas may have occurred to you in a random order, but you certainly cannot present them to your reader like that. You can use the concept of a hierarchy of ideas with top level, second level and lower level points using approaches to organise and order your ideas. This technique, brainstorming (as illustrated above), or the traditional outline can be used to get your material organised.

STEP 3: DRAFTING

From your outline, you can produce a rough draft. You should write this without worrying about correct spelling, punctuation, grammar, sentence structure, etc. Focus on what you want to communicate and not how you are writing. Separating the creation and editing stages of writing makes an enormous difference to the quality of your final product. You should aim to get into a 'drafting attitude'.

- Avoid thinking about spelling, punctuation, paragraphing, finding the best word, etc. while you draft.
- Work from a typed copy if you possibly can.
- Don't force yourself to write in a beginning-to-end order.

If you can, get someone else to read through your rough draft with the aim of telling you:

- what is not clear
- what they need to know more or less about
- which parts they liked
- which parts they think should be left out.

By doing this, you are trying out your writing on a receiver. What is perfectly clear to you may not be clear at all to your receiver. If you cannot arrange for someone to read through your draft, try to leave it for a while. Time away from your writing allows you to see it in a new light when you return to it. When you come back to it, try to put yourself in the shoes of your reader.

STEP 4: EDITING

Change roles at this stage and become the editor of your own work, finally concentrating on **how** rather than **what** you have written.

You need to ask yourself:

- Does it achieve my communication objective?
- Is it likely to get the response I want?
- Is it written appropriately for my readers?
- Are ideas organised clearly?
- Have I been consistent in format?
- Are my sentences and paragraphs well constructed?
- Have I written as concisely as possible?

To edit well you need to start with the large issues first. The first five of the questions above are macro-editing issues, which we deal with later. The last two are about micro-editing. You may prefer to undertake this on a wordprocessor.

STEP 5: PRODUCING YOUR FINAL VERSION

Having worked through your draft, you are ready to produce a final version. Now you must consider the format and layout conventions for presenting your letter, memo or report. If you have done your drafting on a wordprocessor or computer, this step is much easier and makes the task of proofreading much more efficient. It also allows you to see your work in a variety of layouts and print styles if presentation is particularly important. You will learn more about wordprocessing in Unit 6.

If your work is being typed by someone else, make sure you give very clear instructions to the typist. Many large organisations have standard ways of doing this. Alternatively, write your instructions enclosed in square brackets. This is a signal to the typist not to type these words.

In the sections on letter, memo and report writing, we will deal with the specific formats for each kind of document.

STEP 6: PROOFREADING

Proofreading is different from editing. Proofreading is your final check that everything is perfect before it goes to your readers. You can use a spellchecker and grammar checker on your computer, but you will still need to check carefully, these tools are not foolproof! You will see how to get the most out of your wordprocessing software program in Unit 6.

Do a final check for:

- typing errors, omissions, repeated words, lines left out, etc.
- spelling errors – use your wordprocessing software's spelling checker, but beware of words which may slip through, such as were/where, to/too, their/there etc. also, for UK work be aware of American versions of spelling.
- punctuation errors – note these will probably be overlooked on a wordprocessor, although the grammar checker may pick up some.
- layout errors – spacing, headings, margins, numbering, etc.

The typist may be able to do this but if the document has your name or the name of your firm on it, **you** are responsible for its final form.

Problems finding your own errors? Try reading what you have written aloud. This forces you to process what you are reading in a different way.

Summary of the steps in the composing process

There are six steps in this approach to writing: prewriting, organising, drafting, editing, producing a final version and proofreading.

For short writing tasks, some steps will take little or no time. For major writing tasks, such as formal analytical reports, each step may take one or more writing sessions. This approach gives you a good procedure for tackling your writing tasks both at work and in your studies. Please use it.

1.2 Macro-editing: highlighting, emphasising and connecting ideas

You now need to focus on the first step in the editing process – improving the structure of documents and paragraphs. The four principles that apply to documents and paragraphs are:

- unity and emphasis
- organisation and highlighting
- connection or coherence
- appropriate length.

UNITY AND EMPHASIS

Unity means that your writing concerns a central idea or subject. Emphasis means that your main ideas are placed in a key position or emphasised for your reader. To achieve unity you need to make sure that you are meeting your communication objective, and only that. If you've added in other information that you just happened to have, then delete it as it is not about your main topic. And by making sure that your main idea is clear you will be adding emphasis.

For a document, it is useful to have an introduction and a conclusion. For paragraphs, you need to group your ideas around a topic sentence that contains the controlling idea of the topic sentence and the paragraph. Start with the topic sentence and then follow with the supporting information, and then end with a conclusion if appropriate. Don't embed the topic sentence in the support material or end with it.

Introductions and conclusions

Most people have trouble writing introductions and conclusions. One reason for the difficulty is trying to write them in the same order as your final piece. Give up this idea and try writing your introduction and conclusion afterwards.

Bentley (1991) offers good advice on the task of writing introductions and conclusions. You will find the *what exists/ why write/ how organised* plan on page 185 of this book very useful (Figure 1). As you can see from this figure, depending on your audience, you can emphasise different aspects of the same information.

The *WHAT EXISTS*	The *WHY WRITE*	The *HOW ORGANISED*	
What exists, is familiar, is shared	Why you are writing – change, issues, reasons	Direct approach: State solution	or Indirect approach: Ask questions
Examples Every employee must understand company policies.	You are a new employee.	Here are five policies.	What should you know?
Business people must communicate with an increasing number of audiences.	Present legislation demands that you report X to the government.	This memo outlines four steps in reporting process.	How should you deal with reporting X?
The copying machine serves the entire third floor.	It has been breaking down daily.	I recommend purchase of a new machine, for three reasons.	What should be done? Here are four options.
Your time is valuable.	You have become more busy lately.	I recommend you take a time-management program.	What can you do? Here are some possible solutions.

Figure 1: An effective introduction includes:
Source: Bentley, 1991, p. 185

For some practice, try the following:

ACTIVITY 2

1 Identify the *what exists/why write/how organised* parts of the following:

The volume of photocopying in this office has increased by 50% in the last three months. As a result our overheads are up and our end of year bonuses will be down. To avoid this situation, I recommend three ways to reduce the volume of photocopying.

2 Rearrange the information to produce:

a a *how organised* plan

b a *why write* plan

---

1 Sentence 1: *What exists*

Sentence 2: *Why write*

Sentence 3: *How organised*

2 a *How organised* emphasis showing high credibility of sender

This memo outlines three ways of reducing the volume of our photocopying which was up by 50% in the last three months. If we don't reduce our overheads we must expect reduced bonuses this year.

b *Why write* emphasis appealing to interests of reader

We are facing lower bonuses this year if we do not reduce our overheads. For example, I have discovered that in the last three months the volume of photocopying is up by 50%. I recommend three ways of cutting photocopying costs.

ORGANISATION AND HIGHLIGHTING

Your document and paragraphs must be well organised, you need to divide up your material in a hierarchical manner. You can show this by various highlighting techniques: subheadings of different levels, capitalisation, lists, etc. In this module, you can see the use of different levels of headings, subheadings, the use of bold or italic or capitals, boxed items, lists with bullets etc. Highlighting shows your organisation and identifies the key points to your reader. And by structuring your work like this you will get your ideas and subsequent writing clear. The computer skills that you will acquire by the end of the module will help you in some of these techniques. Picking out headings and key points in bold, for example, will become second nature. Also, you will be able to format data and information into charts and tables with ease. However, wordprocessing and graphic techniques will only enhance your content, they will not magically make it correct. Remember they are not a substitute for getting it right, they just make the execution and final appearance and legibility better.

1.3 Writing effective paragraphs

A 'well constructed paragraph is like a document in miniature'; they should both exhibit the same characteristics. It is, in fact, easier to learn about the concepts of unity, emphasis and connection using the paragraph than using a whole document. Once you understand the concepts, it is relatively easy to transfer them to whole documents. Here, we concentrate more on the paragraph than on the document.

One of the easiest and most effective ways of achieving clarity in your writing is to concentrate on the construction of your paragraphs. If your paragraphs are well constructed and linked to each other properly, your writing will be clear and easy to understand and it will flow well.

To write an effective paragraph, pay attention to:

● its unity

● the inclusion of a clear topic sentence and a controlling idea

● its coherence.

UNITY
In English, the paragraph deals with one idea or one complete section of an idea or topic. If you introduce material not directly related to the paragraph's topic you run the risk of confusing the reader.

ACTIVITY 3

Read the following passage and identify a sentence that should NOT be present.

Parrots and mynah birds are famous for their ability to reproduce human speech. Mynah birds can imitate human vowel sounds better than parrots, but parrots can remember a larger vocabulary. The record is 100 words. The parrot, with its vivid green and red feathers, is more brightly coloured than the black mynah bird. Many parrots learn to associate particular words with specific actions. They may say 'good-bye' when someone leaves the room or 'hello' when the telephone rings. It is difficult, however, to show that such words have a real meaning for the parrot. They, certainly do not serve among parrots for communication, which, after all, is the function of language. (Bander 1978)

The sentence that should not be there is: 'The parrot, with its vivid green and red feathers, is more brightly coloured than the black mynah bird.' The rest of the paragraph sticks to the topic of speech introduced in the first sentence.

TOPIC SENTENCES

English paragraphs tend to follow a straight line of development. This usually begins with a topic sentence, the sentence containing the central idea of the paragraph, followed by a series of sentences developing the central idea. Kaplan concluded that paragraphs are developed differently in different cultures (1975). See Figure 2. For example, he sees the Chinese approach to paragraphing as following a more circular line of development.

To write a good paragraph in English you need to be clear about the idea you want to communicate. This idea can be expressed simply in a topic sentence. In business communication, it is wise to place this topic sentence at the beginning of your paragraph whenever you can. This serves to make your idea clearer by warning the reader of what this paragraph is about. At times, however, a topic sentence can be placed effectively in either the middle or at the end of the paragraph. These two positions can be particularly effective in persuasive writing. Wherever it is placed, the topic sentence should control the development and the content of the paragraph. Study the diagrams in Figure 2 to get a good idea of this concept.

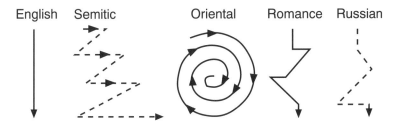

Figure 2: Different approaches to paragraphing

CONTROLLING IDEAS

Nothing improves business writing quite so much as understanding and applying the concept of controlling ideas in paragraphs. You can make each topic sentence clearer and your paragraphs more tightly constructed by adding an idea which controls what should and should not be in the paragraph.

ACTIVITY 4

Identify the controlling ideas in the following topic sentences:

1 There are only two ways of getting thin.

2 We would like you to consider the advantages of signing a 12-month contract for our services.

> 3　The use of chemical pesticides can be harmful for animals and plants.
>
> 4　As head of sales, Ms Brown had many responsibilities.
>
> 5　A business letter's attractive appearance is an important aid in gaining the desired response from your reader.

Controlling ideas have been underlined, and these will then determine the information which should be developed within the paragraph, and the information which should be omitted.

1　There are only <u>two ways</u> of getting thin.

2　We would like you to consider the <u>advantages</u> of signing a 12-month contract for our services.

3　The use of chemical pesticides can be <u>harmful</u> for animals and plants.

4　As head of sales, Ms Brown had <u>many responsibilities</u>.

5　A business letter's attractive appearance is an <u>important aid</u> in gaining the desired response from the reader.

COHERENCE OR CONNECTION

The third feature of an effective paragraph is called 'connection' by Bentley (1991). Connection or coherence in your writing is what makes it flow easily and helps your reader move smoothly from one point to the next. An English paragraph is coherent if its ideas are clearly related to each other and are presented in a logical sequence. You can do this by:

- **transitions** – these are words or phrases that 'stick' your ideas together, examples include: and, in addition, also, but, however, although, on the other hand, for example, therefore, in conclusion, before, earlier, after, later, etc

- **highlighting** – using subheadings, lists etc as we discussed earlier

- **identity signals** – these continue on a theme and are often pronouns, for example: The managers of the company. . . . *They* will. . .

- **parallelism** – this is stating equally important ideas in the same grammatical form, for example: To do fulfil the order . . . Make . . . Pack . . . Send . . . . *Perhaps* can also be used in this way.

APPROPRIATE LENGTH

There are no straightforward guidelines on the length of paragraphs or documents. Generally speaking shorter is better, but shortest is not necessarily best. If you follow our guidelines on constructing paragraphs and documents, then hopefully you will have cut out all the unnecessary material.

1.4 Micro-editing: sentences and words

The last aspect of your editing is sentence structure and choice of words. You should be brief, simple and correct. You may be tempted to copy standard business phrases or jargon from business correspondence. Avoid using phrases such as:

'It has been brought to our notice'

'Trusting this action meets with your approval'

'Thanking you in anticipation'

'We are in receipt of your letter'

'We enclose herewith'

'In reference to the captioned heading'.

Many of these are used in UK businesses and government departments. Some may even have letters, reports and memos using language like this as model correspondence. Modern trends, however, are moving away from wordy, formal and difficult to understand language in business communication. If your manager still insists on this old style you will have to comply.

We do not wish to go into a detailed analysis of English grammar here, but you should note some key points in sentence structure:

- watch your sentence arrangement
  - emphasise the important words
  - place the verb near the subject
  - place modifiers correctly, these connect parts of the sentence together
- watch your sentence length
  - add variety and rhythm
- use vigorous verbs
  - avoid overusing nouns
  - avoid overusing weak verbs
  - avoid elongated verbs
- avoid overusing passive verbs
  - for example, 'an important decision was made by Jo' is more formal and less direct than the 'active' form of the same sentence 'Jo made an important decision'

And note some key points in choosing words:

- be concise
  - watch your prepositions
  - watch your repetitions
- be simple
  - avoid pompous words
  - avoid unnecessary jargon: professional jargon, euphemisms and cliches as they create communication barriers, remember barriers from Unit 2
- be correct
  - choose the most appropriate words for your purpose and check dictionary definitions to ensure that you are using words correctly
  - check your grammar.

For more information on this kind of detail consult an English grammar book, Bentley (1991) or Hefferman and Lincoln (1990). Keep in mind that the only way to improve this aspect of your editing is to practise, so do Review Activity 1 carefully.

REVIEW ACTIVITY 1

1 Rewrite the following sentences so that they emphasise the important words. These are underlined.

a Many employees list a **full insurance programme** as one of their most important benefits.

b An effective sentence contains not only a subject but a **vigorous verb** as well.

2 Reposition the verb nearer the subject in the following sentence.

a Business students, if they are to get a job in today's competitive job market, must possess the necessary communication skills.

3 Rewrite the following passive sentence into the active voice.

a All the profits should be reinvested immediately.

4 Revise the following sentence, correctly placing modifying words and phrases.

a His salary increase nearly was £200.

5 Rewrite the following sentences for more brevity and simplicity:

a In your memo of January 3, you requested that I prioritise the main factors.

b A managerial employee must give authorisation for a secretary to send a communication on paper bearing the company letterhead prior to the time the letter is sent.

6 Rewrite the following sentences to eliminate repetitious phrasing:

a The sum total of out net gains is one million pounds.

b This product has a character of a uniquely individual nature.

7 Rewrite the following sentences to eliminate pompous words and jargon.

a Please affix the appropriate signatures and forward said documents to the undersigned.

b Functional logistical flexibility necessitates a balanced approach to issues of employee non-work time and its scheduling.

Taken from Bentley (1991)6 Rewrite the following sentences to eliminate repetitious phrasing:

a The sum total of out net gains is one million pounds.

b This product has a character of a uniquely individual nature.

7 Rewrite the following sentences to eliminate pompous words and jargon.

a Please affix the appropriate signatures and forward said documents to the undersigned.

b Functional logistical flexibility necessitates a balanced approach to issues of employee non-work time and its scheduling.

Taken from Bentley (1991)

Summary

You have seen that to write effective business correspondence you need to:
- define your communication objective and analyse your reader
- use the process writing approach to gather and organise your ideas, draft, edit and produce a final version
- concentrate on writing well constructed paragraphs
- aim to write as clearly and as directly as possible, eliminating wordiness and unnecessarily long words.

SECTION 2

Writing Letters, Memos and Faxes

Introduction

In this section, you can practise applying what you have learnt so far about communication strategies and principles to the writing of business letters and memos. In business, the traditional way of preparing written correspondence involves the sender or writer dictating the letter or preparing a handwritten draft. The draft is then typed up by a secretary, checked by the original writer, retyped, proofread, signed and finally sent off through the post. This method is becoming less common because of the rapid development of office technology. Now that wordprocessors and computers are so commonplace in business organisations, senders are undertaking the whole process of producing business correspondence themselves. They plan, draft, edit, redraft and proofread on a personal computer or a wordprocessor (as you may do for your assignments). Letters, memos and faxes may be sent electronically from computer to computer without ever being printed.

Even though modern technology is changing the production of written correspondence, the principles behind effective written communication remain the same. Regardless of how they are produced, letters and memos should always be written for a specific purpose to a specific receiver. They are successful only if the receiver gives the response the sender wants. If the tone of your letter or memo sets up resistance in the receiver, the message you are sending may be ignored and the purpose of your letter or memo be misunderstood. If your letter is poorly presented, your reader may feel insulted that you have gone to so little trouble; he or she may even have doubts about your own or your organisation's credibility.

Each letter or memo is really an exercise in public relations. A letter involves important people, including clients and customers outside the organisation. The memo involves people with whom you have to continue to work inside the organisation. Because they are written, both can be filed or reproduced and, therefore, can become a permanent record of the standard of your work and a measure by which your competence can be judged.

2.1 Function of business letters and memos

You should always think carefully about choosing the channel and medium appropriate for your purpose. You met this in Unit 2 in our discussions on various channels and media and particular situations. Because writing letters and memos costs considerable time and effort, you should always work out if the advantages outweigh the disadvantages before you take on the task of writing. It may be more efficient to pick up the telephone. In deciding, you should consider several points:

Cost. Writing letters costs a good deal more than just the paper, the envelope and the postage. Regardless of whether a letter is produced by a writer and a secretary, or composed and sent electronically, through e-mail by the writer, the greatest cost is labour. If writers do not write clear, concise correspondence that achieves its purpose the first time, the costs escalate dramatically.

Letters and memos as a permanent record. Once you have written a message it can be filed or stored either as a paper record in a filing system or electronically as a wordprocessor file. This filing gives you a record of action taken. In most business transactions, the recording of action is essential. You will learn more about using your computer for filing later in the module.

Instant feedback versus time to choose your words carefully. Oral and, in particular, face-to-face communication, gives the sender immediate feedback. Non-verbal communication is an important part of feedback that is not available in a written communication. On the other hand, writing gives the sender time to 'fine tune' exactly what he or she wants to say and gives the receiver the opportunity to check the situation out before replying.

2.2 Business letter

The ability to write effective letters is one of the most valuable business communication skills you can have. Knowledge about acceptable formats, appropriate frameworks (or structures), effective beginnings and endings, and finally, good presentation will help you feel confident about your ability to write good letters.

The seven basic elements of a business letter are:

- **heading** – your return address or letterhead and the date
- **inside address** – your reader's name, title and address usually typed at the left-hand margin
- **salutation** – this can be formal: *Dear Sir or Madam;* semiformal: *Dear Mr Brown;* or informal: *Dear Alan.*
- **subject line** – identifies the topic for your reader, it may include a reference number for easy identification.
- **body** – the text itself.
- **closing** – this can be formal: *Yours faithfully;* semiformal: *Yours sincerely;* or informal: *Regards,* followed by your name and position. The closing should match the salutation.
- **signature** – you need to sign it above your name and title!
- **references** – these indicate any enclosures, or copies to other personnel, or the typist.

The subject line and the references are optional.

Format

Because of the growing international nature of business in the UK, there are many different styles of letter formats. Most formats are acceptable, so the style you choose will probably depend on your organisation's preferences.

The framework

Before writing a business letter, you need to answer the two basic communication questions:

- What is my communication objective?
- Who is my reader?

When you have answered these questions, you will be able to decide what kind of letter you need to write. Your letter will usually fall into one of three categories:

- routine, neutral or good news letter
- bad news letter
- letter to persuade or convince.

Suitable frameworks for each type are:

1   Routine, neutral or good news letters

Direct approach: Clear direct statement of good news

Necessary details

Main idea or look towards the future

2   Bad news letters (for example, refusal of credit)

Indirect approach: Buffer

Facts or reasons leading to bad news

Bad news

Pleasant or neutral statement

3   Letters to persuade or convince (for example, a sales letter)

Attention getter: Use of motivational techniques

Action step

Beginnings and endings of letters

Some people have difficulty with beginnings and endings of letters, so they tend to rely too much on using very formal, traditional phrases, such as:

- We are in receipt of your communication of the 13th instant.
- Receipt is acknowledged of your letter of 12 December.
- In reply to your letter of 10 September, I am directed to advise you . . .
- Assuring you of our best attention at all times.
- Trusting this meets with your approval.

The beginning. If your letter is a reply, you can acknowledge your correspondent's letter very simply:

- Thank you for your letter of 13 December.
- On 13 December you enquired about. . .

Do not waste your time quoting from incoming letters. For example:

> Thank you for your letter of 13 December in which you requested information about possible tours in the European region during August and costing between £800.00 and £1,000.00 per person.

After all, if you are writing a reply, it is obvious that you must have received the letter. Remember, the shorter the better. State your business as quickly as possible.

The ending. The ending, like the beginning, is important because it is the part of the letter that is most likely to be remembered. It should not just fade away, nor should it be too abrupt. It should summarise the contents of the letter and clearly indicate what action the receiver should take. There is no need to add rather old-fashioned concluding phrases like the last two in the list above. If you do feel the need to write a concluding sentence, try something simple like:

- We hope you find the suggested alternatives helpful.
- Thank you for writing to us.

ACTIVITY 5

The following letter illustrates ineffective ways of beginning and ending. Try rewriting it to make it more effective.

> Dear Sir,
>
> Receipt is acknowledged of your letter of 24 instant, in which you asked about the advisory booklets on self-assessment taxation produced by this company.

It is felt that the introductory booklet would be of the greatest value to you at this point in time. Accordingly, a copy of same is being forwarded to you under separate cover.

This publication is being forwarded to you free of charge. Should it be your requirement to obtain other of this company's publications, however, it will be necessary for you to be charged a small fee.

Assuring you of our best service at all times.

Yours faithfully,

Here is an alternative:

Dear Sir

We are happy to send you, free of charge, Introduction to Self-Assessment, the first in our series of advisory booklets on taxation. We hope it meets your needs.

We strongly recommend this series of six booklets to you. They have assisted many of our clients in maximising taxation concessions. Each booklet sells for £2.50.

We have enclosed an order form to assist you in placing further orders.

Yours faithfully

Presentation elements in business letters

Presentation in this context means how the letters look. This is also called 'metacommunication'. *Meta* in Greek means 'beyond' or 'in addition to'; so, 'metacommunication' is something 'in addition to the communication'. Poorly presented letters give a poor impression of the organisation or individual they come from.

As the originator of a business letter, you should make sure that the letter is of appropriate quality before it leaves you or your office:

- free of spelling and punctuation errors
- free of corrections
- set out in an accepted format
- on good quality paper

- placed well on the page
- complete with all necessary enclosures.

Good presentation cannot make a poorly written letter effective; however, poor presentation can make a good business letter quite ineffective.

2.3 Memorandum

You saw in *Unit 2* that communication within an organisation is essential for the effective running of that organisation. The memorandum or memo is an integral part of the communication system of any organisation. It is one of the most common ways messages pass up and down and across the various parts of the organisation. It can go from office to office, branch to branch, manager to subordinate and vice versa.

FUNCTION AND LANGUAGE
The memo is particularly useful in the following situations:

- getting a message through to someone who is difficult to contact
- confirming agreements and arrangements made in meetings or on the telephone
- making sure information will not be forgotten or misunderstood
- providing a record of directions, instructions and/or responsibilities.

Memos are used to:	Examples of simple, effective language to use in memos
● give information	The managing director needs . . .
	The Annual Report is due on . . .
	John Freeman is responsible for . . .
● ask for information	Could you please . . .
	Do you know if . . .
	Could you let me know if . . .
● request action	Would you mind . . .
	Please see that . . .
	Can you please . . .
	I would like you to . . .
	I would appreciate it if . . .
● explain	The reason is . . .
	This happened because . . .
	The problem was caused by . . .

Basically, letters carry messages that go **outside** an organisation; memos carry messages **inside** an organisation. You can apply almost everything you have learnt about writing letters to writing memos. However, the function of the memo as a medium of internal communication creates differences in format and style.

FORMAT

Because the memo is not going to be posted, there is no need for a letterhead or an inside address. Nor does it need a salutation (Dear. . .) or a complimentary close (Yours sincerely). Most organisations have pre-printed memo forms, the standard layout of which will look something like this:

```
Date:        31 July 1991

To:          Alex Leigh, Personnel Branch

From:        Maria Cheyne, Office Manager

Subject:     Guidelines for Leave without Pay
```

The essential information provided by these four headings may be presented in a variety of formats and in a different order, according to a company's requirements or preprinted memo forms.

The body. In memos, you will often find points numbered. This is especially useful in longer memos where the receiver may wish to refer to specific points when replying.

Subject lines. The subject line is the element that causes the most problems. It needs to be neither too broad nor too specific. It should not be a complete sentence.

ACTIVITY 6

Improve the following memo subject lines:

1   My recommendations for the training and promotion of staff in our company

2   How to send e-mail to other personnel in the office

3   What you need to do for the Annual Report

You could have improved as follows:

1   Training and promotion of staff

2   Sending internal e-mails

3   Requirements for the Annual Report

STYLE

The following factors make a memo writing style different from that of letter writing:

- The memo writer knows more about the reader. Even if the organisation is large, the memo writer will usually know something about the reader and his or her favoured amount of detail. The writer may know what background knowledge the reader is likely to have and how the reader fits into the organisation as a whole.

- Because the memo writer works in the same organisation, the writer can use vocabulary that may not be known to people outside the organisation.

- The memo writer does not have the secondary task of projecting the image of the organisation.

However, memos do project the writer's image. Your memos can be used as a measure of your competence and be kept as a record. And they still need to meet your communication objective.

STEPS FOR WRITING MEMOS

Writing clear and effective memos is easy if you follow these steps:

1   As always, determine your communication objective and audience.

2   Identify the central idea you want to get across to your reader.

3   Work out the relationship of all your information to this central idea. Arrange your material so it is presented logically.

4   Cut out all material that is unnecessary for your purpose.

Morgan (1970) gives an example of this approach. Consider the following draft memo:

```
A lot of staff in the office have been complaining
about the lighting over their desks. It just isn't
good enough for them to see by, and they have been
making a lot of mistakes in their typing. Also,
their eyes have been getting sore.

I have looked into this matter and, after taking
some measurements with a light meter, and checking
on what is adequate lighting needed for a typist's
desk, I have decided that we need more light in the
office.
```

> The best way would be to fit four new lighting units
> to the ceiling. Each unit should have three 40
> watt fluorescent tubes in it. This would give
> adequate light to each desk.

This memo is rambling, contains unnecessary information and is organised in a time order – not the best for this type of memo.

1 Pick out   The central idea is that more light is needed.

2 Work out   Supporting ideas are:

- complaints by staff
- details of the new lighting proposal.

3 Cut out   There is little material that can be cut out but the references to 'adequate light' can be made more specific; and the whole style can be tightened up.

A revised version in full memo form follows:

Date: 4 February 1996

To: Jane Fox, Office Manager

From: Andrew Smith, Clerk, Main Office

Subject: Lighting in Typists' Office

Additional lighting is needed in the typists'
office. The typists have complained several times
that the light is inadequate for accurate work.

At present, each desk receives only 50 watts; a
standard lighting manual states that about 75 watts
is the optimum level.

To achieve this, four units, each with three 40 watt
fluorescent tubes, should be fitted to the ceiling
in addition to the present lighting units. This
work can be done by the company's maintenance staff
and should take two days.

The revised memo, which contains more information, is considerably clearer and shorter than the original.

ACTIVITY 7

Using the principles of effective business writing covered in this section, rewrite the following memo in order to gain the desired response.

Your rewritten memo should demonstrate your ability to:

- write clearly and concisely
- use the 'you' approach
- use a positive approach
- cover the subject completely
- write using correct grammar, spelling and punctuation
- use appropriate and correct memo format
- organise ideas well.

Supply any additional details you think are necessary.

To: All plant managers

From: Assistant director

RE: What is needed for the annual Division Report.

I need information from all you plant mangers immediately to prepare the Annual Division Report. What I want is the major accomplishments of you plant during the year, what major problems you've got next year, do you have any objectives for next year and what about last year? How are you going to actuate them. I also want to be informed about organisation planning, community relations, quality control, health and safety, personal management and cost of operation. I have the expectancy that this information will be organised in such a manner so it can be put strait in my report. So make sure everyone proofread it and get all the grammer and spelling right for once. And I want you also to write about anythinng else I might think is important. Make sure you get it the right length and in on time as I do not have any time to waist. This report has got to be positive to show that we act as a team.

The memo has the following problems:

Tone: All 'I attitude'

Organisation: Hard for managers to know what is really wanted

Vocabulary: Unnecessarily long, difficult words (e.g., actuate, expectancy)

Format: Errors in format

                   No date

                   'Re' is old fashioned

Proofreading: Spelling mistakes (manager, personnel, straight, grammar, anything, waste)

                   Mistakes in capitalisation

Suggested answer

To: All Plant Managers

From: Assistant Director

Date: 6 August 1996

Subject: Preparation of Annual Division Report

It is time again to prepare the Annual Division Report. This year I am looking forward to reporting on the hard work and successful operations of all plants. In particular, I would like to stress *organisation planning, community relations, quality control, health and safety, personnel management* and the *cost of operations.* We will also be looking to the future and your plans for next year.

As usual, I would appreciate your help in providing me with information. It will save me a great deal of time if you could give me the information written in such a way that I can put it straight into the report. I can then acknowledge your contributions in the report. For this to work well, you would need to write a paragraph under each of the headings below. If you type your information on your personal computer, you can use the spelling and grammar checker and either give me your work on disk or transfer it electronically to me. I can then paste your work straight into the document.

```
As my deadline is 4 October, I will need your
information by 30 September.

Headings for report

1995-1996

a. Objectives

b. Major accomplishments

c. Problems

1996-1997

a. Major objectives

b. Anticipated problems

c. Strategies

Thank you for your co-operation.
```

Note the use of lists and italics and bold to highlight. You should become familiar with using these kinds of techniques as you become more competent at using your computer, or you need to instruct a typist if this is how you are working.

2.4 Fax and other electronic means

Both nationally and internationally much business correspondence is transmitted by facsimile or fax. Faxing is a way of life. Faxes can simply be letters transmitted electronically rather than by post or internal memos from one part of the organisation to another. They can be sent directly from and received by computers, without ever existing as a hard copy. An extension of this is to send your message via e-mail, this tends to become an informal exchange rather like actually talking to someone. The technology can be used to send more formal documents, even large ones can be sent by a process called file transfer. However, there may be some problems as formatting that you have put in may not be read by the receiving computer.

Electronic Data Interchange (EDI) takes this electronic communication a stage further and allows direct communication between say, a supplier and a manufacturer, on ordering, delivery and invoicing. The organisations must agree on a standard procedure and format for communication. It enables a business to run with very little paper communication. However, it is beyond our scope here.

FORMAT

All faxes should have a transmission sheet as their first page. Most companies have their own preprinted transmission sheets which ask for the following information:

- Receiver's name, address and fax number
- Sender's name, address and fax and phone numbers
- Date
- Number of pages
- Reference number (less common).

A typical fax transmission sheet is given in Figure 3.

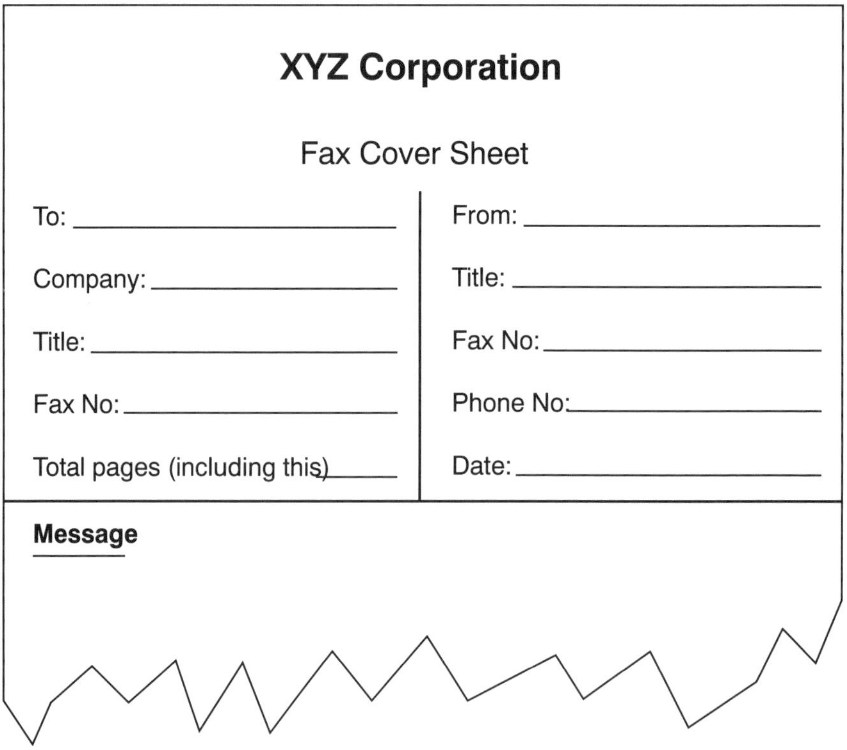

XYZ Corporation

Fax Cover Sheet

To: _____   From: _____

Company: _____   Title: _____

Title: _____   Fax No: _____

Fax No: _____   Phone No: _____

Total pages (including this) _____   Date: _____

Message

Figure 3: Typical fax transmission sheet

It is helpful if you can fit your message on the transmission sheet to reduce costs and to keep all information together. If the information you are faxing is important, you may want to follow up by sending the original document by post. This is called a confirmation copy; you should note on the transmission sheet that you are sending it.

ADVANTAGES AND DISADVANTAGES

Advantages: Using faxes can eliminate some of the major disadvantages of letters – cost and time – while retaining the advantages: providing a permanent record and allowing time for both sender and receiver to consider the message.

- It is cheap.

- It is fast. The speed of transmission means there is little delay between the sending and the receiving of the message.

- You are left with the original for your records.

- You can send copies of documents which include graphics.

- Your message does not have to be typed. It does, however, need to be legible.

- You are likely to get a fax in reply, speeding up feedback.

Disadvantages: Most of the disadvantages of the fax are being overcome by current advances in technology.

- Fax paper does not make a good permanent record for filing as the paper disintegrates with time. This problem is now being solved by the production of fax machines using ordinary bond paper. If you need a permanent copy, photocopy your fax. If a fax is received by your computer, you can file it directly or print it out if you need a hard copy.

- Sometimes fax copies are not clear and pages are missing. Again, advances in fax technology are making faxing more reliable; any transmittal problems are also avoided by computer to computer transfer.

- Because fax machines are usually shared, a fax may get lost with someone else's correspondence. The solution is to have your own personal fax machine!

- Called 'the curse of the 1990s' by some, the overuse of faxes generates a lot of unnecessary paper and uses up energy. For example, some people may telephone, fax and mail the same information.

THE LANGUAGE

Unlike telexes, faxes do not need any special language. Because they are simply letters, all the techniques that you have learnt about writing clear, concise, well organised letters applies to writing faxes too. Like letters, there is no need to use old fashioned terms such as: 'at your earliest convenience', 'as per your fax' or 're your fax'. It is also odd to write about documents or information being 'enclosed'. Writers commonly adopt a more informal tone on fax transmission sheets than they do in letters sent by post.

ACTIVITY 8

Rewrite the following sentences to make them more suitable for a fax.

1   As per our fax of 13 December 1996, you are advised that the shipment will arrive in the UK on 23 March 1997.

2   Please find enclosed a map of the location of the venue for the aforementioned meeting.

> 3 We would be most obliged if you could see your way clear to giving this matter your urgent attention.

Your answers should be something like this:

1   Your shipment will arrive in the UK on 23 March 1997.

2   I am sending you a map to help you find the meeting venue.

3   As this matter is urgent, we would appreciate it if you could reply (act etc.) as soon as possible.

REVIEW ACTIVITY 2

1 What are the usual parts of a business letter?

2 Identify three categories of letters. What kind of opening would you use in each?

Summary

This section has introduced two major business writing applications: the letter and the memo, either of which can be transmitted as a fax. To write effective business letters and memos, you need to be certain about your communication objective; know about your readers; use accepted formats; organise your ideas in an appropriate framework; pay particular attention to beginnings and endings; use appropriate language; and present your letter or memo as professionally as possible.

SECTION 3
Writing Effective Reports

Introduction

In this section, we introduce you to the skills needed to write effective business reports. We provide you with guidelines for writing effective, well-structured reports with relevant content and good style.

Managers have always needed information in order to make sensible decisions. In business, it is common to use reports for assembling and conveying information. Your ability to gather, organise and present information in a report format is, therefore, likely to be an important factor in your career path.

3.1 What is a report?

You might think of a business report as a lengthy document with a special format and elaborate graphics – the type you see being produced on television commercials by teams of executives with the help of a computer. Some reports are like that, but others are short and simple. A report can be any length, ranging from a one-page memorandum report to a book-length report on which the future of a company may depend. It is not length but function that defines a report.

FUNCTION

A business report is usually authorised or assigned; that is, the job of preparing a report is given to an 'expert' who is in close contact with the particular problem, or to a person who is in the right position to collect information and data. If you are that person, you will need to know how to go about the task.

The function of a report is to convey ideas and information clearly, concisely and accurately from the mind of the writer to the mind of the reader. This requires the report writer to:

- collect accurate data
- organise and analyse data objectively, draw conclusions, and sometimes make recommendations
- write clearly and concisely
- understand exactly what the reader wishes to know and convey that information in a form he or she can understand.

USES

Organisations find reports useful for many purposes. Some common uses are:

- recording work done
- assessing a situation
- assessing new ideas
- indicating future action
- solving problems
- keeping people informed.

The following definition takes all these factors into consideration:

> 'An effective business report is an orderly, objective presentation of factual information with or without analysis, interpretation, and recommendations. It is planned to serve some business purpose, usually that of making a decision.' (Treece 1989)

3.2 Types of reports

Your purpose and your audience will determine the type of report you will need to write. There are two kinds of written statements that can be made: those that tell the reader about something and those that tell the reader to do something. This idea is very helpful in classifying reports. **Informational reports** (the TELL style) tell the reader about something and **analytical reports** (the SELL style) tell the reader to do something. Both informational and analytical reports can be presented in a **formal** or **informal** format.

Informational reports present information with no attempt to analyse data or make recommendations. Their purpose may be to provide an accurate record or to explain, for example, a new procedure. The important task here is to select and emphasise the most appropriate facts.

Analytical reports present data, analyse and interpret that data and make recommendations. Sometimes, they aim to persuade the reader to the writer's point of view. These reports are sometimes known as 'leading' reports because they lead the readers towards making a decision – the one the writer wants them to make.

FORMAL REPORTS

This type of report has several parts. A formal report has a preliminary part which may include a covering memo or letter (sometimes called a letter of transmittal), table of contents, list of tables and a synopsis or abstract. Usually it also has supplementary parts including a bibliography and appendices.

The language of formal reports can be different from informal reports. In formal writing you generally do not use:

● contractions, for example, 'won't', 'it's'

● incomplete sentences

● slang or colloquial vocabulary, for example, 'OK'.

There is some debate about whether it is appropriate to write formal reports in a first or second person active style (I, we, you). Many people feel the impersonal passive writing style (there is, it is) provides a more objective and unbiased tone. Organisations usually have policies about the level of formality required in their reports so you should always check. A good rule is to be as informal as you are allowed to be.

INFORMAL REPORTS

These are sometimes presented in a letter or memorandum format. They usually do not include letters of transmittal, tables of contents, etc. They do, however, still need some sort of summary statement. The language can be relatively informal.

3.3 Report formats

Reports vary in the parts they include and the order in which the parts appear, particularly, with regard to the best position for the conclusion and recommendations. Many view that these parts should come early in the report so that the busy reader can decide early if the report is worth reading or not! You should find out if your organisation has a preferred report format. You may also wish to construct templates or structures for those reports that have consistent or specific outlines or sections. You will find this easy to do when you have developed your computer skills later in the module.

FORMAL REPORTS

Formal reports are the type that worry most people. They are usually a large task, involving investigation or research, and include several more parts than the letter or memo report.

Cover page. A very basic title page for this report could look like this:

Corporate Arts Support at High Tech Corp
Prepared for Mr Arthur Hailey
Managing Director
Drafted by Mark Floyd
Public Relations
23 September 1996

Letter or memo of transmittal. When sending your report to the person who authorised it, you should write either a cover letter or memo to accompany it. This person is involved in other work and could be very puzzled when your report turns up in the in-tray. In this case, because this report is being sent inside the company, a cover memo is appropriate. For example:

```
To:        Arthur Hailey, Managing Director

From:      Mark Floyd, Public Relations

Date:      23 September 1996

Subject:   Report on Corporate Arts Support

Here is the report you asked me to write on possible
ways to enhance the company's image by linking its
name with arts funding.

I am confident that through the four steps outlined in
this report, we can develop an effective programme
that benefits both the arts and our company.

Thank you for the opportunity to research this
interesting area of public relations. Should you
decide to implement the programme, I would like to
work on the project team.
```

The contents page would probably be something like:

Contents

3.4 Other report formats

In business, shorter reports in either memo or letter report format are more common than the long formal report. Both memo and letter reports require the same writing and organisational skills as longer formal reports.

MEMORANDUM REPORTS

'Memo' reports are used when the report is brief and for internal reference only. These reports are very common and are usually needed when change is proposed. They usually follow this organisational pattern:

1   Proposal

2   Description of present system

3   Advantages of the change versus its cost to the organisation.

Note that the framework of this report uses the direct approach for the ordering of ideas, probably because the report writer has predicted that the reader will agree with the proposal. How would you change the order if you anticipate opposition to the proposal? The following is an example of a memorandum report:

MEMORANDUM

To: Mary Lamb, Personnel Research Director

From: Christopher Challen, Assistant Manager, Catering

Date: 18 May 1997

Subject: *Communication problems at shift change in the main kitchen*

To ensure adequate instructions are passed on during changes of shift, I propose a ten-minute overlap of all employees at shift changes in the hotel's main kitchen.

The problem

Since the opening of our main kitchen, we have been experiencing major start-up problems at the beginning of each shift. The problems are usually concerned with unreported breakdowns in kitchen equipment or with shortages in ingredients because of unanticipated customer demand.

At present the head chefs are responsible for communicating job-related information. Much of it is done through work notes which each head chef maintains. They make entries throughout the day regarding orders and the functioning of equipment. At the time of the shift change, the incoming head chef first reads the work notes and seeks any necessary clarification before the outgoing head chef departs.

There are several problems with this system. A head chef will often forget to record vital information and, as a result, the incoming head chef will not be aware of it. Head chefs are not always told by their team about equipment or supply problems, so such problems are often not recorded. Head waiters are subsequently not being briefed about shortages. Some head chefs must leave promptly in order to catch the hotel bus and do not have enough time available to assist the incoming head chef or head waiter.

Advantages of a ten-minute overlap

This would make the exchange of information at shift changes easier and more thorough. Not only could the head chefs exchange work-related information, but individual kitchen workers and head waiters could also pass information to their incoming counterparts. Being made aware of any problems with equipment upon coming to work would enable a kitchen hand, for example, to adapt to the situation. Order chefs would tell their replacements the important details of the current supplies, and head chefs would no longer have to depend entirely on the work notes for information from the previous shift. Head waiters could brief their waiting staff on what dishes they should encourage patrons to order.

Costs

The change would increase payroll costs by approximately 4%, since each kitchen employee would be paid for eight hours and 20 minutes per day rather than for eight hours. The benefits to the hotel would be worth it. While it is difficult to determine how much the present situation has cost the hotel, the expense has been considerable. Unclear instructions in the work notes plus supply changes which were not conveyed to the succeeding shift have cost the hotel much in terms of both pounds and frustrated kitchen staff, not to mention the effects on our clientele and our reputation.

Recommendations

1 That a staff meeting of all main kitchen employees be called to explain the purpose of the 10-minute overlap in shifts.

2 That a 10-minute overlap in shifts begin as soon as possible and no later than 1 July 1997.

Other common situations in which the memo report is used are:

- **periodic reports,** where daily, weekly or monthly updates are needed to keep others informed. As this type of report is usually addressed to the same reader(s) on a regular basis, there is usually no need to provide an introduction. Numbered points should be used and each report should aim to supply updated information in the same order as previous reports to help the reader find information quickly. Periodic reports can be useful for informing people about meetings.

- **progress reports,** which are usually sent upwards in an organisation to inform management about the progress of a project. If a series of progress reports are needed, they should each follow the same format to help the reader.

LETTER REPORTS

If a short report is going outside the organisation, the report is usually presented in the letter report format. Letter reports, like business letters, are presented on letterhead and include the date, inside address, salutation, body and complimentary close. The difference is that very often the business letter is trying to sway the reader (especially in sales letters) to a specific viewpoint in order to reach the communication objective of the writer. The letter report needs to present information objectively and provide a range of options or recommendations for the client. The structure of a letter report and its parts will vary according to its purpose and contents.

The opening sentence will usually refer to the authorisation and purpose of the report. For example:

> Here is the report you requested on June 18 on the feasibility of purchasing residential properties in the UK.

> As you requested on June 18, I have compiled the following report listing a number of options for your investment portfolio.

The main body of a letter report will set out the information required. This will usually include an analysis of the situation being studied or a presentation of relevant findings. This will be followed by a set of recommendations if required. If the report reader is likely to read only the recommendations, this section should be positioned before the findings section, where the reader can focus on it immediately. The last section of the report, the closing, will usually offer further assistance and express courtesy and goodwill.

The main text of a letter report can usually be clarified by the use of sub-headings and numbered points. An appropriate style for the letter report will be determined by the reader/writer relationship but, in general, it should be as informal as possible. The following is an example of a letter report.

Perfect Properties
UK's leading property consultants
1 King's Way, London EC1 5PQ
Tel: 0171-602-3456, Fax 0171-602-3458

10 April 1997

Charles Wells
General Manager
Smith International
123 Harbour Street
London W11B 5EG

Dear Mr Wells,

Proposed purchase of property in Spirit Quay
In your letter of 1 April, you asked us to supply you
with details of suitable properties available for
purchase in Spirit Quay. Having carried out an
extensive investigation of all prestige properties
available in Spirit Quay, I find only two properties
that come close to meeting your requirements.

Property 1: 45 Spirit Quay
This is a very large, three-storey, freestanding
residence, facing the sea. It was built in 1950.

Number of bedrooms:	Six (three double, three single)
Parking:	Space available for three cars in an attached carport
Helpers' quarters:	Has two rooms, a separate kitchen, shower room
Recreational facilities:	A 25-metre in-ground swimming pool
Other features:	A large, somewhat overgrown garden
	Close to the Spirit Quay shopping complex
Price:	£800,000 (negotiable)

Property 2: 76 Reach Road, Spirit Quay
This property is a four-storey residence with a view
of the harbour from the top two
floors. It was built in 1985.

Number of bedrooms:	Five (three double and two single)

Parking:	Space available in attached garage for two cars with on-site parking for two more
Helpers' quarters:	Has two bedrooms with cooking facilities, shower room
Recreational facilities:	A spa pool set in the terrace on the third floor
Other features:	A large terrace with a harbour view on the third floor. Built-in bar in reception area.
Price:	£650,000

Summary

The two properties are quite different in style: the first is old and rather run-down but with great potential for renovation. Renovations could cost up to £40,000. Depending on your preferences, you may regard the garden as either an advantage or a disadvantage.

The second is smaller, more modern and is in immaculate condition. The view does not compare well with the first property but from the upper floors and the terrace it is still good. Built on a very steep slope, it has no usable garden but does have a large, attractive terrace with built-in flower beds and courtyard trees.

Recommendations

As the styles of these two properties are so different, I recommend that you view both. They represent excellent investments at the quoted prices. I look forward to showing you these two properties. Please let me know when it is convenient for you to inspect them.

Yours sincerely

Amy Taylor
Sales Manager

3.5 Approach to writing business reports

Writing reports is much easier if you approach the task in an organised way. The following plan is based on advice given in the *Training Handbook* of the Australian Public Service Board. There are nine useful steps in preparing both formal and informal reports:

1 Consider the aim of the report and write down your statement of purpose.

2 Think about who will read your report by completing an audience analysis.

3 Work out your action plan.

4 Gather and organise the material.

5 Analyse the material and decide on your conclusions.

6 Decide on your recommendations.

7 Make a writing plan.

8 Write the draft.

9 Edit and prepare the final copy.

DEFINING YOUR PURPOSE

Writing reports is usually a major task, so you must be very certain that you fully understand the report writing task you have been given. If you don't, you run the risk of putting a lot of hard work into solving the wrong problem. As you know from your other writing activities, the first step is always to identify your communication objective.

It is really the job of the person assigning the task of writing the report (usually a manager) to recognise, isolate, and define the problem clearly and precisely. However, we do not live in a perfect world and sometimes people further up the organisational ladder do not communicate their requirements very clearly. What steps can you take to make sure you understand your report writing assignment properly?

● Write down, in specific terms, the aim of your report. This forces you to clarify your thinking. You should show this to the person who has assigned you the task of writing the report in order to confirm that you both agree about its purpose. This statement of purpose can be used as the opening sentence in the introductory section of your report.

● Find out if any work has been done on the problem in the past. You do not want to waste your time 'reinventing the wheel'. If work has been done, make sure you find it.

- Find out how your report will be used. Will it be presented to a committee, will it be read only by the manager, or will it be filed away for future reference?

- Find out the expected scope and size of the report. This will help you decide on the degree of detail needed. Don't spend a month and then find out your boss only wanted a two-page report.

- Find out when the report is needed. A report submitted after the decision is taken is a waste of everyone's time.

- Find out what facilities you can use, for example, computer data searches, clerical support, and if you have a budget for the task.

- If the report is a major task, ask for written authorisation.

ANALYSING YOUR AUDIENCE

In *Unit 2,* you learnt that analysing your audience is a basic and vital strategy in producing effective business communication. In report writing, you must focus on the needs of your audience or you run the risk of your report never being read or understood. We have devised the following Audience Analysis Sheet. Use it whenever you have a major writing task or presentation to do.

An important part of audience analysis is working out your strategies for overcoming anticipated problems with your audience. For example, if your report is going to recommend the purchase of a new computer system to a board of directors with no knowledge of computers, you will need to be very careful about your use of computer terminology. In this situation it may be advisable to include a glossary of technical terms.

If you find you circle several 'Don't knows', it may indicate that you do not know enough about your target audience.

Audience Analysis Sheet

---

1   Who are your readers?

   Primary: Age:
   Secondary: Sex:
   Key decision maker: Educational level:

2   How similar are your readers to you in their educational background?

   Similar   Not similar   Don't know

3   How similar are your readers to one another in their educational backgrounds?

   Similar   Not similar   Don't know

4	How much background knowledge do your readers already have in the subject you are writing about?		
	A lot	A little	Don't know
5	How similar are your readers' values and yours?		
	Similar	Not similar	Don't know
6	How useful is your material to your readers?		
	Useful	Not useful	Don't know
7	How do you rate your credibility?		
	High	Low	Don't know
8	Is there any reason your readers will not want to accept your message?		
	Yes	No	Don't know

WORK OUT YOUR ACTION PLAN

Decide what you will do, how you will do it, and when you will do it. How do you intend to begin the task? How will you gather material? How much time will it take and how much time do you have? At work, the writing of a report often has to be fitted around other tasks, so time management is extremely important. Be clear about whether your report is informational or analytical and whether it is to be formal or informal in format and writing style.

GATHER AND ORGANISE YOUR MATERIAL

Prepare to collect your data. For example, you might like to use a card system or your computer. Whatever system you use, collect all the stationery (index cards, folders, etc.) or computer file information you need before you start. You will find more help about this in Unit 8 on databases.

You can gather your data from either primary or secondary sources. Primary data is information that has not been gathered and recorded by someone else. The most common primary sources in business are questionnaires, surveys, observation, and interviews. Secondary data comes from interpretations of others in such sources as Government, professional associations, market research companies, books, journals, reports, files, newspapers and library resources.

Once you have gathered your material, sort it out and organise it. Throw out any irrelevant material that doesn't meet your primary purpose. If you keep it you may be tempted to use it. Group your ideas and begin to order them according to the needs of your reader. Also decide if you will use any graphic aids such as graphs or diagrams.

ANALYSE THE MATERIAL AND DECIDE ON YOUR CONCLUSIONS

If you have gathered information from primary sources such as questionnaires or interviews you need to interpret your findings and check on their reliability. You must interpret information in a way that helps the reader.

Having analysed your findings, you can draw conclusions. You should know these before you start writing your report. Conclusions are really a set of summaries of what your findings reveal. In an informational report, however, analysis is not necessarily required, so a summary usually replaces the drawing of conclusions.

DECIDE ON YOUR RECOMMENDATIONS

Recommendations state your suggested course of action and should be based on your conclusions. They should not be a surprise to the reader. They should be practical and action-based so that your reader can make use of them. In formal reports, recommendations are often presented in a list beginning with the word 'that'. In informal reports, they are often presented in paragraph form. Not all reports give recommendations.

MAKE A WRITING PLAN

Write a comprehensive outline of your report. If you are working on a computer, find out if the software package you are using has an outline facility – a created template structure. This enables you to switch between the outline and the text of your report easily. Computer outlining is highly recommended for report writing.

WRITE THE DRAFT

Write your draft, preferably at one sitting if it is a short report. This helps the report to flow well. There is great value attached to a 'drafting attitude'. At this stage, concentrate on what you want to say, not how you are saying it. Leave the editing and proofreading until after you have your ideas down on paper. Remember the general guidelines on business writing in Section 1.

EDIT AND PREPARE THE FINAL COPY

Using all you have learnt about editing, work through your report, editing for communication strategies first, then for the mechanics, such as sentence structure, spelling, punctuation, grammar and word choice.

There are two other aspects of report writing that you should consider:

- use of graphics in reports
- presentation of reports.

3.6 Using graphics

Reports are often enhanced by graphic aids such as charts, tables, illustrations or graphs. Sometimes data, particularly statistics, are easier for the reader to understand in a table, chart or graph format than just stated in words.

You should try to position a graphic aid as near as possible to the text it explains or illustrates. However, if you have large amounts of data, this might destroy the flow of your report by distracting your reader. Place these aids in an appendix, and include a summary statement in the body of your report. If you are preparing your own material, the computer skills you learn later in the module will help you with charts and tables. Again, the techniques themselves will not make poorly organised material any more understandable; they are not a magic way to achieve success!

HOW TO USE GRAPHICS IN REPORTS

1   **Label and number your graphic aids.** 'Tables' may be numbered separately from other illustrations, or 'figures'. Or you can number all kinds of graphic aids consecutively throughout your report as 'figures'.

2   **Use appropriate titles for your graphic aids.** Titles of tables usually appear above the table; titles of charts and figures are usually below.

3   **Acknowledge your source of information.** Remember, if you take material from other sources, you must acknowledge that source. This is usually done below the graphic aid but it can be placed under the title. This is also necessary if you adapt a graphic. Remember plagiarism in business as well as your studies.

4   **Create a table of figures.** If you have used graphic aids in your report, this table goes immediately after your table of contents.

USING COMPUTERS FOR CREATING GRAPHICS

The use of computer graphics programs has revolutionised the production of graphics. Data can now be converted to graphical form with the press of a key. For example, you can easily discover if your data will be more effectively presented as a pie, line or bar graph. However, this ease of production has its dangers. Remember, graphic aids should only be used if they make things easier for your reader, not just because they can be easily produced. As a good communicator, you should always consider the use of your reader's time. After you have studied Unit 8 you will have a clearer idea of some of the simpler types of graphics that you can use in a report.

3.7 Presenting reports professionally

Finally, consider how to present your report. It needs to be legible. Legibility relates to how easy or difficult your report is to read not handwriting! We have found the following checklist very useful. It has been adapted from *How to Write for the World of Work* by Pearsall and Cunningham (1982). Comments have been added in brackets. Keep these points in mind:

● Use good quality paper, heavy enough to make the typing stand out. (Or as good as you can manage.)

- If copies are required, make them by the best reproduction process you have available. Carbon copies are generally undesirable. (If you have the choice, try to print your report on a laser printer rather than a dot matrix printer. Material printed on dot matrix printers does not usually photocopy very well.)

- Maintain at least one-inch margins all around.

- If you are going to put your report in a binder or have it spiral bound, leave two inches of margin on the left-hand side. (Some wordprocessing packages have a special setting for you to print your report with facing pages.)

- Use legible, plain type. Avoid script and fonts with fancy lines and flourishes. If you are using a wordprocessor or computer with a number of font options, choose a font with serifs. (Serifs are the small bits on the ends of each letter. Research has shown that fonts with serifs are more legible because the eye can more easily distinguish the letter shapes.)

- Enclose graphics in boxes.

- If the sequence of a list is random (as this one is), use bullets (•). If the order is important, use numbers.

You will learn more about the techniques of formatting using your wordprocessor in Unit 6.

REVIEW ACTIVITY 3

Joyce Smith works for a safety consultant. She has been called out to make an assessment of a photographic studio which has suffered extensive damage due to a gas explosion in a neighbouring shop. Three areas of the studio have suffered extensive damage. All areas contained equipment, filing systems, large amounts of chemicals, storage and development tanks.

Joyce is to prepare a report to include assessment of the hazards and recommendations for making safe the studio and dealing with the hazards. This report will be for the studio owners.

Prepare an outline of the sections/headings Joyce might use. What do you think might be included in an appendix?

Summary

Reports are essential in business for equipping managers with the information they need to make sensible decisions. The report writer must constantly keep in mind the function of the report and through careful formatting and organisation make the information in it easily accessible to the reader. You will find report writing more manageable if you follow the nine-step process outlined in this section. Finally, the addition of graphics and extra care taken in the presentation of your report will improve its effectiveness. The activities will give you the opportunity to practise your writing skills. Remember the more you practise, the better you will become at communicating through writing.

UNIT REVIEW ACTIVITY

Gold Coin Bank

Gold Coin Bank is a small, privately owned bank which has been operating in Jersey, Channel Islands for over forty years. The bank prides itself on offering high quality services to its clients, many of whom are international. It is very important that the staff working in the Customer Services Department maintain this standard. Recently, there have been a few problems with more customer complaints; more demands have been placed on the customer services personnel and on the computer staff. The Bank Manager, Mr Martin Rush, has therefore decided to recruit a new Customer Services Manager to help improve the services offered to customers. The new manager is Jill Paine. Existing staff in the Customer Services Department include Issy Wright, Senior Personal Account Advisor, and Cindy Thomas and Ron Field, Personal Account Advisers.

Prepare an outline memo report for Martin Rush (Bank Manager) from Jill Paine (Customer Services Manager) about introducing a new Customer Services System. Along with the new system some other bank services will also be offered. These include a multi-currency account and tax and insurance advice in addition to the mortgage advice and small business planning advice currently offered. Each customer will be allocated a Personal Account Adviser who will channel advice to the customer from the various service areas, instead of the customer having to make individual enquiries to the Customer Services Department.

In preparing her report, Jill conducted some market research (see Exhibit 1). Think about what kind of detail she will put into the memo report for Martin, but you don't need to write the full report. Identify Jill's communication objective for this memo report to Martin.

If Jill's suggestions are implemented, Martin wants her to present the report to the Board of Directors. In Unit 4, we look at her presentation to the Board in more detail.

Exhibit 1: Results from the market research campaign. The numbers listed represent percentages of persons interviewed.

	US		Japan		UK	
	Yes	No	Yes	No	Yes	No
1 Would you be interested in a multi-currency account?	90%	10%	75%	25%	80%	20%
2 If yes, why?						
Pay off mortgage in home country 24%	82%	18%	65%	35%	76%	
Pay off life insurance premiums in home country 60%	75%	25%	55%	45%	40%	
Pay children's education fees 25%	59%	41%	44%	56%	75%	
Support parents 98%	3%	97%	45%	55%	2%	
Currency speculation 85%	24%	76%	6%	94%	15%	
3 If no, why not?						
No need 5%	80%	20%	95%	5%	95%	
Too difficult to understand 84%	10%	90%	55%	45%	16%	
4 What other services would you like from your bank?						
Tax advice 25%	91%	9%	55%	45%	75%	
Small business planning 70%	35%	65%	6%	94%	30%	
Mortgage 85%	25%	75%	5%	95%	15%	
Life Insurance 86%	15%	85%	10%	90%	14%	
Medical Insurance	91%	9%	55%	45%	94%	

Unit Summary

In this unit you have covered many aspects of business writing from informal memos and faxes to large formal reports. You have been given a number of techniques and guidelines to help you with the detailed aspects as well as overall structure and format. However, you will only improve your writing skills with practice. Don't be afraid to try out some of the techniques in your studies and in your business life. In your general or study reading look out for good and bad examples of writing and what features hold your attention and help you to understand the ideas. Instead of just throwing away circulars, or despairing about the letters from the bank manager or Inland Revenue, use them! Look at the format and note the wording. Is it bad news? Or is it trying to sell you something? Practice your own writing on replies. You will find writing essays for your assignments easier too. Remember that successful communication through writing is an essential part of business and of everyday life.

References

Australian Public Service Board (1985) *Communicating in Writing,* Australian Government Publishing Service, Canberra

Bander, R G (1978) *American English Rhetoric,* Holt, Rinehart and Winston, New York

Bentley, M (1991) *Mary Munter's Business Communication: Strategy and Skill,* Prentice Hall, Singapore

Kaplan, R B (1975) 'Cultural thought patterns in inter-cultural education' *Language Learning,* 16 (1 & 2)

Morgan, D H (1970) *Effective Business Letters,* McGraw-Hill, Sydney

Pearsall, T and Cunningham, D (1982) *How to Write for the World of Work,* Holt, Rinehart and Winston, New York

Treece, M (1989) *Communication for Business and the Professions,* Allyn and Bacon, Boston

Recommended Reading

Bentley, M (1991) *Mary Munter's Business Communication: Strategy and Skill,* Prentice Hall, Singapore

Clampitt, P G (1991) *Communicating for Managerial Effectiveness,* Sage, London

Hefferman, J A W and Lincoln, J E (1990) *Writing: A College Handbook,* W W Norton, New York

Stanton, N (1990) *Communication,* Macmillan, London

Locke, L F, Spirduso, W W and Silverman, S J (1987) *Proposals that Work,* Sage, London

Answers to Review Activities

Review Activity 1

1 a A full insurance programme is one of the most important benefits to employees.

   b An effective sentence contains not only a subject but also a vigorous verb.

2 a Business students must possess good communication skills if they are to get a job in today's competitive market.

3 a We should reinvest all the profits immediately.

4 a His salary increase was nearly £200.

5 a On January 3, you asked me to list the main factors in order of importance.

   b Letters on company letterhead must be authorised by a manager before they are sent out.

6 a Our net gains are £1,000,000.

b   This product is unique.

7   a   Please sign and return.

b   To keep the company running flexibly we have to balance and coordinate people's leave.

Review Activity 2

1   The seven parts of a business letter are: your address or letterhead, receiver's address, salutation, subject line, body, closing, and signature, references. The subject line and the references are optional.

2   Three categories of letters are: good news, bad news and selling. You would use a direct approach to emphasise the good news for a routine or pleasant letter; a buffer, or indirect opening for a bad news letter; and an 'attention getter' for a letter to convince or persuade.

Review Activity 3

You could use the following outline for the report:

Cover Page:

Company Name
Prepared for: Client Name
Title of Report
Drafted by Joyce Smith

Contents Page:

```
Section/Title

1.  Introduction

2.  Examination of Specified Areas

3.  Conclusions Drawn From Examinations

4.  Recommendations

5.  Bibliography

6.  Appendix
```

Suggested Report Outline:

```
1.  Introduction

2.  Examination of Specified Areas

    2.1 Area 1

    2.2 Area 2

    2.3 Area 3

3.  Conclusions Drawn From Examinations

    3.1 Area 1

    3.2 Area 2

    3.3 Area 3

4.  Recommendations

5.  Bibliography

6.  Appendix
```

The appendix could be used to provide the current Health and Safety regulations covering procedures for dealing with the particular hazards encountered.

In addition Summary Sheets of the nature of the chemicals, their properties and hazards, that were contained within the studio could be outlined in an appendix.

Unit Review Activity

GOLD COIN BANK

Memo report

Jill's communication objective for this report is 'Convince Martin that her new ideas for customer services should be adopted'. This report should be in memo format. It could be set out something like this.

MEMORANDUM

To: Martin Rush, Bank Manager

From: Jill Paine, Customer Services Manager, Central Branch

Date: 10 November 1996

Subject: Introduction of new Customer Services System in Central Branch

1.0 Introduction

2.0 Background

3.0 What is the new system?

4.0 What are the new services?

5.0 How the new system affects

    5.1   Customers

    5.2   Customer Services staff

    5.3   Computing Department

6.0 Conclusion

```
7.0  Recommendations

8.0  Appendix
     Market Research Results
     Multi-currency Account
     Tax guidance for foreigners
     Life insurance policies
     Work flow in Customer Service Department
```

You should note that this is just a recommended outline. You may find that your outline is slightly different.

UNIT 4
PRESENTATION AND SOCIAL INTERACTION SKILLS

Introduction

How ever talented you are and how ever good at your job you are, you will not be able to achieve very much unless you can deliver your message and yourself effectively. In this unit, firstly we look at the process of delivering an effective oral presentation. Related to this skill is the skill of running effective meetings and of interacting with your work colleagues. Meetings are obviously important features of organisational life. You learn more about these skills in this unit. Finally we bring together all these communication skills that you will need in your business life to develop your own personal skills of self-presentation in an interview situation and through your curriculum vitae. We also identify the features and importance of an organisation's culture as this affects all communication within it and your approach to it.

Objectives

By the end this unit, you will be able to:

- describe the features of an effective oral presentation
- prepare and deliver an effective business-related oral presentation, supported by appropriate visual aids
- describe the advantages and disadvantages of group meetings
- describe the role and characteristics of an effective group leader and of an effective group participant
- identify the key elements affecting small group communication
- implement strategies for improving the productivity of group meetings
- write an effective job application and follow-up letter
- prepare a concise and well organised curriculum vitae
- prepare for, and participate in, a job interview
- understand the communication of the organisation's culture
- identify how organisational culture affects job selection.

SECTION 1
Oral Presentations

Introduction

In this section, we take you through the process of preparing for and delivering an oral presentation supported by appropriate visual aids. The emphasis in this section, as in the report writing section, is on learning by doing.

The ability to speak effectively is highly valued in the business world. There are many occasions when you may be required to speak to a group: promoting or selling a new product, process or service; presenting progress reports or proposals to small or large meetings; participating as a member of a team presentation; or addressing a conference or a convention. Your credibility with your employers and your colleagues is easily enhanced or diminished by your public speaking ability.

One of the most common forms of speaking to groups in business is what is known as the 'oral presentation' or simply the 'presentation'. In business presentations, the speaker usually not only speaks but also uses other means of communication, such as computer assisted presentations, overhead transparencies, charts, slides or video, as well as engaging in a question and answer session either during or after the presentation. The presentation may be directly or by videoconferencing, for example.

Even though giving presentations is common and relatively straightforward, most people, even very experienced and skilled speakers, are very nervous about speaking before a group of people. In fact, being nervous is probably a necessary ingredient of a good presentation. Extreme nervousness, however, can be a big problem. The best way to control it is to be very well prepared. This section will equip you with a procedure for preparing any business-related presentations you might be asked to give. In your study programme, you may also be asked to do a small presentation as part of the assessment. This section will also help you with this.

1.1 Preparing your presentation

Preparing a business presentation depends on the same strategies as other forms of communication. You must know your communication objective, analyse your audience, and structure the main points with your objective and audience in mind. With presentations, however, you also need to know how to produce and use visual aids for support, rehearse your presentation efficiently, and deliver it effectively.

The task of preparing a presentation is more manageable if you work in the following phases:

- analysing your objective, your audience, the occasion and your central theme
- organising your ideas
- developing your visual aids and delivery notes
- rehearsing.

STEP 1 – SETTING YOUR COMMUNICATION OBJECTIVE

This is possibly the most important phase. Even carefully prepared talks and speeches can fail badly if speakers do not know what response they want from the audience and the presentation is not appropriate for the audience and/or the occasion.

Like all effective communication, presentations depend on defining your communication objective. For example:

As a result of my presentation, my audience will _____.

Remember the Unit Review Activity from Unit 3, as well as preparing the written memo report at Gold Coin Bank, Jill is required to present the new system after its implementation to the Board of Directors. This is the communication objective, Jill wrote before giving her oral presentation to the Board:

As a result of my presentation, my audience will understand and be impressed by the new Customer Services system in Central Branch.

This is different from her communication objective for preparing the memo report for her boss about the same subject which was to persuade Martin to implement the system. Don't make the mistake of thinking that she could just read out the memo report that she had prepared! The objective, the audience and the mode of delivery are all different. Obviously, some of the information will be the same but presented from a different perspective.

STEP 2 – ANALYSING YOUR AUDIENCE

It is important to do this step when you prepare for presentational speaking, as you did in preparing for report writing. Because an oral presentation is not a permanent record in the same way that a written report is, you have some different concerns when analysing your audience. For a presentation, you are only concerned with your immediate audience, the ones in front of you. However, you may know your boss or someone important is going to attend your presentation – not to learn about your topic, but to see how you perform. Perhaps a video of your presentation may be made. Unlike reports, the number of people in an audience is significant to presentations. Your delivery manner should be very different for audiences of five or of 50. From a practical point of view, it will certainly affect your choice and use of audio-visual aids.

Here is the Audience Analysis Sheet that Jill filled in before preparing her presentation to the Board. Notice that Martin is not the 'primary' audience, as he was with the report, but he is an important party and Jill will need to do a good job in front of her boss, even though he is not making a decision this time about implementing the system.

Audience Analysis Sheet

1   Who is your audience? *The Board of Directors*

Primary audience: *Chairman & Board members* Age: *45-65*

Others: *Martin Rush*   Sex: *Female & male*

Key decision maker: *Chairman*   Number in the audience: *6*

2   How similar are they to you in their educational backgrounds?

(Similar)   Not similar   Don't know

3   How similar are they to one another in their educational backgrounds?

(Similar)   Not similar   Don't know

4   How much background knowledge do they already have in the subject you are speaking about? *They know a lot about the bank and they know that we have had problems in our Dept. However, they do not know what specific problems we've had.*

A lot   (A little)   Don't know

5   How similar are their values and your own?

(Similar)   Not similar   Don't know

6   How useful is your presentation?

(Useful)   Not useful   Don't know

7   How do they rate your credibility? *I am the manager of the Customer Services Dept. and I was hired to solve these problems.*

(High)   Low   Don't know

8   Is there any reason why they will not want to accept your message? *Although they want me to solve problems, they are also reluctant to make big changes.*

(Yes)   No   Don't know

If you find you have circled several 'Don't knows', it may indicate that you do not know enough about your target audience.

Write brief notes below on how you intend to overcome any problems this analysis of your audience has revealed.

4.   *I will have to give them some background information about the specific problems we have had in the Customer Services Dept.*

8.   *I will have to give them concrete evidence to prove that the new system is working and that the changes were necessary*

You should complete an audience analysis sheet for each major presentation or report that you do. Remember that you will need to do more research into your target audience if you circle several 'don't knows'.

STEP 3 – ANALYSING THE OCCASION

As well as knowing your audience, you need to know the facts about the situation or occasion at which you are speaking.

Some questions to ask:

1   Why have **you** been asked to speak?

2   Is anyone else speaking, and, if so, what about?

3   Is there any background information you need to know (for example, history of event, previous speakers in a series of presentations, etc.)?

4   Where will you be speaking? Will the venue present any difficulties (size, lighting, seating etc.)?

5   How many will be in the audience? Where will they be coming from?

6   What audio-visual facilities are available?

7   Who is in charge of organising the presentation? Do I have to do it? Or do I just need to show up at the right time? How long am I expected to speak for? Is there a question-and-answer session?

Jill Paine has answered these questions below in preparation for her presentation to the Board of Directors.

1   Why have you been asked to speak?

   Because I implemented the new system at Central Branch.

2   Is anyone else speaking, and, if so, what about?

   No, no-one else is speaking, but Martin will introduce me.

3   Is there any background information you need to know (history of event, previous speakers in a series of presentations, etc.)?

   Yes, I should try to find out how positively the other members of the Board of Directors are likely to feel towards my presentation.

4   Where will you be speaking? Will this present any difficulties (size, lighting, seating, etc.)?

In the board room. I will need to check to see if I can use the overhead projector, and then make sure that all the board members will be able to see the screen easily.

5   How many people will be in the audience?

About six people. Four will be coming from out of town, two are from our office.

6   What audio-visual facilities are available?

An overhead projector or computer which I will use if possible.

7   Martin's secretary is organising the meeting and then the lunch afterwards. I need to be there 15 minutes early. I am expected to speak for 25 minutes and allow 10 minutes for any questions at the end.

STEP 4 – WRITING DOWN YOUR CENTRAL THEME
Write down the central theme of *your* talk in one sentence.

Jill Paine has decided that her central theme is:

'The new customer services system is effective, and could be applied in other branches of Gold Coin Bank.'

Note how this differs from her communication objective, which in this case was:

'As a result of my presentation, my audience will understand and be impressed by the new Customer Services system in Central Branch.'

1.2 Organising your ideas

The second phase in developing a presentation is to decide on the content, and to organise your ideas according to the needs of your audience and your communication objective. Because it is often hard to get started, we suggest you tackle the task by doing the following:

Brainstorm your ideas

One useful brainstorming technique for getting your mind active is to follow these steps:

1   Identify the key words in your sentence describing the theme or central idea.

2   Write these words down scattered over a page.

3   Write down ideas related to each key word.

Remember, when brainstorming, try not to evaluate or judge the importance of the ideas. Just write down all ideas that come into your mind.

ACTIVITY 1

Below you can see examples of Jill's brainstorming for the presentation she will give to the Board of Directors.

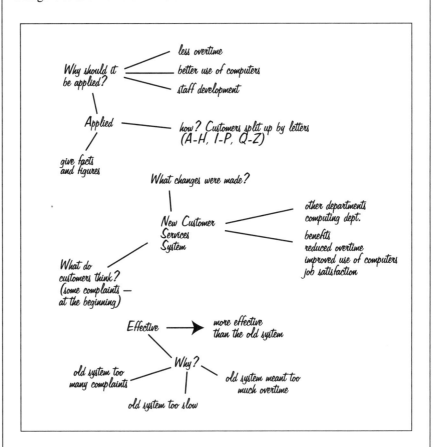

Read Jill's brainstorming notes and circle the key words from her central theme.

Remember the central theme of the presentation you may have concluded that the key words relate to the **New Customer Service System**, the **application** of the system and the fact that it has been **effective**.

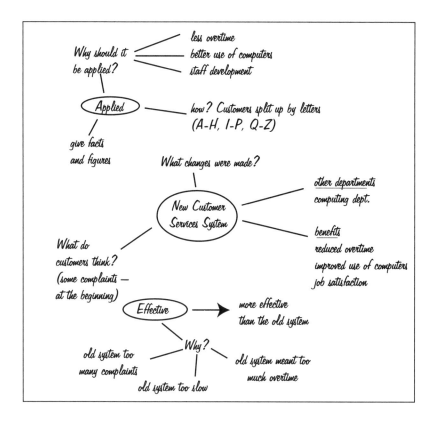

Limit your main points

Having got some ideas down on paper, select the points you will use. Be ruthless! You are far better off having three well-developed points than six half-developed ones. Keep in mind that the listener cannot turn back a few pages to check on your previous points. To be a successful speaker, you must make it easy for your audience.

Support your main ideas

Here is a list of ways to support the main ideas in presentations (Quible et al. 1988):

- explain the topic, information, or ideas
- compare and contrast trends
- illustrate information in easy-to-understand charts, graphs, etc.
- give specific examples to add meaning
- give specific statistics
- quote opinions and conclusions of others
- state similar ideas in different words.

Once you have your data sorted out, you can produce an outline of your presentation. It should contain your main ideas and supporting ideas in the sequence in which you will present them.

Make your main points stand out

You could use three ways of doing this:

- including a preview
- providing clear and explicit transitions
- using internal summaries.

A preview provides the audience with a mental map of the order of your ideas and the overall structure of the presentation. In speaking, you always need a clear plan, and you always need to share it with your audience. Such a preview will lead you into helpful transitions between your main points and the various parts of your presentation.

The best place for your preview is **after** you have gained the audience's attention through your introduction but **before** you begin the body of your presentation. For example, if you have used a chronological arrangement, you might say towards the end of your introduction: 'I will trace the development of project XYZ from its first trials in 1995 through to the multi-million dollar operation we are all witnessing today'. If you have used an order of importance arrangement, you might say something like: 'I will begin by outlining the global implications of this development and end by focusing on implications for the UK.'

Transitional words, phrases and sentences are vital for giving your presentation cohesion and flow. Good transitions also help your audience to follow your train of thought. If you have clearly worked out your structure, you should have no difficulty with transitions in your presentation. In Jill Paine's presentation, for example, she says:

> 'There were three problems with the new system. The first one was . . . '
> 'What all these problems meant was that . . .'

ACTIVITY 2

Match the transitions to the presentation topics. The first has been done for you.

Transitions	Topics
In addition. . . also. . .another. . .	A comparison of the features of two different systems.
Having looked at the. . . of X, let's now examine the . . . of Y.	Outlining a new procedure.
Let's now look at the second step.	The development of a new product.
Then. . . not long after. . . at last. . .	Reasons for changing a procedure.
Furthermore. . . besides. . .	The benefits of a new procedure.

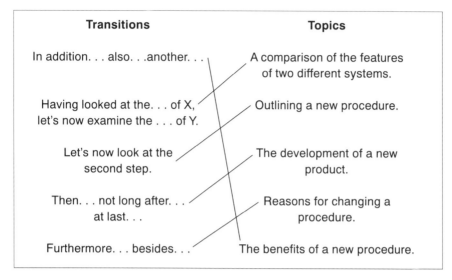

Transitions	Topics
In addition. . . also. . . .another. . .	A comparison of the features of two different systems.
Having looked at the. . . of X, let's now examine the . . . of Y.	Outlining a new procedure.
Let's now look at the second step.	The development of a new product.
Then. . . not long after. . . at last. . .	Reasons for changing a procedure.
Furthermore. . . besides. . .	The benefits of a new procedure.

A particularly important transition is the one leading to your conclusion. Make it very clear to your audience that you are about to begin your conclusion.

> You can use such phrases as: In conclusion. . .   To sum up. . .   Finally. . .
> In summary. . .   The final thought I would like to leave you with. . .

Such phrases give your audience a strong signal that you are about to conclude and are likely to restate your theme or main idea.

Finally, you should note that transitions can be non-verbal as well as verbal. Many speakers use non-verbal transitions very effectively. Examples of non-verbal language used to indicate the beginning of a new section are: pausing for a while; moving away from where you are speaking; referring deliberately and obviously to notes; looking slowly around the audience.

Internal summaries. These are very useful, particularly for long presentations.

Introductions and conclusions
Bentley (1991) writes at length about the importance of an effective introduction and conclusion in any oral presentation. It is true that if you fail to capture the attention of your audience all your efforts in careful preparation will be wasted. Similarly, your conclusion must be memorable or your audience is most unlikely to give you the response you desire. Many people prefer to write these introductions and conclusions after they have thoroughly planned the body of their speech.

STEP 5 – WRITING YOUR OUTLINE
Study the outline Jill prepared for her oral presentation to the Board of Directors:

Introduction to presentation

Opening and introduction of the oral presentation topic
1   [transition] 'There are three main points to my presentation...'
   ● previous system
   ● changes made and staff reaction
   ● advantages of the new system.

Body of presentation
2   The previous system
    [transition] 'I would like to start with the main problems with the old system . . .'
   ● took too long to deal with customer enquiries
   ● too many customer complaints
   ● not enough flexibility for customers
   ● too much overtime.

3   The changes made to the system
    [transition] 'Now I would like to introduce the changes to the new Customer Services System . . .'
   ● assigned customers to each Personal Account Advisor
   ● made each Personal Account Advisor responsible for his or her own clients
   ● offered new account services
   ● how the changes affected the staff in the Customer Services Department.

4   Advantages of the new system
    [transition] 'I would now like to describe the advantages of the new system'
   ● reduction in overtime
   ● use of computers
   ● customers happier
   ● Customer Services staff happier.

Conclusion of the presentation
5   Summary and finish
    [transition] 'So to sum up...'
   ● better products and services to customers
   ● decrease in overtime
   ● decreased dependency on computer department
   ● developed skills of the staff.

STEP 6 – DEVELOPING YOUR VISUAL AIDS

Using visual aids such as computer graphics, charts, overhead transparencies, slides and films can improve the effectiveness of your oral presentation. You also want to prepare this information as part of a written report or as a handout for the audience to take away at the end of the presentation. Relatively simple software packages such as Powerpoint are available to help you develop transparancies, handouts and speaker's notes. You will learn more about preparing graphics in Unit 7 on spreadsheets.

Graphics can:

- add variety and interest to the presentation
- provide useful props and memory prompts for the speaker
- communicate some ideas more effectively
- enable some information to be more easily understood by your audience.

Visual aids must be carefully built in and rehearsed before you deliver your presentation. You must check that the computer works, the visual is appropriate for your purpose, and that the facilities you need are available for the particular type of visual aid you plan to use.

On the next two pages you can see the four visual aids that Jill prepared for her presentation. Note that she uses different formats for the visual aids so they don't all look the same. All of Jill's visual aids will be presented on A4 size transparency paper which will be used on the overhead projector.

Work flow for the Customer Services Department

The number of customer complaints in the Customer Services Department, Central Branch, from January 1996 to September 1996

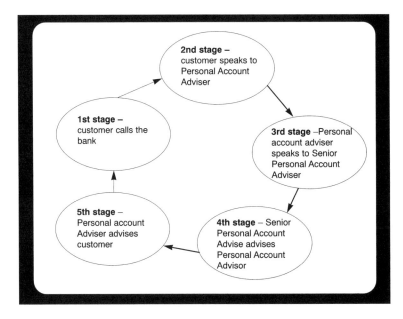

Month	Number of complaints	Number of complaints as a % of total customers
January	12	3%
February	12	3%
March	12	3%
April	16	4%
May	20	5%
June	12	3%
July	8	2%
August	4	1%
September	2	0.5%

The amount of overtime in the Customer Services Department from January 1996 to September 1996

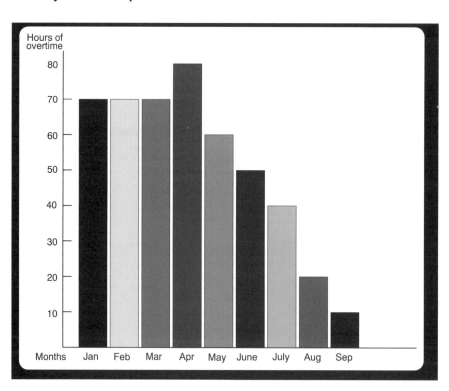

Allocation of customers to staff in the Customer Services Department

Staff member	
Ron Field	Customers with surnames starting with A - H
Issy Wright	Customers with surnames starting with I - P
Cindy Thomas	Customers with surnames starting with Q - Z

STEP 7 – PREPARING YOUR DELIVERY NOTES

Most speakers find delivery notes very useful to remind them of what to do and say during their presentations. It is always better to work from notes than from a written version of your complete presentation. Delivery notes help you to maintain eye contact with your audience. You can put your notes on cards so you can easily read them.

Bentley (1991) suggests you should use one card for about each five minutes of your presentation. On each delivery card:

- have your content written in point form with as few details as possible
- have reminders about when to use your visual aids or make moves
- have transitions written out to help you get from one part to the next
- number your cards
- have your notes written on one side of the card only.

1.3 Rehearsing

Good delivery of oral presentations does not just happen but is usually the result of rehearsal. Practise delivering your presentation to:

- get to know your material well enough to be able to present it without reading it
- find any parts that do not work well
- pause effectively
- incorporate visual aids
- make sure it is the right length
- use your delivery cards and modify them if necessary.

Bentley (1991) has ideas on practising and arranging to give presentations. You can try practising in the room where you will give the presentation; or in front of chairs grouped as they will be in the actual presentation; or in front of a mirror; or in front of a friend or colleague. Remember to plan the actual meeting arrangements carefully too if you are in charge of them, so your audience is at the right place, at the right time, and for the right reason. Decide what you are going to do about latecomers before the event. Perhaps you just need to wait, if the latecomer is the most important person, but you risk the rest of your audience becoming irritable with the time wasting and becoming unresponsive to your message. Perhaps for a small group, you can serve coffee first, if you expect latecomers. For larger groups, interruptions may be more easy to handle. In Gold Coin's case, Jill should check with Martin first to ensure that the Chairman is likely to be there on time, especially as he is flying in that morning.

Check the equipment for showing your visuals, and make sure you know how to work it. Make sure that there is water to drink, and that you have something to rest your cards on. Make sure that the audience has everything it needs, a notepad and pencil, for example.

If you suffer badly from nerves before giving talks or presentations there are several relaxation exercises you can try. These involve relaxing your body, your voice and your mind before you start. Even during speaking, you can help your delivery by relaxing and concentrating on positive reactions from your audience and the information that you want to communicate.

HOW TO REHEARSE

There are many ways you can rehearse your presentation to polish it before you deliver it to your real audience.

- The best and most sophisticated method is closed circuit television or video. If these facilities are available to you, please use them. Nothing is more effective than actually seeing yourself perform.

- The tape recorder is the next best. Do not record yourself until you have practised several times.

- You can use a mirror, preferably full-length.

- You should try to imagine yourself in the actual location of your presentation with the audience as you imagine it will be. Paint a mental picture of the scene with you in it.

- However you decide to rehearse, practise your speech aloud. You need to hear your own voice.

- Rehearse your presentation using your delivery cards. Make sure you have the presentation timed to fit into the available presentation time. You don't want to overrun or underrun. Don't forget to allow time for questions.

1.4 Step 8 – Delivering your presentation

If you follow all the steps outlined in this section, you will be well prepared to deliver your presentation and be less nervous. All effective speakers have to work hard to gain a rapport or positive interaction with their audience. Remember these tips:

- Wear clothes that you feel completely happy with, don't try new shoes out on an important day! If they hurt, it will show in your face! Check your appearance before you meet your audience. Jill has never met any of the Board before and this is obviously an important occasion, so she should wear something appropriate and business-like.

- Smile at the audience. Hopefully, someone will smile back! Martin will introduce Jill at the presentation, she should thank him before she starts.

- Maintain good eye contact. Look at all of the audience but without making them feel uncomfortable.

- Be enthusiastic. If you are not enthusiastic about your topic, how can your audience be?

- Make sure you can be heard. If your audience cannot hear you, you have wasted their time and your own. Be particularly careful that you do not drop your voice at the end of sentences or sections of your talk.

- If you get flustered, slow down, take a deep breath and a drink of water. The audience will want you to succeed, rather than get into more difficulty.

ACTIVITY 3

This activity forms part of Review Activity 1. It will be easier if you start thinking about the preparation and requirements now. Select a subject that interests you. It could be anything – football, eighteenth-century architecture, birdwatching, cooking, a course you are studying, the company you work for. You are going to prepare a short talk to give to friends, family or colleagues on why it interests you so much and how other people could find out more about the topic. Identify your communication objective. Decide on your audience and analyse it using the audience analysis sheet. Make some preliminary notes now. As a first step, tape the first three or four minutes of your draft notes to enable you to hear how you sound and to get an idea of how long it takes for you to deliver a particular amount of information. Or read an article from a magazine or newspaper, but you will find it easier if you have written the words yourself. You probably won't like what you hear! Many of us don't like the sound of our own voices. Try talking more slowly and distinctly, change the emphasis, experiment with some different ways of using your voice and see how it sounds. You will look at some of the details of the presentation in Review Activity 1.

1.5 Handling questions in presentations

Do you want your audience to ask questions during your presentation? Would you prefer them to wait until you have finished? There are advantages and disadvantages to both approaches. You must decide when you want to answer questions and prepare yourself to answer them. If you request that the audience asks questions at the end of the presentation, then you can keep to your delivery cards without being distracted. It does have drawbacks, as audience members may forget their questions and useful input and feedback is not at the most appropriate point in the presentation.

ACTIVITY 4

1 What are the advantages of taking questions during the presentation? After the presentation?

2 Suggest some ways of dealing with questions you cannot answer immediately.

3 How would you respond to difficult questions?

4 How would you deal with unfair questions?

---

1   Taken during the presentation, questions are more meaningful to the questioner and the feedback is more meaningful to you. Audiences may also listen more actively. Taken after the presentation, questions will not disrupt the flow of information or waste time.

2   Possible ways of dealing with questions you cannot answer immediately include:
   ● repeating the question
   ● turning it back to the person who asked it
   ● turning it outward to the rest of the audience
   ● reflecting on the question
   ● writing it down.

If you have no idea how to answer it be honest, you will only make matters worse by pretending. When you are watching or listening to politicians or lawyers being questioned on the television or radio, or the UK Parliament is being broadcast, note how eloquent speakers get out of difficult situations! But be careful what you attempt yourself, they have had years of practice!

3   Two steps for answering difficult questions are:

● compliment

● divert.

Again note how individuals in the media avoid answering difficult questions!

4   Unfair questions should be challenged or rejected.

REVIEW ACTIVITY 1

You will now do some further work on your presentation that you started in Activity 3. So far, you have selected your topic and have an idea of what you want to say, and what you will sound like saying it. You have identified your communication objective and your audience. Run through all the steps we have outlined for preparing your talk, including writing cards and preparing visual aids. As you are unlikely to have the appropriate facilities to deliver your talk with visual aids etc, you could prepare handouts to go with the talk instead. Perhaps you have addresses or more information that your audience needs to follow up the topic. Rehearse. Tape yourself and experiment with the whole presentation. You should try to speak for about 15 minutes. Decide if and when you will invite any questions. And then if at all possible, deliver the presentation. Make all the necessary arrangements to get everyone together at a suitable venue. It doesn't matter if the only place is your living room or the park on a summer evening.

If you are very brave and concerned about your future career, ask your, hopefully sympathetic, audience, how you performed. Maybe your message was fine, but your sister is just not interested in football, or your colleague just didn't understand about the technical aspects of the motor bike that is your pride and joy. Or maybe the red and blue striped tie didn't quite go with the pink shirt you'd specially chosen, or everyone was distracted by your hair standing up at the back or the hem of your dress starting to unravel. Or the address you gave in the hand-outs for the Ramblers' Association was out of date. There are many things that can go wrong! The key is to plan carefully following all the steps we have identified here, and rehearse. And you will get better every time you present in public!

Summary

Careful preparation is the key to successful presentations in business. You should define your communication objective, analyse your audience and structure your ideas logically, as you would for written communication. In addition, you should prepare delivery cards, rehearse, and prepare to answer questions either during or after the presentation. Your presentation can often be improved by skilled use of visual aids.

SECTION 2
Business Meetings

Introduction

In this section, we examine group communication in a business setting. We look at meetings as management tools for generating ideas and making decisions. We explore ways of increasing the productivity of meetings by focusing on: the advantages and disadvantages of meetings as a medium of communication; and on the roles of the leader and the participants.

In this section, we make frequent reference to the 3M Meetings Team. The members of this team are professionals in the Audio-Visual Division of the 3M Company. This team has been analysing, planning, and considering every aspect of business meetings for 30 years.

2.1 Business meetings

There are many jokes about how much time is wasted and how little is achieved in business meetings:

- A meeting is an event at which minutes are kept and hours are lost.
- A camel is a horse designed by a committee.
- A meeting is something we do instead of making decisions.
- A meeting brings together a group of the unfit, appointed by the unwilling to do the unnecessary.

It seems most business people at some stage in their careers have been frustrated by unproductive meetings. And yet, despite this, there is an increasing trend in business to use the group meeting as a decision-making and problem-solving tool. There are many types of meetings, here are a few common ones:

- staff meetings
- student meetings
- union meetings
- workshops
- conferences
- task forces
- committee meetings – advisory, standing, special, *ad hoc*, planning, selection, etc.
- annual general meetings.

Why do we continue to hold meetings when they can be such a problem? And since we persist in spending valuable time in meetings, how can we make them more productive? We attempt to answer these questions.

Before you progress with this section, check that you understand common meeting terminology.

Agenda. A list of items to be covered in a meeting – sometimes in the form of questions.

Hidden agenda. This is often the real motivating force behind a person's actions in a meeting. For example, participants may criticise all suggestions made in a meeting even if they agree with them because their hidden agendas are to have their own suggestions adopted at a later meeting. Or they may use the meeting as a means of favourably impressing others with their knowledge or verbal skills. Or they may have a personal vendetta against the person running the meeting. Issues such as fighting for promotion or budgets, or for making money or quotas are examples of dangerous hidden agendas.

Minutes. A written record of all the activity that takes place at a meeting.

Conference. This term can be used to mean either a convention (usually many people) or an interview with someone. For example:

> She will attend the conference, *Business Technology for the 90s.*

> He had a conference with the director of the company.

Also a conference can take the form of a meeting of a group of people over the phone, using computer conferencing or videoconferencing.

Bentley (1991) states that you should only choose to hold group meetings if:

- you have time to prepare for and arrange the meeting
- your audience has time to attend
- the cost of getting the group together is not prohibitive
- you need a group of people to hear or discuss the same information at the same time
- you want to build a group identity or relationship
- you want group response, which includes non-verbal response and may include consensus.

2.2 Advantages and disadvantages of meetings

The decision to hold a meeting should be taken after weighing the advantages and disadvantages of this medium of communication. It is worth remembering that approximately \$3 billion was spent in 1988 in North America on large business meetings (McMahon, 1989).

To give you some further perspectives on the role of meetings in business, we have included a chapter from Timms, *Managerial Communication: A Finger on the Pulse,* Item 4.1 in your Resources Section.

This is a long reading. Do not try to read it all at this stage. Read the first six pages and stop at the heading 'Types of committees'. Take notes as you go on the advantages and disadvantages of holding meetings, and do the following activity.

ACTIVITY 5

1 Compare your list of advantages and disadvantages with those we have listed below. Make sure you have a thorough understanding of these.

2 Ensure that you understand the concepts of *groupthink* and the *risky shift phenomenon.*

3 In an organisation you know, work out the hourly labour costs of a meeting of a group of employees and executives following the example given in this reading. (Note that the figures given by Timms are based on 1980 salaries and do not include indirect labour or the opportunity costs.)

---

1   Advantages and disadvantages of meetings:

Advantages
- Better quality solutions possible because of the range of skills and experience of participants.
- If a group makes a decision, its members are more likely to co-operate in carrying it out and be committed to its implementation.

Other advantages not mentioned in Timms are:
- Work can be shared.
- Team spirit can be built by enabling all to contribute to a decision.

Disadvantages:
- May become substitute for action.
- Can cost a lot.
- Can produce low quality solutions when groupthink or the risky shift phenomenon are present or when one person dominates.
- Take time which may not be available when a speedy decision is needed.

2   *Groupthink* is excessive like-mindedness. It occurs when group members' desire for group unity outweighs their concern for finding the best solution.

Risky shift phenomenon occurs when the group takes a more risky decision than individual members of the group would.

Both *groupthink* and *risky shift* are explained clearly in the Timms reading. Read the first six pages again if you do not fully understand these two concepts.

3   An example of meeting costs:

If a meeting at the university is attended by five people (Head of Department, a senior lecturer, two lecturers and an executive officer), the hourly cost of labour (in the mid 1990s) works out to approximately £150 per hour. This does not include support staff costs (typing, etc.) or fringe benefits of employment (housing allowances, superannuation, etc.). In business, possibly the greatest cost is in the lost opportunities for business activities while the meeting is going on (that is the oppurtunity costs), especially if key personnel are involved.

2.3 Types of meetings

You should now continue with the Timms reading for an explanation of the different types of meetings. You will find it is often assumed that people know the difference when, in fact, they often do not.

Skim the section *Types of Committees* in Resource Item 4.1. You should then read through to the end of Item 4.1 to build your background knowledge of the key elements in effective meetings and the importance of leadership.

2.4 Holding productive meetings

When the situation requires group action and/or participation, a meeting can be a very effective communication tool. The 3M Business Meetings Team (1987) in *How to Run Better Business Meetings* comment:

'The ideal business meeting is an organizational jewel. It proceeds without wasted motion from opening to adjournment. It is well-planned, has a defined purpose, adheres strictly to a prepared agenda, and proceeds crisply, dispatching each item on the agenda. When it is over, everyone can leave the room knowing something has been accomplished.'

'Good meetings bring forth the best in people – the best ideas, the best decisions, and the best follow-up reactions. Not all meetings are good meetings, but good meetings can happen, and when they do, the company and the individual participants reap the benefits.'

'There is a certain amount of magic when people come together for a meeting. The magic is in the interplay of ideas and personalities that take place in the meeting room. When the interaction is completed, information has been exchanged, old concepts and ideas have been tested and blended, and new ones have emerged.'

So what elements are required to bring about productive meetings?

- There needs to be a clear purpose for holding the meeting.
- They need to be well planned.
- The roles of participants need to be defined.
- They need strong and skilled leadership.
- They need willing and active participants.
- They need clear discussion and decision-making strategies.

The role of the leader (or chairperson) is critical in setting the scene for productive meetings.

2.5 Chairing meetings

As a chairperson (or group leader) you have many responsibilities before, during and after meetings. We address these various responsibilities now.

DEFINING THE PURPOSE
As for all effective communication, you need to define your communication objective:

As a result of this meeting, _____.

Your objective should be limited and precise. For example, Janice Kane of MET Market Research is planning her regular monthly meeting with her staff: John Stephens, Gunter Schmidt and Lauren Bergerac. This company carried out some market research for Jill Paine of Gold Coin Bank. Janice's meeting objective is:

As a result of this meeting, we will identify the major problems with the market research survey we recently completed for Gold Coin Bank, and we will suggest some solutions to the problems.

2.6 Preparation before the meeting

A successful meeting depends in part on good preparation. The steps needed are:

- preparing and sending out an agenda
- notifying all participants in plenty of time
- choosing and preparing an appropriate venue

- making sure the meeting will not be interrupted

- checking on meeting requirements (room size, number of chairs, visual aid equipment, tea-making facilities, etc.).

All these steps are simply common sense, but it is important that you remember to do them. Setting an effective agenda, however, takes some skill.

SETTING AN AGENDA

An agenda is a plan of the flow of business or discussion. It helps participants prepare for a meeting and keeps it on track. So important does the 3M Meetings Team consider agendas that their only rule about meetings is: **Never begin a meeting without a written agenda**. Agendas vary according to the type of meeting and the level of formality.

Let's go back to Janice Kane planning the meeting to discuss the Gold Coin Bank Market Research survey with John, Gunter and Lauren. She sent the following agenda to them.

MET Market Research

Meeting to discuss the Gold Coin Bank Market Research Survey to be held in Meeting Room 1 on Thursday 12 May, 1996 at 2.30 pm

Agenda

1 Minutes of the meeting held 10 April 1996

2 Matters arising from the minutes

3 Recruitment of interviewers

4 Effect of the outbreak of influenza on interviewers

5 Feedback from Gold Coin Bank

6 Any further business

7 Close of meeting

The 'call to meeting' memo

The agendas can also be incorporated into a memo (known as a 'call to meeting' memo) sent to participants. For example:

MEMORANDUM

Date: 2 May 1996

To: John Stephens, Gunter Schmidt and Lauren
             Bergerac

From: Janice Kane

Subject: Gold Coin Market Research

A meeting will be held to discuss the Gold Coin Bank
Market Research Survey on Thursday 12 May at 2.30 pm
in Meeting Room 1. The agenda is as follows:

1   Minutes of the meeting held 10 April 1996

2   Matters arising from the minutes

3   Recruitment of interviewers

4   Effect of outbreak of influenza on interviewers

5   Feedback from Gold Coin Bank

6   Any further business

7   Close of meeting

2.7 During the meeting

The chairperson has two distinct roles during the meeting itself. Bentley (1991) refers to these as 'task' and 'process' functions. For meetings to be effective both functions must take place. Task functions might include defining problems or ensuring it has the necessary information. Process functions could include ensuring that everyone contributes to the discussion or ensuring that the group resolves differences of opinion in an effective way. However, both are not always performed by the same person. Frequently, one person is seen as a task leader and another as the process leader of the group. Some leadership theorists believe that really great leaders are those who manage both roles well.

TASK FUNCTIONS
The chairperson steers the meeting so that the agenda is covered in the allocated time. This includes introducing the purpose of the meeting at the beginning and summarising the decisions or findings at the end. The chairperson must also decide how discussion is going to be organised in order to arrive at decisions.

The chairperson is also responsible for deciding how decisions will be taken by the group. Four ways are described: **decision taken by leader; decision by majority rule; consensus; and unanimity**. You should be able to recognise these in action in any meetings you attend.

PROCESS FUNCTIONS

The harder function for the chairperson is making sure everyone participates in the meeting and that the group meeting process runs smoothly. Sometimes called *group maintenance,* it can take the form of encouraging participation, reducing conflict and/or motivating participants.

In handling the process functions of a meeting, the style of leadership is very important. Item 4.1 touched only briefly on leadership theory. You will be studying it in some depth in other modules. In this module, you only need to relate it to the communication process. As we discussed earlier, tailoring the way you communicate to your audience is a basic communication concept. In a group situation, handling the diversity in the audience is the problem. The leader or chairperson must constantly consider how different all the participants are, and, at the same time, appear to treat everyone in the same way – a very difficult task!

One such difference is some participants' hidden agendas, which can easily sabotage a meeting. A person may cause an uncomfortable or awkward atmosphere on purpose, usually to embarrass the speaker or chairperson. Skilled leadership is necessary to make sure hidden agendas do not take over. When chairing meetings you need to watch out for difficult questioners and participants whose main aim is just to be difficult.

The chairperson should keep everyone to the agenda, and ensure that decisions are actually made where needed. He or she should stop any bickering, and anyone wandering off the subject being discussed. He or she should advise the offending participant to raise the matter at the appropriate agenda item, or under any other business. He or she should make sure that everyone has the chance to speak and that the meeting is not overtaken by one or two noisy and forthright individuals. All this can be hard to do diplomatically, and to achieve the aims of the meeting!

ACTIVITY 6

At Gold Coin Bank, Jill Paine, the Customer Services Manager, and her staff, Issy Wright, Ron Field and Cindy Thomas hold a weekly Monday morning staff meeting. Jill has decided to plan her next meeting very carefully as previous ones have not gone very well. In this activity, you will help Jill prepare for the meeting. Read the freewriting Jill did (below) to help her get started planning the meeting.

Look at the agenda for the MET Market Research meeting (p. 171). Using this agenda and the information from Jill's freewriting, prepare an agenda for Jill, for circulation to Ron, Cindy and Issy.

Jill's freewriting to help with the meeting.

Well, this week I'll write an agenda. We didn't achieve much last week. I want to get more out of meetings in future especially when we come to installing the new system. So what's happened this week? Ah, Ron was very good at dealing with a difficult customer. I can talk about that. Also, Issy has worked hard on that new international account. I can talk about that too. I have just received a message from Flora in Personnel. She has told me that there are some changes to the medical benefits for employees — I can get her to talk about that at the meeting. Good. Now, Cindy was quite angry at the meeting last week. I'll involve her more in the meeting. What can I ask her to talk about??? Oh, I know — she has redesigned the computer input slip for the new system. I can ask her to explain the changes to Ron and Issy. Good.

What else? Ah yes, a difficult one — Mr Clark wants us to organise a cocktail party for our customers to introduce the new services. That won't be popular with Ron and Cindy as we will have to stay late that night, and spend time organising it all. Oh I know — if I get Ron, Cindy and Issy to discuss it in the meeting and to suggest a good day, and some ideas for the venue and food etc., they may not mind getting involved.

Where shall we have the meeting? My room is the best. The date will be Monday 12 June and we will start at 10 am.

What else? How can I get everyone involved in the meeting? Oh I know, rather than me talking about Ron dealing with a difficult customer, I can ask him to explain it. That means both Ron and Cindy will talk about something. That leaves Issy. I can get Issy to talk about the work she has done on the new account. How long should they talk? About five minutes each, I think.

Anything else? Issy is on holiday next week so we must decide who will look after her clients. One more thing? Oh yes, I know. I had better start off the meeting more positively. Perhaps I could talk about how the meetings will be run in the future. Oh that's good. I have planned the meeting. Points to remember about previous meetings

Points about previous meetings
1   At the beginning of the meetings, Jill has not stated clearly what was to be discussed. The participants were confused about what they should talk about, so someone had to ask for further clarification. Jill had not thought about what she really wanted to achieve, and, as a result, the meetings were wasting everyone's time.

2   Jill knows that Cindy has negative feelings about attending meetings, so in the future she should make sure Cindy is involved positively in meetings. Cindy does not want to waste time, so Jill should stress to her that the meetings are useful, and will help her in her job.

Agenda

Weekly Staff Meeting at Gold Coin Bank to be held in Jill Paine's office on Monday 12 June at 10 am

1 Introduction to the new style of meetings — aims and objectives

2 A reception to launch the new system (Jill — five minutes)

3 Cover while Issy is on holiday (Jill — three minutes)

4 Computer data input for the new system (Cindy — five minutes)

5 Dealing with difficult customers (Ron — five minutes)

6 Development of the new international account (Issy — five minutes)

7 New medical scheme (Flora French from Personnel — 10 minutes)

8 Any other business

9 Close of meeting

ACTIVITY 7

Go back to the description of the sales meeting at the beginning of Item 4.1. Using what you have learned in this unit so far, write down what you think is wrong with this meeting.

Some of the problems with this meeting are:

- late start
- welcome address achieves no purpose here
- poor preparation of venue
- agenda has not been distributed to all participants

- chairperson does not keep to the agenda
- purpose of meeting is not clear
- chairperson allows the meeting to be sabotaged.

2.8 After the meeting

Chairpersons' responsibilities do not end with the meeting. They must make sure that the minutes of the meeting are completed usually by an appointed meetings secretary, circulated and filed and that any follow-up action takes place.

MINUTES

Minutes provide a permanent record of what took place in a meeting and of what courses of action were decided upon by the group. They usually include:

- name of group
- date, time, place of the meeting
- names of members present and of those who sent apologies
- name of chairperson and recording secretary (usually at the end of the minutes)
- brief summaries of reports, if any, by those listed on the agenda
- highlights of solutions presented and decisions made
- time the meeting finished and the date and time of the next meeting.

The minutes of a personnel staff meeting held at Gold Coin Bank follow. You may have to write minutes yourself, so note the different verbs used to record what is said in meetings. These verbs have been highlighted for you.

Minutes of the Personnel Department staff meetin held on 12 April, Room 123

Present: Amy Taylor (Chairperson), John Childs, Sara Thomas (from Accounts), Brian Fraser, Stephen Bentley, Lee Shelton and Mary Smith.

   Apologies from Winnie Charles.

1   The minutes of the last meeting held on 13 March were approved.

2   Matters arising from previous minutes. From item 3, Mary Smith **reported** that all reallocations of office space were now complete and all staff seemed happy in their new locations.

---

3   John Childs **summarised** current problems in data retrieval in the Personnel Department. Most problems result from a lack of training for users of the new software.

4   Sara Thomas from Accounting **reported** the improvements made in her department as a result of the XYZ training programme.

5   After discussion, it was **resolved** to ask senior management to provide the Personnel Department with a training package similar to that used in the Accounts Department.

6   Brian Fraser **reported** that the *Kirkdale Palace* had been booked for the annual dinner on 4 June and that the cost would be £20.00 per person.

7   With no other business, the meeting finished at 4.00 pm. The next meeting will be on 14 May at 2.30 pm.

Mary Smith
Secretary

FOLLOW-UP

It is the chairperson's job to see that any decisions made by the group are implemented by appointing committees or individuals to carry out the action. The chairperson should decide:

- Who will do what?
- By when?
- What resources are needed?
- Who will obtain them?
- How?
- From where?

In this meeting, for example, the chairperson would need to follow up the request to senior management for the training programme.

2.9 Participating in meetings

Although the greatest responsibility for a meeting's success lies with the chairperson or leader, the participants have responsibilities too. Bentley (1991) sees three functions for the group: explaining ideas; reacting to the ideas of others; and helping the chairperson to keep the process going.

It is difficult to fulfil any of these three functions without some preparation before the meeting. One of the main reasons for poor meetings is lack of preparation by the participants. At a minimum, the agenda must be thoroughly read and thought about. You should have your ideas ready before you go into a meeting. At times, more extensive preparation is needed. You may have to make a short presentation, or you may know you will be called on as the expert on a particular topic. If you need to prepare an idea to present to a meeting, the following formula from the 3M Meeting Management Team may help.

1   Think the idea through and feel sure it will work before presenting it.

2   Think out an organised presentation of the major benefits. Indicate weaknesses, but show how they are outweighed by the benefits.

3   Be prepared to defend the idea. Know where it may be attacked and have answers ready for possible questions.

4   Show how the idea can be implemented.

During the meeting your responsibility is to contribute to the discussion, not only putting forward your own ideas, but building the ideas of others. Herbert Meyer, writing in *Fortune* magazine, summed up the skills needed by participants in this way:

'What they need is the ability to think on their feet, to make their cases clearly and briefly, to convince doubters that their fears are groundless, to disagree agreeably, and above all to shut up when there is nothing more to say.'

REVIEW ACTIVITY 2

During the next week at work or university take special note of any agendas and minutes of meetings you come across. They might be meetings that you are involved in, or an open meeting agenda put up on a notice board, or a company shareholders' meeting announced through the national press. Evaluate the agendas using the ideas discussed so far.

Summary

Because of the costs in time and money, the most important question that we should ask about holding a meeting is: Is it really necessary? If group involvement and/or group decision making are required, the meeting can be a most effective managerial tool. The success of the meeting will depend, to a large extent, on the skills of the chairperson (or group leader), who must make comprehensive preparations before the meeting, control both task and process functions during the meeting, and follow-up afterwards. The meeting participants need to prepare for the meeting and take active and supportive roles during it.

SECTION 3

Self Presentation for Job Selection

Introduction

In this section, we aim to help you communicate effectively in order to get the job you want. You will learn how to:

- assess your own strengths and weaknesses for the job market
- write a two-part job application package
- prepare for a job interview.

We focus on you and your career needs. You probably would not be following further studies if you were not interested in improving your employment prospects. Now that you have begun to acquire some business skills, you will be able to focus what you have learned about these skills into your academic study in order to achieve the job that you want.

In the UK, people change their jobs frequently as they see opportunities for advancement, for more interesting jobs, or for higher salaries. In such a mobile employment market, employers, who have little time available for interviews, will select (shortlist) applicants on the basis of:

- their job application letters
- their application forms and/or their curriculum vitae.

It follows that the better the quality of your job application, the more likely you are to get an interview. Once you get that interview, you need a different set of communication skills to get the job! We look at these later.

3.1 Assessing your strengths and weaknesses for the job market

If you do not already have a personal job search file, it is a good idea to start one. You can put all your job search material in it, including the material you generate in this section. You will find it very useful to have all your job search material together. A simple folder will do. However, using a computer, may be a more streamlined and efficient way to create a job search file.

ACTIVITY 8

For your job search file

You should include:

- education (academic and extra-curricular achievements)
- work experience (full- and part-time)
- organisations to which you belong
- special training
- in-service courses
- special interests.

Also consider the following personal qualities:

- ability and willingness to accept responsibility
- sense of humour
- ability to make decisions
- ability to work with other people
- ability to persevere
- dependability
- courtesy
- maturity
- flexibility
- physical health
- neatness and appearance
- ability to handle conflict
- initiative
- ability to work without supervision
- creativity
- energy
- leadership.

For any of these qualities you possess, try to think of an example to prove your point. Brainstorming produces data for your curriculum vitae (cv) and can help you with material for your job application letters. It will also help in an interview situation if you are asked to defend anything you have said.

Please note that we are not suggesting that you include all this material in your job application package. It is, however, useful for you to have thought about the particular qualities you can offer an employer. You can then select those qualities that are appropriate for the particular job you are applying for.

Include in your file any certificates, diplomas and degrees that you have received for any of your education or training; if it is impossible to include the original, include a photocopy and indicate where you have put the original for safekeeping. Include any testimonial letters, or letters of thanks for any activities – helping with the college play, or village carnival, or local hospital fundraising, for example. Include any certificates etc for sports or leisure achievements. Note down all your achievements whatever they are, you will forget them and they may come in useful one day.

3.2 Researching the job you want

Once you have identified the job you wish to apply for, you need to gather some information about the specific company and position, perhaps it's not the right one for you in any case as you will see when we look at organisational culture later in the unit. If you have narrowed your search down to a particular advertised job, the best sources of information usually are:

1   The contact officer. Some advertisements give the name and phone number of a person who is available to answer questions about the job.

    You can ask for:
    ● a description of the job
    ● the areas of responsibility
    ● an organisation chart
    ● a list of the criteria that will be used to select the successful applicant (may not be available for relatively junior positions)

    You may also be directed to request an application form.

2   Someone working for the organisation who supervises the advertised position or who has previously worked in it. It will not hurt your chances at all to be seen as keen to learn about the job. (However, remember that actually canvassing support for your application may disqualify you.)

3   Someone who works for the firm in a different position. You can ask them about the organisation's policies, etc.

4   The organisation's annual report or other printed information.

5   Newspapers, local, regional or national, or the business press if it is a large corporation, for any information about the company you are applying to work for. You will appear very impressive at an interview if you know some news about the company.

6   Identify the company's products or services in the marketplace and get to know as much as you can about them through your own or your friends' or family's experiences. Get a feel for the type of company they are through their products, advertising and public relations. Do you want to be associated with this company and its approach?

On the whole, personal contact will give you better information than printed material.

3.3 Job application package

Once you have completed your brainstorming and gathered information about the job, you are ready to work on your job application package. This package consists of two parts:

1   **Your curriculum vitae (cv).** Also known as the 'resume' or 'data sheet'. Curriculum vitae are generally considered to be more detailed than resumes. Data sheets are usually even briefer than resumes.

This can be used as the basis for all your job applications. You should be prepared, however, to alter the emphasis you give to various parts to suit the specific job you are applying for. This is easier if you have it stored on a computer. You may find that the company requests you to fill in an application form. You should do this carefully and neatly with the information in your cv, and attach additional summary sheets if necessary. Don't send your cv as well!

2   **The cover letter.** Also known as the 'covering letter', the 'job application letter' or the 'transmittal letter'.

In this letter you highlight your particular qualities, work experience and abilities relevant to the specific job you are applying for. A new letter should be written specifically for each job application. The job advertisement may request you to handwrite it, in which case, do so, but legibly!

PREPARING YOUR CURRICULUM VITAE
A cv is not just for listing your educational and work experience. It should sell your abilities, talent and potential. If possible, follow these suggestions:

● Because you will be using your cv to apply for different jobs, keep a copy of it on a computer or wordprocessor. This allows you the flexibility to make changes to your cv in order to make it more appropriate to specific jobs.

- Keep your cv concise. Very lengthy cvs are not appreciated by busy employers trying to sift through large numbers of applications. Remember, employers are most interested in recent and relevant work experience and qualifications.

- Begin your sentences with action verbs.

  Instead of:

  I was responsible for the development of a new system for staff training.

  write:

  Developed a new system. . .

  If you write like this, it will give the impression that you are an active person who gets things done.

- Don't crowd the page.

- If you have considered having your cv commercially prepared, please note:

  1 Because of layout and style, it is usually very apparent to employers that you have not written your own cv. If the job you are seeking requires good written communication skills, prospective employers might immediately question your writing ability.

  2 You are less flexible to adapt your cv to a specific job if you have had it prepared in this way.

  3 Prepare your own cv in order to demonstrate your skills.

Note the following points about some cvs:

- Even if you have relatively little work experience, you can make a little relevant experience look quite good.

- The final cv may fit on one page.

- Referees' names, addresses and contact numbers may need to be added.

ACTIVITY 9

Choose the sentence from each pair that highlights the applicant's achievements and is well expressed:

1 a I was responsible for the ordering and sales of all hardware products.

   b Achieved a 20% increase in hardware sales during my management of our Sales Department.

2 a Can competently operate word processing, database, spreadsheet applications and statistics packages.

   b I am competent in the use of a range of computer packages.

---

3 a Responsible for incoming and outgoing mail.

  b Responsible for handling up to 800 articles of mail daily, including cataloguing and distribution to 18 sections.

4 a Gained valuable experience in processing learning materials and working as a team member while working to support myself during university vacations.

  b I have no experience except for a part-time position as a clerical assistant during the university vacation.

---

1   (b) is both clear and succinct, demonstrating performance. It does not refer to 'I' and begins with an action verb.

2   (a) is rather more specific than (b) and is more applicable to business.

3   (b) indicates the range and breadth of responsibilities.

4   (a) is extremely positive and hints at enthusiasm and good self management.

3.4 Types of curriculum vitae

There are many different types of cvs, but the most common are **chronological** cvs and **functional** cvs.

- **Chronological cvs:** A chronological cv lists your educational qualifications and work experience in time order. There are advantages in using a reverse chronological order as this focuses the employer's attention on your most recent experience. This type of cv is probably the most commonly used in the UK.

- **Functional cvs:** Another type of cv gaining popularity is the functional or classified cv. This kind of cv is built around qualifications and abilities rather than on time periods of education or on years of work experience.

Issy Wright's cv, which follows, is an example of a functional cv.

Issy Wright

3/42 Special Apartments
Beech Road
Hartness DE4 5PC
Telephone: 0123 4567

Objective:	To work in a small business in order to gain experience of the different aspects of business management.
Past work experience:	Have been working for Gold Coin Bank, Central Branch for 10 years. Positions held: secretary (two years), Personal Account Adviser (three years), Senior Personal Account Adviser (three years). I am currently a Senior Personal Account Adviser in the Customer Services Department.
	Customer relations: Responsible for looking after approximately 130 customer accounts. Familiar with dealing with customer enquiries and problems.
	Bookkeeping/financial work: Assist Manager of Customer Services Department in preparing budgets and monthly statistics for the central finance department.
	In-house training: Responsible for training new staff through oral presentations.
Computing skills:	Knowledge of IBM compatible systems. Also familiar with Microsoft Word, Excel and Works software systems.
Education/training	**BA (Hons) degree:** Have completed five courses toward a BA Hons degree at the University of Everpool.
	Managerial training: Have attended courses on time management, leadership styles, management by objectives.
	Communication training: Attended in-service courses on public speaking, presentational skills and report writing at The Centre for Professional and Business English, University of Everpool.
	Banking: Have completed Stages 1 & 2 of the Chartered Institute of Bankers.
Personal:	Born 1960. Excellent health. Married with one child (5 years old). Hobbies: reading and walking.
References:	Mr Martin Rush General Manager Gold Coin Bank 13 Bond Street St Helier Jersey *(Current employer)*	Mrs W Scott Lecturer in Finance Everpool University Sandridge Road Everpool BE18 9KL *(Lecturer, banking examinations)*

ADVANTAGES OF FUNCTIONAL CVS

1   Functional cvs enable you to address the job specifications listed in the job advertisement directly.

2   This form of cv can assist the employer to focus more easily on what he or she is looking for.

3   The focus is on what skills you have, rather than what you have done in the past.

DISADVANTAGES OF FUNCTIONAL CVS

1   Many employers (particularly in the UK) are not used to this kind of cv.

2   If the employer is concerned about work history, then this type of cv will not easily provide him or her with that information.

Read Resource Item 4.2 for more advice on getting your cv noticed.

ACTIVITY 10

For your job search file

Using the brainstorming you did earlier as data, produce a cv (in either the chronological or functional style) suitable for use as the basis for future job applications. Remember you must be honest, even if something didn't work out very well. However, you can play down particular experiences and situations, and emphasise others. File the cv and note the date you prepared it. You should keep it updated with any new developments, even if you are not actively looking for a job. You will find it much easier to polish it when you need it for a particular purpose. You will find it easier to cut out irrelevant material than to try and add in new material for a specific job.

3.5 Preparing your cover letter

The second part of your job application package is the cover letter. As you plan this letter to accompany your cv or completed application form, keep the following in mind:

● Be positive. Emphasise your strengths.

● Use the 'you' approach. You must aim to convince the employer that he or she will benefit by employing you.

● Do not complain about previous employers or employees.

● Do not mention salary, fringe benefits or working conditions in this letter. You can ask your questions in the interview.

- Use simple, straightforward language. Avoid phrases like 'May I present my qualifications for your consideration.'

- Refer to your cv or the application form.

- Emphasise the qualities, experience and abilities which make you especially suitable for this specific job.

ACTIVITY 11

Improve the following sentences from cover letters.

1 Enclosed herewith please find my attached cv.

2 It suits me to be interviewed on Friday October 14 between 4 pm and 6 pm.

3 If I am not suitable for the job above I will consider any other you have available.

4 I have already thought of several ways of improving your sales figures by reading your annual report.

5 Please do not contact these referees without checking with me first.

---

1 Replace by: 'I have enclosed my cv.'

2 The applicant should not try to organise the interview time in this letter. Omit.

3 This wording makes you sound desperate for the job. Omit.

4 This sounds very arrogant. Omit. You will probably get opportunities to express good ideas at the interview.

5 Do not choose referees that you are not confident about. Ask them first for permission to use them as referees.

ACTIVITY 12

Below you can see another example of a cover letter – the letter Issy sent with her cv to Sam Stone at Snappy Business Services. Read this letter now.

> Ms Issy Wright
> 3/42 Special Apartments
> Beech Road
> Hartness DE4 5PC
>
> 18 November 1996
>
> Mr S Stone
> Managing Director
> Snappy Business Services
> 232 Results Building
> Hennessey Road
> Manchester PE14 9TG
>
> Dear Mr Stone
>
> I am writing to enquire about the position for Administration Manager within your company which was advertised in the *Manchester Morning Post* last Saturday.
>
> I know of your company through my position as Senior Personal Account Adviser for Gold Coin Bank. Although I am not directly responsible for your account, I have handled enquiries on your account in the past.
>
> I have 10 years of experience in banking, with duties in both management and administration. As you can see from my cv, I am used to dealing with customers as well as undertaking administrative and accounting duties and, therefore, feel I can offer a great deal to the position of Administration Manager within your company.
>
> I have enclosed a copy of my cv and look forward to the opportunity to meet you to discuss my application.
>
> Yours sincerely
>
>
>
> Issy Wright
> Encl.

Using a suitable framework and Issy's letter as a guide, write a cover letter for a position of your choice. File it or keep it on computer to save your time later on.

3.6 The job interview

If your cv or application form and covering letter have achieved their purpose, you will be asked to come to a job interview. You are very unlikely to be the only person selected, so you need to continue to 'sell' yourself. The job interview requires extremely careful preparation. Remember the problems of stereotyping and perceptions from Unit 3.

When preparing for an interview, the following checklist may be useful (Sligo 1982):

1   Know about the company you are applying to join. Research its products, services, locations, growth and prospects. See the final section of this unit for more help on this.

2   Know your own qualifications and work record in detail. Be familiar with the facts mentioned in your application package.

3   Have all necessary papers ready and organised for easy access. It is very unsettling if you cannot produce the required documentation just before or during an interview.

4   Anticipate questions your interviewer might ask and practise answering them.

5   Jot down questions you would like to ask the interviewers.

6   Turn up prepared. Know the time, the location and, if possible, the interviewers' names.

7   Decide early what you will wear. Remember, the interviewer can form an impression about you from how you look and what you wear. Remember the issues of first impressions and frozen evaluations from Unit 3. Don't wear or do anything outrageous just to get noticed in an interview. You might be remembered, but you won't get the job!

8   Don't be unnerved by a panel interview. Different individuals will have different questions to ask you. You will get better at them with practice!

Be prepared to deal with the following kinds of questions.

Closed questions. These are direct and give you little freedom in how to respond. When an interviewer asks a closed question he or she is usually looking for factual information. Examples: *How long did you work for Gold Coin Bank? What was your salary in your last position?* Do not try to expand on answers to these kinds of questions.

Open questions. These questions are deliberately designed to get you talking. You should take the opportunity to answer fully. There are usually no right or wrong answers to open questions. Examples: *Tell me about yourself. Why do you think you are suitable for this job? If you found an employee stealing, what would you do?* These kinds of questions are used to test your ability to communicate and think. Do not answer with just one sentence. You are being given the opportunity to show your talents.

3.7 Following up the job interview

Sending a follow-up letter after an employment interview is a more common practice in the USA than in the UK. However, it may be useful to follow up in this way if you feel you can overcome any deficiencies in the interview.

The advantages of writing a follow-up letter are:

- It can give you a psychological advantage.
- It shows you are keen about the job.
- It keeps your name prominent in the interviewer's mind.

If you turn down a job offer, you should write to the interview panel to thank them for their time and give brief reasons for refusing the job. You may want to apply to the same firm at some later stage!

REVIEW ACTIVITY 3

1   How is selling a product similar to finding a job?

2   Write a follow-up letter for an imaginary interview for any advertised job that interests you. Keep it in your job search file.

Summary

You have now created a job search file that contains a typical covering letter, your updated cv and a typical follow-up letter. You will now always be ready to polish these in applying for real jobs when appropriate. In addition you have some guidelines for presenting yourself in an interview situation. As you will see in the next section, the knowledge of the culture of an organisation is an important factor in successfully getting a job and indeed in doing well in the organisation.

SECTION 4

Organisational Culture and Recruitment

Introduction

Working for an organisation you are affected by and become part of the culture of that organisation. To function effectively, you need to be aware of it and particularly how to use it to facilitate good communication and an environment for change. When you first approach a company in a job application or even in a sales situation, you will avoid a lot of unnecessary work and disappointment if you take the culture of the organisation into account. In this section, we look first at what culture is and how it is manifested, and what to look out for.

4.1 What is organisational culture?

Organisational culture is the basic assumptions and values which are shared by, guide and shape individual and business behaviour in that organisation. You may find this rather hard to grasp initially, but you will see as you go through this section that culture is the people who work for the organisation and the people themselves make up that culture. You will also see that it is a very important part of the organisation and binds it together. It particularly affects communication which has been a key theme in this module so far. As an individual in the organisation you are affected by it and part of it.

Schein (1991) provides us with a framework for culture at three levels of awareness. We can describe the first level of **tangible elements of culture** or **artefacts** as symbolic evidence of 'the way we do things around here'. They include stories, metaphors, myths, heroes, logos, slogans, rituals, ceremonies, etc.

The second level of **shared values** is not so visible but employees in a strong culture will be aware of them; for example, integrity and loyalty might be highly valued. These values concern moral and ethical codes and shape, predict and explain behaviour at the surface level. They affect how people behave and what they do in particular situations. Beliefs are close to values and concern what people believe is or isn't true. **Attitudes** connect these values and beliefs to personal feelings. You may feel positive about the company's approach to honesty and pilfering in the factory, but negative about its emphasis on team working as you may like working by yourself.

The deepest level of culture occurs as **basic assumptions** – these are 'taken-for-granted' truths and values that have become automatic in the company. They are the fundamental aspects of the culture and may concern human nature, the organisational objectives, and the environment. For example, an emergency service strives to save lives, it would be inconceivable that an ambulance would not rush to the scene of an accident as quickly as possible at all times of the day and night. This is what we would regard as the basic assumption of the service.

Managers' interests in culture stem from the four areas which Martin and Siehl (1990) identify:

1   Culture provides a **history** which can be used by members as a guide for their own behaviour at work.

2   Culture can help to establish **commitment to management values**.

3   Cultural norms and values can be used as **control** mechanisms by management.

4   Culture might possibly be related to **productivity and profitability**.

Some organisations might already have a strong culture which they wish to retain; others might have cultures which are still embryonic. In both cases, there is a need to at least maintain if not develop these cultures. Culture is extremely difficult to change as we need to change the basic assumptions even if we manage to change the other two levels of culture, so we need to approach the influence which management can exert over culture realistically and carefully.

4.2 Selection of candidates

An organisation is its people. Then the obvious way in which culture with shared values and meanings can be maintained, is to ensure that the people who are hired are the 'right' people in the first place. Do they share the same attitudes and beliefs as the organisation? In some companies with strong cultures, this is becoming as important as relevant qualifications and skills. Nissan, for instance, has a strong work ethic in its production areas. There is an important commitment to tasks which is physically demanding and which requires endurance. It is extremely useful for this type of company to choose people who are keen to work hard. With the plentiful supply of well trained workers in an area which has high unemployment, there is no lack of suitable candidates and the company can afford to be selective.

You would not apply for a job as an ambulance driver if you were not prepared to respond immediately to an emergency call even if it came at an inconvenient time, say just as you were coming off your shift. You would accept the basic assumption of being an ambulance driver.

4.3 Reputation

Even before a candidate walks into an interview situation at a company such as Nissan, he or she will be aware of certain cultural aspects of the company. As the potential recruit, perhaps you have asked friends and acquaintances about working there. You might have queried:

- how 'hard' the working life is
- how 'Japanese' it is – is there exercise at the beginning of the day, for instance?
- are people rewarded for being good at their job or for long-term loyalty, or both?

Local newspapers might have mentioned the plans of the company; or the importance which it places on its values; quality, for example, might be apparent. The company is very visible through its products. The Nissan Micra and Bluebird cars have both been highly recommended in car magazines in recent years for their quality and reliability. Quality products do not just happen – they require a dedicated approach to quality throughout the organisation.

A reputation helps to transmit both explicit and implied cultural values. Within the car industry, a good reputation is paramount to successful sales. It also says much about the company to the prospective worker. Consider the company, Skoda, which is now part of the Volkswagen group. It has attempted to transpose its once poor reputation for quality to that of its new owners by encouraging potential buyers with the words: 'Before we changed the car, we changed the company' (advert for Skoda Felicia in *Daily Mail Magazine,* Saturday 20 May 1995). The advert ends with three brief 'soundbites'. 'We heard the criticisms. We changed our company. Now, are you open enough to change your mind?'.

4.4 Job adverts

When a company places adverts for its jobs, these also provide some information to the candidate about the type of culture and values espoused by the organisation.

ACTIVITY 14

Consider the following three imaginary job advertisements and identify any key words and phrases which indicate the organisations' values.

Advert 1

Purchasing Professionals
£25,500-£28,250 + car + benefits

To support XYZ's further European development we are looking for individuals with initiative, commitment and flexibility to enhance our professional purchasing team in the following areas:

Production Component/Materials Purchasing: Working closely with our European Technology Centre, key plant interfaces and suppliers you will develop Sourcing Strategies on a European-wide basis. You will be responsible for selecting and developing suppliers to enhance delivery, development and management performance against quality, cost and business improvement targets.

Facilities and General Purchasing: You will source and develop suppliers of capital equipment, services and other indirect materials in order to support a diverse and dynamic production environment.

You will need considerable experience in the engineering industry and considerable personal initiative and drive for this challenging position.

Call the Personnel Officer on 0141-247-6754, for further details and an application form. The closing date for applications is 21st December 1996.

Advert 2

Maintenance Officer
Salary £12,915 to £15,624 (under review)

HOAM is a leading regional housing association and consultancy. Following expansion we now require a qualified and experienced full-time Maintenance Officer to provide a high standard, comprehensive maintenance supervision and administration service to approximately 800 properties and a range of clients throughout the north east.

You must have an HNC level qualification in building studies or equivalent and at least 3 years' experience in the construction industry. You must be able and prepared to travel throughout north east England and to work sympathetically and sensitively with a wide range of elderly and other clients.

HOAM supports equal opportunities and we particularly welcome applications from members of ethnic minority communities.

Call the personnel Officer on 0121-123-4567 for further details and an application form.

Advert 3

Cash Collector
£10,074 to £10,643 + Car + Benefits

PATECH is the premier electronic leisure supply company in the UK and part of a major PLC with ambitious plans for further development. Opportunities now exist in the Birmingham area.

Duties include the collection, conciliation and documentation of cash from a wide range of electronic equipment located in our customers' premises.

Applicants must be numerate and physically fit. A current driving licence is essential. Experience is preferred but full training will be given.

Benefits include a competitive salary, an excellent pension and life assurance scheme, participation in the Company share ownership scheme, sick pay, four weeks' annual holiday, service bonus, profit-related pay scheme, and various other group discounts and allowances.

If you feel you meet the requirements of this challenging opportunity, then please apply in writing to . . . .

We are an equal opportunities employer.

Advert 1

The engineering industry is highly competitive and innovation and the ability to respond quickly to change is essential. XYZ's culture reflects this in its advert through the use of words such as:

- initiative
- flexibility
- delivery
- quality
- cost
- business improvement targets
- dynamic
- challenging
- drive.

Loyalty is expressed through the words:

- commitment
- professional.

Advert 2

We are continually told that we are in the 'Caring 90s'. Organisations have followed the recent surge of public opinion and attempted to adopt these caring values. HOAM talks of the need to:

- work sympathetically and sensitively

and it goes further than the simple 'we are an equal opportunities employer' of PAYTECH by its positive action in particularly welcoming:

- members of ethnic minority communities.

Advert 3

The cash collector advert demonstrates a focus on the individual, as opposed to the team, in what would appear to be a tough environment.

Values are demonstrated by the words:

- ambitious
- development
- physically fit
- challenging opportunity
- performance-related pay.

You should learn to 'read' job advertisements with care. You need to recognise what messages an advert is sending about the company and whether it is an appropriate job or company for you to apply for. If it is the right company and the right job, then you first need to tailor your covering letter and cv to meet the job requirements and the company culture indicators. At the interview you can continue the 'selling yourself' process in the particular environment.

4.5 Job and person specifications

With large corporations, it is no longer the case that the job advertisement is immediately followed by a single one-to-one interview leading to either acceptance or rejection of the candidate.

It is quite usual for the company to send the candidate written material in advance of any meeting. This would often include information about the company, a job description and, more revealingly from your point of view, a person specification. A plan may list 'special aptitudes', 'interests' and 'disposition' amongst its criteria (see Torrington & Hall, 1992). Through these means, the potential candidate will glean further details on the organisation's culture, the type of person and commitment the company is looking for and whether he or she will 'fit in' – perhaps even to the point of 'de-selecting' themselves. A company may even ask for a draft proposal for, say, a new marketing strategy before it makes the next selection. This selects fairly effectively anyway as many candidates will drop out as they don't have the time, inclination or ability to do this, or they may think it's a waste of time or expecting too much.

4.6 Interviews and the selection process

There are opportunities in the interview and through the whole selection process for transmitting cultural values. Some of the values might be apparent in the selection process itself. How tough is it? How many stages of interview are there?

As the prospective candidate, you will observe the surrounding settings and gain an impression of the organisation through symbols such as:

- photographs – the product, aerial view of large site, team and chairman
- company magazines
- trophies – quality, charity
- decor – spartan, opulent
- building size and importance
- building layout – open plan, closed offices
- number of personal computers and other high-tech equipment
- dress – formal, informal
- activity – busy, quiet.

It is quite common, even before final selection has taken place, for candidates to be taken around the workplace and shown the various departments and rest and social facilities. In addition to the interviewing panel, candidates may be allowed to talk to staff.

The surroundings and ambiance experienced during the selection process convey very strong messages about the culture to a newcomer whether these are consciously absorbed or not. The buildings themselves are quite literally concrete symbols. And their messages affect long-serving employees just as strongly as newcomers – a phenomenon that is particularly highlighted when changes are proposed or occur.

REVIEW ACTIVITY 4

Read the case study, *Soapworks,* and answer the questions that follow it. This is a long article, but it will give you an interesting insight into the culture and organisation of a successful company. When you are next in your local high street, take a look round a branch of Body Shop and get a feel of the culture that it is transmitting. Remember too that this shop is a franchise, so the culture has to be relayed from Anita Roddick right through to the retail floor.

Soapworks

Just east of Glasgow, on the main road to Edinburgh, lies a great sprawl of grey council blocks, thrown up on bare fields. This is Easterhouse and it houses 55,000 people. Supported by a handful of churches, boarded-up pubs, barricaded shops and a surfeit of schools, the dreary blocks of flats were built after the war when the councils cleared the Glaswegian slums and had to house 75,000 people. Twenty years ago, gang warfare brought a notoriety that today is maintained by a drugs culture where solvent abuse-related deaths are common.

Unemployment is high here; 56% of the men are out of work. There's an industrial estate at Queenslie in the middle of Greater Easterhouse, but it's pretty quiet. The Glasgow factories, steel works and shipyards that used to employ residents have disappeared. Companies like Olivetti which once employed thousands locally have long gone. Who can blame them?

Indeed, it's all too easy to write off a place like Easterhouse, lacking as it does any superficial allure. Parts like these have been recognised by the European Community as the nearest thing to Third World conditions in the developed West. But, fortunately, not everyone here has given up. There are jewels to be found – the Calvi project, for example, shows what can be made of these drab blocks to change them into desirable homes. The council, meanwhile, wages an endless war on the all-pervasive damp that afflicts so much of the housing in the area. And there are phalanxes of council and community workers fighting for improvements.

It was one of these interested parties, Chris Elphick of Community of Learning Initiatives, who stood up at a meeting in London late in 1987 and accosted Anita Roddick, founder of Body Shop International. She was giving a talk to the Business Network, a group of people which looks at running business in a holistic way.

Roddick is one of Britain's most publicly unorthodox managers. When her husband decided to spend a year horse-trekking across South America in 1976, she started a small shop in Brighton to support her family. She sold a handful of naturally based toiletries, adapted from materials she had seen being used in less developed countries. Packaged in urine sample bottles with hand-written labels and offered in five sizes the products were an immediate hit. Today, she and her husband Gordon, who is chairman of the company, run a £220 million empire with 350 shops in 34 countries. The company owns 13 of these shops; the rest are franchises, the factor that enabled Body Shop's stupendous expansion.

The company is imbued with the Roddicks' principles of honest trading, value for money, a high level of support for the environment and the community and a total belief in the people who work for the company. As

Anita, who is fond of epigrams, says, 'I employed workers, but people came instead.' So Roddick is uniquely equipped to give a talk about holistic business, for she practises what she preaches. At the Business Network meeting, Elphick suggested that she might care to go and practise some of it in Easterhouse. She immediately arranged to visit Scotland in January. 'What struck me was that there was so much skill here,' says Roddick, recalling her visit. 'I just decided instantly – it's wonderful, you can do that when you're at the top.' On her return to headquarters in Littlehampton, Sussex, she told her husband that he should go and see it for himself. He came back and said, 'Right, let's put in a soap factory and we'll put 25% of the profits back into the community,' and that was it. Done.

'Going into Easterhouse we were dealing with hard traditional socialists with no real belief in change,' says Roddick. 'You go in and you're suspect because you're business. So we got in all the councillors from the area and talked. I think passion persuades – if they were doubting before, they certainly weren't afterwards. We said, you're getting a factory and employment and you're not dealing with a traditional company. We bombarded them with the Body Shop. They came in like lambs. They asked about unions, I told them you only need unions if management are bastards. We like to talk to people one-to-one if there's a problem.'

Having convinced the community of their good intentions, the Roddicks then had to figure out who in the company would run the factory. Gordon Roddick and director, Stuart Rose were heavily committed to the operation currently being set up in the US, while Anita Roddick spends much of her time looking for new products, which includes travelling for at least two months each year. Eric Helier, the manufacturing director recently appointed to the board, was a natural choice as one director, and Michael Ross, a franchisee who owns two shops with his wife in Aberdeen and Dundee, had expressed a wish to work on a wider front within the company. Ross, who helped find the 36,000 sq.ft Scottish Development Agency site at Queenslie Industrial Estate, was appointed managing director of the factory, which was christened Soapworks.

Next, Ronnie Morgan was hired as factory manager. Morgan had spent 20 years as an engineer and latterly in senior management in the construction industry. Made redundant after a take-over of the business he was running, he suffered a traumatic time looking for another job. After a brief stint in Australia, he came back looking for the right job in Scotland. He remembers going for the interview in Littlehampton with Gordon Roddick: 'I was the only guy dressed in a suit and tie – I lost the tie very quickly.' Morgan came moulded as a traditional manager, but says, 'I found I fitted in very easily with the ethos, the feel for Body Shop. We hold views in common.' He reflects, 'I was sufficiently cynical to wonder if the whole environment thing they support was a gimmick, but I honestly don't believe it is. Body Shop is a tremendously honest company; people genuinely believe in what they are doing.'

Morgan wasn't alone in his initial suspicion of the company. Recruiting was a harrowing time for those involved. 'We were looking for personality really that would gel into a team. We can add the training,' says Ross. 'We went for a balance of sexes and ages. I was almost dreading that moment, starting recruitment. You don't come away from an experience like that unmoved.' They interviewed 100 people, all unemployed, for 16 jobs. 'The employees are the ambassadors for this – they're crucial,' Ross adds.

Yvonne Anderson, 30, from Easterhouse and Linda McGovaney, 21, from nearby Garthamloch, part of Greater Easterhouse, came to the Body Shop from a training scheme run by Poldrait, a publicly funded employment training group. 'Employment training is a bit of a con,' says Anderson 'You're given to understand you'll get what you want, but they put you into what they have for you. We were treated as ignorant people, patronised. So there was a certain amount of suspicion to begin with – these English people coming up.' McGovaney nods in agreement.

Both women say they'll feel more secure when the first year in the job is up. They are naturally further unsettled by the new factory's teething problems but are happy working for Body Shop. The job has strings – no smoking (nearly everyone is a smoker), and rather healthier food with more salads than they would personally choose. 'I like something a bit more substantial myself,' says McGovaney. But the factory is spotlessly clean and the facilities pleasant. 'It's a really good, caring company,' says Anderson. They are interested in making sure that people know what's going on.' McGovaney adds, 'Anita is really down-to-earth and Gordon is really nice. It's good to work for people like that.'

The five most skilled staff, including Morgan himself, his office administrator, a graduate chemist, the production supervisor and the maintenance engineer, came from just outside the Greater Easterhouse boundary. The rest live in the area. They started work in October. It had taken just eight months from Roddick's visit, to get the factory up and running.

That first week in October was, in fact, spent at the Body Shop Training School in London. 'It was brilliant,' says Linda Bruff, Soapworks' bubbly receptionist. She was delighted to get the job – even though her brother is a manager with Safeways and her sister is a dealer on the Glasgow stock exchange, she felt that she had been discriminated against by potential employers just because of where she lives. 'The training was more practical; learning things about yourself, mind games to see how you coped. It wasn't them and us. We were made to feel welcome, made to feel part of Body Shop, to feel at home.'

This was followed by a week in the factory at Littlehampton, shadowing workers there to see how the company operated. The aim was to mould a disparate group of people – single parents, long-term unemployed, an ex-soldier, a 16-year-old school leaver – into a team. The result: 'We all started here knowing each other,' says Bruff. 'All we had to do was learn our jobs properly.'

It is inspiring to listen to these people talk about their work. Even though Soapworks is designed to employ 100 people eventually, and the current 25 rattle round in it, there is a busy, happy atmosphere. They want to do their jobs well and get to grips with new machinery that doesn't always do what it's supposed to do. There are constant references to 'the family', which is how they view their group. 'I thought we might have big problems here,' says Ross, who was originally given dire warnings about Easterhouse. 'I thought we'd have to spend 90% of our management time on it, but we haven't. They're good people to work with and it's been very rewarding.'

But it really isn't all that surprising. The people who work at Soapworks are treated well and with respect by their employer. They are made to feel their role is important, and they are told what is going on and why, both informally and in a more formal monthly meeting with Morgan. As a relative newcomer to the company he walks a delicate balance between the superficially laid-back Body Shop style and the more paternal role of the traditional factory manager. He won't stand for any nonsense, but some of his workforce might be surprised at how much he knows about their lives outside the factory, and how much he cares about them.

Perhaps it has sometimes been hard for Morgan, and it has certainly proved difficult for other business traditionalists in the city, industry and the press, to understand what makes the Body Shop work. It demands that the observer step outside a 'normal' mental framework and look at the company in a different way. After all, how many companies build environmental and community issues along with community work into their mainstream business? And how many companies would choose to set up a new factory in one of the blackest spots in the country and commit themselves to ploughing a quarter of that factory's profits back into the community? Sadly, all too few.

That 25% figure was pulled out of the air at random, as Roddick, Ross and Morgan all confirm. Ross is committed to ensuring that it is 'a significant amount – not just peanuts'. He reckons the factory should be in profit in 18 months, maybe two years. Until then, his concern is to get Soapworks running at full stretch; on current equipment producing 3 million bars of soap this year. 'I asked for a budget,' says Morgan of his original interview, 'but they didn't seem to have one. It seems like the company has so much money that it doesn't have to look after it. That's not true, they look after it very carefully. They don't present me with money in the way I'd like them to, but I suppose there are certain things it's not necessary for me to know. I reconcile myself to it. I want the information but I don't need to know it. I have to trust Michael [Ross]; he knows what he wants me to do.'

Ross explains, 'We've got budgets and business plans, but they've been revised about six times. We've got to be flexible, not guided by bits of paper. We know how much we'll commit this year, and next year, but we want to leave room to add things.' As it happens, Morgan has never been refused whatever he has considered necessary, and by not knowing what's available he probably takes even more personal responsibility than usual for keeping what he spends to a minimum.

The speed with which Body Shop has set up Soapworks is extraordinary – eight months compared to an industry standard of about 18 months – especially considering that it has never made soap before. While 98% of Body Shop products are made in the UK, only about a third are made by the company itself, at the facility in Littlehampton. 'As we get bigger we need to secure lines supply and ensure that we know about the products we are selling,' says Ross. 'With soap we see sales increasing 50-60% a year, and even given full production here we'll only meet a fifth of our demand in a year. So we'll continue to subcontract, and we are concerned that our suppliers are confident in us, too.' For Soapworks' future, a dry powder plant is being considered, for making talcum powders and related products, along with a bath salt filling line and certainly a second soap line.

But even before the plant makes a profit, Body Shop already has contributed to the community. Every year the company holds an international conference for all franchisees. Last year the franchisees were told about Easterhouse. Roddick spoke of her dismay at the terrible lack of facilities in the community, not even a playground for the children. The response was immediate: £23,000 from their own pockets which was put into an account towards having a playground built.

Heather Forster, who like her husband Rob is an environment and community projects co-ordinator for Body Shop, is responsible for getting the playground built and managed. 'The idea was not for anyone from BSI [Body Shop International] to co-ordinate it,' she says. 'The idea was for someone like CLI [Community Learning Initiatives] to do it. Someone from the community has to carry the can for and run it'. Forster has involved local schools in designing equipment for the playground, and commissioned community architects in Glasgow to design it. A site has been found in the middle of Easterhouse and a steering committee staffed by members of the community has been set up. Since Roddick's initial contact with Easterhouse was via CLI, it is fitting that one of its team, Pat Boase, is responsible for co-ordinating the project locally. He has already delivered one playground in the Glasgow area and is currently trying to convince the regional and district councils along with the SDA, to fund this project's completion.

All the Body Shops are involved in community work of some kind, whether it's working with old people, handicapped kids or prisoners, or whatever staff choose. Both the central company and franchisees give staff time off in working hours to do it. Forster helps advise and inform employees on what they can do. Of course, it costs the company money, but the rewards are considerable. As Forster says, 'We have to make money to do something, but there's no reason for earning money if we don't do it.' This is Roddick's utter conviction and one she has instilled throughout her company. Steve Maguire, Soapworks' storeman, puts it most succinctly: 'They've got t'get before they can gie.'

To cynics, Roddick points out, 'Altruism in business is disarming. But the bottom line is you keep your staff – and good staff are hard to get and keep, especially in retailing.' Body Shop has a commendably low turnover of staff. 'We had an audience of young females in the company and community work opened up a well of caring. They're looking to do more than just earn their daily bread.' It's not, though, a female preserve. While the new staff at Soapworks won't be starting community work until the factory is running smoothly, Maguire comments that one of his colleagues, Paul, had already set up a football match with Soapworks staff and unemployed friends. The Soapworks team rented a pitch and provided the strips and probably bought the drinks afterwards.

It's a curious phenomenon that Body Shop seems almost too good to be true. Once tagged 'the share that defies gravity', the company has been able to circumnavigate the pervasive insipidity of most 'health products'. While its wares are based on natural and often ancient treatments for 'cleansing, polishing and protecting the body', they are presented in a compelling way which informs the consumer about relevant and topical, moral and environmental issues. Of course, the company is riding the current 'green wave', but it was there long before the general public had expressed such an interest in green issues. In the five years since its flotation, the company has increased both its turnover and profits by a factor of nine to £46.2 million and £9.3 million respectively.

The reason for Body Shop's success is not a closely guarded secret. It can be attributed to two major factors. First of all, the company operates on principles and values that most individuals feel entirely comfortable with. Most of us don't earn money for the sake of earning money; we work so that we can afford to live and do the things we want to do. But most companies earn for the sake of earning; profits are bottom line, an end in themselves. Yet why should companies, which after all simply employ individuals, be any different from people? Why not earn so that you can spend the money on things that matter – informing and educating people, supporting your local community, paying decent prices for Third World goods, as well as providing decent dividends for shareholders? That is precisely what the Body Shop does, and extremely successfully at that.

The second major factor is that while the company and its founders appear to be flouting the traditional ways of doing business, they actually operate with extremely sound and well-recognised methods. Body Shop asks customers what they want and delivers. Since its earliest days the company has never diluted its image – it keeps it concentrated and clear by communicating it through training, videos, newsletters and meetings with staff from top to bottom of the company. It even bought its own video production company, Jacaranda, last year to step up its communications abilities as the company expands. Its staff are highly trained and motivated, and they are given the chance to excel. Yvonne Anderson says she would like to be an 'ideas person' in the factory, while Wee Willie, at 16 the youngest member of the Soapworks family, is nursing a clear ambition to run the factory one day. Both will get their chance.

But Body Shop never forgets that it is money that enables it to do what it wants. Behind the apparently casual image, every movement of every penny is carefully tracked. And while Roddick proudly points out that Body Shop has never advertised or marketed its products, she is nevertheless an instinctive marketer.

Suspicious observers analyse Body Shop on their terms, sure that the company must be hiding something. Yet even a cursory glance reveals excellent business principles embedded in all its operations. What the critics have not grasped is that unlike many traditional businesses which struggle to integrate these principles, Body Shop, almost by accident, was built on them right from days of the first shop. The Roddicks' astuteness rests not on an ability to fool outsiders, but in spotting a good idea and exploiting it for all its worth. If you don't look at the business and its good deeds in this light, you just won't see it. In the traditions of the Quakers, Body Shop wants to trade as fairly as possible and benefit the world around it.

Roddick believes in an ethical code of behaviour for the global citizen – and that means multi-national companies. She believes in empowerment of people through jobs, work, honest earnings. 'Our idea of success,' she says, 'is the number of people we've employed, how we have educated them, and raised their human consciousness, and whether we've infused them with a breathless enthusiasm. Products in industry are no more than a by-product. I mean how can you take a moisturiser seriously – it's not the body and blood of Christ, it's water and oil. All we're doing is trading, but, like the Quakers, trading in an honest way, and that brings a morale and a sense of purpose. I don't know how we'd have succeeded without it.' As for Easterhouse – 'Its like love – the more you put in the more get out.'

(Anne Ferguson, *Management Today,* May 1989, pp. 94-100.)

Outline the culture of Soapworks and consider the relationship between culture and skills. Use the following headings to interpret observations: *Careful selection of entry level candidates, Reputation, Interviews and the selection process, The workplace itself: rules and regulations* and *Caring attitude.*

Summary

In this section, we have considered culture in the organisation and the many ways in which the assumptions, values and artefacts which it embodies may be communicated to those within and external to the company. We looked at what it means to you as a prospective employee and how you should make judgments about the company and whether you want to join it or not. You analysed some job adverts to highlight possible cultural values. Reputation and even building design can communicate a great deal in terms of the priorities and ways of operating within organisations.

When you apply for your next job, remember to follow the steps outlined in this section. After having researched the position you want, take care to prepare an effective job application package, consisting of a cv and an application letter. Prepare yourself both mentally and physically for the job interview, and be aware of the purposes behind the questions asked. Finally you should investigate and take into account an organisation's culture. Good luck with your job hunting!

Unit Summary

This rather diverse unit brings together many skills that will help you throughout your working life. They all concern communication in some form, and rather than the writing approach that you took in Unit 3, here we are more concerned with the spoken word. We developed ways of preparing an oral presentation, then went on to getting the most out of meetings either as a participant or a leader.

You have put together your own job search file with a covering letter, a cv and a follow-up letter. And through our perspective of culture in the final section you will be able to assess job advertisements and the organisation concerned more effectively. We have not included a unit review activity to help you with these ideas. Clearly with these very personal skills you will learn them most efficiently and quickly by actually doing them in the real world.

References

Bentley, M (1991) *Mary Munter's Business Communication: Strategy and Skill,* Prentice Hall, Singapore

McMahon, T (1989) 'How successful are your meetings?' *Drake Business Review,* Vol. 3, no. 2

The 3M Meeting Management Team (1987) *How to Run Better Business Meetings* McGraw Hill, New York

Martin, J and Siehl, C (1990) 'Organizational culture and counterculture: an uneasy symbiosis', in Sypher, Beverley Davenport, *Case Studies in Organizational Communication,* The Guilford Press

Quible, Z K, Johnson, M H and Mott, D L (1988) *Introduction to Business Communication,* Prentice Hall, Englewood Cliffs, New Jersey

Schein, E H (1991) *Organizational Cultures and Leadership,* Jossey-Bass, San Francisco

Sligo, F (1982) *A Guide to the Employment Interview,* Faculty of Business, Massey UniversityPalmerston, New Zealand

Torrington, D and Hall, L (1992) *Personnel Management: A New Approach,* Prentice Hall, Englewood Cliffs, New Jersey

Recommended Reading

Bentley, M (1991) *Mary Munter's Business Communication: Strategy and Skill,* Prentice Hall, Singapore

Bolton, R (1986) *People Skills,* Simon & Schuster, New York

Brown, A (1995) *Organisational Culture,* Pitman, London

Handy, C (1993) *Understanding Organizations,* fourth edition, Penguin, Harmondsworth

Pascale, R (1992) 'The paradox of corporate culture: reconciling ourselves to socialization', *California Management Review,* 27, 2 Winter 1985, p. 38, as used in Luthans, Fred (1992) *Organizational Behaviour,* McGraw Hill, New York

Stanton, N (1990) *Communication,* Macmillan, London

Answers to Review Activities

Review Activity 3

1   In selling a product you need to know it well, just as you need to know yourself well in writing a cv and succeeding in an interview situation. You need to believe in the product and yourself, in either case. You need to match the product to its market and you need to match yourself to the job and the organisation.

2   A follow-up letter from Gina Velaquez after an interview with Jill Paine at Gold Coin Bank.

Ms Gina Velaquez
66 Mead Road
St Peter Port
Guernsey

20 December 1996

Ms J Paine
Customer Services Manager
Gold Coin Bank
13 Bond Street
St Helier
Jersey

Dear Ms Paine

I am writing to thank you for interviewing me yesterday for the position of Personal Account Adviser in the Central Branch of Gold Coin Bank.

I would like to let you know that I am very interested in the position, and that I think I can use my past experience in banking to contribute a great deal to Gold Coin Bank. As you know, I am very interested in continuing my banking career, especially in the Customer Services area. I would be happy to relocate to Jersey.

I look forward to hearing from you next week regarding your decision.

Yours sincerely

Gina Velaquez

Review Activity 4

Careful selection of entry level candidates

Soapworks chose people who were likely to be receptive to the socialising process:

- We were looking for personality really that would gel into a team.
- They interviewed 100 people, all unemployed, for 16 jobs.
- The employees are the ambassadors for this – they're crucial.

There is, in effect, a person specification.

Reputation

It is likely that all of the recruits had an idea of the caring and 'green' image of Body Shop, the parent company, probably through buying the products for themselves or for their families.

Interviews and the selection process

Dress is featured at managerial level, for example, Ronnie Morgan's interview, 'I was the only guy dressed in a suit and a tie – I lost the tie very quickly'.

There are clearly 'no-nonsense', 'let's call a spade a spade' values with managers prepared to 'roll up their shirt sleeves'.

The workplace itself: rules and regulations

The green, caring and paternal values are evident in the workplace:

- no smoking
- healthy eating – salads, etc

Caring attitude

'All the Body Shops are involved in community work of some kind'. Staff are given time off to do these activities. Such activities are clearly looked upon with favour by senior management.

UNIT 5

AN INTRODUCTION TO COMPUTERS AND WINDOWS 3.1

Introduction

In this unit you will learn how to operate your computer, store and retrieve your work and protect it against accidental damage. We assume that you will be using Windows version 3.1.

Operating systems and graphical user interfaces are special computer programs that control all parts of the computer, including the screen and the keyboard. Windows, a graphical user interface, was designed to offer a helpful and intuitive way for you to control the computer.

In this unit, we begin by looking at what operating systems are and what they can do. You then find out how you can use them for management tasks including:

- preparing disks for use
- setting up structures for storing your data
- controlling elements of the screen display and the computer's behaviour.

You need to be able to perform these tasks before you can do any work with a program such as a wordprocessor. By working through this unit, you will be well prepared for the material in the rest of the module.

Objectives

By the end of this unit, you will be able to use Windows to:

- format and copy disks
- create and manage filing structures
- control elements of the screen display
- run applications (such as a wordprocessing program)
- load, store and print information
- use menus, icons, windows and the mouse pointer, and use multi-tasking to run several applications at once.

Versions of Windows

Windows is being developed all the time. This unit assumes that you are using Version 3.1. Version 3.1 of Windows offers some improvement over version 3.0. If you are using Windows 3.0 you will still be able to use this material though you may notice very slight differences in the way your screen looks. Version 2.0 or Windows 95, are substantially different versions and cannot be applied to the work in this unit. If you are using a version numbered less than 3.0, you should upgrade to a more recent version.

SECTION 1

An Introduction to Windows

Introduction

A computer needs basic instructions in order to run at all. For example, it needs to know how to interpret anything you type, and how to display information on screen. It also needs to be told when and how to load a program you want to use, and how to allocate its memory. These fundamental tasks are performed by the **operating system**.

Many people find that an operating system is not particularly easy to use. For this reason, a special type of program called a **graphical user interface,** or GUI (pronounced 'gooey') has been developed. This uses pictures and options you can choose from lists displayed on the screen. Many people find it easier to use a GUI to communicate with the computer. Windows is a GUI.

In this section we look at what the operating system does, and why you need to know something about using it.

1.1 What is an operating system?

A computer operating system is a type of control system. It manages the resources of the computer and tells it how to perform tasks. It also gives you a means of communicating with the computer and giving instructions. As such it forms an interface between you and the computer.

– The tasks the operating system performs can be divided into three broad areas:

- It controls how the computer operates, including:
  - displaying information on the screen
  - interpreting anything you type on the keyboard
  - reading information from disks and writing to disks
  - interpreting mouse movements.
  - You do not need to know about these unless you make changes to the computer such as fitting a different monitor or screen.

- It controls the allocation of memory or processing power to tasks.
  - Using Windows, the computer can run more than one program at a time, switching between tasks as necessary. The computer does this on its own without any instructions from you.

● It enables you to communicate with the computer so that you can make it perform tasks and it can give messages to you, telling you if you have made a mistake and answering your questions.

– This is the function of the operating system that you will concentrate on here.

1.2 Turning on your computer

It may not be immediately obvious how to turn on the computer, and, once turned on, whether it is behaving correctly.

ACTIVITY 1

Please note, most computers will not start properly if there are floppy disks in the disk drives. Therefore, before switching on your computer please ensure that all disk drives, i.e. the slots in the front of the machine, are empty.

Find out how to turn on your computer. There may be a button on the front, side or rear of the main box (which contains the computer's 'brain' or Central Processing Unit). You may have to turn on the monitor, i.e. the display, separately. Even if the computer was turned on when you arrived, find out how to do this in case you ever need to turn it on yourself.

1 Describe here what you have to do to turn on the computer you are using.

2 Describe what happens when you turn on the computer. Look out for indicator lights, and anything on the screen display.

You may have to press a button and/or flick a switch in order to turn on your computer. When you have turned on the computer it is likely that the following will happen:

● One or more indicator lights will come on. One of these may be a disk indicator light, which may flash to indicate that the computer is reading software from the disk drives.

● You will hear a whirring noise as the fan starts up. The fan keeps the computer cool and helps prevent it overheating.

● You may hear some noise from the disk drive as the computer reads a disk.

● You may hear a clicking or ticking noise as the computer performs a memory check.

● The screen may flash, and then briefly display some text. Often this will be too quick for you to read. Do not worry if this happens most messages only confirm that the machine is performing correctly.

The computer may immediately load Windows and show a screen looking like Figure 1.

ACTIVITY 2

If Windows has not started automatically, try one of the following to start it manually :

– typing 'win' and pressing the return key (large key on the right hand side of the keyboard) sometimes marked 'enter'

– alternatively a menu may come up and you can select an option from this

or you may have to go through a signing on process to identify yourself as a legitimate user

finally, if all else fails, ask for help.

What ever happens when you switch on a computer

Don't Panic

Someone will be able to show you how to activate Windows on your computer.

A screen similar to Figure 1 indicates that your computer is running Windows correctly. You may find more, or less, on your screen depending upon what software (i.e. computer programs) has been installed on your particular computer.

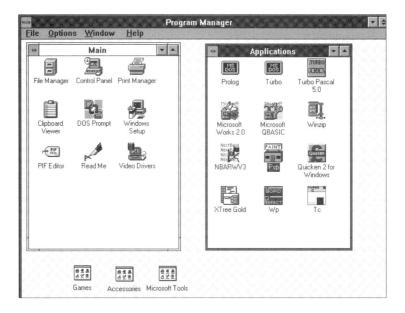

Figure 1: Program Manager window opened as typical

If it does not look anything like the above, it may look like Figure 2. (This is how it would look if it has not been customised.) Figure 2 still shows the Program Manager window but in this case the window has been reduced to its minimum size, i.e. 'iconised' and its contents can no longer be seen.

Figure 2: Screen with Program Manager iconised

1.3 What is a graphical user interface?

Unlike a traditional operating system, instead of requiring you to remember and type commands, a GUI shows pictures, called icons, and lists of options on the screen. This allows you to instruct the computer by moving a pointing device around the screen and activating buttons rather than typing a set of special commands. You type less, and make more use of a pointer and mouse buttons.

LOOKING AT A GUI

When you load Windows, a screen something like Figure 3 appears.

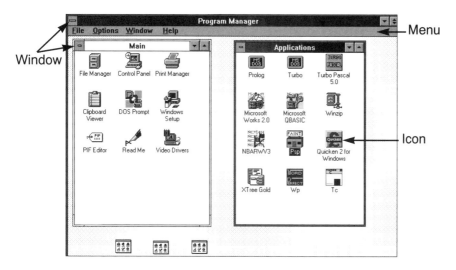

Figure 3: Program Manager

The main components of GUIs are:

● Windows

● Icons

● Menus

● Pointer.

From these, the acronym WIMP has been derived. You may see a GUI referred to as a WIMP user interface.

Figure 3 shows a window, some icons and a pointer. The pointer moves around the screen as you move the mouse, which is beside the computer.

You can use the pointer to:

● select icons

● display menus

● select an option from a list.

Your main way of communicating with the computer using a GUI is by moving the mouse and pressing its buttons to select what you want to do with the icons and menu options. You will occasionally need to type something, such as the name you want to give to some work you are saving, but you will not need to type in specialised instructions for the computer.

Microsoft Windows is the name of the software package used to control the machine. A 'window' is the name given to a rectangular object on the screen. Both of these are often called 'windows'. They can usually be distinguished by the context.

SECTION 2
Controlling Windows

Introduction

With Windows you will be dealing with pictures, menus and dialog boxes rather than typing commands. You will make choices and give answers by clicking on buttons and on items in lists of options. Once you are proficient in the basics, you will use the same techniques in your continuing work with disks and programs.

In this section you will learn about, and try many important techniques you need in order to use Windows. You will continue practising these throughout this unit so they will soon become familiar.

2.1 The Windows screen

The Windows screen is called a desktop and you will carry out all your work on it. On the desktop in Figure 4 is a window with the title Program Manager. If, instead of a window, there is a small picture labelled Program Manager, don't worry (Figure 2). You can display the window later. First look at the parts of the window shown.

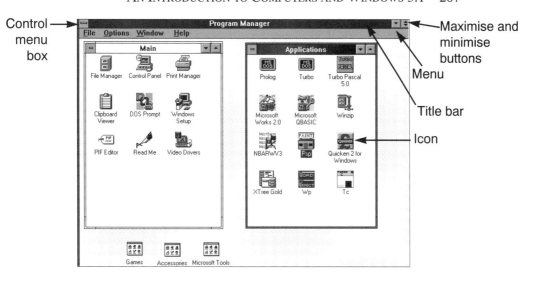

Figure 4: Program Manager window with labels

The title bar shows the name of the window.The control menu box calls up a menu relating to the whole window.

The minimise and maximise buttons let you alter the size of the window. The menu bar shows the names of other menus you can call up from the window. The icons represent programs and work i.e. files stored on the computer.The activities in the rest of this section will help you to explore this window and its components, and find out about using Windows.

2.2 The mouse

You will be using the mouse a lot in your work with Windows to point at, move and select items on the screen. The mouse can be set up for a right-handed or left-handed person. If you are right-handed, you will use the left button on the mouse; if you are left-handed, you will use the right button. In Activity 3 you will set up the mouse to suit you.

THE MOUSE POINTER
The mouse pointer, which moves on the screen as you move the mouse with your hand, is an important aspect of using Windows.

2.3 Restoring the Program Manager window display

Before you do Activity 3, make sure you have a screen similar to that shown in Figure 1. If you do not, you may have several other windows on the screen, or an icon labelled Program Manager.

If you have other windows, cluttering up the screen, you will need to close them. To close a window:

> point to the control menu box (a horizontal line in the top left corner of the window),

> without moving the mouse, press and release the left-hand mouse button twice in rapid succession.

This is called double-clicking. Double-clicking on a control menu box will close the window. Do this on each window in turn until you get back to the display shown in Figure 1.

If you have an icon labelled Program Manager you will need to enlarge it. To enlarge an icon double-click on it.

Double-clicking on icons that represent iconised windows will display the window at its normal size.

Sometimes the mouse pointer will change to a different shape as you are working. You can still use it in the same way as you use the arrow.

2.4 Exiting Program Manager

Whenever you want to stop using the computer you will need to exit Program Manager. You do this by clicking once on the control box (Figure 4). A menu will appear: choose (i.e. click on) exit. A box will appear asking if you wish to Exit Windows, choose Yes.

You will want to leave Program Manager and come back in to continue your work on this unit at another time. You need to start Windows if it is not already started. If you need help ask your tutor or Resource Centre Manager.

2.5 Windows tutorial

Windows 3.1 has an in-built tutorial to teach fundamental mouse and window control skills. Working through this will take approximately 20 minutes.

ACTIVITY 3

Work through the Windows tutorial. Using the mouse select Help from the Program Manager menu, i.e., move the mouse over the word Help and press on the left mouse button once. Now select 'Windows Tutorial' and follow the instructions given.

All computer packages running under Windows will have similar help facilities. These will often be enough to help you through the basics (and some of the more advanced features) of using the package, without the need to use a manual. These help systems are invaluable when working in an environment without manuals. To learn the basics of a computer package activate the Help system (after running the package in question) and then select Contents. To find specific help on a particular topic activate the help system and then select 'Search for help'. This will be covered in more detail later.

2.6 Moving a window

You may sometimes want to alter the position of a window on the screen. Moving and resizing windows are very common activities to arrange the contents of the screen for convenience.

ACTIVITY 4

Move the mouse pointer up to the title bar of the window. Now press and hold down the mouse button and move the mouse.

You can see that the window moves around with the pointer for as long as you keep the button pressed. When you release the button, the window stops moving. This technique is called **dragging**.

2.7 Resizing a window

There are two ways of changing the size of a window:

- dragging the borders with a mouse
- switching between the current size and a maximum size.

DRAGGING BORDERS TO CHANGE WINDOW SIZE

ACTIVITY 5

1 Move the mouse pointer so that it is over one of the window borders. Draw the new shape of the pointer.

2 Next move the pointer until it is over one of the corners of the window. What shape is it now?

3 Move the pointer back over a window border at the side of the window.
   Now what has happened?

4 Then move the pointer onto a window corner again and drag the corner in
   and out. What happens?

---

1   When you move the mouse pointer over a window border, the shape of the
     pointer changes to show that you can drag the border and alter the size of the
     window. Over a side edge, the pointer changes to a pair of arrows pointing left
     and right; over the top or bottom edge, it changes to a pair of arrows pointing
     up and down.

2   When you move the pointer over a corner of the window, it changes to a pair
     of arrows set diagonally. This shows that you can drag the window corner in
     and out.

3   When you drag the window border, it moves with the mouse pointer until you
     release the mouse button and the window is then fixed at its new size.

4   When you drag a window corner, you can change both the height and width of
     the window at once.

Now try another way of changing the size of a window.

SWITCHING TO CHANGE WINDOW SIZE

ACTIVITY 6

1 Move the mouse pointer over the button in the top right corner of the
   window that shows an arrow pointing upwards. Click on this by pressing
   and then releasing the mouse button. What happens?

2 Look at the button you just clicked on. What does it look like now?

3 Click on it again. What happens?

1 When you click on the 'maximise' button, the window is redrawn at a larger size so that it fills the screen. This is its maximum size.

2 At the same time, the icon shown on the top right button changes. It now shows an arrow pointing upwards and an arrow pointing downwards. This shows that if you now click on the button, the window will be made smaller.

3 When you click on the 'maximise' button when the window is already at full size, it returns to its previous size. The icon on the button changes back to just an arrow pointing upwards.

ACTIVITY 7

There is a button with an arrow pointing downwards next to the 'maximise' button. This is the 'minimise' button. Click on it now. What happens?

When you click on the 'minimise' button of a window, the window shrinks right down to an icon. All the window parts that you have looked at disappear, and you see just an icon in the lower left of the desktop. This icon represents the window.

ACTIVITY 8

Using the mouse, double-click on the icon you have just created. What happens?

When you double-click on the icon of a window, the window opens at the size it was before you turned it into an icon. (If this did not happen you may have left too much time, or moved the mouse, between clicks.)

2.8 Using menus

Menus are an important feature of Windows. A menu is a list of options from which you can choose tasks you want to do or settings you want to make.

ACTIVITY 9

1 Move the pointer over the word File in the menu bar. Now click the mouse button. What happens?

2 Move the pointer off the menu and onto the desktop. Now click the mouse button or press the Escape key (marked Esc) on the keyboard. What happens?

3 Next click in the menu bar on Options, Window and Help in turn. What happens?

4 Click once on the icon labelled Accessories.

5 Move the pointer up to the button showing a horizontal line in the top left corner of the 'Program Manager' window. Click on the button, and copy the menu down here.

1 When you click on a menu name in the menu bar, such as File, a menu appears.

2 When you click outside the menu or press Esc, the menu is removed without choosing any options.

3 You can click on other menu titles to bring up other menus, and the menu already displayed will be removed each time.

4 From an icon representing a closed window you can also display a menu. The choices shown relate just to that window.

5 When you click on the control menu box in the top left-hand corner of a window, a menu appears like the one in Figure 5.

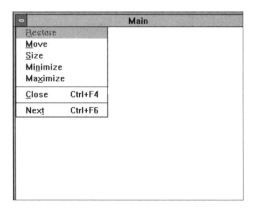

Figure 5: Control menu

This menu lets you make choices about the window itself.

There is a letter underlined in each menu option; this is the letter you need to type to choose the menu option by using the keyboard, though usually, you will want to choose a menu option by clicking on it with the mouse.

ACTIVITY 10

1   Display the control menu again. Using the mouse, click on 'Move'. What happens?

2   Try pressing the arrow keys on the keyboard. Press 'Enter' when the window is in the desired position.

3   Now use the mouse to click on the title bar and then try moving the window.

4   Which seems to you to be the best way of moving a window?

5   Display the control menu again. This time choose 'Size' by pressing 'S' on the keyboard. Again, use the arrows on the keyboard to alter the window. Write down what you have to do.

6   Display the menu and click on Maximise. Now display the menu again. What do you notice?

1   When you choose Move from the menu, the pointer changes shape to a four-headed arrow.

2/3   You should have found two different ways of moving the window, one by using the arrow keys on the keyboard and the other by putting the pointer over the title bar and dragging the window. (You would not have been able to move the window if it had been maximised as this would then fill the screen and leave no space in which to move it.)

4   You probably decided that the mouse pointer method was quickest. Most people decide that it is not worth using the menu option Move as it is simpler just to drag the title bar with the mouse. (When using the computer you will often find that the same result can be achieved in several different ways. Just use whichever you prefer.)

5   When you choose Size, the pointer again changes to the four-headed arrow. However, when you move it over an edge or corner, it changes to the pair of arrows you have seen before. Again, you can resize a window by either dragging an edge or a corner using the mouse or by selecting 'Size' from the menu and then using the arrow keys on the keyboard. Note when using the mouse neither 'Size' nor 'Move' need to be selected from the menu.

6   When you click on Maximise, the window changes to its full size, the same as it does if you click on the Maximise button. When you look at the menu again, you will see that the Maximise option is now shown in grey text. An option that is 'greyed out' like this cannot be selected; you cannot choose Maximise because the window is already at its maximum size.

ACTIVITY 11

1 Display the Control Menu again and choose Minimise. What happens?

2 Move the pointer over the icon and click the mouse button to display the menu for the icon. What do you notice about this menu?

3 Click on Restore to restore the window to its previous size.

1   When you click on Minimise, the window shrinks to an icon.

2   The menu available from the icon is the same as the control menu because the menu still relates to the whole window, even though the window has been iconised.

3   Whenever you have changed the size of a window, you can restore it to its normal size using the menu option Restore. When the window is at its normal size, Restore is greyed out in the menu.

2.9 Using the Help menu

Almost all windows applications, and Windows itself, provide help systems, partly to give you an overall guided tour of how that particular piece of software works but also to answer any specific queries you may have. It's a bit like having a book built into the computer.

ACTIVITY 12

1 With Windows Program Manager maximised select the Help menu.

2 Next select Contents.

3 After reading the page that pops up, close this new window.

4 Select the Help menu from the Program Manager again and this time select 'Search for help on...'

5 Notice that there is a list of topics available. Using the mouse select 'Applications, starting'.

6 Activate the button 'Show Topics'.

7 Highlight 'Applications, starting' in the lower windows and then press 'Go to'.

8 Finally after having read the page generated close down the Help system.

2   Using the Help menu and contents is a good way to get an overall introduction to the piece of software you are using.

3   The window that pops up gives an brief overall description and then shows major subtopics. After clicking on the underlined subtopics the computer will show you information on the subtopic requested and then goes on to highlight other related topics.

4   'Search for help..' is a mechanism for allowing you to get help on a particular topic. Firstly, you specify your general area of interest and then the specific topic within that area on which you would like help (see Figure 6). These help systems are not just available in the Program Manager but in almost all packages that run under Windows.

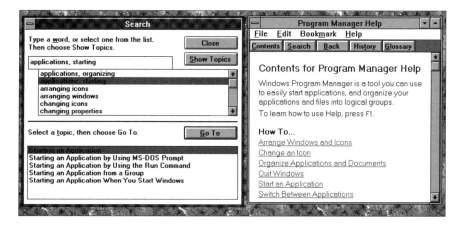

Figure 6: Search window and its generated Help page

2.10 Using icons

Each icon in the display represents something. In the window you have been looking at, there are probably icons labelled Accessories, Games, Main and possibly many others. An icon may represent:

- a single item, such as a computer program (including games)
- a group of items, such as several programs that have been grouped together.

The three icons, Accessories, Games and Main in the Program Manager window are group icons – they each represent a group of programs.

ACTIVITY 13

Double-click with the mouse pointer on the icon labelled Accessories. What happens? What do you think you can do now?

When you double-click on a group icon, a new window opens showing icons for all the items in the group. This may replace the window you could see before, or open on top of the old one.

The icons in the Accessories window each represent a single program or application. You can now double-click on any of the icons to begin running that program. Alternatively, you can click once on an icon and then choose Open from the File menu. You can move these icons around, and move or resize the window.

ACTIVITY 14

1   Assuming your computer has a Calculator icon then double-click on the Calculator icon, or click once on it and then use Open to start the calculator working. Describe here what happens.

2   Using the pointer, click on the calculator keys 6, then 4 and then sqrt. What happens?

3   Click on the Minimise icon in the top right corner of the calculator window. Now move the icon around by dragging it on the desktop. Double-click on it. What happens? How do you think this can be useful?

1   When you double-click on the Calculator icon, a new window opens. The original window remains on screen this time. The new window looks and works like a calculator (see Figure 7).

    The Calculator icon represented not a window but a computer program. This program was activated by double-clicking on the icon. When activated the calculator program displayed a window on the screen which has many of the properties associated with the other windows you have worked with.

Programs running under Microsoft Windows always run within a window of their own.

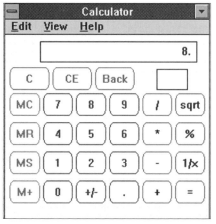

Figure 7: Calculator window

You can use the calculator by clicking on the buttons you want to use.

2   When you use the sequence 6, 4, sqrt, the calculator works out and displays the square root of 64, which is 8.

3   When you click on the Minimise icon, the calculator shrinks to an icon on the desktop. It may be hidden behind the Program Manager or any other window currently using the full screen. You can move the icon around on the desktop now. When you double-click on the Calculator icon, the Calculator window opens again showing the same numbers in the display as when you minimised it. This is very useful because it means that you can have desktop 'accessories' available on your desktop all the time, but they do not need to be present as full-size windows. Instead, you can keep your desktop tidy by having them present as icons and only restoring them to their full size when you need to use them. Being able to have a clock, calculator, notepad and calendar on your desktop means that your Windows desktop can emulate a real desktop; you can pause from your work on an application to do a quick calculation, check the time or note an appointment in your calendar.

ACTIVITY 15

1 Double-click on the Clock icon in the Accessories window. (You may have to move the Calculator window aside first.) See if you can change the display from analogue to digital. Describe here what you did.

2 Next try to close the Clock window. What did you do?

3 Open the clock again, and click on the Minimise button. What happens? Do you think this will be useful to you?

To change the display from analogue to digital, you need to click on Settings in the menu bar to display the menu and then choose Digital.

2   There are, at least, two ways to close a window. You can:

●   choose Close from the Control menu (click once on the button in the top left corner and then choose 'close')

●   double-click on the Control menu button.

Close the Calculator window using either of these methods.

3   When you shrink the clock to an icon, it remains active as a clock. You do not need to enlarge it again to see the time. This can be useful as it means you can have a small clock visible on your desktop all the time.

You can change some other things about the clock, too. You can use Options from the menu to choose whether to display seconds and/or the date as well as the time in hours and minutes, you can set the font (style of lettering) when the clock is using a digital display, and you can remove the title. Experiment with these if you like. If you remove the title bar from the clock window, the control menu button disappears. To bring back the title bar and button, double-click at the top of the clock.

Another option, only on some versions of Windows, is keeping the Clock window at the front of the screen display all the time. This means that it will always be shown 'on top' of any other windows that overlap it.

2.11 Arranging windows

You have already tried opening one window when you have another open. How the windows are arranged will depend on the setting made in the Window menu.

ACTIVITY 16

Close the Accessories and Clock windows if you have these open, so that you are starting with just the Program Manager window on screen.

1 Open two or more windows, for example Accessories, Start-up or Games. Now choose Cascade from the Window menu (you may need to move some windows out of the way to see the menu bar of the Program Manager window). Sketch the arrangement of the windows.

2 Next choose Tile from the Window menu. Sketch the arrangement of the windows.

1   When you use Cascade, the windows are arranged on top of each other, as shown on the right in Figure 8.

2   When you use Tile, the windows are drawn narrower and spread across the screen side by side, as shown on the left in Figure 8.

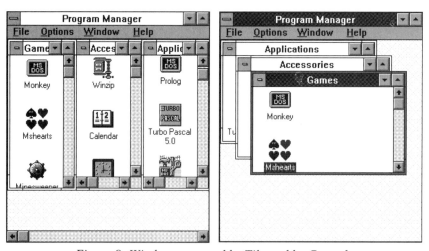

Figure 8: Window arranged by Tile and by Cascade

Close the windows you have opened in the activity.

2.12 Scrolling through a window

When you come to use applications running in windows, you will often find that you cannot see all your work in the window at one time. You therefore need a method of changing the part which is visible in the window. This is called scrolling. You can experiment using the Accessories window.

ACTIVITY 17

1 Open and shrink the size of the Accessories window until all the icons no longer fit in the window. What happens to the window borders?

2 Try each of these operations and describe what happens:

   (a) Click on the arrow icon at the bottom of the right-hand edge or at the right of the bottom edge of the window. What happens?

   (b) Drag the solid block between the two arrow icons. What happens?

   (c) Click in the space between the arrow icon and the block. What happens?

---

1   When the contents of a window cannot all be seen at once, Windows adds scroll bars and scroll arrows to one or two sides of the window. You can use these to scroll the window contents, moving other areas into view. A window with a vertical scroll bar looks like Figure 9.

Figure 9: Window showing scroll bars when not all contents are visible

2   (a) If you click on an arrow icon, the window contents scroll in small steps.

 (b) If you drag the block along the scroll bar, you can move straight to the other end of the window contents, or to any place between the extremes. You have full control.

 (c) If you click in the space between the block and the scroll arrows, the contents scroll by in jumps.

2.13 Using dialog boxes

So far you have given the computer instructions by choosing options from menus and clicking on buttons and icons, but the computer has not sent you any messages. When the computer needs to ask you a question or tell you that you have made a mistake, it uses a dialog box. This is a special window that appears just for as long as it is needed. It has text, buttons you can click on, sometimes lists that you can choose from, and sometimes text fields for you to type in.

ACTIVITY 18

1   Double-click on Notepad icon in the Accessories window. This opens a text editor i.e. a very simple word processor. Type some text, just your name will do. Now double-click on the control menu box, or display the menu and click on Close. Sketch the dialog box that appears.

2   What do you think will happen if you click on:

 (a) Yes

 (b) No

 (c) Cancel?

3   Click on No.

1   The dialog box looks something like Figure 10.

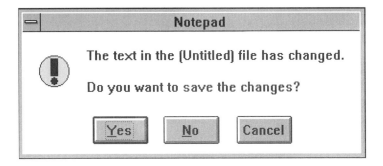

*Figure 10: Dialog box displayed when trying to
close an unsaved file from Write*

2   (a) If you click on Yes, Windows will give you the chance to save your
document before closing the window.

(b) If you click on No, the window will be removed and your document will
be lost.

(c) If you click on Cancel, Windows will not close the document, and you will
be able to carry on working on it and save it if you want to.

2.14 Program Manager Main group window

The Program Manager Main group is important as you will use it to ensure the work
you create is safely stored and can be retrieved when needed.

ACTIVITY 19

Close any windows except the Program Manager window. Now open a
window for the Main group. List the icons you can see:

You will see these icons:

- ● File Manager
- ● Control Panel
- ● Print Manager and various others.

You will need to use only the File Manager and the Control Panel in this unit.

The File Manager is used to:

- move, copy, delete and rename files (see Section 5)
- organise your files and programs into groups (Section 6)
- manage disks and directories (Section 6).

The Control Panel is used to change settings such as:

- the date and time
- the colours used in the screen display (Section 7)
- whether the mouse is set up for a right-handed or left-handed person (Section 7).

2.15 Resetting the date and time

You already know how to display the clock. It may or may not show the correct time. You can set the clock and the date stored by the calendar by using a special group of programs that give you control over many Windows settings and settings that affect how the computer operates. To use these programs and make settings, you need to display the Windows control panel.

ACTIVITY 20

You should have the Main group window on screen still. If not, open it again. Double-click on the Control Panel icon to open this window:

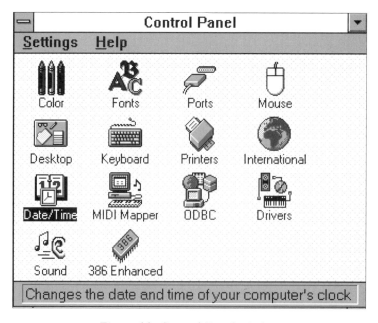

Figure 11: Control Panel window

ACTIVITY 20 Continued

Double-click on the Date/Time icon to open a window that allows you to change the date and time:

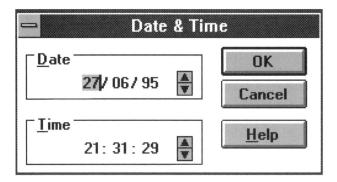

Figure 12: Date and time window

The clock on your computer may be set up to use a 12-hour format, in which case it will show AM or PM.

ACTIVITY 20 Continued

1 Move the pointer over the Date or Time. What happens?

2 You will see that the first figure is highlighted. Look at the date and decide whether this is the month or the day. In the example shown here, the first figure is the day, but your computer may be set up to show the month first. Type a different number. What happens?

3 Now click on another element of the date or time. What happens? You can now delete the figures in the element you have clicked on and type new figures. Alternatively, you can click on the up or down arrow to change the value by one at a time. If you are using a 12-hour clock format, always use the arrow icon to change the hour if there is a change from morning to afternoon (or afternoon to morning) as Windows will change the AM/PM setting automatically if you do this.

4 Set the date to 23rd August 1995 and the time to 10.42 and 35 seconds.

Describe here what you did:

5 When you have finished experimenting, set the date and time to the correct values and click on OK, or just click on Cancel to restore the original values updated to the current time.

1 When you move the pointer over the areas showing date and time it changes shape. This shape shows that it is in an area in which you can type text. It is usually called an **i-beam**.

2 When you type with a figure highlighted, the new figure you type replaces the figure in the dialog box. You may have noticed a flashing vertical line to the right of the highlighted figure; this is the **caret** or **cursor,** and shows where text you type will appear.

3 When you click elsewhere in the date or time field, the caret is placed at a new position and you can delete another figure and type a different value.

4 To set the date to 23 August 1995, you would need to delete the day figure and type 23, click to place the caret in the month figure, delete it and type 8, and click on an arrow icon to change the year.

To set the time to 10.42 and 35 seconds, you would need to:
- Click to place the cursor or caret on the hour figure, then click on one of the arrow icons as many times as necessary to change the hour.
- Click to place the caret on the minutes figure, delete it and type 42.
- Click to place the caret on the seconds figure, delete it and type 35.

You could have used the arrow icon for one or more of these. Windows automatically keeps track of a change from AM to PM or PM to AM if you use the arrow icons to change the hour, so you do not need to change the AM/PM setting yourself.

Summary

In this section you have learnt about the main features of Windows and practised using some of them. You will find that they quickly become familiar and easy to use as you use the computer more and more.

SECTION 3

Using Computer Disks

Introduction

You will need to use floppy disks with your computer. Even though your computer probably has a hard disk fitted, you will need to use floppy disks to make copies of your work, to move any programs or data around from one computer to another, and to load new programs onto the computer. In this section you will learn how to 'format' a floppy disk under Windows i.e. to prepare a disk for use, and how to make a copy of a disk and give it a name. You will also set up a schedule for making back-up copies of your disks regularly to make sure your work is always safe.

3.1 Preparing a disk to hold information

Before you can use a new floppy disk to hold any information, or data, you need to prepare it. This preparation is called **formatting**. Usually floppy disks are sold unformatted because different types of computer need the disk to be formatted differently. Formatting prepares the tracks (lines) on the disk to hold data in the way in which the computer is going to present the data. A disk formatted on a PC is not the same as a disk formatted on a Macintosh or Acorn computer, although all the disks are identical when you buy them.

When you format a disk, any data already stored on it is irretrievably lost. Although you need to format a new disk before you can use it, be careful if you reformat a disk you have used before. Make sure you have a copy of any information that you want.

Disks are denoted both by their physical size (usually 3.5 or 5.25 inches) and also by the amount of information they can store in thousands or millions of bytes, Kb or Mb (usually 360Kb, 720Kb, 1.22 Mb or 1.4 Mb). One single byte of storage will normally be enough to store a single letter of the alphabet. The 3.5 inch disk is neither floppy or round! Disks are also either high density or double density.

	3.5 inch	5.25 inch
Double Density	720 Kb	320 Kb
High Density	1.44 Mb	1.2 Mb

ACTIVITY 21

1 Your computer may accept any of the following disks. Ask someone who is familiar with your machine specification which of the following it can take: 3.5 inch 720K (double-density) 3.5inch 1.44MB (high-density) (this is the most common variety) 5.25 inch 360K (double-sided, double-density) 5.25 inch 1.2MB (double-sided, high-density).

2 How many disk drives does your computer have?

3 Record below the types of disk you can use in each drive of your computer. If it is not your own computer, you may need to ask someone who knows more about the computer.

A disk drive that can accept 1.2MB disks can also take 360K disks; a drive that can take 1.44MB disks can also take 720K disks. The reverse is not true.

You can try formatting now. You will need a new floppy disk of an appropriate type for your computer for the next activity.

ACTIVITY 22

Put the disk into the disk drive slot of your computer. If your computer has two floppy disk drives one will be called drive A (or A:) and the other drive B (or B:). You will need to know whether you are using drive A: or B:. Use drive A: if you can.

If it is a 3.5 inch disk, there is an arrow moulded into the top left corner of the disk to show you which way to put it into the drive. When inserting a disk into a horizontally mounted drive, the arrow must be on the top of the disk and pointing towards the disk drive slot as you insert it. When inserting disks into vertical slots care should be taken to insert them gently in case they are the wrong way around.

If it is a 5.25 inch disk, there are two small semi-circular notches out of the side you need to put into the disk drive. Hold the disk so that the moulding of the case is smooth on the top surface. (The other side has seams around the edges.)

1 Push the disk into the drive until it clicks into place.

> 2 To format a floppy disk from Windows, you need to use the File Manager. To start the File Manager, open a window for the Program Manager Main group and double-click on the File Manager icon. Do this now.

The File Manager window opens. Inside it is another window. This shows the contents of one of your disks. It has a button for each disk drive you have, and one of these will be highlighted. In the space below it there is a list of all the directories on that disk.

The window looks something like Figure 13, though yours may have different disk drive buttons and will show different lists of directories and files. If it is a new disc then it will not contain any information.

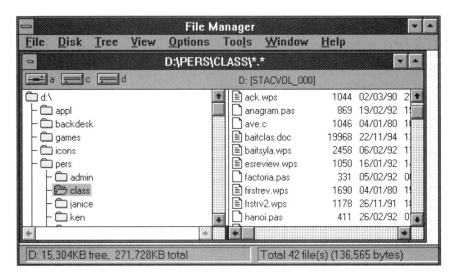

Figure 13: File Manager window

In Figure 13, on the left there is a list of the contents of the root directory of the disk. The root directory is the main directory on a disk and every disk has one. A directory is like a folder in which files and other smaller folders can be stored. All other directories and all files are stored within the root directory. It is called the root directory because, if you imagine a directory structure as being similar to a tree, the root is the base of the structure as shown in Figure 14. On the right of Figure 13 is the contents of the directory highlighted on the left, i.e. 'class'. When trying to locate anything that has been stored on a disk the root directory is a good starting point. From this appropriate subdirectories can be repeatedly chosen until you have homed in on the item to be found.

The root directory can always be found in the left at the top of the window. It is denoted by the (\) symbol. In Figure 13 this is d:\ the root directory of drive 'd'.

A: and B: usually denote floppy disk drives. On machines where only one floppy disk exists 'B' is usually unused. Found on the front of machines, these drives initially have no disks inside them but can have disks inserted at will by the user. C: usually denotes a hard disk. These are located inside the machine and are not easily removed. They do however store much more than floppy disks can store and work much more quickly. Hard disk drives are the usual place where the computer stores 'Windows' and application programs such as Microsoft Word, a large wordprocessing program. Floppy disks are often used to store personal files. This is especially true if you are likely to be working on several different machines and wish to transfer these files between machines. D:, E: and other drive letters may be used to denote extra hard disk drives, CD ROM drives or other storage media (including drives stored elsewhere to which the computer is connected through a network).

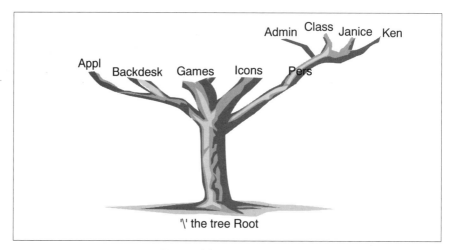

Figure 14: Tree structure

If your computer shows only one of the windows, you can display both by choosing the option Tree and Directory from the View menu.

ACTIVITY 22 Continued

1 Move the pointer up to the menu bar of the File Manager window itself and display the menu called Disk. There is an option Format Disk or Format Diskette. Even though the current drive shown in the directory window may be C, do not worry. The computer will assume that you want to format a disk in drive A. It will not reformat your hard disk. Click on the Format option.

2 Write down here what happens next. (Follow the instructions the computer gives you.)

The computer displays a dialog box like the one in Figure 15 for you to set some options.

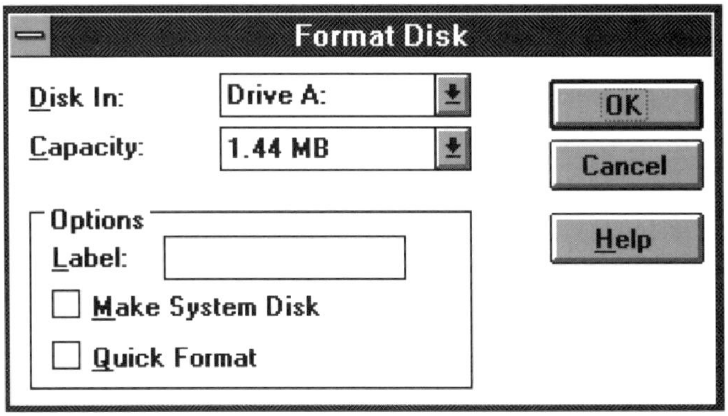

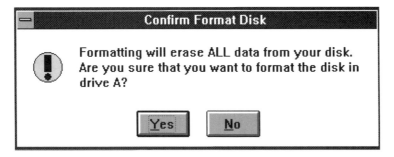

Figure 15: Window for disk formatting options

If your computer has more than one floppy disk drive, you can click on the arrow (pointing down) beside the first user selectable option 'Disk in' to display a menu offering the floppy disk drives available. If your computer has a high density disk drive, you will be able to choose from the menu displayed when you click on the button beside Capacity whether to format a 720K disk or a 1.44MB disk.

ACTIVITY 22 Continued

Choose the formatting option that is appropriate for the type of disk you are using. Ignore the other options for now and click on OK when you are ready.

The computer first displays a warning dialog box to tell you that you will lose all the information on your disk if you format it.

Figure 16: Format confirmation dialog box

ACTIVITY 22 Continued

Click on Yes to continue. This will delete all the information on the disk.

If you have made an inappropriate choice (asking to format a 720K disk to 1.44MB, for example) the computer will display a dialog box showing an error message. If you have set up your formatting request properly, the computer begins formatting the disk. The dialog box on screen shows you how it is progressing with a message that updates as formatting proceeds.

ACTIVITY 22 Continued

When formatting is complete, the dialog box changes to ask whether you want to format another disk. Click on No.

Finally, remove and label the disk.

You now have a blank disk that is empty but is correctly formatted for your computer.

3.2 Copying disks

You will often need to make copies of disks, for example:

● when you have bought a new program and want to make a copy to use, keeping your original copy safe in case anything goes wrong with your working copy

● to keep a secure back-up copy of your work, in case anything happens to the copy you are working on **(strongly recommended)**

● to exchange files between people working in a group.

When you copy information from one disk to another, the computer reads the data from one disk, stores it in its memory, and then writes it to the next disk.

If you have only one floppy disk drive of the appropriate sort on your computer, you will have to:

● put the disk you want to copy from into the disk drive

● tell the computer to copy information from it

● when the computer displays a message telling you it is ready for the second disk, replace the disk with the one you want to copy to.

Depending on how much free memory your computer has, you may have to switch the disks in the disk drive several times as the computer copies parts of the information stored. If you have two disk drives to use for copying, it will be quicker and you will not need to switch disks.

The next activity involves making a copy of the disk that comes with this module. You will then be able to keep the original disk safe and use the copy you have made to work on the module.

ACTIVITY 23

1 In the lower left corner of the disk that comes with this module there is a small plastic slider. Move this to uncover a hole. This will write-protect the disk that comes with this course. Now put the disk into the floppy disk drive. This will be referred to by the computer as the 'source disk', because it is the source of the information you are going to copy.

2 Put the source disk in the disk drive and keep your blank disk ready; you will need it soon. The blank disk will be referred to by the computer as the 'destination' disk by Windows.

3 With the source disk in drive A:, choose 'Copy disk' from the Disk menu of 'File Manager'.

4 A dialog box appears warning you that you will lose all the information on the destination disk. Click on Copy.

5 The next dialog box tells you to put the source disk in drive A:. If you have not already done so, do this now and then click on Continue.

6 The computer begins to copy information from the disk into its own memory, showing in a dialog box how it is progressing. When the computer is ready for the second disk, it will display a dialog box asking you to insert the destination disk. Click on OK when you have done so.

---

1 Opening the slide protects the disk from accidental erasure just as removing the tabs from a blank cassette prevents any new recording being stored on that tape.

6 The computer should now copy the information onto the destination disk. This can be confirmed by using 'File Manager' to check the contents of this disk.

3.3 Naming a disk

You can give each of your floppy disks a name, or label, which the computer will use when listing the information on the disk. This is useful as it identifies your disks and you print out lists of the contents of your disks later.

ACTIVITY 24

1   Copy the module disk that you have just made into the disk drive. Think of a name that you want to give the disk. It can be up to eight characters long. You can use letters and numbers, but **not** punctuation marks or spaces in the name.

2   Click on the option 'Label Disk' from the 'Disk' menu of 'File Manager' to display a dialog box similar to Figure 17.

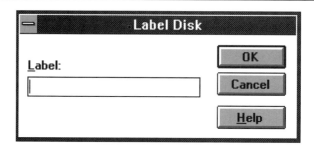

Figure 17: Label Disk dialog box

ACTIVITY 24 Continued

Type the name you want to use for the disk in the 'Label' box and click on OK.

The directory window will now update to show the new name of the disk. Of course, this will only be visible when examining the disk using software such as File Manager within Windows.

It is a good idea to stick a paper label on your disk and write your name, module and disk contents on it. This can then be returned to you if you accidentally leave your disk in the machine at the end of a session.

3.4 Keeping back-up copies of disks

You have already made a back-up copy of the module disk during the activities in this section. It is important to keep a back-up copy of anything important that you have on disk in case you lose or damage your working copy. When you get a new program or some information from someone else, you should always make a copy of the disk and work on that, keeping the original disk safe as a back-up copy. When you do your own work with the computer, you should make frequent back-up copies, which will be duplicates of your work, so that you do not lose too much if something happens to your working copy.

ACTIVITY 25

Besides physical damage to a disk, why would you back-up your information? Write down your reasons below:

- You may make a mistake while working on your disk and perhaps delete some information you wanted to keep.
- You may make changes to your work and then decide to go back to the original version.
- You may lose your working disk. (It is very easy to leave your disk in the computer when you have finished working and to forget about it. If you are working somewhere other than your own home, it may not be there when you come back.)

It is possible for disks to become corrupted either because a computer virus has attacked the disk or because the disk has been damaged by being dropped, being placed in an area of excessive heat or near a magnetic field. *Sooner or later this will happen to you,* your computer will report a disk error when you try to use one of your disks. You may then not be able to get your information from the disk and will need to use your back-up.

Even if you keep most of your work on the hard disk of your computer, it is wise to keep back-up copies of all your work and the programs you use (these will probably be as the programs were supplied originally). It is not common for a hard disk to become corrupted, but it does happen. It is possible for you to delete something by mistake from the hard disk, too.

To be useful, back-up copies of your own work need to be recent, so you will have to work out how often you need to make back-ups. If you are working on a large document and spend all day at the computer, making a back-up copy only once a week will not be enough. You could lose a whole week's work, and it is unlikely you can remember everything you added during a week.

ACTIVITY 26

Consider the factors that affect how frequently you should make back-up copies of your work. What questions should you ask in deciding how frequently you should make back-up copies.

You probably came up with some of the following questions:

- How quickly do you work?

- How much work are you prepared to recreate if necessary?

- How difficult would it be to recreate your work?

- How inconvenient would it be for you to have to redo work? (This may depend on how busy you are and whether your time working on the computer is limited.)

- How much time do you spend working on the computer each day.

Thinking about these questions will help you decide how often you need to make back-up copies. For example, if you work solidly on the computer all week, you will need to make back-up copies every few hours. If you have limited access to the computer, or little time to spend working on it, you will not want to have to waste any of it duplicating work you have already done, so you will want to make frequent back-ups. If you work very slowly with the computer, perhaps thinking most of the time, and then typing a little, and you print out your work at the end of each session, you may decide to make back-ups only every day or so. How frequently do you plan to make back-up copies of your work? Try to stick to your decision to make back-ups frequently. It is easy to have good intentions but not to bother in practice. The first time you do lose some of your work, you will realise how valuable the back-ups are.

In industries where computers are used all the time and to store important information, a system of triple-level back-ups is often used. This consists of using three, or more, disks in turn to make back-ups on successive occasions. For example, if you decided to make a back-up each day, you might use disk 1 on Monday, disk 2 on Tuesday and disk 3 on Wednesday. On Thursday, you would use disk 1 again, overwriting the copy you made on Monday. On Friday, you would reuse disk 2, and so on.

ACTIVITY 27

1 What are the advantages of the three-disk system?

2 What other precautions could you take to keep your back-up disks safe?

1   The three-disk system offers extra security in two important ways:

If anything happens to the most recent back-up, it is possible to restore work from the previous day's back-up. Although a day's work is lost, it is better than having no back-up at all, or only an old one.

If you make a mistake during the day and do not notice it until after you have saved the back-up, you can restore a version without the mistake. Even if you fail to notice the error for two days running, it is possible to correct the mistake with three back-ups.

2   You could make two back-up copies at a time, so that if anything happened to one disk you would still have the other. However, it is not particularly likely that your working copy and your back-up copy will get lost or damaged at the same time. A better precaution is to keep your back-ups and originals separate. This will minimise the chances of both sets being damaged or lost at the same time. If you keep three levels of back-ups, it is a good idea to keep these disks separate too. Try to keep your sets of disks not just in different disk boxes, but in different rooms or even buildings. Do not carry all your back-ups and originals around with you. If you have to travel to use the computer, you should keep at least two sets of back-ups so that you can carry one with you and leave one at home.

3.5 Disk copying and the law

We have suggested that you should always make a copy of any new program you buy and put the original disk away safely. However, you must read the licensing conditions of new programs carefully and make sure that you only make and use copies as you are allowed to. Generally, you are not allowed to:

- make copies to give to someone else

- use a program on more than one computer at once

- lend copies to someone else to help them decide whether they want to buy the program

- sell copies to anyone else

- copy the program onto a network without permission from the software company that produced the program.

You are allowed to:

- remove your copy of a program from one computer and then use it on another computer

- make a back-up copy in case your working copy is damaged.

If you want to use several copies of a program on a network, you should apply to the software company for a site licence. You will probably have to pay for this, and it will specify the number of copies you are allowed to use.

If you break any of the conditions of the licensing agreement, you may be prosecuted. The Federation Against Software Theft (FAST) has the right to search computer installations to check that software is not being illegally copied and used, and can impose large fines if it finds any illegal use. Individuals can be fined too, so be careful.

ACTIVITY 28

Which of the following do you think would be in breach of the licensing conditions of a piece of software?

1 Rachel has loaded a word-processing program on her portable computer and typed in some reports. She gives the computer to her secretary to make amendments to the report, using the program.

YES/NO

2 Tony has two identical computers at home, one upstairs and one downstairs. He has bought a copy of a flight simulator game and loaded it on both computers.

YES/NO

3 Alice's mother wants to borrow a copy of the spreadsheet program Alice uses. Alice makes copies of the disks and lends them to her mother. Her mother uses the program for a week and then deletes the copies.

YES/NO

4 Adrian is worried that his toddler may destroy the disks that hold his database program. He makes 15 back-up copies and keeps some in his house, some at work, and sends some to his father for safekeeping.

YES/NO

5 Thomas has created a design for a garage using a drawing program. He saves his design on a disk. His friend also wants to build a garage and asks if he can borrow the design. Thomas lends him the disk with the design on it.

YES/NO

1   Rachel is not breaking the law. She has installed a single copy of the software on one computer; it does not matter who uses the computer.

2   Technically, Tony is breaking the law. Although he is unable to use both computers at once, he has installed the program on two computers when he is allowed to install it on only one.

3   Alice and her mother are breaking the law. Even though Alice's mother deletes the copies when she has finished evaluating them, she should not have used them in the first place.

4   Adrian is allowed to make as many copies for security as he wishes. He may have difficulty convincing FAST that all his copies were kept for this purpose, but he is not breaking the law if none of the extra copies is ever used and he does not intend them to be used.

5   Thomas can give the drawing he has created to anyone as long as he does not also pass on a copy of the program. The data you create with a program is not

generally subject to any restrictions on distribution. (His friend would need to have some software capable of understanding the diagram. He may even need to have the same program.)

Summary

In this section you learned how to format a disk and make a copy of it. You looked at why you need to make back-ups, and decided how frequently you will do so. You are also able to abide by the law when making copies of disks.

SECTION 4

Launching Applications

Introduction

Using Windows you will want to run, or 'launch', application programs that have been purchased and installed on your computer.

4.1 Starting, finishing and minimising applications

To start, or launch, an application move the mouse over the icon representing that application and double-click.

ACTIVITY 29

1   With Windows Program Manager maximised find and open a window called Microsoft Office. If a window with this name does not exist find an alternative such as Applications.

2   Next find the icon representing the program Word 6 and double-click on this icon.

---

3 Wait for a while and the program should load and run in its own window.

4 Activate the File menu and list below the options that you think are general and may also exist in other application programs.

5 Now activate the Help menu. List below the options that you think are general and may also exist in other application programs.

6 Using the familiar bar at the top left of the window close the application down.

---

2 You should now see the program getting ready to run.

3 All windows applications look and work in similar ways – this makes it easier to learn a range of packages. Looking at the Word application you should be able to recognise a familiar window with its control bar, menu, maximise and minimise buttons. From the menu you should be able to activate the familiar help system.

4 In many application programs there is a File menu with the same options that exist in this menu. Thus having learnt how to use one program many of the skills are the same when using other programs. Some of the common options include :-

New – this creates a blank sheet when starting a new report or letter,

Save – having created a document this stores it on disk,

Open – opens a document from disk for further editing,

Print – this prints a document out,

Print preview – this shows how the document will look when it is printed,

Exit – this closes the application down.

5 Similarly, in most applications there is a 'Help' menu. Common options here include:
   ● Contents – this gives an overview of the package
   ● Search for help on – this allows the user to look for help on a specific topic.

6   Closing an application down will also take a short time. When an application closes, all data from within that application will be lost unless previously stored.

ACTIVITY 30

1 Reactivate Word. Type in a few words and then instead of closing this application minimise it.

2 Look for and activate the application Excel 5.

3 Minimise the Excel application.

4 Finally minimise windows Program Manager itself.

---

1   When the program is minimised it will no longer be visible though it will still be active in memory and all data within it will still be intact. Minimising an application is much quicker than closing it but does not free up the computer systems resources (e.g. memory) being used by that application.

3   When both Word and Excel applications have been minimised they will be represented by icons. However these icons will be obscured by the Program Manager window.

4   By minimising the Program Manager you should be able to see the icons that represent the Word and Excel applications still active in memory (Figure 18).

Figure 18: Active, yet minimised programs

ACTIVITY 31

1 Reactivate the Word program by double-clicking on its icon.

2 Examine the words typed in.

3 Minimise Word again.

4 Finally reactivate the Program Manager.

---

2 When Word is reactivated it should still contain the text you typed into it earlier.

4 With the Program Manager enlarged to its full size the Word and Excel windows are again obscured.

4.2 Using Windows Task List

A list of applications currently in memory can be obtained by activating the Windows Task List. Using this list, an individual application can be selected either to shut it down or to reactivate it after it has been minimised.

ACTIVITY 32

1 Ensure that, as in the last activity, Word and Excel have been activated but minimised and that the Program Manager is maximised and therefore is obscuring the Word and Excel icons.

2 Using the keyboard press 'Ctrl' (the control key) and while holding it down press 'Esc' (the escape key).

---

2 This should activate the Windows Task List (Figure 19).

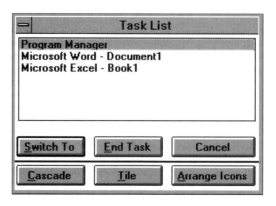

Figure 19: Windows Task List

ACTIVITY 32 Continued

1 In the Windows Task List highlight Microsoft Word and then use the mouse to select Switch To.

2 Reactivate the Windows Task List and this time highlight Excel and using the mouse select End Task.

3 Use the Task List to switch between the Program Manager and Word.

4 Finally Close Word.

---

1   This is one way of reactivating a minimised program that has been hidden by another window.

2   This is one way of closing down an application.

3   This is one way of switching between two applications. For instance you may wish to stop working on an assignment that you are word processing while you temporarily use the calculator program. This is one way of getting back to the word processor after you have finished with the calculator. An alternative way of switching between applications is by holding down the 'Alt key and pressing the 'Tab' key (which is just above the 'Caps Lock' key and often marked with left and right arrows). This switches between all active applications one at a time.

4.3 Running multiple copies of an application

ACTIVITY 33

1 With the Program Manager maximised, locate and activate the Calculator, found within the Accessories window.

2 Move the Calculator into the top left hand of the screen and then click the mouse on the Program Manager window.

3 As the calculator cannot now be seen, double-click on the icon within the Accessories window again.

4 This time move the Calculator into the upper right hand side of the screen and then click the mouse on the Program Manager window.

5 As the Calculator cannot now be seen, double-click on the icon within the Accessories window for one more time.

ACTIVITY 33

6 This time move the Calculator into the lower right hand side of the screen and then click the mouse on the Program Manager window.

7 Finally minimise the Program Manager.

2   We know from past experience that by clicking on the Program Manager window this window is brought into the foreground and thus sits on top of the Calculator window. The calculator is still active in memory even though we cannot see it.

3   We may think that by double-clicking on the calculator icon from within the accessories window that we are bringing the calculator back so that we can use it. This is not the case. We are in fact launching another copy of the calculator. One way of reactivating the calculator would have been to use the Windows Task List ('Ctrl'+'Esc').

6   We now have three copies of the Calculator program running in the computer's memory even though we cannot see any. This is wasteful of the computer's resources. Each copy of the program uses up some of the computer's available memory. If the program had been a larger application such as a word processor then running multiple copies of the same application would waste vast amounts of memory. Eventually as the computer starts to run out of memory it would slow down significantly and be incapable of working with large data files (e.g. documents in the word processor). **There are almost no situations where running multiple copies of an application in memory is advantageous and care should be taken to avoid doing this.**

7   By minimising the Program Manager we can clearly see the three copies of the calculator (Figure 20).

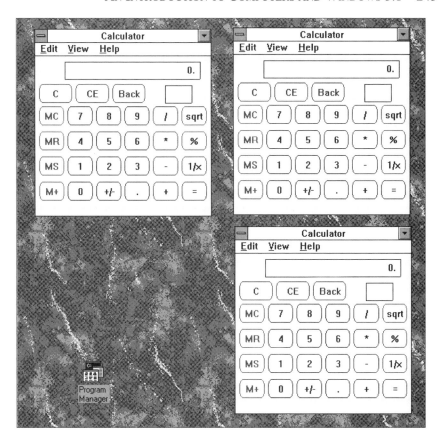

Figure 20: Multiple calculators running in memory

ACTIVITY 34

Close down ALL copies of the calculator and restore the Program Manager.

Summary

In this section you have learnt how to launch applications, how to switch between applications and how to ensure that only one copy of each application is active. Windows applications have many similarities and therefore knowledge of one helps when you are learning others.

SECTION 5

Working with Files

Introduction

Information that you use with the computer is organised into files. A file may be a letter, spreadsheet, drawing or other item of work that you have created. In this section, you will learn how to handle files in Windows, how to create, copy, rename and delete files, and how to find out information about files.

Files are usually organised into groups in a system similar to a filing cabinet in an office. You will look at filing structures in detail in the next section. You will learn how to store and display a catalogue of files in a directory.

2.1 What is a file?

When you begin work on the computer, you will want to save your work so that you can use it again later, print it out, or store it for future reference. Any saved piece of work is stored as a **file**. The type of information held in the file depends on the sort of program you used to create it. If you are using a word-processor, you will create a **document file**, such as a letter, report or essay. If you are using a spreadsheet program, you will create a **spreadsheet file,** and a database will create a **database file**. You may also be able to create graphs from a spreadsheet and graph or report files from a database.

The computer refers to each file by its own name. You will need to give a file a name when you save it for the first time. You can reuse this name the next time you save it if you want your new version to replace your old version, or you can save the file with a new name to preserve the old version.

Files are stored inside directories. A directory does not store any data of its own, but holds files, and sometimes other directories. Figure 21 shows a typical set of directories on someone's computer disk. On the left hand side is a picture of the directories. The directory 'class' (which is itself *inside* the directory 'pers') is highlighted. On the right hand side is a list of files inside directory 'class'.

d:\					
appl	ack.wps	1044	02/03/90	21:57:08	a
backdesk	anagram.pas	869	19/02/92	19:39:38	a
games	ave.c	1046	04/01/80	16:51:26	a
icons	baitclas.doc	19968	22/11/94	13:31:20	a
pers	baitsyla.wps	2458	06/02/92	11:05:32	a
admin	esreview.wps	1050	16/01/92	14:52:48	a
class	factoria.pas	331	05/02/92	00:05:18	a
janice	firstrev.wps	1690	04/01/80	15:21:44	a
ken	frstrv2.wps	1178	26/11/91	18:34:32	a
lect	hanoi.pas	411	26/02/92	01:10:14	a
mary	hnd5msch.wps	1958	28/04/94	19:10:24	a
progs	into.txt	5566	20/03/92	11:49:12	a
referenc	know_rep.wps	8144	19/06/92	08:28:48	a
sw	martial.wps	2586	22/05/93	22:21:46	a
utils	mksheet.wps	1952	23/11/93	21:11:22	a
	mrkapr92.wks	2271	07/05/92	14:54:36	a
	mrkapr92.wps	3250	20/05/92	09:52:04	a

Figure 21: Directories and files

You can think of a directory on a disk as similar to a folder in a filing cabinet draw. You can store documents and sub-folders in it, and keep your work organised by filing each document appropriately.

ACTIVITY 35

1 Put your working copy of the module disk in the floppy disk drive of your computer. If the File Manager is not open you will need to open the Main program group and then double-click on the File Manager icon.

2 When the File Manager window is on screen, click on the icon for drive A: This displays a catalogue of the disk. Sketch the contents of the window in a similar fashion to Figure 21.

3 Display the View menu and check that the option All File Details is ticked. If it is not, click on this option. What happens to the display?

4 If All File Details is clicked, click on Partial Details... to display a dialog box. Try turning off some or all of the options and clicking on OK. What can you do?

---

2   The directory window (on the left) should show the Root directory of your floppy disk (as in Figure 22) and its contents.

Figure 22: Root directory

3   Using Windows 3.1, you have full control over the display of File Details in the window on the right. You can set Partial Details to show any or all of the following:

- size of the file in bytes

- date it was last modified

- time it was last modified

- file attributes – these describe some special kinds of files, and are discussed in the next section.

4   If you set all these options off, the window will just show a list of file names.

FILE NAMES AND DETAILS AND WHAT THEY MEAN

When you did Activity 35, you will have found that the File Manager can show you not just a list of file names but also extra information about a file.

Directories and files have different icons as shown in Figure 23. (In fact there are several different kinds of file icons, but directories are always the same.)

Figure 23: Directory icon and file icon

In Windows a file has a **name** and (usually) an **extension**. The file extension comes immediately after the file name, separated from it by a full stop (.) and tells you what type of file it is (e.g. a word-processor document).

In the last column in the list of files, A stands for Archive. (This is involved in the management of 'back-up' data, and of no concern to us at this stage.) You may also see the letters:

- R for a read-only file – you can look at its contents but not make any changes.

- H for a hidden file – you cannot even look at this file.

- S for a system file – again, you cannot look at this file as it serves some internal technical purpose.

Often, only A and R files are included in directory windows, but someone may have changed the Windows setting that controls which are included.

Because directories on a disk are arranged in a *hierarchical* fashion – i.e. each directory can have other directories branching off from it – we refer to this structure as a 'tree'. Remember that the first directory of your disk is the *root!* A typical Windows directory tree is shown in Figure 24.

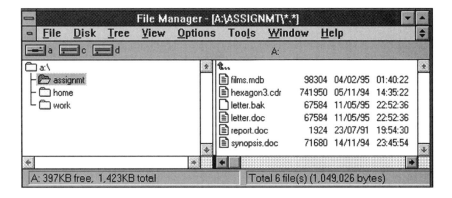

Figure 24: A typical Windows directory tree

ACTIVITY 36

Look at the directory tree above in Figure 24 and answer the following questions.

1 Which items are directories?

2 Write out the file names of the files which may be documents.

3 When was films.mdb last modified?

4 How large are the three document files?

---

1   The directories are called assignmt, home and work.

2   The document files are called letter.doc, report.doc, synopsis.doc and letter.bak. The file extension doc signifies document files. (The file extension bak is for a back-up – letter.bak is a back-up of letter.doc.)

3   films.mdb was created at 1.40 in the afternoon on 4 February 1995.

4   The document files are 67584 bytes (letter.doc), 1924 bytes (report.doc) and 71680 bytes (synopsis.doc).

CHOOSING FILE NAMES AND EXTENSIONS

When you want to save a piece of work for the first time, you will need to give a file name for it. File names may be up to eight characters long. File extensions are usually three characters long. You can use any of the letters from A to Z and any numbers from 0 to 9 in a file name. You can also use the characters ! # $ % ( ) & – _ but you may not use any spaces or the characters : ; , . < > / \ + =. The computer will not let you save a file with a name that contains these 'illegal' characters. There are also a few combinations of characters that you are not allowed to use as file names as they are already being used for other purposes. These are:

AUX, COM1, COM2, CON, LPT1, LPT2, LPT3, PRN, NUL

You can give a file name in upper or lower case (capitals and small letters), but Windows will convert it to lower case only.

There are many different file extensions for different types of file. Those you are most likely to see early on in your work with the computer are:

DOC for a word-processor document file

TXT for a 'pure' text file without any of the formatting provided by a word-processor

XLS for a spreadsheet file produced by Microsoft Excel

MDB for a database file produced by Microsoft Access

EXE for an executable file (a file containing a *program,* which requires 'executing' so that you can use it).

When you refer to a file, you must always include the file extension, or else the computer will not recognise the file.

When you save or retrieve a file using an application program (such as a word-processor or database), you will not need to specify the file extension as it will be added automatically to the file name you give. This is a good way for the computer to make sure that it always give files the right file extension.

ACTIVITY 37

Tick which of the following are acceptable file names?

JASLET.TXT

PM.FILE.TX

TG_LET.TXT

LetYoung.txt

LetYoung2.txt

CON.BAK

config.sys

let/1/ajs.txt

You should have ticked the following acceptable file names:

JASLET.TXT (which becomes jaslet.txt)

TG_LET.TXT (tg_let.txt)

LetYoung.txt (letyoung.txt)

config.sys

The rest are not acceptable because:

PM.FILE.TXT has the illegal character full stop (.) in the name; PM_FILE.TXT would be acceptable

LetYoung2.txt has nine characters in the name

CON.BAK uses the illegal name CON

let/1/ajs.txt uses the illegal character /

5.2 Creating and storing a file

You can easily create a file of your own to store in a directory; you use an application program supplied with Windows.

ACTIVITY 38

You are going to activate a simple application program, create a file and save it onto your floppy disk. *This is a vital skill that you will use almost every time you use a computer.* You will need to make sure that your floppy disk has been formatted, is not write-protected (i.e. that the hole is closed) and that it is in the disk drive.

1 Close the File Manager window and open the Accessories program group window. Double-click on the Notepad icon.

2 Display the View menu. If there is no tick next to the Word Wrap item, click it. If the tick is there press the Esc key to cancel the menu without activating any item.

3 Type some text, just a line or two will do. Do NOT press Enter (Return) when you reach the right-hand margin – just carry on and see what happens.

4 When you have typed some text, display the File menu and click on 'Save As'.

---

1. The Notepad window appears.

2. The Word Wrap option is what is known as a **toggle**. If it is OFF (not ticked) then clicking it sets it ON (ticked), and vice versa.

3. Because you ensured that Word Wrap was ON, when your typing reaches the right hand margin of the window it automatically 'wraps round' to the beginning of the next line.

4. You will see a dialog box similar to Figure 25.

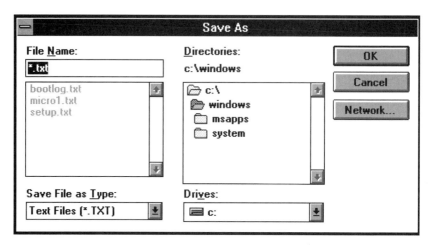

Figure 25: Save as dialog box from Notepad

The Save As dialog box has several components:

● A box for you to type the name you want to use for the file.

● A line showing you your current disk drive and directory (here it is the 'windows' directory on the 'C:' drive, i.e. c:\windows).

● A list of directories for you to choose from.

● A box listing the files already present in your current directory.

● A box labelled Save File as Type; this shows a file type, and has a button to the right for you to click on to display a menu of the options available. You can save your file as a text (.TXT) file, or as another type, in which case you will need to specify a file extension when you choose the file name.

● A box labelled Drives, with an icon for the current disk drive (probably the hard disk drive) and a menu button that displays a menu listing all the drives available on your computer.

● An OK button for you to click on when you have chosen the file name and directory.

● A Cancel button for you to click on if you decide not to save the document.

● A Network button – this is only needed in unusual situations when you want to save on to a different computer.

For now we will keep things fairly simple and save your file on to your floppy disk.

ACTIVITY 38 Continued

1 Click on the button next to the drive name, and from the list which appears choose 'a:' – the floppy disk drive.

2 Think of a name for your file which obeys the rules described above. Type it in to the File Name box. Do NOT include a full stop or extension.

3 Press the OK button.

1 After a pause while the computer looks at your floppy disk, the directory box changes to show the contents of your disk.

2 You don't need to include an extension, because like most programs Notepad will add the appropriate one (.TXT) for you.

3 The computer pauses again while it writes your new file on to the disk. So long as this operation is successful the dialog box then disappears. If an error message appears, check:

   ● that your disk HAS been formatted, is NOT write protected and IS in the drive

   ● that the filename you gave was in agreement with the rules above.

   If it still won't work, keep calm and seek assistance!

5.3 Retrieving a file

On many occasions you will not be creating new files but will wish to retrieve a file you have already created to make changes and improvements to that file.

ACTIVITY 39

1 Close the text editor you were just using by double-clicking on the horizontal line in the top left of the window.

2 Reactivate the text editor you have just closed. Load the file you created in the last activity by:

   ● selecting the Open option from the File menu

   ● selecting the disk drive where the file was stored

- selecting the Open option from the File menu

- selecting the disk drive where the file was stored

- selecting the directory where the file was stored (probably the root directory)

- double-clicking on the correct file name

3 Make a slight change to the text you originally typed in (e.g. add one word), and then select File Save.

4 Finally close the text editor down.

1   Clicking on the Control bar closes down the application associated with that particular window. This is true for all programs including the File Manager and the Program Manager. It is good practice to close all windows before you switch off your computer.

2   To load a file previously created, *which you will need to do on a regular basis,* you will need to find the file. This will be easy if you practise the following good file management techniques.

- Label your disks appropriately

- Create directories with suitable names (games for games, taxretns for tax returns etc.)

- Store your file on the appropriate disk and in the appropriate directory

- Give your files meaningful names (e.g. sub1ass3 for subject 1 assignment 3).

3   Selecting the Save option will store your new document with the same name as before and on the same disk, so this time you will not be asked for a name and location. This will overwrite, i.e. destroy, the old version and replace it with the new file. If you want to keep the old and new versions then use the Save As option instead.

5.4 Copying a file

You will often want to make a copy of a file, either copying it onto a different disk using the same file name or making a copy on the same disk with a different name. You may want to copy a file onto a different disk to keep as a back-up copy, or to to use on a different computer. You may want to make another copy on the same disk if you want to make a modified version of the file and keep your original as well.

ACTIVITY 40

First you will make a second copy of a file on the same disk. You will need to put your working copy of the module disk in the floppy disk drive of your computer. It must not be write-protected.

You will need to use the File Manager again. There are two ways to copy a file in Windows. The one you are going to use now is useful if you want to copy a file within the same directory.

1 Using File Manager open the Windows subdirectory from your course disk by clicking on it in the left hand window. You should see the icon for the file File1.txt, and click on the file to highlight it. Now choose Copy File from the File menu. It displays a dialog box with a field showing the original name of the file and a field for you to type a new name.

2 Without giving a name for the new file, try clicking on OK. What happens?

3 Try again, and this time type the name File1new.txt in the text field labelled To:. This is the name that will be used for the copy. Click on OK when you are ready. What happens?

2   You cannot copy a file without giving a new name for it, as Windows assumes you want to use the same name as the file already has, and this is not allowed. The computer displays a dialog box telling you it cannot copy the file. When you click on OK, both the warning and the Copy dialog boxes are removed from the screen.

3   When you give a file name for the copy, the computer makes the copy in the same directory and you can see that it has been added to the list in the window.

If you were now to open the copy, 'File1new.txt', make some changes to it and then save it again, this would not affect 'File1.txt' at all.

Perhaps you are more likely to want to make a copy of a file onto another disk. You will do this frequently to keep back-up copies of your work.

ACTIVITY 41

1 Put the module disk in the floppy disk drive of your computer. You are going to copy a file from this disk onto the hard disk.

2 Using File Manager open the Windows subdirectory from your working disk in drive A:.

3 *Double-click* on the icon for drive C:. This will open a *new* window for drive C: instead of changing the drive shown by the current window.

4 Now display the Window menu; at the bottom of it you will see a list of windows you have opened during this session with the File Manager. The window you are currently looking at is ticked. Choose the option Tile. All the windows in the list will be displayed in an arrangement.

If there are several versions of the window for drive A: or C:, close all but the most recent (you can identify it by its number, as the most recent has the highest number in the title bar). Use Tile again to enlarge your remaining windows when you have just one window for each of drives A: and C:.

Your screen should look something like Figure 26.

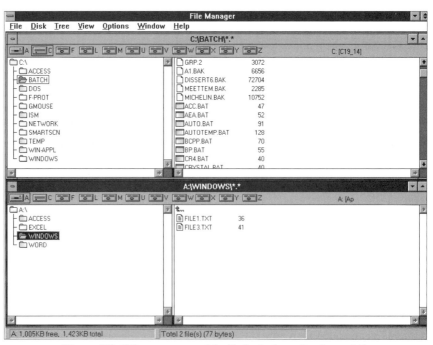

Figure 26: File manager with tiled windows for A: and C:

ACTIVITY 41 Continued

5 Click on the icon for File1.txt and then press and hold down the mouse button while you drag the icon for File1.txt from the window for A: into the window for C:.

6 When the file icon is over a directory icon, you will see a rectangle around the icon. You can move this so that it is over a directory icon in the drive C: window. While it is not over a directory icon, there will be no rectangle. When you release the mouse button, the file will be copied into the directory its icon is over. Copy the file into the disk C: root directory. Does the computer ask any questions?

5   When you select the file, its icon and file information is highlighted in reverse colours. As you drag the file, the pointer changes shape to show a file icon. If you move the pointer to somewhere that you cannot drag the file, the pointer changes shape again to a No Entry sign.

6   When you drop a file icon over a directory icon, the file will be copied into the directory so long as they are on different disks. (Otherwise the file will just be moved. To *copy* a file to a different directory on the *same* disk, hold down Ctrl while you drag it.) This technique is called *drag and drop*. The computer may first display a dialog box asking you to confirm that you want to copy the file to the directory. It then starts copying, displaying a dialog box for you to cancel the copying if you change your mind. When copying is finished, the directory window may be updated to show the new copy of the file. (The display will only be updated if a directory window for the directory you have used is already open on the screen.)

You are now going to copy a file from one floppy disk onto another floppy disk.

You will first have to copy your file onto the hard disk, swap disks, then copy the file from the hard disk to the new floppy disk and finally delete the copy placed on the hard disk drive. There will often be a subdirectory set-up on the hard disk drive to allow you to store temporary files such as these. This temporary directory may be called 'temp'.

ACTIVITY 42

1 Using the File Manager open two directory windows, one for your floppy disk and one for the hard disk. Choose a location where you can store a temporary file on the hard disk (e.g. 'temp' on C: if this directory exists on your computer).

2 Select a file from your floppy disk and drag the icon to your chosen location on the hard disk. Wait for the copying to finish.

3 Take out your floppy disk and replace it with the disk where you want the copy to be stored.

4 Select the file from the hard disk and drag it to the floppy disk window. Again, wait for it to be copied.

5 Select the file on the hard disk, now no longer required, and delete it by pressing the Delete key.

6 Finally close the File Manager.

If you have two floppy disk drives you can copy the file directly from one disk to the other without using the hard disk drive at all.

COPYING A GROUP OF FILES USING WINDOWS

You can easily copy a group of files at once using Windows.

ACTIVITY 43

Close the directory windows you currently have open and display a directory window for the hard disk and a floppy disk.

1 Click on a file icon. Now, with the Shift key held down, click on another file icon, not adjacent to the first. What happens?

2 Now hold down Shift again and click on any one of the selected icons. What happens?

3 Try dragging an icon in the group (but do not actually drop it in another window, because we don't want to do a copy at this stage – instead, drop it on to the File Manager title bar where it will appear as a 'No Entry' sign and have no effect).

4 What do you think this allows you to do if you *did* drop it on another directory?

5 Click on an icon *without* holding down Shift. What happens?

---

1   Clicking on two icons with Shift held down selects the two icons you click on and all the others between them in the directory window.

2   If you click with Shift held down on one of the selected icons, the selection changes.

3   The pointer shape changes to show a group of files.

4   You can drag the whole group of icons to copy them all to another disk or directory.

5   Clicking on an icon without shift will cancel the group and revert to a single file selection.

ACTIVITY 43 Continued

6 Now click on a file icon. Hold down Ctrl key and click on another file icon, not adjacent to the first. Click on more icons. What happens?

7 What shape is the pointer if you try to drag the group? Sketch it below.

8 Hold down Ctrl again and click on one of the highlighted icons. What happens?

---

6   Clicking on two icons with Ctrl held down selects both icons, but none of those between them. You can add further icons to the group by clicking on them with Ctrl held down.

7   If you drag the group, the pointer shape changes to show a group of files.

8   If you click on a highlighted icon with Ctrl held down, that icon alone is deselected.

5.5 Renaming a file

You may sometimes need to change the name of one of your files. For example, if you had two versions of a report you had typed called REPT_NEW.TXT and

REPT_OLD.TXT, and then created a third version, you might want them to be called REPT_1.TXT, REPT_2.TXT and REPT_3.TXT. You can easily change the name of a file.

ACTIVITY 44

You are now going to change the name of FILE1NEW.TXT to FILE2.TXT. You will need your disk containing this file in the floppy disk drive.

1 Click on the icon for file1new.txt to highlight it. Now choose Rename from the File menu to display a dialog box with a field showing the original name and a field for you to type a new name for the file.

2 Type the name file2.txt in the field for the new name and click on OK. What happens?

You will have found that the computer renames the file without asking you to confirm it. The directory window is redrawn with the file icon showing its new name.

5.6 Deleting a file

Sometimes you will want to delete files from the hard disk or a floppy disk.

You are now going to delete one of the copies you have made. When you delete a file and continue to use your disk, it is usually irretrievably lost, so make sure you really do not want it, or have another copy, before you delete any of your own files or programs.

(It *may* be possible to retrieve accidentally deleted files as long as no further use is made of the disk until the file is recovered. Seek assistance if this happens.)

ACTIVITY 45

Highlight the icon for file3.txt and choose Delete from the File menu. What happens?

The computer may give you one, or two, chances to change your mind, depending on how it is set up. To delete the file, click OK or Delete on the first dialog box and, if there is a second, on Yes. When the file has been deleted, the directory window is redrawn to show that it is no longer there.

If you have not already done so you should delete the copy of File1.txt which you created in the root directory of the C: drive in Activity 41. Clean up your litter before you leave!

5.7 Moving files in Windows

Windows offers a quick way to move files from one directory or disk to another. This has the same effect as making a copy of a file and then deleting the original.

- To move a file to a different directory on the same drive, just drag and drop as above. The file is moved rather than copied.

- To move a file to a different drive, hold down the Shift key while you drag and drop. Unlike Activities 41 and 42, the file is moved and no longer exists in the original location.

Summary

In this section you have learnt about files and file names and how to copy, rename and delete files. You will usually want to organise your files into a directory structure to help you to keep track of your work and find things easily. The next section explains how to create and manage directories and gives you the chance to design a directory structure suitable for your own work.

SECTION 6

Filing Structures

Introduction

Once you begin working seriously with Windows you'll soon find yourself creating many files – either on floppy disk or on the computer's hard disk.

Obviously, you need to organise files so that you can find specific items easily at a later date. In this section you will learn how to build and maintain filing structures to keep your work organised. A filing structure is built from directories, subdirectories and files.

6.1 Designing a filing structure

If you just save all your files onto a floppy or hard disk without thinking about their order, you will soon have just a long list of files. This would be just as foolish as piling up all your papers on your desk without making any attempt to keep them in order. To work efficiently, you need to organise your work on disk just as you need to organise the paperwork on your desk.

Windows lets you create **directories** in which to hold your files. A directory is like a folder. In an office you can put several documents inside a folder, and you can put several folders in a filing cabinet. On your computer, you can build up a similar filing structure using several levels of directories, i.e. you can have folders within folders (within folders)!

When you look in an office for a document, you first identify the right filing cabinet, then the right drawer, then take out the correct folder, and finally the document you want. On a computer, you would need to identify the right disk, open the right sequence of directories and finally open the file you want.

Figure 27 is an example. A solicitor keeps clients' files on floppy disks. She has a disk for divorce cases, on which she divides her clients into husbands and wives. Within each of these directories, she has a directory for each client. Within those directories, she has directories for evidence and for correspondence with the client. These directories contain text documents.

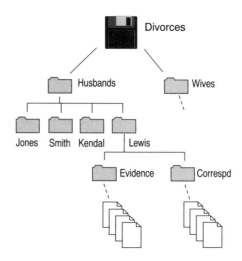

Figure 27: A filing structure

Figure 27 illustrates only one husband's (Lewis) complete directory. Each of the wives' and other husbands' directories would also contain subdirectories called Evidence and Correspd, and each of these would contain documents.

ACTIVITY 46

Imagine you are publishing a weekly student newspaper. You have a floppy disk for each issue. On each disk, you want your filing structure to include:

● adverts for accommodation, pubs, and others

● main stories

● news items on different academic departments

● regular items including editorial, reviews of videos, books and records, coming events, and competitions (chess, crossword, etc.).

Sketch a possible filing structure.

Here is one possibility.

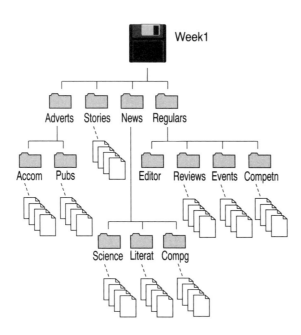

Figure 28: A filing structure for Activity 46

Yours may be different, but as long as you have followed the basic principles of grouping materials sensibly and dividing the whole into directories and subdirectories it is probably just as good.

CREATING A DIRECTORY STRUCTURE

Once you have designed your structure, you need to create it. When you create your structure on the computer, your directory names cannot have more than eight characters.

As you begin to create, move, copy and delete directories, you will, inevitably, have to move up and down the directory structure. For example, you may create your first directory in the *root directory* of a disk. If you want to create another directory inside this one, you will first have to open this directory and tell the computer you want to create the next one inside it. These points will become clearer once you try creating directories and moving around the structure.

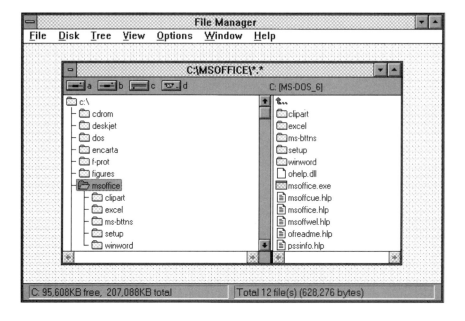

Figure 29: The File Manager window

In Figure 29, you can see an example of the window that appears when the File Manager application is running. There is another window, showing the contents of one particular drive, inside the File Manager window.

The title bar in the drive/document window indicates the drive and the directory being viewed. Below the title bar is a row of drive icons (in Figure 29 the document window is currently looking at drive c:). Below the drive icons, the drive window is split into two halves; the left hand side is the directory tree and the right hand side is the contents of the directory (an expansion of the directory highlighted on the left hand side). Either side may have scroll bars so you can move up and down the window when there are too many items to see all at once.

The first icon in the directory is usually an upwards arrow followed by two dots.

This symbolises the 'parent' directory – the directory which *contains* the directory highlighted in the tree. In what circumstances would there *not* be any parent directory?

ACTIVITY 47

You are going to create a directory, called mydir, in the root directory of the module disk.

1 Insert your course disk in drive a: and start the File Manager application by double clicking on the File Manager icon in the Main window

2 Check to see if drive a: is highlighted. If not, click on the drive a: icon (just below the menu bar).

3 Check to see that the root directory (a:\) is highlighted, if not, click on the root directory icon.

4 Click on the word File on the menu bar, look down the menu displayed below File and click on the option Create Directory.

5 A dialog box is displayed, with a blank field for the new directory name.

6 Read what it says in the dialog box carefully, it tells you on which drive and in which directory it will create the new directory (for example, a: means the floppy disk drive, \ means the root directory).

7 Type **mydir** in the field and click on OK. What happens?

(If you wanted to create the directory on the hard disk, the dialog box should say drive c:. If it did not you would need to Cancel the dialog box and click on the icon for drive c: to make it the current directory.)

When you create a new directory, the File Manager window is redrawn to show the new directory. You are not asked to confirm that you want to create the directory.

If you were to create another directory now, it would be placed, like mydir, in the root directory of the disk. To place a new directory *inside* mydir (i.e., create a subdirectory), you first need to open mydir. Remember, Create Directory always creates the new directory immediately inside the highlighted directory.

You are now going to create a directory inside mydir, then another inside that, and then return to the root directory to create another directory that will be at the same level as mydir in the filing structure. This structure is shown in Figure 30 (though your disk probably has additional directories in the root apart from mydir and anotherd).

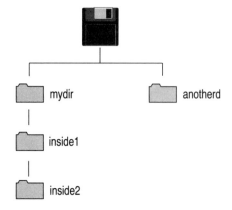

Figure 30: The filing structure to be created

ACTIVITY 48

1 Click on the icon of your new directory, mydir, to make it the 'current' (highlighted) directory.

2 Now use Create Directory again to create a new directory inside it called inside1. (There must not be a space between 'inside' and '1', because spaces are not allowed within directory names.)

3 Now create another directory inside this one called inside2. (Remember to open 'inside1' first.)

4 Create another directory in the root directory called anotherd. Write how you did it below.

---

3   To create the second directory inside the first, you need to click on the icon of inside1 and then use Create Directory, giving the name inside2. You will see the new icon appear in the directory window for inside1.

4   To create another directory in the root directory, you need to click on the icon for a:\ (to make this the 'current' directory) and then use Create Directory, giving the name anotherd.

6.2 Looking at directories

You have already looked at directories several times and seen that they contain files and/or further directories. Occasionally you may come across blank (i.e., empty) directories, but this need not concern you now.

Windows offers several ways of presenting information about the contents of a directory; you may sometimes want to look at the information in a different way, or sort the files in the directory into a different order.

ACTIVITY 49

Can you think of any shortcomings so far about the way the computer shows you the contents of directories? Try to list a few examples in the space below.

For example:

- You may find it annoying that you have to click on a directory to see what is inside it, and then click on subdirectories inside that directory to see their contents.

- You also might not like the order in which the files are listed.

Several of the problems you may have identified with the directory displays in Windows may be overcome by the selection of different options from the Tree and View menus on File Manager's menu bar.

ACTIVITY 50

Try these options from the Tree menu and describe what happens in each case.

1 Put the module disk in drive a: and click on the drive a: icon. Click on the root directory icon (a:\) and choose Collapse Branch from the Tree menu. What happens?

2 Next choose Expand One Level from the menu. What happens?

3 Then click on mydir and click on Expand Branch. What happens?

4 Click on Collapse Branch again, and then on Expand All. What happens?

5 Complete the following to make up a checklist of what these menu options do.

   Use Expand One Level to:

   Use Expand Branch to:

Use Expand All to:

Use Collapse Branch to:

6 You may have noticed that some of the directories in the display are marked with a + sign. Have you worked out what this means? (If you do not see any + signs, choose Indicate Expandable Branches from the Tree menu. Can you tell what the + means now?)

---

1   The options in the Tree menu let you expand and remove parts of the directory tree in the same window.

You were asked to begin by using Collapse Branch from the root directory so that you would be left with just the root directory icon itself on screen. You will have this regardless of the settings previously made on your computer. Collapse Branch removes the display of directories and files contained in the directory that is current when you choose the option.

2   When you use Expand One Level, the directories contained *within* the current directory are added to the display. No subdirectories within these directories are shown, though. The directories inside the root appear when you choose this option.

3   When you click on Expand Branch, any directories within the current directory, and all levels of subdirectories within them, are displayed.

4   When you use Collapse Branch, the directories you have just displayed are removed again. When you use Expand All, the contents of all directories and subdirectories are shown. For a complex structure, this can take a few seconds to display.

5   You might have completed the checklist like this:
   ● Use Expand One Level to:
     show the next level of directories inside the current directory
   ● Use Expand Branch to:
     show all levels of directories within the current directory
   ● Use Expand All to:
     show the whole directory tree
   ● Use Collapse Branch to:
     remove the display of directories within the current directory.

6   The + sign shown on some directories when Indicate Expandable Branches is turned on shows that these directories contain sub-directories and can be expanded to show more of the directory structure.

6.3 Some searching operations in File Manager

File Manager also offers a Search option, under the File menu, which searches for files and can select several files at once. The Search option is extremely versatile, it will search several different directories or even a whole disk.

ACTIVITY 51

1 Making sure that your module disk is in drive a:, start File Manager and click on the drive a: icon. Do not open or click on any directories.

2 Choose the option Search from the File menu. This displays a dialog box like that in Figure 31.

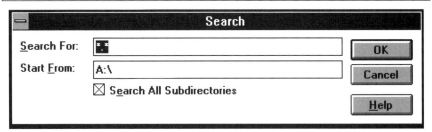

Figure 31: Search dialog box

In the Search dialog box:

● there is a Search For field (to enter the name of the file to be found)

● there is a Start From field (telling you the level that the search starts from)

● there is a small box marked Search All Subdirectories (if it has a cross in it, it indicates that all directories 'below' the start point will be searched).

ACTIVITY 51 Continued

You can use Search to find just one file, or find several files by using a 'wildcard' (a * in the file name) which will match files with a range of names. Try looking for a single file first.

3 Delete anything written in the Search For field and enter file1.txt. Click on the small box, to search all subdirectories. Click on OK. What happens?

4 Try the search again, using a wildcard: type *.*in the Search For field. This means 'any filename, any extension'. What do you expect will happen? Click on OK and find out whether you are right.

1 When you search for file1.txt, the computer searches for this file on the module disk in drive a: and, when it finds it, opens a window showing the full name of the file, including the directories you have to open to find it.

2 When you search using a wildcard, the computer finds all the matching files and directories and then lists them in the window it opens. These may be held in several different directories. In practice, to be useful a wildcard will usually need to be a bit more selective than *.* was, as in the next activity.

If, instead of just finding files, you want to select them so that you can go on to do something else with them, you can use the option 'Select Files'. This operates only on the files in the current directory, though.

ACTIVITY 52

With the module disk in drive a:, click on the icon of the directory 'word' and then choose Select Files from the File menu.

This displays a dialog box with a field for you to specify file names using text and wildcards.

Type *.txt and click on OK.

1 What happens?

2 How do you think this may be useful?

3 See if you can work out how to deselect just one of the files but leave the others selected. Explain here what you have to do.

---

1 All the files with extension .txt are selected and their icons are shown highlighted.

2   This may be useful if you wanted to select a group of files to copy or delete, but wanted to check which files would be affected before going ahead with the operation. If you just used Delete or Copy with a wildcard, you would not necessarily have the chance to make a decision about each file. (This actually depends on the setting of the Confirmation option, in the Options menu.)

3   To deselect a single file, use Select Files again, type the name of the file you want to deselect (or enough of the name, combined with wildcards, to identify only that file) and then click on the Deselect button.

6.4 Exploring different ways to view directories and files in File Manager

Because the ease of use of Windows is so heavily dependent on the appearance of the screen, it is not surprising that Windows offers you so much control over the screen display.

Similarly, File Manager has many different ways of presenting you with the same, or other, information about the files and directories on any of the disk drives.

You can modify how File Manager presents information to you through the View menu. The View menu has many useful options for the different display of information.

The next activity gives you the chance to experiment with some of the display options under the View menu.

ACTIVITY 53

Try out all the options in the View menu that you have not used already and write down here what each one does.

1   Tree and Directory

2   Tree Only

3   Directory Only

4   Split

---

5   Name

6   Sort by Name

7   Sort by Type

8   Sort by Size

9   Sort by Date

10 By File Type

You should have found that the options have these functions:

1   **Tree and Directory:** displays the directory tree in a window on the left side of the screen and a list of the contents of the current directory in a window on the right side of the screen (i.e. the 'normal' view).

2   **Tree Only:** displays only the directory tree window.

3   **Directory Only:** displays only a list of the contents of the current directory.

4   **Split:** displays a line which you can move from the left to right and then place by clicking the mouse button to specify the division of the screen into the tree and directory windows.

5   **Name:** shows only the names of the items in the directory.

6   **Sort by Name:** sorts the contents of directories into alphabetical order by name.

7   **Sort by Type:** sorts the contents of directories into alphabetical order by type (i.e. file extensions).

8   **Sort by Size:** sorts the items in directories into order of their size in bytes.

9   **Sort by Date:** sorts the items in directories into order of the date they were last modified.

10 **By File Type:** decides which items will be included in a directory window (for example, files, directories, programs) so you can 'filter out' types you are not interested in.

Summary

In this section you have learned about file structures and directories, and have learnt how to manage files and directories to help you keep your work well organised.

This section and the previous section are closely linked. You have covered a lot of ground, the material is very important and you will often use these techniques. As you find real uses for the tasks you have learned to perform, you will find that they become more meaningful and easier to remember.

SECTION 7

Computer Viruses

Introduction

In one sense a virus is just another computer program. Whereas other programs, when they run, perform a function for the user, a virus's main purpose is to make copies of itself – just like biological viruses. Unfortunately, viruses don't just make copies of themselves, they do other things too. Most of the things they do are relatively harmless, like putting up a message saying 'Your computer is stoned'. (In fact, far more trouble is caused by so-called 'bugs' in legitimate programs!) Although many viruses are harmless, there are enough dangerous specimens in circulation for you to need to know what to do to either avoid them or 'disinfect' your disks and computer. A serious virus 'attack' could mean losing all the work you have done on the computer!

7.1 Types of virus

There are two basic types of virus: **file viruses** and **boot sector viruses.**

● File viruses attach themselves to executable and command files (.EXE and .COM files). Everything on a computer – programs, data, etc. – is a file. Your word-processing application, or your accounts package, is an executable file. File viruses change an instruction at the beginning of an .EXE or .COM file so that when you try to run it, the computer jumps to the virus and executes that first, copying the virus into memory. Another instruction then sends the computer back to the application to continue the execution of the program you thought you were going to run. To a user, the delay is unnoticeable.

● Boot sector viruses work similarly: the virus modifies the special area called the 'boot sector' on the hard or floppy disk. When you turn on the machine (or press Alt-Ctrl-Del to reboot), the computer loads the virus code into memory and executes it before continuing to start up, apparently as normal.

GETTING 'INFECTED'

One of the easiest ways for a computer to get infected is for you to leave a floppy disk infected with a boot sector virus in the machine's floppy drive. When the machine is switched on or rebooted, the message:

Non-system disk or disk error

Replace and press any key when ready

appears on-screen. In a millisecond, the virus has been read out of the floppy's boot sector into the computer. The fastest infecting viruses will then infect every executable file you open. So, you should

---

never leave a disk in a machine's floppy drive

---

when you turn off or on, or reboot, or leave the computer.

Remember that viruses have to get into your computer in the first place; they arrive attached to other software. Computers have been infected by files downloaded from the Internet, and by floppy disks from all kinds of sources; friends, magazines, and even, on occasion, commercial software and pre-formatted floppy disks.

The easiest way to get a floppy disk infected is to put it into a drive of a computer that you haven't first checked for viruses. This could mean **any** computer, so **always** check the state of any machine you are going to work on.

7.2 Prevention

Prevention is better than cure. Some simple prevention rules for anyone using a personal computer are:

1   Any floppy disk should be write-protected before it is inserted in a disk drive. Slide open the write-protect window on 3.5 inch disks.

2   Find out if the computer you are going to use has up-to-date anti-virus software. (You may need to ask for help with this.) Use this software to scan for any

viruses on the machine. If the machine does not have anti-virus software or if it is out of date, use a different machine.

3   Scan your write-protected disk for viruses before doing anything else.

4   If you work on a computer at home, follow the same procedure there that you would do at work or at college, or anywhere else. Disks taken from one computer to another should always be treated as dangerous; follow steps 1 to 3.

5   If at work or college, etc., report suspicious behaviour to the appropriate technical or support staff. If routine tasks cause unexpected results, a scan for viruses should be one of the follow-up actions.

6   Develop a routine for backing up **clean** copies of software and data. Back-ups are critical, but if you've had a virus attack, you must scan the back-ups before you use them to make sure they're clean.

7   If you have your own computer but do not have an up-to-date copy of anti-virus software, think about investing in one.

ANTI-VIRUS SOFTWARE

There are two types of anti-virus software, **scanners** and **check-summers**.

Scanners do precisely that: they scan files and memory for viruses. Most scanners do this by 'pattern-matching'. The majority of viruses have recognisable 'signatures' in their code, which can be compared to a database of such signatures which forms part of the scanning software. Because, sadly, new viruses are being written all the time, **it's critical to ensure that scanners are updated regularly**.

It makes sense to have an anti-virus package that scans files automatically when you go to open them, even if this entails a little extra waiting time.

Check-summers compile a database of 'check-sums' so they can tell afterwards if executable files are modified. This approach has limitations. If your system is already infected with a virus when you install the check-summer, the program will log as normal the infected version of the files. Some commercial software packages write user configurations to executable files; the check-summer will flag such changes as abnormal.

Generally, the best approach is one that combines the two types: the check-sum provides a check on specific files or infections by unknown viruses, while the scanner can identify what's infecting your system so you can tell what kind of damage you're likely to have to clean up.

Windows adds another problem. In case of infection, you need to be able to shut the machine off and reboot from a write-protected floppy disk. Whatever happens, you can't run Windows from a floppy. So any anti-virus package must include utilities you can run under DOS in a crisis. Ideally, you should check your system every time you start it up.

7.3 Getting rid of viruses

The natural reaction when you discover that either your computer or your disk has a virus is to panic. Don't. Carefully work out a plan before you do anything that might spread the virus. If you are at work or college, or elsewhere, find and inform the appropriate authority. If you discover the problem at home, or have a PC at home that may be infected, use a (legitimate) copy of anti-virus software, carefully following its instructions, to disinfect your PC.

Generally, to disinfect your PC, you will need to 'boot up' a clean machine; that means you will need a write-protected system floppy disk. (A system disk is one with your CONFIG.SYS and AUTOEXEC.BAT files on it, plus whatever utilities the anti-virus software has suggested you include on it.) Most anti-virus packages include creating this disk as part of the installation routine. If you haven't already got a clean system disk you should create one as soon as possible.

Summary

An awareness of viruses is just as important in protecting your work as is keeping up-to-date back-ups. You need to know:

- how to minimise the risk of infection
- how to detect infection
- how to deal with infection if it occurs.

SECTION 8

Changing Your Windows Settings

Introduction

Once you are using the computer frequently and confidently, you may find that there are some settings or options you make every day and that you would like to be automatic when you turn on the computer. You can make settings and save these changes so that they are used each time you run Windows.

If you are using a computer on a network it may take its settings from a central 'server' computer rather than storing them on its own disk. In this case you will be able to change settings as described in this section, but you will probably not be able to preserve your settings between work sessions as they will be lost when Windows is closed down.

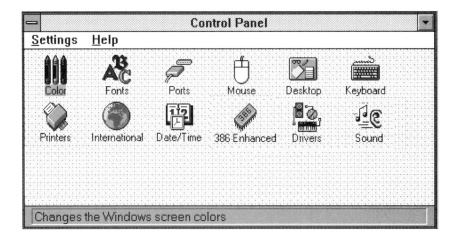

Figure 32: Windows Control Panel

8.1 Controlling Windows Control Panel

There are many settings that you can customise in Windows to make the computer easier to use. To customise the settings, you need to use the Control Panel program.

Do not change any settings made with the Windows Setup program unless you know what you are doing; these control the hardware and software the computer expects to find and you must not set these to invalid options or values.

ACTIVITY 54

1 Double-click on the Control Panel icon (in the Main group window).

2 Click once on each icon in turn and look at the status line at the bottom of the window. This gives a brief explanation of what each program does.

3 Write a list of the icons you can see.

The Control Panel window will look something like Figure 32. The icons may include the following:

Color:	changes the Windows screen colours
Fonts:	adds and removes fonts, and sets True Type options
Ports:	specifies communications settings for serial ports
Mouse:	changes settings for your mouse
Desktop:	changes the look of your desktop
Keyboard:	specifies the keyboard repeat rate and delay
Printers:	installs and removes printers, and sets printing options
International:	specifies international settings
Date/Time:	changes the date and time of your computer's clock
386 Enhanced:	optimises Windows for '386 enhanced mode'
Drivers:	installs, removes and configures 'device drivers'
Sound:	assigns sound to system events.

You can experiment with many of these. However, some of them you should not change unless you know what you are doing. You can open a window for any of them, but if you look at Fonts, Ports, Printers, Drivers, or 386 Enhanced, click on the **Cancel** button without making any changes.

COLOR PROGRAM

The Color program lets you change the colour scheme used for the different parts of the screen display. You can choose from a menu of Windows colour schemes, or you can choose new colours for individual parts of the screen display. It will also let you define your own colours, if you want to.

ACTIVITY 55

Double-click on the Color icon and experiment with the dialog box that appears.

1 What happens when you change the colour scheme?

2 What happens when you click on the button Color Palette ?

3 How would you change the colour used for the Menu bar?

---

1   When you choose a different Color Scheme, all elements in the screen display (e.g., title bars, active and inactive windows, menu bar, text, highlighted text, etc.) will have their colours changed.

2   When you click on the button Colour Palette >>, more options appear in the window. You can then choose new colours, or even define your own, for any individual screen element.

3   To change the colour of the menu bar, you need to click, in the following order, on: Colour Palette >>, Screen Element, and Menu Bar. You can then click on the colour you want to use.

MOUSE PROGRAM

The Mouse program lets you control the speed at which the pointer moves and how quickly you have to give two clicks for Windows to register a double-click.

ACTIVITY 56

1 Double-click on the Mouse icon.

2 Experiment with altering the speed of the mouse and the double-click speed. Any changes take effect immediately, so it is easy to experiment.

3 To test the double-click speed, try double-clicking on the box marked TEST. It will highlight when you give a successful double-click.

4 Turn on Mouse Trails. What does this do? Why might you want to use it?

5 Why do you think it may be useful for someone to swap the left and right buttons on a two-button mouse?

---

4   Mouse Trails makes the mouse leave a trail of 'shadow' arrows as it moves. This facility may be useful if you have difficulty seeing the mouse, for example on the LCD display of a portable computer.

5   A left-handed person or someone with impaired hand movement or missing fingers may want to swap the mouse buttons to make the mouse easier to use.

DESKTOP PROGRAM

The Desktop program lets you change the appearance of the desktop and choose a screen saver (a moving picture or pattern displayed on the screen when you have not used the mouse or keyboard for a while).

ACTIVITY 57

1 Double-click on the Desktop icon.

2 Inside the Screen Saver box, find the Name: box and click on the right hand side button; choose a screen saver from the list and click on Test.

3 A screen saver helps preserve your screen by preventing a static image being burned into the screen if you leave the display the same for a long time. (This is not a danger with LCD screens.)

4 Choose a wallpaper pattern, click on Tile and then OK. What happens?

4   The pattern you choose for wallpaper is repeated across the background of the screen.

KEYBOARD PROGRAM

The Keyboard program lets you control how long you have to hold down a key before the computer assumes you want to repeat the character, and the rate at which the character is repeated again if you keep the key held down. This is a particularly useful setting to control if you have difficulty using the keyboard. You can only use this program if the computer is fitted with a keyboard that can vary its speed.

ACTIVITY 58

1 Double-click on the Keyboard program icon.

2 Experiment with setting the delay (how long the computer waits before first repeating a character) and the interval (how long it then waits between repeats).

Begin with slow speeds and increase them gradually.

INTERNATIONAL PROGRAM

The International program lets you control the keyboard layout and the country settings (such things as date and time formats, and currency symbols).

ACTIVITY 59

1 Experiment with changing the country setting to Mexico, Taiwan, Norway and Brazil. See which elements change.

2 Click on the button marked Change beside Date. What changes does this allow you to make to the way date is displayed?

3 Look at the Long Date Format section of the dialog box. What happens if you type something in one of the fields that does not have a menu button?

2   Change lets you set the following for short and long date formats:

● the order in which the elements of the date appear (day-month-year, or month-day-year)

● the character used to separate the elements (25/12/96 or 25:12:96)

● whether a zero is added before a single-figure day or month figure (01/01/97)

● whether the century is included in the date (1997 or 97)

● whether to include the weekday name in long-format dates

● whether the day and the month names are abbreviated in long-format dates (Sun 11th Jan or Sunday 11th January)

● any text you want to use between the date and month and the month and year in long-format dates.

If you want to use a non-British/American keyboard with your computer, you will need to get a keyboard in the language you want, fit it and then change the keyboard layout option using the International program. If you just change the option with the program, some of the characters produced will not match the symbols on the keys when you press them.

Summary

In this section you have learned how to set up the computer as you want it. You can make many choices about the appearance of the screen, the keyboard repeat rate and other elements when using Windows. However, although Windows will preserve the settings you have made from one day to the next, if anyone else makes any changes, then their settings will override your earlier ones and you will need to make them again when you next use the computer.

Make a note of any settings you would like to make (or change) and anything else you wish to remember or discuss from your work on this section.

Unit Summary

In this unit, you have learnt some basic skills in setting up your computer, opening applications, using and copying disks and protecting against virus damage. You are now in a position to investigate some software programs in the next three units.

UNIT 6
WORDPROCESSING WITH WORD 6

SECTION 1

Getting started with Word
Introduction

Welcome to this unit on wordprocessing. We introduce you to wordprocessing skills using Microsoft Word (version 6). We start with the basic techniques so it is fine if you have little or no experience of wordprocessing. However, if you already have good wordprocessing skills you can apply more advanced techniques in later parts of the unit.

Throughout the unit you will work on documents learning the techniques needed to use the wordprocessor effectively. You will spend time assessing the results of your work, evaluating whether something works or not, and if not, how best to change it. You will be able to use your wordprocessor as a means of communicating effectively to produce the documents we identified in the early units of this module.

We have used certain standard ways of presenting information:

- When you are asked to select a command from a menu the symbol I is used to separate the menu name from the command. For example File I Save means select the Save command from the File menu.

- To carry out an operation using the keyboard angled brackets are used to indicate which key or keys to press. For example: <Enter> means press the key marked 'Enter' (or 'Return' or '⏎ '), whereas <Ctrl End> means hold down the 'Ctrl' key and press the 'End'.

Objectives

By the end of the unit, you should be able to:

- create new documents in Word and open existing documents
- enter, delete and edit text
- save and close files
- open up and work on more than one file at a time
- set the margins, page size and orientation of documents, and insert headers and footers including automatic page numbers
- format text including: new paragraphs; tabs; indentation; alignment (to the left, right or centre, or justified); and apply borders and shading
- apply typographical features including: bold; italics; underline; superscript; subscript; and capitals
- set line and paragraph spacing
- create bulleted and numbered lists

- insert page breaks and keep lines and paragraphs together

- use Cut, Copy and Paste commands to move text around within and between Word documents

- apply automatic checking tools, such as spell checking, grammar check, thesaurus, and search and replace

- have the confidence to explore and experiment with other facilities available such as indexing, inserting footnotes, setting up tables, mail merge

- print your work and preview it on screen before printing.

SECTION 1

What Can Your Wordprocessor Do?

Introduction

In this section we introduce you to Word and take you through the basics.

Word 6 (hereafter called simply Word) must be correctly installed on your PC. Your PC should also be connected to a printer so you can print out documents you produce as you work through the unit. (In some circumstances the printer may be shared between a number of computers and accessed via a **network**.)

1.1 Opening documents

You will start by creating a new Word document and getting a feel for how this program works.

ACTIVITY 1

1 Turn on the computer, 'log on' (if necessary), start up Windows and launch
   Word 6 by double-clicking on its icon. You may find it in Microsoft Office.
   You will remember this from Unit 5.

You have now opened up your first Word file. What you see will be similar to
Figure 1. (If the toolbars or ruler are different or missing this is because someone
has changed the 'View' settings, which you will learn to do yourself shortly.)

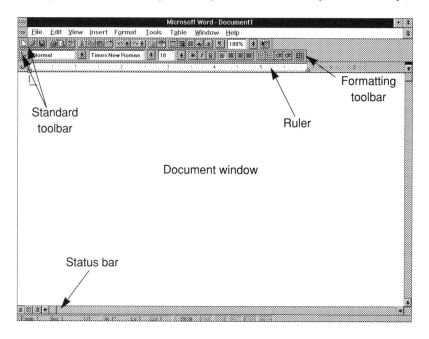

Figure 1: Word with a newly-opened empty file

You will see that the main text area is completely blank except for a flashing
vertical bar and a solid horizontal line in the top left. Somewhere in the screen you
should also see either a vertical bar with little bars on each end or an arrow.

| This is the cursor: you can work at the place where it is flashing to enter
    or delete text.

__ This bar indicates the end of the file. Initially it is right underneath the first
    line because the file is empty.

I   This is the pointer. It is controlled by the mouse. As you move the mouse
    around it will move in the corresponding direction (so long as it is over
    the text area and not too far to the left – otherwise it turns into an arrow
    as described below).

You may also see this symbol ¶ next to the cursor. Ignore this for the time being,
or get rid of it by clicking the button with the same symbol on the toolbar. You will
look at what it means in Section 6.

1.2 Entering and deleting text

Once you have opened a document you can type in whatever you like. To enter text all you have to do is to type it onto the screen. The cursor moves with you as you type words.

When the cursor reaches the end of a line it automatically moves to a new one. This is called 'wrapping round'. You can *force* the cursor to move to a new line (for example, at the end of a paragraph) by pressing the key marked 'Enter' (or 'Return' or '↵'). But within paragraphs you should *not* press Enter – just let the text wrap round itself when it reaches the right margin.

ACTIVITY 2

1 Type a short paragraph of text three or four lines long, describing your experience of computing on this module so far. Don't forget full stops at the end of each sentence.

2 Press Enter to start a new paragraph.

3 There is no space between this paragraph and the first one so press Enter again.

4 Now you have started a new paragraph with proper spacing. Type another short paragraph describing what you hope to learn in the rest of this module.

If you want to delete any text, you press the backspace key. This is the key with an arrow pointing to the left. It is in the top right corner of your keyboard.

ACTIVITY 2 Continued

5 After finishing your second paragraph try deleting the last word. (You will need to press the backspace key once for each letter of the word.) Then type the word back in again.

6 Look at your screen and check:

a) Where the flashing cursor is now.

b) Where the __ bar is.

c) Where the pointer is.

You now have the text of your first document. To type in that text you did not actually need to use the mouse. You could do it all with the keyboard. The flashing cursor and the bar should have moved as you typed in text and will now be at the end of the text. The pointer is probably in the same place as when you opened the new file.

1.3 The mouse

The mouse is an important part of Word. You need to become skilled in using it.

ACTIVITY 3

1 Take hold of the mouse. Without clicking on its button move it around on your table or mouse mat. You should see the pointer on the screen move in exactly the same way as you move your mouse.

2 Move the mouse so that the pointer is over the toolbars. Now move it down onto the text. What happens?

3 Move the mouse slowly to the left towards the edge of the screen. What happens?

You should have found that moving the mouse changes the shape of the pointer or cursor according to which part of the screen it is in. The pointer takes three different forms.

2   It is ↖ while it is over the toolbars and then ⌶ when it is actually over the text.

3   It is ➚ when it moves off the text area onto the invisible **selection bar** to the left of the text area.

This change of shape is designed to help you. In the text area the vertical form lets you position the pointer accurately between words, letters and other characters. Off the text area, the arrows let you point to and select options or sections of text (as we will see later).

POSITIONING THE CURSOR WITH THE MOUSE

When you typed in the text for Activity 2 you saw the flashing cursor move as you typed in the different words. Look at the screen now. You should see that the cursor is waiting and flashing at the end of the last word. You can also move and position the cursor using the mouse.

ACTIVITY 4

1   Move the mouse so that the pointer is positioned at any place in the first paragraph of the text you typed in for Activity 2. Click once on the button on the left side of the mouse.

What happens? You should see that the cursor is no longer flashing at the end of the last word but has been positioned in the first paragraph at the exact place where you moved the pointer to.

ACTIVITY 4 Continued

2   Use the mouse to move the cursor in front of the very first word you typed in. (You will probably find that you have to be very careful about how you positioned the mouse. If you go too far to the left the cursor turns into an arrow.)

3   Move the cursor so it is level with the one-line space you left between the two paragraphs. Position the cursor so that it is about 1 cm to the right of the left margin. Click once on the left button of the mouse.

The cursor should now be flashing right up against the left margin. There is no text in this line so the cursor moves to the beginning of it.

ACTIVITY 4 Continued

4   Use the mouse to position the cursor in between the last word of the first sentence in your second paragraph and the full-stop which ends it.

5   Experiment with the mouse positioning the cursor in different parts of the text you have typed in.

It may take you a little time to get used to the feel of the mouse, but before long you should find it easy to move the cursor around quickly to the point you want to go to.

THE MOUSE AND MENUS

An important feature of Word is its menus which let you access many different functions. The menus may be operated using either the keyboard or the mouse, but the mouse is the easier method to begin with so we will concentrate on that. Each word on the menu bar gives you access to a menu of options. We will refer to these as, for example, the File menu, the Edit menu, and so on.

Each menu is made up of a list of options or commands, e.g. the New command, the Open command.

ACTIVITY 5

1 Move the mouse so that the pointer is positioned somewhere on the menu bar. You will see the pointer change to an arrow. Move the pointer so that it is positioned anywhere on the word File. Click on File. You should now see a list of words appear.

This is what is called a menu (or 'drop-down' menu). It looks like Figure 2.

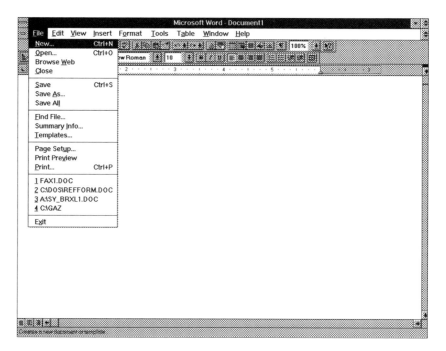

Figure 2: The File menu

Each item in the list is a different option letting you use a particular feature of the program. Do not worry about what each item on the list means but a quick look down the menu will show you that many of them are self-explanatory. For example:

- **New** opens up a new document for you.

- **Open** lets you open up an existing Word file.

- **Close** is the command you choose if you want to close the file you have been working on.

- **Save** lets you save on disk the file you have been working on.

ACTIVITY 5 Continued

2 Click once on Open. The File menu will disappear, the pointer will change momentarily into an hour glass and then open another window. This window has the title 'Open' and contains a series of smaller boxes each offering you different options about what action to take. This sort of window is referred to as a **dialog box**. You could go on to select a Word file to open (but instead – in the next step – we will just close the box for now).

3 Move the mouse so that the pointer is positioned on the button labelled Cancel. Click once on this button. The dialog box will disappear and you will be back in the main text file.

4 Open up the File menu again by clicking the mouse on the word File in the menu bar. Suppose you change your mind: you do not now want any of the commands available under this menu. So how do you remove the menu? The quickest way is to move the mouse away from the open File menu to any other part of the screen. Click once on that part of the screen and see what happens. You should see the File menu simply disappear.

5 Experiment by opening up all the different menus along the menu bar.

You may have guessed by now that the menus form groupings of commands. For example:

● **File** menu contains different commands for doing things with whole files.

● **View** menu contains commands that alter the way the file appears on your screen.

● **Tools** menu contains a mixture of different functions.

● **Help** menu contains different options for getting help in using the program.

ACTIVITY 6

1 Open up the View menu. You should see Figure 3.

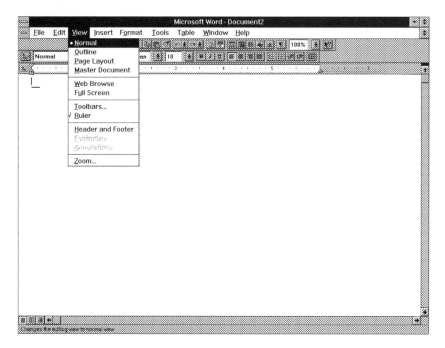

Figure 3: The View menu

Notice that in this menu the commands appear in different formats:

● Some of the items have a bullet (●) to the left of the command

● Other commands have a tick. (✓).

Both of these indicate that the option is currently in use. Some commands appear as faint grey type. This means that the command is not currently available.

Some commands have three dots (an 'ellipsis') after them. These lead you to a dialog box containing further options. Those without the dots, such as Save, simply carry out that command.

ACTIVITY 6 Continued

2 Click on the Ruler command.

You will see that you can make the ruler appear and disappear. Notice that when you click on the View menu it closes and you have to open it up again if you want to access the command again. When the ruler is displayed the name is ticked on the View menu. When it is not displayed there is no tick.

Toolbars can also be made to appear/disappear by clicking on the Toolbar command. If a particular toolbar is currently displayed there is an 'X' in the box to the left of its name. By clicking on this box, the 'X' will appear and disappear. The usual toolbars initially displayed are the Standard and Formatting toolbars, but your computer may have been set up to show a different selection.

ACTIVITY 6 Continued

3 Experiment by choosing different combinations of toolbars and clicking on the OK button. When you have finished experimenting change the choice of toolbars back to Standard and Formatting.

By a combination of the Ruler and Toolbar commands, you can choose what is displayed above your document. With them hidden there is more room to view the main text file but it makes it more difficult to access the functions contained on them.

ACTIVITY 6 Continued

4 Look at the first three items in the View list. They are Normal, Outline and Page Layout. Click once on Page Layout. This command gives a view of the text as it would appear on a page. You may not be able to see any great difference at the moment.

5 To see the effect more clearly open up the View menu again and click on the Zoom command. This opens up a dialog box with a number of smaller boxes. One of these is Zoom To. This lets you choose how big to display the text. Click once on the button next to 75%. Then click once on the OK box to the right. The text will shrink to three-quarters its actual size.

6 Click on the Zoom command again and choose Whole Page. Click on OK.

You will now be able to see the complete page. You are viewing the page as it will appear when printed out with the margins on each side and at the top and bottom. This command is very useful for getting an overall picture of how your document is looking.

ACTIVITY 6 Continued

7 Open up the View menu again. Click on the Normal command.

The view changes back to the standard display. With long documents you will find that it is quicker to work in Normal view – the program takes longer to display files with several pages in Page Layout view. However, Page Layout view does give you a better impression of how your document will finally appear.

ACTIVITY 6 Continued

8 Open up the View menu again. Click on the Zoom command. In the dialog box, click on the button next to 200% and then click OK. You should now see the text at twice the original size.

9 Change the magnification back to 100%.

By now you should be getting used to opening menus and choosing commands using the mouse. You have also seen some of the options that Word gives in terms of viewing documents.

1.4 Saving files

So far all the information in the file you created is stored only in the computer's memory. It is not stored on the disk and would be lost if the power failed or the computer 'crashed'. Saving the document will create a permanent record of the information as a Word file. You covered this in Unit 5.

ACTIVITY 7

1 Open up the File menu.

Click once on Save. You will see a dialog box open. This gives you various options:

● Where to store the document (on the computer's hard disk or on a floppy disk using the Drives box).

● Which directory to save the file in (using the Directories box).

● Which file format to save the file as (using the Save File as Type box). You can choose from a range of options but you most likely want your file to be a Word file. In this case you would leave this box in its default setting which is the one automatically chosen by the program. In this case it is Word Document.

● What to call the new file (in the File Name box).

2 Make sure your module disk is in the floppy disk drive.

3 Where will you store your file when you save it? The best option might be to store it on your own personal module disk. To do this:

(a) Put your disk in the external disk drive.

(b) Look at the Drives box. Click once on the arrow pointing down to the right of the box. A menu will appear which lets you choose between the floppy disk (drive a:) or the hard disk (drive c:).

(c) Click on a:

4 Select the directory 'Word'.

5 Decide what to call your file. Place the cursor in the box under File Name. Delete any text that is already in the box and insert your new file name.

You should aim to use a name that will unmistakably identify this file and its contents. Many people use their own name in their first file, for example 'Pat1'. This is not very useful, especially when you come to create more files. When you reach 'Pat49', you are unlikely to remember what is in each file!

Remember from Unit 5:

● You can use up to eight characters for your file name.

● Do not use the following characters: * ? , : ; [ ] + | / \..

● Do not leave any spaces in the file name.

The computer will automatically add an extension to the file name, shown by a full stop plus three letters. This identifies what type of document the file is. Files in Word are automatically given the extension .doc, which identifies the document as a Word document.

If you share PCs with others you may not be able to use the same PC as and when you want to, but a floppy disk can be used with whatever PC may be available. (Another possibility is that you may be able to store your files on a network drive accessible from many different computers.)

ACTIVITY 7 Continued

6 You are now ready to save your file. Do this by clicking on OK with the mouse. (Note that this button is 'framed' with an inner border. This means you can achieve the same effect as clicking on it by pressing Enter.)

Your first file is now saved in the place where you want it to be saved. You will notice that saving the file does not close it. It stays open for you to carry on working on it.

'SAVE' OR 'SAVE AS'?

Once you have saved a document you can continue working on it. The file that is stored on your hard or floppy disk is the version as it was when you last saved it. If you want to update your file to save the latest version you can do that by simply clicking on Save in the File menu.

ACTIVITY 8

1   Add another paragraph, at the *start* of the file currently open, describing briefly what previous experience of computing you had (if any) before beginning this module.

2   Now go to the File menu and click once on Save.

When you go to Save you do not get a dialog box. All that happens is that you see the pointer turn into an hour glass shape and the machine makes a few noises. On using the Save option, you only get the dialog box when you save a file for the first time. This is because subsequently Word assumes you want to save in the same place and with the same name, replacing the previously saved version.

ACTIVITY 9

1   Click once on the Save As command in the File menu.

2   You should see that the same dialog box comes up as appeared when you saved your file for the first time. The Save As command enables you to create *another version* of the file you are working on. You can change the name, location and type of the file using the options in the dialog box.

3   Press Cancel to clear the dialog box from the screen, since we don't actually want to save another version at the moment.

When you use the Save As command and give a different file name and/or location (i.e. drive/directory) you create a new version of the file you are currently working on. The old version will then be left as it was when you last Saved it. If you subsequently use Save it will be the *new version* you are replacing (or 'overwriting') on disk.

Save As is particularly useful when you want to create several files which contain mostly similar text but with some differences; for example, sending similar letters to several different people. You can edit, then Save As, then edit again, then Save As again, and so on, ending up with a separate file for each different letter. It can also be useful when you have opened a document to revise it but want to leave the old version intact on disk for future reference. You would do this on amending your cv and covering letter in Unit 4 and identifying which versions you sent to which companies.

SAVING FILES: GOOD PRACTICE

Like most aspects of using computers there are certain principles of good practice which are important to follow.

You should save a new file very soon after creating it. Some people even save their files before writing a word because they feel uncomfortable working in an unnamed file which only exists in the computer's memory.

Having saved it once you should then save it regularly as you work to store what you have written. This is because, in the event of a catastrophe such as a power failure or a computer failure (or a user failure such as accidentally deleting all your text!) any work done after your last Save exists only in memory and will be lost. If you save every 10 or 15 minutes you will only ever lose a small amount of work.

Regular saving is something that Word can help you with by automatically saving your work at specified intervals. (Your computer might already have been set up to do this.) If you want to investigate this facility, choose the Options item from the Tools menu, then click on the Save tab which selects one of several 'pages' of options. Look to see whether the 'Automatic Save Every __ Minutes' option is selected (with an X to the left), and if so what time interval has been specified.

1.5 Closing files

ACTIVITY 10

1 First of all Save the file you have been working on.

2 Open the File menu and click once on Close. What happens?

The text should disappear as the current window closes. You will notice that the menu bar and ribbon have changed – each now displays less information (because many commands are not applicable when there is no document being edited). Although no text files are open, you are still inside the program Word.

ACTIVITY 11

1 Click once on the File menu and look at the menu that drops down. You can see that you have a number of options for the next action to take.

- You can open (create) a new file by clicking once on New.

- You can open (retrieve) an existing file by clicking once on Open.

- You can search for an existing file by clicking on the Find File command.

2 Now look at the bottom of the drop-down menu. You will see a list of four items. These are the last four files that have been opened.

You should see the name of the file you created at the start of this section. (Note that the name of your file will be preceded by an indication of where it is located, for example, drive **a:**.) However, if someone else has used the computer in the meantime your file may no longer be included among the last four files opened.

ACTIVITY 11 Continued

3 Click once on the name of your file located at the bottom of the File menu. What happens is that that file is opened directly. This is a useful short cut for accessing files you worked on recently and want to work on again. (If your file is not listed you will have to use the Open option from the File menu.)

4 Make some changes to your file by adding or deleting some text. Then go to Close. You should see a dialog box which asks you: 'Do you want to save changes to [your file name]'. You have four options:

Yes   This will automatically save the changes and close the file as though you have done a Save first.

No   If you press this, the document will close, but you will not lose any changes you made since you last saved the document.

Cancel Pressing this will return you to the main text file. You may have changed your mind about closing the document, or you may have pressed Close by mistake.

Help   This gives you help on saving changes.

Be very careful when answering the 'Do you want to save changes' box, especially if you decide you do not want to close the file at all. In this situation it is all too easy to press No when you should press Cancel. No means: 'No, I do not want to save the changes'. It does not mean: 'No, I do not want to close the file'.

5 Now press the appropriate button to close your file, saving the changes you made to it.

If you try to save a file to a floppy disk drive without a floppy disk in it, you will find that the computer simply will not let you. Similarly, if you are working on a file that was saved on a floppy disk and take the floppy disk out, you will not be able to save the changes. The computer will alert you by displaying an error message on the screen.

1.6 Exiting Word

As you now know, you can close files down and open other ones while still staying inside the main program Word. When you come to the end of your work session you will need to leave the program and shut the computer down.

ACTIVITY 12

1 Open up your file again.

2 Make a few changes to the file and then close it down straight away, saving the changes.

3 Now click on the File menu. In the drop-down menu you should see Exit. Click once on this command. You have exited the application and are back in the Program Manager. You are back to where you were before you did Activity 1.

4 Launch Word again and open up your file once more.

5 Make a few more changes to the file.

6 *Without saving the changes* click on File|Exit. You will get the same dialog box as before asking you if you want to save the changes. In other words the program will always remind you about saving changes either when you Close the current file or when you Exit Word.

7 Click Yes to save the changes and exit Word.

Now you are back at the Program Manager. If you want to stop working you can turn the machine off, knowing that your document is stored on disk for future retrieval.

Summary

You have been through the basics of using Word including getting in and out of the program itself, saving files to disk and retrieving files from disk.

SECTION 2

Finding Your Way

Introduction

This section will help you to find your way around Word. You will look at how to move about inside the program and inside documents. You will also look at how to arrange windows on your screen in a way that makes it as easy as possible for you to work.

As you work through this section you will open up and work on a file supplied on the module disk. The file is called: Cast.doc

2.1 Introducing the toolbar

In Section 1 you learned how to carry out a number of basic operations. You looked in particular at using the menus to access different commands. Word gives you different ways of doing the same thing. For instance, there are often keyboard-only equivalents of the commands in the menus. The program is also good at providing short cuts. The toolbar offers you many useful short cuts.

ACTIVITY 13

1 Go back into Word. A new blank file will be created automatically. Close that file.

2 You are now inside the program Word but no files are open. You should still be able to see the formatting toolbar. (If you are not sure which part is the formatting toolbar look back at Figure 1.)

3 Click on the first icon at the left edge of the toolbar:

4 You should find yourself in a new Word file.

5 Close the file.

6 Click on the second icon: . You should find yourself in the Open dialog box ready to search for the file you want to open. Click on Cancel to remove the dialog box.

If you don't know the purpose of an icon, simply position the cursor over the icon without clicking and within a few seconds a description should be displayed.

Already you can see that the toolbar is a quick way of carrying out commands. Several of the commands you learned in Section 1 have icons on the toolbar. Word has been designed so that the most common commands are accessible with the toolbar.

Here is a list of the icons you can already begin to use:

Toolbar icons

Icon	Function	Equivalent menu command
	Open a new document	File I New
	Open an existing document	File I Open
	Save the document	File I Save

You can customise the toolbar by taking off some icons and adding others not shown on the standard toolbar. You might find that the toolbar on the machine you are using does not match the one described here. This could be because someone has customised the toolbar or it could be that you are using an older version of Word.

ACTIVITY 14

1 Create a new document and type in the following text:

Toolbar icons are the simplest way of carrying out commands. They make life very easy.

2 Click on the *left-hand side* of the icon that looks like this: .
Everything you have done will disappear. This icon is the Undo command. It enables you to reverse the last action you performed. In this case the last action you performed was to type in the text above, so the Undo button reversed that. The Undo command can also restore text you have accidentally deleted, for example.

3 Now press the *left-hand side* of the icon that looks like this . The text will reappear. This icon is the Redo command. This function is useful if you Undo something and then realise that you wanted the undone action done after all!

4 Go to Edit and click once to view the drop-down menu. At the top you should see the command Undo Typing. Click on that and the text will disappear.

5 Go back to Edit. This time you should see the words Redo Typing. Click on that and watch the text reappear.

6 Close the document *without saving the changes.*

Repeatedly clicking Undo will work backwards through a series of your most recent actions.

There are certain things you cannot undo. You cannot undo Save or Exit, for example. Once you have saved something it is saved.

PRINT BUTTON
There is a button on the toolbar which enables you to print out your documents.

This is the Print command and when selected the computer automatically prints out all the pages in the active document. The menu equivalent is to select File | Print.

The **Print** icon allows you to print all the pages in your document. However, File | Print offers you a range of different options such as how many copies to print and which pages to print if you do not want to print them all. These options will be covered fully in Section 6.

2.2 Moving around documents

The work you have done so far on this unit has been with relatively short documents. The whole document has fitted easily onto the screen. But what happens when you start working with longer documents? How do you move about within the document when all of it is not visible?

SCROLLING
The technique of scrolling helps you see more of a long document.

ACTIVITY 15

1 Open the document Cast.doc using the method described in Activity 13. This document is a draft programme for a show being put on by a local Light Entertainment Society. It is two pages long. At the moment you should be able to see most of the first page. You want to see what is on the second page.

2 Move the cursor to the right of the screen onto the vertical bar shown in the diagram below. This is the scroll bar. At the top of the bar you will see a thick black bar (1), then a box with an 'up' arrow in it (2), and below that another box (3). At the bottom of the screen there is a box with a 'down' arrow in it (4).

3 Click once on the down arrow (4) at the bottom of the scroll bar. When you click on the down arrow your view of the text in the document moves down by about one line.

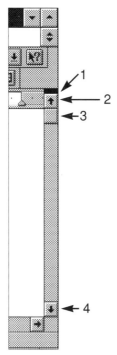

4 Click and hold on the down arrow. Your view of the text will move down continuously for as long as you hold down the arrow button. This technique of moving through a document is called scrolling. You should also notice that your position in the document is marked by a box (3) moving down the scroll bar.

5 Scroll back up to the beginning of the document by clicking on the up arrow (2) and holding. Watch the marker box move gradually back to the beginning of the document.

6 Make a note of what text is on the bottom line of the screen.

7 Click once on the scroll bar anywhere below the marker box. With this technique you move through the document a screen-length at a time – the text you noted is now right at the top of the screen.

8 Use this technique to move quickly to the bottom of the document. Then move back to the beginning.

9 Once you are back at the beginning of the document click on the marker box at the top of the scroll bar and hold. Using the mouse drag the marker box down the scroll bar. When you are half way down the scroll bar let go of the mouse button. You should find that the top of the new screen view is about half way through the document.

10 Practise using the different methods of scrolling up and down the document.

There are three main techniques you can use to scroll:

1   clicking (or clicking and holding) on the up and down arrows

2   clicking on the scroll bar itself

3   dragging the marker box.

If your document is Zoomed to a size where the page is too wide to fit on the screen, you can use the *horizontal* scroll bar to move left and right in just the same way as the vertical scroll bar moves up and down.

MOVING THE CURSOR

So far we have looked at how to view different parts of the document on the screen. However, to actually make changes at a particular place we need to move the cursor into position.

There are a number of ways of moving the cursor around the screen. Many of them are based around the four arrow keys positioned on the right side of your keyboard. On most keyboards they look like this diagram.

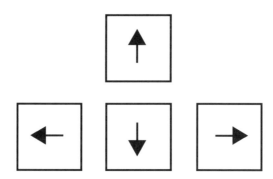

Each of the basic arrow keys moves the cursor *one character* in the direction indicated.

You probably also have a set of keys labelled with the following commands:

Command	moves the cursor
<Pg Up>	up one screen-length
<Pg Dn>	down one screen-length
<Home>	to the beginning of the line
<End>	to the end of the line

In addition, holding the control key ('Ctrl') down and pressing one of the above keys adds more possibilities:

Command	moves the cursor
<Crtl ↑ >	up one paragraph
<Crtl ↓ >	down one paragraph
<Crtl → >	one word to the right
<Crtl ← >	one word to the left
<Crtl Home>	to the beginning of the document
<Crtl End >	to the end of the document.

GO TO

In Word the Go To command in the Edit menu is another quick way of moving around a document. This brings up the Go To dialog box. On the left-hand side is the Go to What box. In this box you scroll up and down the box until you find the type of item you are looking for (e.g. Page, Line, Equation). Then to the right of this box you enter the name/number of the item. Click on either the Next or Previous button to start the search forwards/backwards.

This moves the cursor directly to the start of the chosen item. In a two-page document it may be just as quick to scroll to the place you want. However, the longer the document you are working on, the more useful the Go To command is.

ACTIVITY 16

1 Open up the document Cast.doc (if it is not still open from the previous activity).

2 Use the arrow keys to move the cursor to the end of the word 'present' in the third line of text. Add an 's' to the word.

3 Move the cursor down to the word 'Technicolour' using the arrow keys and delete the 'u' to give the American spelling as in the title.

4 Move back to the beginning of the line. Add an extra carriage return here by pressing <Enter>. What is the quickest way of getting to the start of the line?

5 Move to the end of the document. What is the quickest way of doing that?

6 Go to the start of page 2. What is the quickest way of doing that?

7 Practise using all the different movement keys. Then, in the space below, note down what you have to press to carry out the actions described.

Action	What you have to do
Up one line	
Down one line	
One character to the right	
One character to the left	
To the start of the line	
To the end of the line	
To the start of the document	
To the end of the document	
To the start of the next paragraph	
To the start of the previous paragraph	
Up one screen-length	
Down one screen-length	

As you become familiar with your wordprocessing package you will develop your own style of working. Some people just use the mouse to get around. Other people use only keyboard commands. Many people use a mixture of the two.

2.3 Highlighting text

In all wordprocessing programs you can manipulate individual words, sentences or paragraphs to make them appear as you want them to. For example, you may want to make a word in bold type or to underline a heading. To add features like this, you need first to highlight (or 'select') the part of the text that you want to manipulate.

Text that is highlighted or selected usually appears as white text on a black background on the screen (i.e. the opposite of 'normal' text). This is called 'reversed out'.

ACTIVITY 17

1 Open up Cast.doc again (if necessary), then move the cursor to the start of the word 'Joseph'.

2 Hold down the <Shift> key and press the right arrow key <→> six times. You should see the whole of the word Joseph highlighted as white on a black background.

3 Letting go of <Shift>, press the left arrow key <←> once. You should see all the text go back to normal and, because you pressed the left arrow key, the cursor moves to the left-hand end of what was selected.

4 Highlight the words 'Joseph and his'. Then let go of <Shift>, but this time press the right arrow key <→>. This time the text goes back to normal, but the cursor moves to the right-hand end.

5 Highlight the words 'Joseph and his' again. When they are highlighted, let go of <Shift> and press the Backspace key. All the highlighted words will be deleted.

6 Undo the last action, using the Undo command in the File menu, or by choosing the Undo icon from the toolbar.

Step 5 in Activity 17 shows how you can manipulate text once you have highlighted it. In this case the manipulation was to delete, but you can use highlighting to alter the appearance of text.

You can combine the <Shift> key with any of the cursor-movement commands described earlier in this section to select larger areas of text. For example, if you position the cursor at the start of a paragraph and then hold down <Shift> and press <Ctrl-↓>, the whole of the following paragraph will be highlighted.

OTHER METHODS OF HIGHLIGHTING

Activity 17 used the arrow keys in combination with <Shift>. If you are using a mouse there are several different options available to you. Here is a summary of them.

- To highlight a word place the pointer over the word and double-click.

- To highlight a sentence position the pointer over any point in the sentence, hold down the <Ctrl> button and click once.

- To highlight paragraphs and longer pieces of text place the pointer at the start of the text you want to change or delete, click and hold. Drag the mouse across and/or down to the end of the text you want to change and release the mouse button.

- If you have a large area to highlight – perhaps several pages place the pointer at the start of the desired text and click once, move the cursor to the end of the desired text, then hold down the Shift key and click again. All the text in between will be highlighted.

- To un-highlight text click once with the mouse anywhere on the text. The text will go back to normal and the cursor will be positioned at that point.

USING THE SELECTION BAR

The selection bar is an invisible area in the margin to the left side of the text. When you move the pointer into this area it turns into an arrow pointing to the top-right. Clicking in the selection bar highlights lines of text at a time.

- To highlight a line click once in the selection bar.
- To highlight several lines click once in the selection bar, hold and drag down with the mouse.
- To highlight the whole document hold down the <Ctrl> key and click once in the selection bar with the mouse.
- To un-highlight text click once with the mouse anywhere on the text. The text will go back to normal and the cursor will be positioned at that point.

ACTIVITY 18

1 Use the mouse to do the following:

Select the word 'Pharaoh' in the cast list.

Select the whole of the cast list from 'Joseph' to 'Judah'.

Select and delete the word 'green' in the Acknowledgements.

Select the words 'Mrs Potiphar' in the cast list.

2 Unhighlight the text and then select all the text in the file using the selection bar.

3 Select and delete the sentence 'Jessie Joiner ... sets' in the Acknowledgements.

4 Select all the text in the file and delete it.

5 Type in the following text:

```
Cancelled because of food poisoning.
```

6 Close the file, *without saving any of the changes.*

2.4 Opening several documents at once

In Word it is possible to open up several documents at once. This can be useful if you need to refer to one document as you are working on another one or if you need to work on both at the same time.

ACTIVITY 19

1 Open up Cast.doc once more if it is not still open.

2 When it is open, also open up the document you created in Section 1.

3 You have two documents open, but you should be able to see only the last one you opened. This is the *active* document. If you were to open another document, that would become the active document.

4 Open the Window menu. At the bottom of the menu you can see a list of all the files currently open. The one ticked is the one that is currently active.

5 Now select the other (inactive) document from the list in the Window menu. You should see that the first file you opened (Cast.doc) becomes the active file, while the other one has become inactive and hidden from view.

6 It is possible to view both the documents at the same time. Go to the Window menu and select Arrange All. You should see that the screen divides to enable you to see both the opened documents. Note that only one is active (Cast.doc). You can tell which is the active one by looking at the menu bar. Inactive documents usually appear shaded a darker grey. You will also notice that the cursor only flashes in the active window.

7 It is possible to move from one document to the other, either by simply clicking on the inactive document with the mouse or by selecting it from the Window menu via the keyboard. Practise moving from the active document to the other one, and back again, using both methods.

8 Close one of the files without saving any changes. The remaining file will still only occupy half the screen. Maximise the window containing this file by either clicking on its Maximise button or choosing Maximise from its control menu.

When you have two or more documents open at once there is not much room for the windows. To get the biggest view of the documents you can try hiding the ruler (using the Ruler command in the View menu), and any of the toolbars.

Every document you open in Word is in a window of its own *within* the main Word window, but because the document you are working on is normally maximised you may not be aware of this. However, you can minimise, restore and maximise these document windows in just the same way as you manipulate application windows themselves, using buttons or the control menu on the title bar.

Summary

In this section we have introduced some of the most important techniques needed to operate the program, including how to navigate through large documents and how to position the cursor and select text where you want to make additions, deletions or alterations. You now have the basic skills needed to learn about some of the powerful facilities Word provides to enhance the appearance of documents you create.

Section 3

Basic Styles

Introduction

In this section you will start to make use of wordprocessing programs to make documents as attractive and readable as possible. This is all part of being an effective communicator as you saw in the earlier units. You will be introduced to features which control the overall format of documents you want to produce. You will also learn how to manipulate text by changing its style, size and character.

Throughout this section you will be encouraged to think about suitable ways of using the wordprocessing features you learn about. This is so you will know when, as well as how, to apply a particular feature.

As you work through this section you will open up and work on a number of files supplied on disk. You will also create and save new files. The files you will need to work on are: **Umbria.doc, Lire.doc, Restrt.doc, Newslt.doc.**

Throughout this section and the rest of the unit remember the theoretical material you covered in Unit 2 on communication, and the more practical written material in Units 3 and 4. You should be able to combine the techniques you learn here with the practical applications you will need in business.

3.1 Preparation

To start this section you will work on one particular document which is supplied as a Word file. The text in the file is the raw material. Your aim will be to make this document attractive and easy to read.

ACTIVITY 20

On the disk supplied with this unit is a file labelled Umbria.doc. Open this file in Word.

You will see that the file consists of a page or so of text about the northern hill towns of Italy. This text is taken from a *Which?* magazine article about holidays in Umbria. Spend a couple of minutes looking at this document. Imagine that you want to present it in an attractive format to a group of people you are accompanying on a holiday to Assisi.

In what ways could you make the document more attractive and easy to read? List some ideas here.

Did you think of any of these ideas?

- Try to fit the text neatly onto one page.
- Divide up the longish paragraphs into shorter ones.
- Make the headings stand out using a bigger, bolder type.
- It may be better to present the different 'sights' in the form of a list. The names of the sights could be emphasised by using a different form of type, such as bold or italics.
- The figures presented in the paragraph on weather would be better presented as a table.

DOCUMENT FORMAT (PAGE SET-UP)

Before you begin to work on the text itself it is important to spend time thinking about the overall format of the document. Aspects of the document you need to think about are:

- What width do you want the margins to be at the top and bottom and on each side?

- What size of paper will your document be on? (You will almost certainly want to print out documents that are A4 in size.)

- What orientation will your document be? It can be portrait (longer than wide) or landscape (wider than long).

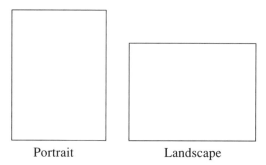

Portrait   Landscape

MARGINS

Margins are the distance between the edge of the paper and the edge of the text. You can choose the margins for every side of every document you produce. Word sets automatic or default margins, usually at 1.25 inches (or 3.17 cm) for the left/right margins and 1 inch (or 2.54 cm) for the top/bottom margins.

To change margins, go to the File menu and click on the Page Setup command. You will see that at the top of the dialog box are four pages of options given to you: Margins, Paper Size, Paper Source and Layout.

If the margins page is not activated, you click on the 'tab' marked Margin to activate the page. You can enter your preferred margins in the boxes labelled Top, Bottom, Left and Right. (Ignore Gutter, Header and Footer for now). There are two ways of doing this:

1   Highlight the existing number in the box, delete and replace (or overtype) with your preferred figure.

2   Use the up and down triangular buttons on the right of each box to increase or decrease the size of the figure by small increments.

You can also choose whether to apply the margins to the whole document or just part of it, using the Apply To option, though normally margins will apply through a whole document.

ACTIVITY 21

Look again at Umbria.doc. You want to produce an A4 document, portrait, with margins of 3 cm all round.

Follow the instructions given below to achieve this.

1 Check that the ruler is measured in centimetres. To do this, go to the Options command in the Tools menu. You will see a dialog box. On the General page, at the bottom, you will see the words 'Measurement Units' in the centre bottom of the screen. You can now select Centimetres as your basic unit. Then press OK.

2 You are now ready to put in the correct margins. Go to File|Page Setup. Choose the Margin page if it is not already activated.

3 Highlight the figure in the Top box by dragging the mouse across it.

4 Now type in 3.

5 Press <Tab>. You will see that this automatically highlights the figure in the next box (Bottom).

6 Type in 3 again and then press <Tab> to highlight the Left box.

7 Do this once more for the final box (Right).

8 You want to set these margins to Apply To the whole document, so choose that setting accordingly.

9 Click on OK. The text in Umbria.doc will automatically realign to its new margins. Look at the rule. The left marker should be at 0 while the right marker is on 15 cm. This is correct as the width of an A4 page is 21 cm. Subtracting two margins of 3 cm each equals 15 ($21 - 6 = 15$).

PAPER SIZE

The second option in the Page Setup window is for Paper Size. Open up the window again and click on Paper Size page. You will see another set of options available to you.

ACTIVITY 22

1 In the Paper Size window look at the Paper Size box. It should currently say A4 (210 x 297 mm). Click once on the arrow to the right of the box. A menu will appear of other possible sizes. You are unlikely to want anything except A4, the standard page size used throughout Europe. Click once more on the same arrow to remove the menu.

2 The Orientation box is for selecting whether to have your page as portrait or landscape. The portrait button should currently be activated. Select landscape and click on OK. After a few moments you should see the text realign to a margin of 23.7 cm, as it is now running across the greater width of the A4 landscape page. In fact, in order to see the right margin, you may need to scroll right, using the bottom scroll bar.

3 Change the orientation back to portrait.

You have now set the basic page layout for your document and you can start to work on the text itself. Whenever you create a new document spend a minute or two working out what the most suitable format will be.

3.2 Paragraphs

In Activity 20 you identified a few things you could do to make the information sheet about Umbria more attractive. An immediate first step is to sort out the paragraphs. Remember from Unit 3 that paragraphs should have a main theme or idea and a topic sentence.

ACTIVITY 23

1 The paragraph under 'Assisi' is too long. Create three paragraphs by adding two carriage returns before 'By contrast' and again before 'The pedestrianised main square'. This leaves a clear line space between each paragraph.

2 The paragraph under 'Sights' can be turned into a list with four items in it, each one describing one place of particular interest. Add one carriage return before each item in the list.

3 The paragraph under 'Food' is also too long. Create three paragraphs out of it. The first paragraph should be about local produce. The second should be about truffles. The third should be about wines.

---

4 The figures in the paragraph under 'Weather' are best presented as a table. To start getting this ready insert carriage returns to ensure that every month from April to October appears on a new line.

Make sure you positioned the cursor accurately, right up against the first letter of the first word of your new paragraphs. Otherwise you might accidentally take over an extra space that comes before that word.

Now close the file, saving the changes you have made.

Even if you are still relatively new to wordprocessing, you should have found that activity fairly simple. Remember that you have the choice when positioning your cursor either to use the mouse, or to use the arrow keys.

3.3 Tabs

Tabs are a way of precisely aligning text in columns. They are particularly useful for setting out information in tables. Look at the following information, also included in the *Which?* magazine article (though not in the extract in your file). There are four columns of text. The 'Town' column is aligned with the left margin but each of the other three columns is aligned to a tab to create a neat, easily-read table of information.

Town	Restaurant	Telephone	Price (2 courses)
Citta di Castello	Amici Mei..............	(075) 8559904	£14.00
Gubbio	Federico da Monte	(075) 9273949	£14.00
Montefalco	Coccorone...........	(0742) 79535	£14.50
Perugia	Falchetto..............	(075) 61875	£15.00

TYPES OF TABS

Look at the horizontal ruler near the top of your screen. (See Figure 1 if you are unsure which part of the screen is the ruler. If no ruler is displayed choose Ruler from the View menu.) On the left-hand side you will see an icon ▨. This is the left-hand tab icon. Click on this a number of times and you will see the icon change each time until it changes back to the left-hand tab icon. There are four icons as follows:

▨ is a left-hand tab: text aligns with its left-hand edge at the tab marker.

■ is a centre tab: text aligns so that the centre of the text is at the tab marker.

■ is a right-hand tab: text aligns with its right-hand edge at the tab marker.

■ is a decimal tab: it is used for columns of numbers, which will be aligned by their decimal points (or where the decimal point would be, if one is not actually shown).

SETTING TABS

When you open a new Word file the program sets tabs in the file according to its default setting. This default setting is 0.5 inches or 1.27 cm. These tabs are just visible as faint dots at the base of the ruler. When you place tabs of your own they will override the default tabs.

To set a tab you click on the tab icon until it is the type of tab you want and then click once on the ruler at the point where you want to place the tab.

Look at this in an actual file.

ACTIVITY 24

Open up a new document. The cursor will start flashing ready for you to enter some text. Before writing anything look at the ruler to check that you can see the row of default tabs on the ruler.

1 Press the tab key on the left side of your keyboard. It will look something like this:

You should see the cursor line up directly underneath the first default tab stop. At the same time an arrow may appear between the margin and the tab stop. Check that both these things have happened. (If you cannot see the arrow, press the ■ icon on the toolbar. This enables you to see many features such as tabs, spaces and paragraph markers which are not normally shown explicitly. You can turn these display features off by pressing the same icon again.)

Delete the tab you have inserted by pressing the backspace key near the top right of your keyboard.

2 Now insert the following tab markers on the ruler:

● a left tab at 5 cm

● a decimal tab at 10 cm

● a right tab at 12 cm.

When you placed the first tab you should have noticed that all the default tabs to the left of it disappeared. The ones to the right remain in place until you place your second and third tabs. Default tabs are in effect overridden by your own choice of tabs.

To reposition a tab marker you place the pointer over it then hold down the mouse button and drag it to the new position on the ruler. To remove a tab marker you drag it off the ruler completely.

ACTIVITY 24 Continued

3 Move your left tab to 4 cm.

4 Move your decimal tab to 10.5 cm.

5 Delete your right tab.

When you deleted the right tab you should have seen the default tabs reappear to the left as far as the decimal tab.

ACTIVITY 25

Open Lire.doc. This document contains a table giving a quick guide to conversions between £ Sterling and Italian Lire, which you want to include in your information sheet on Italy. At present the different columns are not aligned. There are actually four columns in this table. Now carry out the following steps to align the columns accurately.

1 Highlight all the lines that make up the table. Once all the lines are highlighted any tabs you insert on the ruler will affect all the lines that are highlighted.

2 Insert the following tabs markers:
   ● a right tab marker at 2 cm
   ● a decimal tab marker at 3 cm
   ● another decimal tab marker at 5 cm
   ● a left tab marker at about 5.7 cm.

   The text in the table should now be aligned. Save the document.

3 Now replace the decimal tab at 5 cm with a left tab at 4 cm. You should notice that the figures do align but they align from the left. In this table it does not matter too much but in other tables of figures it may be vital to have the figures aligned along the decimal point (for example, if you want to add them all up).

4 Experiment with other tab settings and alignments to check that you can add, delete and move tabs of all four kinds.

5 Close the document without saving the changes from step 4.

TABS DIALOG BOX

In addition to using the tab icons on the ribbons and the rulers you can set tabs using a dialog box which comes up when you click the Tabs command under the Format menu. This box enables you to set the tabs with greater accuracy and offers more choice about the format of your tabs. You may wish to experiment with some of the options here.

LEADERS

There is just one more aspect of using tabs that you need to know. This is the use of **leaders**, which are dots or lines that lead the eye from one part of a line to another.

ACTIVITY 26

Open the file Restrt.doc.

1 Highlight all the lines that make up the table.

2 Double-click on any of the tab markers. The Tabs dialog box should pop up and the first tab position should be highlighted in the list on the left. Click on the 8.5 cm tab in the list. Now look at the Leader box. Click on 2 .... and then press OK. You should now see that a row of dots connects the names of the restaurants with their telephone numbers. This is a row of leader dots.

3 You have a choice about the style of leader you use. Double-click on any of the tabs again, select the 8.5 cm tab in the list on the left, and this time press 4 in the Leader box. Press OK and see the dots change into a solid line.

4 Close the file without saving the changes.

When would you use leaders? You will often see leaders in the contents pages of books going from section or chapter titles to the relevant page numbers. Any document which has a long list of items with figures will benefit from these.

3.4 Styling text

An effective and quick way of making documents look attractive and professional is by applying typographical features. 'Typographical features' are things such as bold, italic and underlined type. In Activity 20 you already identified some of the ways in which you could apply styling features to the text in **Umbria.doc**. And you will recall from Unit 3 that these features are useful for highlighting key words, headings, subheadings etc.

BOLD, ITALICS, UNDERLINE
To add features such as bold, italics and underline to any parts of an existing text first **highlight** or **select** the word or words that you want to change. (You looked at highlighting text in Section 2.)

ACTIVITY 27

1   In Umbria.doc we want to make all the headings bold. First highlight 'Northern Hill Towns of Umbria'. What ways of doing it are there?

(Have you decided what is your preferred way of selecting text? How did you do it this time.)

You may have considered these ways of selecting text:

● place the cursor before 'Northern' and drag to the end of the line

● click once in the selection bar to the left of the line which will highlight the whole line

● click once before 'Northern', hold down <Shift> and click once more after 'Umbria'.

To apply new styles to the selected text you can then either:

● click on the formatting buttons **B** **I** or **U**

● or choose the Format|Font command then choose the Font page.

Like all the formatting buttons, they will appear 'pressed in' when activated and 'popped out' when not activated.

ACTIVITY 28

1 Make all the headings in Umbria.doc bold by selecting each in turn and pressing the Bold button on the toolbar.

2 In the paragraphs under the heading 'Sights', underline all the names of the four sights that are mentioned.

3 In the paragraph on 'Food' put all the names of foods given in Italian into italic type.

4 In the last line italicise 'Which?'

5 Save the changes. You may like to print out your document to see the effect directly.

Already you should see that these features make the document easier to read and more attractive. Below is a summary of how these features can be used in the following ways:

Bold: used in headings to make them prominent; to give emphasis to key words in a text; for display, such as posters, overhead projector transparencies.

Italics: used to give emphasis to words, phrases or sentences; as a feature of headings; for foreign words; for the titles of books and journals and others.

Underlined: used to give emphasis to words, phrases or sentences; as an alternative to italics in titles of books and journals.

These features must be used carefully. Overuse creates visual confusion and can become annoying to the reader.

ACTIVITY 29

1 In the document Umbria.doc make the three paragraphs under 'Assisi' into bold.

2 Underline all the text under 'Sights'.

3 Italicise all the paragraphs under 'Food'.

4 Read through the document.

5 Close the document without saving the changes.

Looking at this version of the document, you should see how adding these features inconsistently and to large areas of text made it more difficult to read.

ACTIVITY 30

1 Open Umbria.doc. Look at the list under the heading 'Sights'. You underlined the names of the four different sights. Underlining often does not look attractive, especially when the underlining lies very close to the text above it. Instead of underlining change the names of the four sights to bold.

2 Close the document, saving the changes.

3.5 Aligning text

Text can be aligned in several different ways:

Left Aligns the text to the left margin, leaving the right side ragged, or uneven.

Right Aligns the text to the right margin, leaving the left side ragged.

Centre Centres the text between the margins, leaving both sides ragged.

Justified Spreads the text evenly across the whole page, so that there are straight margins on both left and right.

The alignment you prefer can be selected through the four alignment buttons on the Formatting Toolbar. These are located just to the right of the bold/italic/underline buttons. Choose which alignment you want following the illustrative icons on the buttons below.

FORMATTING TOOLBAR ALIGNMENT BUTTONS

  is the left-alignment button

  is the centre-alignment button

  is the right-alignment button

  is the justification button.

ACTIVITY 31

Look again at Umbria.doc.

1 The text is currently left-aligned. Highlight the entire document and justify the text.

2 Centre the main heading at the top of the page and add a line space after it.

3 Make the final line in the document, the credit line, right-aligned.

4 Experiment with different alignments to see what effect they produce.

CHOOSING HOW TO ALIGN TEXT

As with using text features, such as bold, italics and underline, you need to be careful about how you use alignments.

Left alignment is the main style used in many letters, leaflets and other documents which have reasonable amounts of text.

Right alignment is less common. It may be appropriate in a leaflet where you can align text along the left side of a photograph or diagram, or right-align your address at the top of a letter.

Justified text is often used in legal documents, dissertations and books. Its straight lines and neat edges are more formal. You might also use justified text in other documents, such as letters or leaflets.

Centred text is used mainly for display purposes or in documents which do not have a large amount of text that has to be read through. Centring is often used in headings. It would also be suitable for posters or invitations, and in children's books where the text is very short.

It is also possible to use a mixture of styles in one document. If you do this, you have to be careful that your document retains a balance so it does not look jumbled.

3.6 Fonts

A font is a style of type. We can also call them 'typefaces'. Word contains a selection of fonts. It is also possible to buy additional fonts from computer suppliers for a wider selection of styles.

Examples

Courier

A common typeface which resembles a typewriter, and like a typewriter each letter and space takes up the same amount of space. This is called a 'fixed-width' or 'non-proportional' font.

Times New Roman

Another common typeface. Fonts like Times are called serif fonts, because they have small strokes finishing off letters. These serifs help move the eye forward. For this reason many people choose serif fonts when creating documents with a lot of text. Like most modern fonts, Times is a 'variable-width' or 'proportional' font where wide letters like W take up more space than thin letters like I.

Arial

Arial is a sans serif font. This means it does not have the little finishing strokes so the letters are plainer. Sans serif fonts are relatively modern.

Script

There are many fonts that are designed to look like handwriting, some neater, some messier. Here is one of the messier ones!

Selecting fonts is easy. The current font (which is probably Times New Roman) is shown on the Formatting Toolbar in the font box: look left from the bold/italic/underline buttons, ignore the box containing a number, and the next box is the current font name.

ACTIVITY 32

1 Create a new file and type in the following text:
   Did the quick brown fox really jump over the lazy dog?
   Or was it just an excuse to type out all the letters?
   1 2 3 4 5 6 7 8 9

2 Highlight all the text. Then click on the arrow to the right of the font box and you will see the available fonts listed (though you may need to scroll the list to see them all). Select one of the fonts in the list. Notice the difference that this makes to the text in the document.

3 Change the font to some of the others available on your computer. Think about the circumstances in which you might choose to use each one.

4 Find your favourite font in the list. Save this last version of your text as Fonts.Doc.

SIZES

ACTIVITY 33

1 Open your file Fonts.Doc, if it is not still open. Highlight all the text and change the font to Times New Roman.

2 While the text is still highlighted look at the box to the right of the fonts box. This is the type size box. It probably currently says 10. This means that the type size of the text is 10 'points' (abbreviated to 10 pt). Click once on the arrow to the right of this box. A menu will now appear listing a range of sizes, and there is a scroll bar to move above or below the initial list. Click on the number 18. The menu will disappear and the text will change to the larger size. This text is obviously very easy to read but is rather impractical as you get far fewer words to a line.

3 Change the font size back to 10 pt. You may have to use the scroll bar to scroll back up to 10. Click once on 10 and the text will change and automatically realign.

4 Close the file without saving the changes.

Sizes of type are measured vertically in points. The most common sizes for normal text are 10 and 12 points. Anything smaller than 10 pt can be difficult to read. Larger type sizes are useful for headings or for display text such as in posters.

Word allows you to pick a wide range of point sizes.

ACTIVITY 34

1 Open a new file.

2 Type in the following text, in the corresponding type sizes.

Times font, size 8 pt.

Times font, size 9 pt.

Times font, size 10 pt.

Times font, size 12 pt.

Times font, size 18 pt.

Size 24 pt.

Size 36 pt.

---

3 Save the document as Sizes.doc. You might like to print out this page for future reference.

4 Experiment with different fonts and different sizes. Try changing the text to 4 pt and see what it looks like. Change it to 127 pt and count how many words you can get onto a page.

There are a number of things to keep in mind about type sizes.

- In theory, all fonts at the same size are the same height. In other words, 10 pt Times should take up the same vertical space as 10 pt Arial or 10 pt Courier. In practice, however, wordprocessed typefaces often vary in their height.

- Fonts vary considerably in how wide the characters are. Some fonts take up more space along the line than others in the same type size.

The spaces between words and between lines have font sizes as well as the characters you can see.

ACTIVITY 35

Use Times New Roman and Arial for this activity. (If you do not have these on your machine use a similar font instead. These would be a serif face in place of Times New Roman and a sans serif face instead of Arial.)

1 Open Umbria.doc.

2 Make the following changes to the document:

- main text to be 12 pt Times New Roman, justified

- main heading at the top of the page to be 20 pt Arial, bold, centred

- all other paragraph headings to be 14 pt Arial, bold, aligned left

- the last line in the document ('Adapted from ...') to be 10 pt Times New Roman, aligned right.

3 Save the changes, then close the file.

USING FONTS

You will see from the last activity that two different fonts were used in the same document. Mixing fonts needs to be done with great care. It is often effective to use one font for text and another for headings but you must assess how well the fonts go together.

The two fonts used in Umbria.doc complement each other fairly well. The plainer bold Arial is a good contrast to the main font of the text, Times. It is often the case that a serif typeface can be used effectively with a sans serif type.

ACTIVITY 36

Mixing fonts

Look at the following excerpt from the information sheet with some of the features changed around. How successful is this? Write your comments directly onto the text.

- Sights-

- `Basilica di San Francesco`: The basilica is really two churches built against a steep hill. The superb frescoes are attributed to Giotto.

- `Basilica di Santa Chiara`: Visitors crowd to see the painted crucifix that spoke to Francis.

- `In the Basilica di Santa Maria` degli Angeli is the tiny stone chapel where Francis founded his order.

- `San Damiano` has a copy of the crucifix that spoke to Francis.

You probably found the excerpt above unbalanced, ugly and even hard to read. Using Courier so close to Times causes a visual collision that is not pleasant. Using different sizes of text on the same line is also unsuccessful. The dashes either side of the heading add nothing.

As a general rule be thoughtful and restrained in your use of fonts and styling features. The most effective documents are often the ones that use a few effects carefully. Remember that as well as making the document look attractive you are really concerned with making it communicate the message effectively. All effects should be used carefully with regard to the subject matter and actual content.

FORMAT I FONT COMMAND

By now you will be aware that there is often more than one way of achieving something in Word. You often have a choice between using a keyboard command or using your mouse to select from a menu. The Font command from the Format menu offers an alternative way of manipulating text.

The features you have covered are changing fonts and type sizes, bold, italics and underline. As you will see if you choose the Font command, the dialog box lets you do other things, too. We will look at some of those later, though you might like to experiment with some of the options now.

Summary

In this section you have become familiar with many important features of your wordprocessing program. By now you should be able to create documents which use layout and styling features to make them interesting, readable and attractive.

SECTION 4

More Wordprocessing Techniques

Introduction

In this section we look at ways of creating effects by changing the appearance of paragraphs, words and individual characters. You will look at how to create boxes, or borders, around text and how to shade them. You will also use some of the special features of the Format | Font command to alter the size and font of words.

It is important to feel at ease with using the various techniques you have learned before moving on.

4.1 Creating borders and shading

An advantage of Word is that you can add simple graphical features to enhance the look of your document. These kinds of feature include boxes, lines, shadows and shading. They are contained in the Borders and Shading command.

ACTIVITY 37

1 Open the document Quest.doc.

2 Highlight the title at the top of the questionnaire.

3 Select the Borders and Shading command in the Format menu. A dialog box will open offering you two pages which contain a number of features. Of the two pages choose the Borders page. The features on this page are grouped under five headings: Border, Preset, Line, Color and Style.

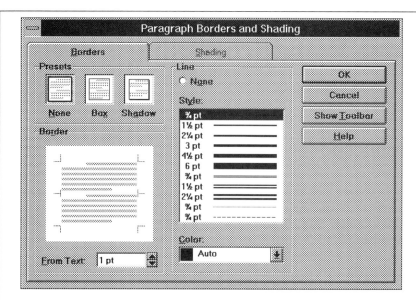

4 In the box marked Border there is a representation of the paragraphs you have highlighted and what border is round them. At the moment there should be no border as the paragraph you highlighted (the title, 'Year One Questionnaire', has no border).

5 Now go to the Presets box above. There are a number of images of pages there which are labelled, for example, None, Box, Shadow.

6 Select the image labelled Box by clicking once anywhere on the image above Box.

7 Three things happen immediately:

   ● In the Presets window, the image of the page above now has a black frame.

   ● Lines have appeared in the Border window to show you what you have selected.

   ● In the Style window, a black frame has moved from the None box to the box containing a thin single line. You have selected a single line box for the highlighted paragraph.

8 Now click OK (or press <Return>) to see what you have done.

In the main file you can see what has happened. A border has been placed around the title, i.e. the paragraph you highlighted. The border goes the whole length of the page within the page margins. Look at the ruler. The border matches up with the margin marker. It should look something like this:

```
┌──────────────────────────────────────────────────────────────┐
│                   Year One Questionnaire                       │
└──────────────────────────────────────────────────────────────┘
```

This is a very simple box and Word offers many more options. Look at a few of them now.

ACTIVITY 38

1 Quest.doc should be open from Activity 37 with a single line border around the heading. Place the cursor at any point in the heading. Go to the Borders and Shading command in the Format menu.

2 Change the line to the thickest possible single line Style available.

3 When you have selected the thickest line the image in the Border box on the left will give you a representation of what it will look like. Now press OK. It should look like this:

```
┏━━━━━━━━━━━━━━━━━━━━━━━━━━━━━━━━━━━━━━━━━━━━━━━━━━━━━━━━━━━━━┓
┃                   Year One Questionnaire                   ┃
┗━━━━━━━━━━━━━━━━━━━━━━━━━━━━━━━━━━━━━━━━━━━━━━━━━━━━━━━━━━━━━┛
```

4 Open up the Borders and Shading command again. This time press any of the double line boxes in the Style box and then press <Return>. You should get something like this:

```
╔══════════════════════════════════════════════════════════╗
║                   Year One Questionnaire                   ║
╚══════════════════════════════════════════════════════════╝
```

5 Open up the Borders and Shading command again. This time look at the Presets box and click on the page icon labelled Shadow. Press <Return>. This time you should see that this gives the box a three-dimensional effect by placing a shadow behind the main box.

6 Change the border back to a plain single line. Then Save your document.

Note that when you are putting a border around one paragraph you do not need to highlight the whole paragraph. Putting the cursor at any point in the paragraph has the same effect.

ACTIVITY 39

1 Highlight the two paragraphs of introductory text below the heading 'Year One Questionnaire' in the document Quest.doc.

2 Using the techniques you learned in Activities 37 and 38 place a thick single-line border around these two paragraphs of text.

3 Highlight the whole of both paragraphs again. Open up the Borders and Shading menu. Click on the box option under Presets. Below Presets in the

box marked Border there is a representation of the paragraphs you have highlighted.

4 Click on the horizontal centre line between the paragraphs, the side markers will change to black arrow heads which tells us the position the line will take.

5 Click a line style under Line. Because you have already selected a thick, single line for the main border, you should get the same for this paragraph dividing line.

6 Now click on OK. You should see that a line has appeared between the two paragraphs of text in your main file. This dividing line will appear every time you create a new paragraph by inserting a carriage return (<Return>).

7 To test this out place the cursor at the end of the first paragraph after 'average'. Now press <Return> twice. You should see two empty boxes appear between the paragraphs.

Activating this paragraph dividing line can be very useful. For example, you might want to create forms or tables with different sections. You can then group text in different boxes.

CUSTOMISING BOXES

Just as it is possible to put in or leave out this paragraph dividing line, it is possible to customise each side of the box.

ACTIVITY 40

1 If you are continuing to work directly from Activity 39 delete the extra lines you put in so that you are back to your two main paragraphs. Now highlight the whole of both paragraphs. Open up the Borders and Shading command and get onto the Borders page.

2 In the Border box, click on one side of the box. Triangular markers appear at the ends of the chosen side. Whenever a pair of markers are visible, it means that you can apply whatever style you want to the line between the markers.

3 In the Style box, choose a style of line by pointing and clicking on the line style you want, this will then be applied to the side of the box which is highlighted.

If you want to select and modify several sides at once, hold down <Shift> while clicking each side in turn until all those you require are selected.

ACTIVITY 40 Continued

4 Highlight the top line. Change this line into a thin double line.

5 Highlight the bottom line and change this to a thick double line.

6 Now change the sides so that there is no line on either side.

You should have worked out that to remove the lines on either side you need to highlight the line in the Border box and then select the item saying None in the Style box.

PUTTING A MARGIN AROUND A BOXED TEXT

A problem with the borders you created in Activity 40 is that the text sits very close to the border. This gives it a rather cramped appearance. It is possible to deal with this by inserting some space between the lines and the text.

ACTIVITY 41

1 In Quest.doc, highlight the two paragraphs that follow the introduction. Turn the border into a thin single-line box.

2 Open the Borders and Shading command if it is not already open. Look at the small box labelled From Text. This box allows you to create a margin between the box and the text. Move the pointer to the 'up' arrow on the right side of this box. Click several times on the box using the mouse. As you click, you should see two things happen:

   ● The number in the From Text box increases.

   ● In the page image above, the shaded lines that represent lines of text move away from the edges of the border.

3 When you have reached 12 pt stop clicking on the arrow and press <Return>. You should now see that there is a 12 pt margin between the text and the border on all sides. However, there is a possible problem. On the left and right sides the extra space goes beyond the page margins you set. You probably prefer to have the border line up with the margin markers. Do this as follows:

4 If you are using the mouse highlight the two boxed paragraphs if they are not still highlighted. Make sure that the ruler is visible above the main document text. If it is not, go to Ruler in the View window and activate it. Click and hold on the left margin marker, and move it slowly to the right.

> When you reach 0.5 cm, release the mouse button. The text block has narrowed to make room for the border.
>
> 5 Now move the right margin marker in by 0.5 cm in the same way. This should improve the overall effect, making the text easier to read.

It is worth remembering that there are 72 points to one inch and 28 points to one centimetre. When you added a 12 pt space around the boxed text you had to compensate by indenting another 0.5 cm. This is only approximate, but it works.

SHADING BOXES

In the Borders and Shading command there is Shading page which adds background shading to paragraphs.

ACTIVITY 42

1 With Quest.doc open, remove the box around the two paragraphs and ensure that the paragraphs are aligned with the margin.

2 Add a thick, single line border to the heading 'Year One Questionnaire'. Make sure that there is a 10 pt margin between the text and the border. Line up the border with the main text margin. Click on OK to view the effect you have created.

3 Return to the Borders and Shading command and open the Shading page. The None button should appear activated as there is no shading. Activate the Custom button by clicking on it with the mouse.

4 Now look at the Shading option which gives you a range of choices. Currently the shading option is Clear. Click on 25% with the mouse. The effect that produced is visible in the Border box. Click on OK again to see it applied to the actual text.

You have now added a shading of 25% to the paragraph. This makes the heading even more prominent and adds extra depth to the document.

When 25% shading is selected, it is 25% of the solid colour which is normally black. Such shadings are often called tints. You can select from as low as 5% right up to 90%. A patch of solid black is 100% and appears in the menu as Solid.

The Shading option offers you a wide variety of types of shading. The percentages give an even shading over the whole paragraph but you can select a pattern, including horizontal, vertical and diagonal lines, and grids and trellises.

ACTIVITY 43

1 Apply the following shadings to the 'Year One Questionnaire' box. Record whether you think each one is attractive and readable and give reasons why.

Attractive	**Readable**	**Why**
10%	Yes/No	Yes/No
80%	Yes/No	Yes/No
Dk Down Diag.	Yes/No	Yes/No
Lt Trellis	Yes/No	Yes/No

2 Select 20% shading as in the illustration below. Do whatever is necessary to achieve this effect.

Year One Questionnaire

You probably found that only the first shading (10%) was both attractive and readable. An 80% shading is too heavy and it makes it hard to read the text. The two patterned shadings also tend to obscure the text, even if they are attractive in themselves.

Background tints above 30% can interfere with the readability of the text. It is a good idea to use bold type in shaded boxes especially for headings.

REVERSED OUT TEXT

Sometimes it is effective to use white text on a black or tint background. This is called Reversing Out and it is easy to do in Word.

ACTIVITY 44

1 Highlight the heading 'Year One Questionnaire' again which should still appear as in Activity 43. Go to Borders and Shading in the Format menu and create a box with a single thick line and solid shading. Go back to the main document to see the effect. You will find that you cannot see the text at all, as it is black on black.

2 Ensure that all the text in the heading is highlighted. (The selected area should appear as a shade of grey rather than black.) Go to Font in the

Format menu. When the dialog box appears ensure you are on the Font page. You should see a box labelled Color somewhere in the middle. Auto will appear in the Color box. Open the Color menu (by clicking on the arrow). Select White. Click on OK.

3 You are now back in the main document. Un-highlight the heading either by clicking with the mouse anywhere on the document or by pressing one of the arrow keys. You can now see the full effect of reversing out the heading. It should appear like this:

Year One Questionnaire

4 Save the changes.

Reversed out text creates an even stronger and bolder heading than ordinary shading. Any text used in this way must be fairly large and bold or it can become swamped by the solid shading around it.

You should now be able to create any effect you want using boxing and shading to result in attractive readable documents.

4.2 Font command

So far we have been concerned with using the Border command under the Format menu. You will now look in more detail at the Font command to alter text in terms of size, font and style.

ACTIVITY 45

1 Open up the document Quest.doc and scroll to the end of the file. Type in the words 'Thank you for your time' at the very end.

2 Highlight all these words. Go to Font in the Format menu. A dialog box will appear. There are two pages – Font and Character Spacing. Ensure you are on the Font page. You have already used several of the options available to you here. Practise using them again by doing the following:

   ● Make sure that the font is a serif font such as Times, Palatino, New Century Schoolbook.

   ● Make the font size 14 pt.

   ● Make the text bold, italics.

When these features are applied the Sample box on the bottom right of the dialog box shows you how the text will appear.

3 Click on OK to see how the text appears in the document.

4 With the words 'Thank you for your time' still highlighted open up the Font dialog box again. Work your way down the Effects box, trying out the different features of Strikethrough, Hidden, Small Caps and All Caps. Look in the Sample box to see the effects created.

5 What is the difference between Small Caps and All Caps?

All Caps makes all the characters into capital letters of the same size. Small Caps makes all the characters capitals but has two different sizes, according to whether or not the <Shift> key was pressed when they were typed in.

When you press Hidden it indicates that these words will not appear on your print-out. They stay visible on the computer screen, but the printer will not pick them up. Probably you will not use this feature much but it could be useful in the following situations:

● You produce a draft document of a report which has certain information missing, is not up-to-date or needs checking. You write a note to yourself in the computer file saying: 'Important: check this data'. By making this text Hidden, you can print out a draft version for other people to read, but your own screen version contains a note in the relevant place which you cannot miss.

● You are writing an essay which contains a lot of statistics and figures you derived from calculations. Using the Hidden command, you can type in details of how you reached particular figures or where you got them from, without them being visible when you print out.

SUPERSCRIPT AND SUBSCRIPT

Other options available to you in the Effects window are Superscript and Subscript.

Superscript raises selected text to a specified point above the baseline, $^{\text{like this}}$.

Subscript lowers it to a specified point below the baseline, $_{\text{like this}}$.

'To a specified point' means that you can state exactly in terms of points how much the text should be raised or lowered.

ACTIVITY 46

1 Open up the document Quest.doc if it is not already open. Highlight the word 'short' in the first line of the first paragraph.

2 Open up the Font command and choose the Character Spacing page.

3 Click once on the arrow to the right of the Position box. A menu will offer you the choice of Normal, Raised or Lowered. Click on Raised. You should now see 3 pt appear in the By box. This means that the selected text will be raised 3 points above the baseline. Click on OK or press <Return> to see the effect you have created. The word 'short' now sits higher than the rest of the line.

4 With 'short' still highlighted open up the Font command again. Click on Lowered in the Position box. This time, use the arrows to the right of the By box to increase the number to 5 pt. Click on OK to implement the changes and go back to the document. This time, the word 'short' sits lower than the rest of the line.

5 Experiment with different settings of Position to see the effects that can be produced. When you have finished experimenting, change the text back to a 'level' setting.

When do you think Raising and Lowering might be useful?

Superscript and subscript are useful in special situations, such as:

- in mathematical expressions: $5^2 + 12^2 = 13^2$
- in other mathematical texts: 'In a sequence of numbers, x_1, x_2, x_3, then the nth number is x_n, and the $(n + 1)^{th}$ number is $x_{n + 1}$'
- to create footnote markers: 'As the author wrote in 1963[1]...' (However, these can also be created automatically using the Insert | Footnote facility.)
- if you just want to create strange effects.

In the first and the third examples, the superscript text is created by making the characters 8 pt in size, and superscripting them by 4 pt.

In the second example, the subscript text is 7 pt in size, subscripted by 3 pt.

The wavy effect in the last example was created by raising or lowering each letter one point different to the letter next to it. This is a laborious process as you must highlight each letter individually and then use the Font command to change the Character Spacing page. However, it can be effective for such things as posters.

THE SPACING OPTION
The Spacing option is the last one to look at in the Character Spacing page of the Font command.

ACTIVITY 47

1 In Quest.doc highlight the whole of the first paragraph. Open the Font command and select the Character Spacing window. Look at the Spacing option which should currently say Normal. Open up the Spacing menu by clicking on the arrow to the right. Here there are three options: Normal, Expanded and Condensed.

2 Select Expanded and set the By box to 3 pt. Click on OK to apply this feature to the paragraph you selected. What do you see and what do you think of it?

3 Go back to the Font command and this time make the paragraph Condensed. Set the By box to 1.75 pt. Click OK to apply this. What do you see and what do you think of it?

4 Change the text back to Normal.

With text that is expanded by 3 pt, you get a spacious effect. This can appear stylish if used carefully. Text that is condensed by 1.75 pt is virtually illegible as all the letters seem to run into each other. Do note, however, that you can customise how far you expand or condense text and achieve subtle changes.

You can only see the full effect of these changes by printing out your document. Often what looks good on screen does not look good on paper, and vice versa.

Summary

In this section you have focused on two main features of the wordprocessing program: the Borders and Shading command; and the Font command.

You have now investigated all the possibilities offered by both these commands. There is a huge menu of options available to you so take care to use them carefully and with thought.

REVIEW ACTIVITY 4

1 Open up the document Notice.doc.

2 Using your own skill and judgement add styling to create an eye-catching and effective poster. Try to use a range of features you learned about in this section without 'going over the top'.

3 Show your version to friends and colleagues. Discuss the overall effect and how well it has worked.

SECTION 5

Formatting Paragraphs

Introduction

You have learnt how to create attractive, stylish and varied text, focusing on the actual format or style of the characters. In this section you will look at ways of formatting whole paragraphs. Most of the features in this section are accessed using the Paragraph command in the Format menu.

The files you will need to work on in this section are Quiz.doc and Cats.doc.

5.1 Paragraph command

The Paragraph command governs the format of paragraphs as a whole. Some of the things it enables you to do include:

- select the alignment of text inside the paragraph e.g. left, right, centre, justified
- indent the text in paragraphs on either side or both sides
- add space before or after the paragraph
- choose the spacing of lines within the paragraph
- make a paragraph start on a new page
- link two paragraphs so that they will never be separated by a page break

- link all the lines in a paragraph so that they cannot be separated by a page break.

This command covers a wide range of possibilities of which you have already used a few in earlier activities.

INDENTATION

When indenting a paragraph, space is added between the paragraph text and the invisible page margin that you set up using the Page Setup box. For example, you have page margins of 3 cm either side in the file Cats.doc. If you indent a paragraph a further 2 cm each side, then that paragraph will be indented a total of 5 cm from the edge of the paper.

ACTIVITY 48

1 Highlight the paragraph beginning 'Forget ...' at the start of the file Cats.doc. Open up the Paragraph dialog box and click on the Indents and Spacing page.

2 Set the indentation Left and Right at 2 cm. You should be able to see the effect of doing this in the Preview box. The black lines show the extra space you have added to either side, compared to the grey lines above and below. Click on OK and see the effect of indenting on the actual paragraph.

3 Look at the Ruler. The markers have become repositioned. They are probably at 2 cm and 13.7 cm. It is possible to achieve the same effect of indentation by simply moving the margin markers using the mouse.

4 Move the pointer so that it is pointing at the right margin marker. Click the mouse button and hold. Drag the margin marker to any point on the ruler. Drag it to 12 cm and release the mouse button. The right edge of the text will move even further in to add more space to the right margin.

5 Use the mouse to move the left margin marker back to 1 cm. The left margin marker is in two parts. Be sure to click on the bottom half when you move the marker. If you find you can only move the top half of the marker this is because you have clicked on the top half only.

6 Open up the Paragraph dialog box again and look at the Indentation box. The new values will be in the Left and Right boxes – something around 1 cm and 3.58 cm.

7 Change the indentation to 0 cm either side and Click on OK.

Shown below are two buttons on the Toolbar which allow you to indent whole paragraphs very easily.

 Click once on this to move the whole paragraph to align at the next tab stop *to the right.*

 Click once on this to move the whole paragraph to align at the next tab stop *to the left.*

HANGING PARAGRAPHS

The left margin marker is divided vertically into two parts because:

- The top half governs the first line of a paragraph only. It can be moved independently of the bottom half by clicking and dragging on the top half.

- The bottom half governs every other line of the paragraph. It can be moved by clicking and dragging on the bottom half.

- You can create features such as hanging paragraphs using this feature. A hanging paragraph is one where the first line aligns with the left margin, but every other line is indented, as in this paragraph.

Hanging paragraphs are particularly useful for creating neatly aligned lists. Note that by using a tab after the bullet you can line up the text neatly and accurately to the lower half of the margin marker.

Indenting the first line of a paragraph is also a very useful feature. It is the standard way of typesetting paragraphs in novels. This can be done by using the First Line option in the Special box.

BULLETS AND NUMBERING

Word provides a convenient short cut to create neatly aligned lists. This is by using two more of the buttons on the formatting toolbar, and the Bullets and numbering command in the Format menu. The buttons on the toolbar are:

 Creates a numbered list.   Creates a bulleted list.

ACTIVITY 49

1 Open the document Cats.doc. Highlight the list of eight items near the start of the document.

2 Look at the two List buttons on the menu. Click on the bulleted list button. A dialog box asks if you want to replace the numbers with bullets. Say Yes. Note that if you were to press <Return>, then you would be saying No, as this is the button with the black frame in this window.

3 You should now have a bulleted list instead of a numbered list. The bullets are probably small and should be bigger. With the list still highlighted, go to the Bullets and numbering command in the Tools menu. Clicking once will bring up the Bullets and numbering dialog box. This gives you various options in terms of style of bullet. Click on the top-centre bullet choice and then click on the Modify button. This displays a screen that allows us to modify many aspects of the bullets. Increase the point size to 18 in the Point Size box.

4 Click on OK to go back to the main document and see the effect of your changes. (It may not be very obvious on screen but the bullets are in fact now larger.)

The list is neat and clear. But looking at the document as a whole, it makes sense to keep the list numbered. All the paragraphs that follow have numbered headings above them. If you have a numbered list, then everything matches up nicely. You can use the numbered list button to change the list back.

ACTIVITY 50

1 Highlight the eight paragraphs that make up the list that is now bulleted at the start of the document. Click on the numbered list button on the Toolbar. You should see a dialog box appear asking you if you want to replace the existing bullets with numbers. Say Yes.

2 The list will change back into a numbered list. Notice that the new numbered list has full stops after the numbers. This is unsatisfactory because the style is not to have the full stops. (Check this by looking at all the numbered headings).

3 With the list still highlighted go to Bullets and Numbering in the Tools menu. Click on the top-left option then click on the Modify button. You can choose what you prefer in terms of:

● **Number:** what sort of numbers to have – Arabic, Roman, letters, upper or lower case.

● **Text Before:** what, if anything, to have displayed before the number. e.g. full stop, a bracket, a colon, or nothing.

● **Text After:** what, if anything, to have displayed between the number and the list.

● **Start at:** what number to start the list at.

Change the Text After to nothing. Do this now by deleting the full stop.

4 When you have successfully changed the list back to a numbered list with no full stops, save the document.

You might want to start a list at a number other than 1, maybe where you have a long numbered list which is interrupted by text. For example, 'Of the 12 member states of the European Community, the first six joined together in 1952 as the European Coal and Steel Community (then comes list with numbers 1 to 6). The next three to join were (then comes list with numbers 7-9) and the last three to join were (numbers 10-12).

Creating lists in this easy way is an extremely useful facility of Word. Lists are excellent ways of presenting information clearly and logically – and are much easier to read than having a long paragraph of complex sentences. As you know from your work using memos, a numbered list makes it easier for your receiver to respond.

SPACING

There are still a number of items in the Paragraph command that you need to look at. The first of these is the part that deals with Spacing on the Indents and Spacing page.

The Paragraph command lets you apply two forms of spacing to a paragraph:

Paragraph spacing specifying a precise amount of space to be added to the beginning and/or end of a paragraph.

Line spacing   specifying exactly how much space is allocated between the lines within a paragraph.

PARAGRAPH SPACING

This is a straightforward operation and allows you to be extremely precise in the amount of space you add.

ACTIVITY 51

1 Open Cats.doc. You have worked so far on the first paragraph and the numbered list following it. Move a bit further down and highlight the heading '1 Farm cats' which currently sits precisely on top of a longer paragraph of about five lines. This is a heading which you want to give some prominence.

2 Change the heading so that it is 12 pt bold. Move the first tab so that it is at 0.75 cm.

This seems like a suitable size for a heading but it is a bit too close to the following text. You can put some space between it and the paragraph, but not as much as a complete line space. Do this using the Spacing option in the Paragraph command.

ACTIVITY 51 Continued

3 Go to Paragraph in the Format menu. Look at the Before and After box (under Spacing). Currently both should say 0 pt. This means that there is no extra space before and after the paragraph. In the After box press the 'up' arrow <↑> once. The value in the box will change to 6 pt. This means that half a line space will be added to the end of the paragraph. Click on OK.

4 Go back to the Paragraph dialog window. In the After box, type 8 pt. Click on OK. The space after the heading increases slightly. This is because 8 points is somewhere between a half and a full line space. You can therefore be extremely precise about how much space to insert.

In Activity 51, you only inserted space after a paragraph. The procedure is similar for inserting space before a paragraph. The only difference being that you use the Before box.

LINE SPACING

As with paragraph spacing, you can be very precise about the spacing of lines within a paragraph.

ACTIVITY 52

1 In Cats.doc, highlight the paragraph below the heading '1 Farm cats'. It starts 'A dying breed'.

2 Go to Paragraph and on the Indents and Spacing page, Look at the Line Spacing box. Click on the arrow to the right of the box to display the drop-down menu. You will see a number of options here:

Auto   matches the spacing to the largest character on the line.

Single   is the standard spacing for text.

1.5 lines adds the equivalent of half a line to the standard spacing.

Double   leaves the equivalent of a full line space between the lines of text.

At Least sets a minimum spacing that can be increased, but not decreased.

Exactly   sets a fixed line spacing that does not change, no matter how large or small you make the text on the line.

> **Multiple**   Allows line spacing to be increased and decreased by any percentage.
>
> 3 Change the Line spacing of the paragraph you have highlighted, so that it is on 1.5 Lines. Click on OK to see the effect that that produces.

Single is the default setting and most documents are perfectly satisfactory left on this setting. There will be occasions when you may want more or less spacing. Where would you want more or less space? If you are writing a draft of an essay or a report that may be heavily corrected a 1.5 or double line spacing will give you or someone else extra room to write in comments and amendments.

Alternatively, you could close up the spacing to create a really tight effect. You could even overlap the lines by setting 12 pt text on exactly 10 points of spacing. This becomes quite difficult to read and should only be used as a special effect, e.g. on posters and display material.

As with paragraph spacing, line spacing can be specified in terms of points instead of lines using the Before and After boxes.

5.2 Pagination

Pagination refers to the way the text is divided into pages. The point at which a page ends is called the page break. The Text Flow page in the Paragraph command gives four options in its box labelled Pagination:

- Page Break Before
- Keep With Next
- Keep Lines Together
- Widow/Orphan control.

PAGE BREAKS
When a document contains more text than can be fitted onto one page Word, like all wordprocessing programs, automatically divides the document up at an appropriate point. These automatic page breaks are shown in the document by a dotted line cutting across the page (in Normal view).

It is also possible to force page breaks at any point you choose. There are at least two ways of doing this:

1. Using the Break option from the Insert menu.

2. Pressing <Ctrl Enter>.

ACTIVITY 53

1 Open Cats.doc. This document is slightly longer than one page so there should be an automatic page break somewhere near the end of the file. Scroll through the document until you find the page break.

2 Insert a page break before the heading in this paragraph: place the cursor at the beginning of the paragraph containing the page break, choose Insert | Break, check that the Page Break option is selected, then click on OK.

3 A dotted line will appear before the heading. Notice that the other dotted line below it disappears. The program has automatically repaginated the document and discovered that it does not need another page break.

4 Undo what you have just done. (If you have forgotten how to do this, look under the Edit menu.) The page break will move back to where it was before.

In case you forgot, you can undo your last action by pressing Undo in the Edit menu.

Forcing a page break is very useful to ensure that each chapter of a book starts on a new page even if there was space remaining on the page or each major section within a report where the previous chapter or section ended.

KEEP LINES TOGETHER

The Keep Lines Together function is useful in ensuring that all the lines in a paragraph stay on the same page.

ACTIVITY 54

1 Open Cats.doc.

2 You decide that you do not want the paragraph containing the page break split up in this way. Place the cursor anywhere in that paragraph. Open up the Paragraph dialog box in the Format menu. Click on Keep Lines Together. A cross should appear in the small box next to it. Now click on OK. What happens?

You should see that the page break has moved between the heading and the paragraph. You have told the computer never to split up this paragraph so it has forced the whole paragraph onto the next page. This can be useful if you have put a border around a paragraph a few lines long and do not want the box to be broken up.

Keep with Next

The Keep With Next function is similar to Keep Lines Together except that it links paragraphs together. For example, you could use it to ensure that a page break does not occur between a heading and the following paragraph.

Summary

In this section you have concentrated on features of paragraph formatting. You have now learned the most important and commonly used features of this wordprocessing program.

Section 6

Other Features

Introduction

The common theme of this section is to learn how to use some other features Word has to offer such as moving text within and between documents, how to insert headers and footers and becoming familiar with several more icons on the toolbar. In this section you will work on the file **Cats.doc**.

6.1 Copy, cut and paste

Word lets you move text around within documents and between documents using the three commands Cut, Copy and Paste. All three are found in the Edit menu.

ACTIVITY 55

1 Open Cats.doc. Highlight the whole of the first paragraph, 'Forget ... following:'. Go to the Edit menu and select Copy. You will not have seen anything visible happen but the program has taken a copy of that text and stored it in a part of the program called the Clipboard. It is now waiting there ready for you to paste it in somewhere else.

2 Move the cursor to the line space after the list of eight items. Now go to Edit and select Paste. You will see that the text you copied earlier has been placed at the point where the cursor was positioned.

3 Undo the last paste. Highlight the paragraph beginning 'These are the basic types ...'. Go to Edit and select Cut. This time you have copied the text to the Clipboard, but you have also removed the original from the document.

4 Move the cursor to the end of the document and select Paste from the Edit menu. The text you Cut earlier will be inserted at the point to which you moved the cursor.

This set of commands is useful for moving text around within a document. It is convenient if you change your mind about where you want a paragraph to appear or if you just want to see what a piece of text looks like in a different place.

When you Copy or Cut text onto the Clipboard, it remains there until you next perform a Copy or Cut command. Then it is lost and the newly copied text takes its place. You cannot store more than one piece of copied text on the Clipboard. Cut or copied text is also lost from the Clipboard when you Exit the program.

As you might expect, there are other quick ways of performing these commands. These include buttons on the toolbar.

TOOLBAR

Cut   Copy   Paste

MOVING TEXT BETWEEN DOCUMENTS

The same Copy, Cut and Paste functions can be used to move text from one Word document to another.

ACTIVITY 56

1 Copy all the text from the start of the document to the paragraph after the list, ending '... their individual characteristics.' Copy this text using either of the methods you have learned.

2 Open up a new document.

3 Paste the copied text into the new document.

4 Close the document, without saving it.

There are two ways to open up a new document. They are to select the New command from the File menu or to use the button on the Toolbar shown here.

It is usually quickest to click on the toolbar.

6.2 Show|Hide

The button which looks like this is called the Paragraph button:

This button does not actually make any changes to your document but it alters your view of it. When activated, the button shows the following symbols within the text:

¶   This symbol indicates the end of a paragraph.

It appears every time you press <Return>, sometimes called a hard carriage return.

⏎   This symbol indicates the end of line, but not a paragraph.

It appears every time you press <Return>, while holding down the <Shift> key; sometimes called a soft carriage return.

→   This symbol indicates a tab.

·   This symbol indicates a space.

These symbols are not part of the text and do not appear when you print a document. What they do is show you detailed information about the how the text is formatted.

ACTIVITY 57

Open Cats.doc once again. If the ⁋ button on the toolbar is not activated, press it. When it is activated you will see a range of symbols appear in the text. Which symbols can you see?

In the document Cats.doc you should be able to see both tab symbols → and paragraph symbols ¶. You should not be able to see any line end symbols ↵ .

In practical terms, there is often no difference between using line breaks and paragraph breaks. However, when you have inserted information specific to a paragraph, such as space before and after, it can make a big difference.

6.3 The ¶ symbol

The ¶ symbol is important as it stores all the formatting information relating to that paragraph. (Information about margin widths, indentations, space before and after, and so on). It is important to realise that any formatting is stored in the ¶ symbol, not in the text itself. When you are cutting and pasting: if you cut and paste just words from a paragraph you will only transfer the words (and not the formatting); if you cut and paste words together with their ¶ symbol, you will also transfer the formatting held in the ¶.

6.4 Headers and footers

Headers and footers are lines of text inserted at the top and bottom of every page to give standard information throughout a document.

The kind of information that generally appears in headers and footers is:

- page number
- book or report title
- section title or other key words.

ACTIVITY 58

1 Open the document Cats.doc once again. You decide that you want to insert a header on every page giving the title of the book and the chapter number: 'The Unadulterated Cat' and 'Chapter 4: Types of cat'. In the footer, you just want to insert a page number.

2 Click on the Header|Footer command in the View menu. This will open up the Header (with the rest of your page greyed out if you have text already on your page). The cursor is automatically placed in the header and you can type in the information you want

   A small toolbar will also appear. We shall look at some of the options on the toolbar in the next activity.

3 Type in the following text to create a header looking like this:

   The Unadulterated Cat Chapter 4: Types of Cat

4 Close the header, using the Close button. Now the screen is once more entirely taken up with the main text file – so where is the header? The header is not visible in Normal page view. Go to View and select Page Layout. You should be able to see the header in its position at the top of the page. Go back to Normal view.

You should now have created the desired header on you document.

ACTIVITY 59

1 Select the Header | Footer command in the View menu. A header will appear along with the Header | Footer toolbar. To switch to the Footer section, click on the first button on the Header| Footer toolbar.

2 In the footer, all you want is the page number, centred on the page. Word will set automatic page numbers. Look at the toolbar, the following buttons are options for page number, date and time respectively:

3 Click once on the page number icon. You should see the number 1 appear in the footer. Centre this number within the margins and add a half-line

space before the paragraph (again to ensure some space between the footer and the main text of the document). Note that you can access the Paragraph command from the Format menu to achieve this. When you have done this, select Close.

4 Back in the main document, select Page Layout again to view the document as it will appear when it is printed out. Scroll right through the document. You can now see both the header and the footer in place.

You might want to put dates and times in the header or footer when you are printing out draft documents. With the date, you can easily identify the version you are looking at.

OPTIONS FOR HEADERS AND FOOTERS

There are a number of options available when inserting Headers and Footers. You can find out what they are by going to Page Setup in the File menu and opening the Layout page. These include:

Different First Page – This lets you set up a separate header/footer for the first page only of the document. This is useful if your first page is a cover page and you do not want to spoil the display effect. You could use this facility for your cover page of a long report.

Different Odds and Evens – In most books and reports like this one the right-hand pages have odd numbers, usually aligned to the right margin, while left-hand pages have even numbers, usually aligned to the left margin. If you plan to copy and bind your report so that printing appears on both sides of the paper, you might want to follow this pattern. Activate Different Odds and Evens and Word lets you set up different headers/footers for odd pages and even pages.

From Edge (this option is found on the margins page of Page Setup) – Lets you specify how close to the margin you want to place the header/footer.

6.5 Printing and preview

One of the buttons on the toolbar offers you a short cut to printing.

 This is the Print command. When you select this icon, the computer automatically prints out all the pages in the active document. The menu equivalent is to select File | Print.

The Print icon only allows you to print one copy of all the pages in your document, whereas File | Print offers you a range of different options.

There is another command which also enables you to view a page before printing: this is the Print Preview command.

ACTIVITY 60

1 Select the Print Preview command from the File menu. This shows you the document as it is ready to print out. You can use this as a final check to make sure that everything is in place and to spot any mistakes.

2 Click on Two Pages to view the document with two pages side by side.

3 Close this view.

4 Go to File | Print. A dialog window gives you various options about what to print, which pages, how many copies, whether to collate copies if you are printing more than one copy, and so on. Select Cancel.

5 Now use the Print icon on the toolbar to print out the document Cats.doc.

If you have any problems printing, you may need to seek advice from the person in charge of your training, a nearby helpdesk, or to consult your manual.

Summary

In this section you have learned additional features of Word. The common theme has been to look at ways of designing and editing your document to produced stylish finished work; and to do so as easily and efficiently as possible. The best way of becoming effective is to to practise on actual documents. On your next assignment, or your next business letter or report, or go back to some of the activities in Units 3 and 4, try out some different options. Vary the layout, highlighting techniques etc to get different effects. When you are happy with a particular style and layout for an assignment, a letter, a memo, for example, you can keep this as a 'template' on your computer and use it each time you have a similar document.

SECTION 7

Finishing your Documents and Moving Forward

Introduction

This section is different from the previous ones which focused on the techniques you need to know to use Word. Here we take a much broader look at ways of working so you can 'polish up' particular parts of a document by checking it for mistakes and making sure everything is as near perfect as possible. This is obviously important before you send out any letters etc, or submit a report to your boss. As you know from your work on communication, errors in written communication reflect badly on the sender.

You will use the file **Telefn.doc** in this section.

7.1 Checking text

When you have finished the basic work on your document you will want to check that the text is correct. You can do this by:

- Printing out the document.
- Read the document through on the screen and check for mistakes before printing.
- Print out the document and read through the print-out (also called hard copy) making any necessary changes on the computer before printing out again.
- Print it out and ask someone else to read through it for comment.
- Circulate the document to a number of different people and ask them to read it.

The amount of checking you do depends on:

- how important the document is
- who it is for
- whether it contains many figures or complicated text.

It is usually worth reading what you have typed on the screen before printing it out whether or not you also plan to check the print-out. Most people find it difficult to spot mistakes on screen. Some of the things that are most difficult to check on screen are:

- spacing errors: too much or too little space between words
- letters that look alike in some fonts: a capital 'i' and a small 'l' and the number '1' can all be very similar
- letters in italics which can be difficult to read.

WHAT TO CHECK

If you are new to wordprocessing you may not spend enough time checking your documents. Perhaps you have never been shown how. There are, after all, many things that you could check for. Some of the most important are:

- **Spelling:** Misspelled words are some of the most obvious mistakes in a document and can create the worst impression.
- **Missed out words or lines:** If the text does not read correctly it is very often because a vital word or phrase has been missed out.
- **Names, addresses, figures and dates:** An incorrect word in the text might be obvious because it does not make sense. It is often difficult to spot a name, address, date or figure that is incorrect.
- **Consistency:** Sometimes you have a choice about how to do things, such as:
  - how to spell particular words, whether to use '-ise' or '-ize' in words such as organise, realise
  - whether to use full stops in abbreviations, such as Dr, Ms, St.
  - whether to use single or double quotes
  - whether to use open or standard punctuation.
- **Figure:** Check that figures 'add up' correctly.
- **Alignment:** Check that you have correctly aligned everything.
- **Foreign words and phrases:** Check that these are spelled correctly and underlined or typed in italics, if necessary.

One quick read through might be all right for a short, simple document. At other times it is more suitable to read through once but then separately, one by one, to look at any figures in the text, to look at the overall layout and alignment and to check any other particular parts that need careful attention.

CHECKING LAYOUT

You have already used the Print Preview option which you can access either via the toolbar or the File menu in Word. This allows a check of the layout and it is often useful to view the pages of a document in this way if you have used features that do not show up in Normal view, such as text in two or more columns or pages with headers and footers.

The Page Layout option under the View menu offers you a similar facility to view text in its actual position.

7.2 Word's checking facilities

Word has a number of facilities that help you check and correct work. Many of these are found under the Tools menu. They include:

- Spelling
- Thesaurus
- Grammar.

SPELLING

The spelling facility in Word is extremely easy to use. However, it does not solve all spelling problems, as you will see.

ACTIVITY 61

1 Open the file Telefn.doc. Select Spelling from the Tools window. A dialog box will appear and Word will start checking the document immediately. The first misspelled word will appear in the Not in Dictionary box. The offending word is 'weappon'. Not only does the spelling checker find the word, but it makes a suggestion as to the most likely alternative and puts that suggestion directly into the Change To box. You now have several options:

- **Change** – just change this one mistake
- **Change All** – change every instance of the misspelling to the correct spelling
- **Ignore** – do not change the word, but look for other misspellings
- **Ignore All** – ignore all instances of the word it has identified
- **Add** – add the word to Word's dictionary so that it never queries it again.

Since this is a clear misspelling, change this example by selecting Change.

2 The spelling checker automatically moves to the next misspelling it has found which is 'dail'. (Note that, having changed the last word another option appears. This is Undo Last, i.e. change 'weapon' back to 'weappon'.)

3 Work through the complete document changing all the wrong spellings you find. As you work through it check your own corrected version of the document to see whether you spotted every mistake.

4 Look carefully at each suggestion that the spelling checker makes. It does not always get it exactly right. Can you find two examples of suggestions the spelling checker made that were wrong?

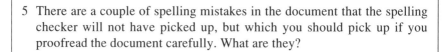

5   There are a couple of spelling mistakes in the document that the spelling checker will not have picked up, but which you should pick up if you proofread the document carefully. What are they?

6   Save the changes you have made to the document.

Did you (or Word) pick up the double word 'you you' in the fifth point under 'Before you telephone'? This is a classic mistake that the eye often misses as it expects to see only one you and so reads only one.

As for inappropriate suggestions, the computer suggested 'extenuation' for 'extension' which is completely wrong. It also suggested 'facile' instead of 'facial'. (If Word has made different suggestions for you this might be because you are using a later or modified version of the dictionary.)

The spelling checker will not have picked up the wrong spelling of 'piece'. As far as it is concerned the word 'peace' exists so it passes over it. In the same sentence the word 'or' (which should be 'of') will also have been overlooked because 'or' is spelled correctly although incorrectly used. It also missed 'breathes' which is correct as a verb, but wrong as a noun and should have been 'breaths'.

What about the mistakes in the two headings 'Understanding what's said' and 'Ending your telephone call'? Oddly enough, the larger the mistake (in terms of size of type), the easier it is to miss.

It is important to remember that using the automatic spelling checker will not correct all mistakes. You still have to make decisions yourself.

THESAURUS
A thesaurus is a reference work that lists words, alphabetically or by subject, giving other words that mean broadly the same thing. These are called **synonyms.** Some thesauruses also list words that mean the opposite: these are called **antonyms.**

Word has its own thesaurus, which is more simply arranged as a list of synonyms. You can select any word in a document and consult the thesaurus to find another word of the same broad meaning. Again, this facility is very easy to use.

ACTIVITY 62

1 Open the file Telefn.doc. On reading the first paragraph you decide that you want another word for 'topic' as you have used this word lots of times already.

2 Place the cursor anywhere in the word 'topic'. Select Thesaurus from the Tools window. A dialog box will appear and Word will automatically suggest synonyms for 'topic'. It might suggest 'issue' which seems reasonable. Therefore, select Replace to change the word automatically from 'topic' to 'issue'. Select Cancel to close the Thesaurus window.

3 Now select 'instrument' in the next line and consult the thesaurus.

   (a) What word is suggested? Do you accept the suggestion?

   (b) If not, what would you replace 'instrument' with?

   Make the appropriate change and return to the main document.

4 Next select 'fuss' in the same sentence. Before choosing a word to replace it look in the Meanings box. Select the option Antonyms. You should now see that the Thesaurus has listed a range of words with the opposite meaning in the box to the right. Clearly you do not want to use any of them. Therefore go back to the Meanings menu and select 'Commotion (noun)' from the menu as this is the meaning of fuss you want to find synonyms for. The list of synonyms reappears. Select one you think appropriate.

   What did you choose?

5 Find a suitable alternative word for each of the following:

   (a) guidelines (end of first paragraph)

   (b) pompous (point 2 under 'Making your point')

   (c) check (point 1 under 'Ending your telephone call').

6 Save the changes you have made to the document.

Here are some suggestions for suitable synonyms:

1   (a) The thesaurus offers 'tool' instead of 'instrument'.

(b) Did you think 'device' is a better choice?

2   The thesaurus suggests 'commotion' instead of 'fuss'. 'Trouble' might be better.

3   The thesaurus in the our version of Word cannot offer any alternatives to 'guidelines'. If this is the case, you either have to think yourself or look up the word in a printed thesaurus.

4   There are many good words suggested under 'pompous' such as 'arrogant', 'fat-headed', 'inflated', 'conceited'.

5   When you searched for 'check', the thesaurus will have identified a lot of different possible meanings, starting with 'barrier'. That is not the meaning you want so you have to look down the list of meanings until you reach 'verify' (verb) which is what you want. When you select it you find a number of suitable synonyms of which 'confirm' seems a reasonable one.

As with so many other features of word processors, the Thesaurus offers some excellent short cuts but your own judgement must still be used to find the most suitable solution to your problem.

GRAMMAR

Word will also check your grammar. The Grammar command on the Tools menu carries out an analysis of your document and highlights any sentences which break rules that have been programmed into its memory.

As with the spell checker, the grammar checker can check either the whole document or a selection of the document. If the grammar checker finds a sentence with questionable grammar or style, it displays it in the grammar dialog box. Words related to the suggested error are displayed in red type. The grammar checker displays suggested corrections in the suggestions box.

There are several options for further action once a sentence has been highlighted by the grammar checker:

- **Ignore** – asks the checker to look for the next 'mistake'.
- **Next Sentence** – asks the checker to start looking at the next sentence.
- **Ignore Rule** – asks to ignore all instances of run-on sentences.
- **Cancel** – takes you back to the main text of the document.
- **Explain** – explains more about the rule it says has been broken.
- **Options** – offers other options about the way the grammar checker analyses the document, such as very strictly or quite casually, and lets you customise the settings.

There are different options available in Word when checking grammar, the program can allow for different styles of writing, for example Casual Writing or Business Writing, where the checker queries things pertaining to the particular style of document being written. These options are available in Grammar in the Tools menu, under the section Options.

If you are unsure about a point of grammar or feel grammar is a weakness then using the Grammar command will give you the extra security of knowing a check has been made. However, the grammar checker can also be very time consuming with very little result. Use it once or twice and make up your own mind about whether it is useful to you.

7.3 Replace command

The Replace command can be very useful in polishing your documents. This can be found in the Edit menu. It lets you carry out a search within the document for all examples of a word or phrase and replace it with another one.

For example, if you were writing a short story and you decided to change the name of the main character from Maureen to Jenny, the Replace command will do this automatically. Simply type 'Maureen' in the Find What box that appears in the Replace dialog box and type 'Jenny' in the Replace With box. The Replace command will also find examples of 'Maureen's' and change them to 'Jenny's'. (Strictly speaking, it will change just the name; the 's remains unchanged.)

ACTIVITY 63

1   Open the document Telefn.doc and make sure the cursor is positioned at the start of the document. To change 'phone' to 'telephone' throughout the document. Open the Replace command and type in the relevant words in the dialog box.

2   Select Find Next to ask the computer to find the next example of the word 'telephone' which it should find in the main heading. The word is highlighted in the text and you now have the option to select Replace or to Replace All. Select Replace – it changes just that one example and then starts looking for the next one, which it finds in the first paragraph.

3   Change that one and then find and replace all examples of 'telephone' in the text. There should be four in total.

4   You could have selected Replace All to carry out the same operation but you should think carefully before using this command. For example, you decide that you actually prefer the more formal 'telephone' to 'phone'. Start by manually replacing the word 'phone' in the main heading back to 'telephone'.

5 Now open the Replace command and type in 'phone' in the Find What box and 'telephone' in the Replace With box. Select Replace All.

(a) What mishap has occurred?

(b) Looking at the Replace dialog window, can you see a way that this could have been avoided?

You should have found that the computer has picked up the '-phone' part of 'telephone' in the main heading and changed that so that you now have 'teletelephone'. Similarly, if you had decided to search for examples of the abbreviation 'eg' to change them to 'e.g.', the Replace All command would have found the word 'begin' and changed it to 'be.g.in'.

To avoid this problem select Match Whole Word only. This would have ignored both 'telephone' and 'begin' when looking for 'phone' and 'eg'.

There are a range of other options for customising your search.

Remember:

- If you highlight a piece of text before going into the Replace box the program will search only through the highlighted text.
- The Find command under the Edit menu can be used when you just want to find text/styles/formatting without changing it.

7.4 Some advanced features of Word

Word is a comprehensive wordprocessing package; it covers an enormous range of potential uses and users. Many of the features will only be useful to a specialised group of users. Here we give a brief summary of some advanced features of Word. Some of these you will be able to use for specialised business use as you develop both your computer and communication skills.

FILE | TEMPLATE
A template is a file where you can store information about margins, page layout, text and heading styles, headers and footers and so on. Whenever you open the template you create a new document with all these pre-programmed styles. You can then work on and save the new document, leaving the template unchanged, ready for the next occasion when you need the same format.

This is useful if you want to use a standard format for documents, such as letterheads, a standard style for essays or reports, an invoice pro forma.

TOOLS I MAIL MERGE

This lets you merge your Word file with a data file so that the two are combined when printing. For example, you can take the text of a letter and combine it with 100 names and addresses in a data file to print out 100 personalised copies of the letter. You might use this for a sales letter or a questionnaire in a business environment.

INSERT I FOOTNOTE

Footnotes are notes of reference, explanation or comment.

- You can insert a reference mark like this [1] anywhere in the text.

- You then write the note and position it either at the bottom of the page or at the end of the document.

- Word automatically numbers all your footnotes in sequence. It will renumber them if you insert or delete a footnote.

This might be useful in writing your assignments or in a lengthy business report. In your further studies it is useful in writing academic theses or dissertations.

EDIT I BOOKMARK

Bookmarks in Word are like real bookmarks. You use them to mark a particular page or piece of text in a book.

- You can insert a bookmark anywhere in a document.

- You can then quickly find that place by telling the computer to find the bookmark.

- The bookmark can be used to create automatic cross-references. If, for example, you want to say 'see the section on borders on page [whatever]', you can create a bookmark at the relevant page, and the program will automatically insert the correct page number when you print out.

- The bookmark can be used to mark numbers that you want to use in a calculation throughout your document. If you change the 'bookmarked' number at any time, all the other references to the number will automatically change too.

Again if you are working on a long essay for an assignment, or a long report, this is useful if you are dealing with numerous references or other text references.

INSERT I ANNOTATION

Annotations are initialled comments that an author or reviewer can add to a document. The reviewer's initials appear in the document as Hidden Text.

This is useful if you are circulating documents for review by other people.

INSERT I FIELD

A field is a set of codes that retrieves and displays information from other places in your document, other documents, other programs, or the computer's own date and time calendar. Fields save you the work of manually updating parts of your document.

This is useful if you are working on documents that regularly need updating or have a large number of references.

INSERT I SYMBOL

You can insert symbols into the text that are not readily accessible from the keyboard. These include: bullets; fractions; non-English letters; and lots of other characters that may be useful. You may need these in particular business environments, for example, technical specifications or foreign addresses.

INSERT I INDEX AND TABLES...

Index

An index can be created for your document by marking particular words or phrases in the text. The computer automatically gathers the references, plus their page numbers, into an index.

Table of Contents

An automatic table of contents can be created for your document. The computer will search for headings (provided they have been given a heading style), gather them together in a table at the start of your document, and add the correct page numbers automatically. You will find these facilities useful for long reports.

INSERT I FILE

You can insert the text from another file into your active one.

INSERT I PICTURE

 You can add graphics to your Word file, which you have drawn in another application. You can then:

- crop and scale the graphic
- apply borders
- position the graphics on a page.

Word also comes with a drawing tool, *Microsoft Draw,* which lets you create and insert new graphics and edit existing graphics. The Toolbar icon is shown above. These facilities are useful in preparing reports and presentations. However, you do need to be quite skilled to get the most out of them.

GRAPHS

 You can create graphs of all sorts using a special tool called *Microsoft Graph.* The icon, as shown on the left, is on the Toolbar. Enter data and the program converts it into whatever form of graph you choose: bar chart, column chart, pie chart, line graph.

INSET I OBJECT

If you create items in other programs, such as charts, graphics and spreadsheets you can bring them into Word using this command. You embed them as 'objects' and can often also edit these objects.

FORMAT I COLUMNS

The text can be arranged in two or more columns on the page, either the whole document or just part of it. When you have only part of your text in two columns, Word separates out that text into a new Section. You can then specify the format for each particular section of the document.

These are useful if you are laying out text in a more complicated and attractive way, particularly reports, tables, newsletters.

TOOLS I ENVELOPES AND LABELS

Use this feature to type in and print out envelopes and labels automatically without having to spend time adjusting margins.

TOOLS I REVISIONS

Creates revision marks which enable a record of every change made to a document to be kept, and later accept or reject each revision.

This is useful if you need to keep track of changes you, or other people, have made to a document.

TOOLS I COMPARE VERSIONS

You can compare different versions of a document when you save them with different file-names. For example, to see changes after you edit a document.

This is useful if you are an editor, administrator, report-writer, and you have updated documents and want to see the changes you have made.

TABLE I SORT TEXT

This automatically arranges lines of text in alphabetical or numerical order.

TOOLS I MACRO

A **Macro** is a custom-made command that will carry out a number of other commands in one go. For example if you want to pick out a number of words in the text that are currently 10 pt Times Italic and make them 12 Univers Bold Superscript, you can record a **Macro** that does this. You only need one action to carry out all the changes.

TABLE

You can create a table in Word where the rows and columns are made up of cells. Each cell has its own text area within which text wraps round. This avoids the problems created by tables made up of tabs when you want to insert or delete text, or change its size.

Borders and shading can be added to the table as a whole or to individual cells. When a table is created using Word a whole set of options becomes active under the Table menu.

You have now an overall view of most of the features of Word. There are other even more specialised functions that the application can perform which you may use with more experience.

If you did not understand any of the descriptions given, you can use the Help option in Word, which gives more explanation and instructions.

7.5 Using the Help menu

Word comes equipped with an excellent Help facility. This is a source of information which you can call up at any time to get help on how to carry out a particular operation.

Word offers different types of help:

- **Help index** – a reference guide
- **Tutorial help** – a learning guide.

HELP INDEX

The Help Index lets you select any particular topic and find out what it is and how to use it. At the top of the Help Index window there is a number of buttons which, like the Toolbar, offer you short cut routes to some very useful functions. These are:

- **Index** – takes you back to the complete list of topics.
- **Search** – brings up a list of related topics.
- **Back** – takes you back, one-by-one, through all the windows you have viewed since opening the Help window.
- **Browse** – takes you, one-by-one, through all the windows in a topic. You can use the two different browse buttons to browse either backwards or forwards.

Help offers you an extremely comprehensive guide to using Word.

TUTORIAL HELP

Tutorial help is available through the Help menu with the two commands of Getting Started and Learning Word.

These both contain a selection of tutorials that take you step by step through various aspects of using Word. They are excellent ways of getting to know aspects of the program as they give you the chance to perform actions within the program itself. They are fully interactive, letting you make decisions and choices.

Summary

You will have discovered that wordprocessing is more than just tapping a few keys and pressing a few buttons. To produce impressive and attractive documents you have to spend some time checking both the overall effect and the details of your document. This section should have helped you become skilled at both these things.

You should now realise that if you use the automatic tools offered by Word you need to handle them carefully as they will never pick up every mistake or inconsistency.

Used carefully and creatively, however, Word is a powerful tool for meeting virtually any document-creation need which you may have.With practice, you will be able to match the techniques in this unit with the communications objectives in Units 3 and 4.

Unit Summary

In this unit, you will have experienced the basics of the wordprocessing software Word 6. Remember that the objective of this unit is not that you should *memorise* every fact and detail. There is simply too much to know about modern computers and their software! Your aim should be to know enough so that most (perhaps 80%) of the time you can get on with your work without delay, and that when you need to use a skill you have forgotten, or perhaps never even come across before, you can find out the answer quickly and easily.

UNIT 7

SPREADSHEETS USING EXCEL

Introduction

Just as a wordprocessing software package is largely a means of processing and formatting **text,** so a spreadsheet is largely a means of processing and formatting **numbers.** This is an oversimplification of what a modern spreadsheet has to offer.

The spreadsheet that you will be using in this unit is Excel. This runs under Windows, that you learnt in Unit 5.

Objectives

By the end of this unit you will be able to:

- use Excel to create a small worksheet
- develop techniques in using spreadsheets
- use formulae and functions
- apply various formats to the worksheet
- create charts of various types
- understand some more advanced functions of Excel
- develop further skills in worksheet organisation.

SECTION 1

Introduction to Spreadsheets

As an example of how a spreadsheet could be used, a European Union directive from Brussels requires all food shops to display the price per kilogram weight of loose food items. Previously the shops had displayed the price per pound weight. This requires a fairly simple calculation to convert from pounds to kilograms. You could use a calculator, but you would have to perform a new calculation for each price. With a spreadsheet you could perform millions of calculations at the same time!

In fact, Excel version 5 has a grid of 256 by 16,384 'cells'; this gives over 4 million cells, each of which can be considered as a multi-function programmable calculator. Moreover the cells can be linked so that the result of a cell can be used by other cells. This can be enormously powerful.

Spreadsheets are widely used for:

- Control of departmental budgets
- Balance sheets
- Decision trees
- Business accounts
- Sales invoices
- Data analysis.

ACTIVITY 1

You will need to be using a computer with Excel installed.

1 You need to be in Windows. If Windows is not all ready open run it now.

2   Find the Excel icon and double click to open the application.

When Excel finishes loading you will see the Excel opening screen. An example is shown in Figure 1.

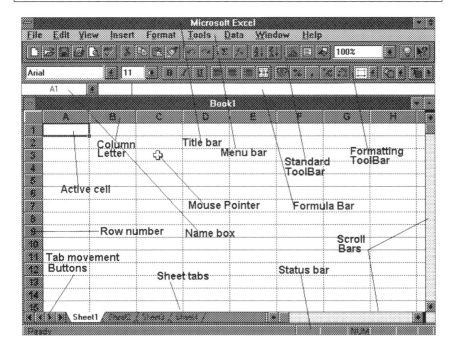

Figure 1: Excel opening screen

The opening screen that you see on the computer may look slightly different from Figure 1 since it is possible to reconfigure Excel. If the screen that you see when you start up Excel is slightly different then don't worry, you haven't made an error.

You should see:

- Title bar
- Standard Toolbar
- Formatting Toolbar
- Active Cell
- Column Letter
- Menu Bar
- Scroll Bars.

The grid that occupies the larger part of the diagram in Figure 1 consists of a large number of 'cells' only a few of which can be seen on the screen at any one time.

1.1 Cell attributes

Each cell has a list of 'attributes'. We will concern ourselves here with just three attributes:

- cell reference address
- cell contents
- active cell.

CELL REFERENCE ADDRESS

At the top of the grid of cells you will see a row of letters ('column letter' in Figure 1) and on the left side you will see a column of numbers ('row number' in Figure 1). Each cell can be referenced by giving the column letter for the cell followed by the row number for the cell. The cell at the top left corner of the grid in Figure 1 is cell A1.

ACTIVITY 2

Use the spreadsheet which is open on the screen. Place the mouse pointer over the appropriate cell and click the left button on the mouse.

1 Click in the first cell in the top left corner – cell A1. Type in A1. Press <Return>.

2 Move the mouse and click in the first box in column D. Type in D1. Press <Return>.

3. Click in each of the following cells and type in the cell address:

- A2
- D5
- B3
- C9
- E14.

CELL CONTENT

Each cell can contain data. The data may be text, a number or a formula. Text is often used to provide 'labels' for columns or rows of data.

ACTIVITY 3

Start with a new worksheet.

1 Using the mouse, highlight cell B1 and type in 'Pre-tax Profits'.

2 In cell A2, type in January

3 In cell A3,type in February

4 In cell A4, type in March

5 In cell B2, type in 5987.95

6 In cell B3, type in 5240.80

7 In cell B4, type in 6347.25

Activity 3 has shown you that a cell might contain text (in this example the label 'Pre-tax Profits') that gives a meaning to a column of numbers. Or a cell might contain a number (e.g. 5987.95) that represents a value.

Your spreadsheet should now look like this:

	A	B	C
1		**Pre-tax Profits**	
2	**January**	5987.95	
3	**February**	5240.80	
4	**March**	6347.25	

The labels show that the number 5987.95 represents the Pre-tax Profit value for January.

ACTIVE CELL

In Figure 1 you will notice that cell A1 has been labelled 'Active Cell'. This means that anything you type would go into cell A1 and become *the contents of* A1. There are two ways of determining which is the active cell:

● The cell has a thicker border than other cells.

● The address is displayed in the Name box (A1 in Figure 1).

When a cell contains a label or a number that is also what you will see when you look at the cell. However, if the cell contains a formula, the cell will display the result but not the formula. This means that it is not always possible to know the contents of a cell by looking at what that cell displays. Formulae are displayed in the formula bar. You will learn about formulae later in the unit.

You may change the active cell by pressing the arrow keys in the appropriate direction or by placing the mouse pointer over the new cell and clicking the left button.

ACTIVITY 4

1 Note the address of the active cell by looking at the address co-ordinates, or by looking at the Name Box (see Figure1).

2 Press the right arrow key.

3 What is now the address of the active cell?

4 Press the down arrow key twice.

5 What is the address of the active cell?

6 Press the up arrow key once and then the left arrow key once.

7 What is the address of the active cell?

You should now see that each press of an arrow key will move the active cell one cell in the direction of the arrow key if that is possible. If the active cell address is B1, then pressing the up arrow key will not change the address (address B0 doesn't exist). Similarly, if the address of the active cell is A5, then pressing the left arrow key will not change the address because there is no column to the left of column A.

In Figure 1 the address of the cell visible in the top right corner of the grid is H1. If you move to cell H1 and then press the right arrow key then cell G1 becomes the active cell and column G becomes visible. Using the arrow keys you can move the active cell to any cell between the addresses A1 (top left corner) and address IV16384 (the bottom right corner). You can view the portions of the grid that are currently off-screen by operating the vertical and horizontal scroll bars, but doing this doesn't change the address of the active cell.

ACTIVITY 5

1 Note the address of the active cell.

2 Click and hold on the right arrow box on the horizontal scroll bar until column Z becomes visible, then release the mouse button.

3 Look at the Name box. The active cell address has not changed.

The cell is the smallest element in Excel that can contain data. The collection of cells that can be made visible using the scroll bars is called a 'Worksheet'.

1.2 Entering and changing data

ENTERING DATA
You can enter three kinds of data into a cell:

- numbers
- text
- equations.

Excel is a fairly intelligent package and will treat data entry that consists only of digits and decimal points (e.g. 23, 41.6) as numbers, and data that contains non-digits as text (e.g. Sales, 123AB600).

One of the most useful and powerful uses of Excel is to apply an equation to a series of figures. If the content of the cell is to be an equation then the first character entered must be the 'equals' symbol (e.g. =5+7, =23.9-15.875).

Activity 6 helps you to explore entering numbers, text and equations into cells.

ACTIVITY 6

Entering a number

1 Make cell A1 the active cell.

2 Type 7321 and press enter.

3 Note the display of cell A1.

4 Note the address of the active cell (it is not A1).

5 Type Excel and then press the right arrow key.

6 Note the address of the active cell (it should be B2).

Entering an equation

7 Press the right arrow key (the result, 35, should be displayed).

8 Note the address of the active cell (it should be B3).

9 Make B2 the active cell.

Note the displayed contents of cell B2 and the displayed value on the formula bar. (The formula bar displays the formula used and the cell displays the evaluated result of the formula.)

CHANGING DATA

There are two ways of changing the data that is already in a cell:

- Overtyping
- Editing.

To overtype the data in a cell you simply make that cell the active cell and then type the correct data and press enter (or an arrow key). The old contents of the cell will be deleted and the new contents will be displayed.

ACTIVITY 7

Continue using your worksheet from Activity 6.

1   Make cell A1 the active cell (A1 should contain the number 7321 that was entered in Activity 6. If it doesn't then enter the number into cell A1 and start this activity again).

2   Type 534 and press enter.

3   Note that the displayed contents of cell A1 have now changed to 534.

4   Make cell B2 the active cell. (B2 should contain the formula =5*7 that was entered in Activity 6. If it doesn't then enter the formula and start this step again).

5   Move the mouse pointer over the formula bar and click when the I-beam is to the left of the 7 in the formula. (If you miss the position you can click again with the mouse or move the cursor with the arrow keys.)

6   Press the delete key once and type 8 (the formula should now read =5*8), then press enter.

7   Note the displayed value for cell B2 (it should be 40).

8   Change the active cell to C1 and enter the formula =B2*2 and press the enter key. (The displayed result should now be 80 for cell C1. You have just entered a formula to multiply the contents cell B2 by 2.)

9   Make B2 the active cell again. Change the formula from =5*8 to =2*8. Note the displayed value for cell B2 (it should be 16).

10 Look at cell C1. What is the value displayed?

The displayed value in cell C1 should be 32 (which is twice the value of B2).

Steps 9 and 10 above illustrate an important feature of Excel. **If the contents of cell B2 are changed, then the displayed value of cell C1 will also change** since we have provided a link between cell B2 and cell C1. By default Excel recalculates cells automatically.

BLANKING CELLS

If you have completed the previous activities then some cells will currently display contents. You will now delete the contents of these cells so that you have a grid displayed with no cell contents. If you have entered data into additional cells then modify the steps in Activity 4 to blank them.

ACTIVITY 8

1 Make cell A1 the active cell.

2 Press the delete key (cell A1 becomes blank).

3 Make cell A2 the active cell.

4 Press the delete key (cell A2 becomes blank).

5 Carry out the appropriate steps to blank cells B2 and C1.

1.3 Constructing a small worksheet

Now that you have a blank grid displayed you can construct a small worksheet. For Activity 9 you are going to construct a small worksheet. It consists of four columns and four rows.

ACTIVITY 9

The first column consists of labels ('Sales', 'Costs', and 'Profit') and the first row consists of labels ('Jan', 'Feb', and 'Mar').

1 Choose cell B1. Type Jan and press the right arrow key.

You should see 'Jan' in cell B1 and cell C1 should be the active cell.

2 Type Feb and press the right arrow key.

You should see 'Feb' in cell C1 and cell D1 should be the active cell.

3 Type Mar and press the right arrow key.

You should see 'Mar' in cell D1 and cell E1 should be the active cell.

4 Choose cell A2. Type Sales and press the <u>down</u> arrow key.

You should see 'Sales' in cell A2 and cell A3 should be the active cell.

5 Type Costs and press the down arrow key.

You should see 'Costs' in cell A3 and cell A4 should be the active cell.

6 Type Profit and press the down arrow key.

You should see 'Profit' in cell A4 and cell A5 should be the active cell.

Your worksheet should now contain the labels. It should look like this:

	A	B	C	D
1		Jan	Feb	Mar
2	Sales			
3	Cost			
4	Profits			

In Activity 10 you will continue entering the numbers.

ACTIVITY 10

1 Choose cell B2. Type 12500 and press the right arrow key.

You should now see '12500' in cell B2 and cell C2 should be the active cell

2 Type 14950 and press the right arrow key.

You should now see '14950' in cell C2 and cell D2 should be the active cell.

3 Type 13590 and press the right arrow key.

You should now see '13590' in cell D2 and cell E2 should be the active cell.

4 Choose cell B3. Type 7500 and press the right arrow key.

You should now see '7500' in cell B3 and cell C3 should be the active cell.

Your worksheet should now contain some of the numbers. It should look like this:

	A	B	C	D
1		Jan	Feb	Mar
2	**Sales**	12500	14950	13590
3	**Cost**		7500	
4	**Profits**			

For this worksheet the costs each month are the same. The next activity shows you how to make the February and March costs the same as those for January.

In the next activity, you will copy cells.

ACTIVITY 11

1 You should still have C3 as your active cell. Type =B3 and press the right arrow key.

You should now see '7500' in cell C3 and cell D3 should be the active cell. You have made the contents of cell C3 equal to the contents of cell B3 (=B3). Remember if the value in B3 changes, so will the value in C3.

2 The active cell is D3. Type =B3 and press the right arrow key.

What value do you see in cell D3?

You will see a displayed value of 7500 in cell D3. By using the equation =B3 you can copy the value of B3 into other cells.

In the 'Profit' row, you do not need to enter numbers at all because Profit is a formula. The profit is calculated as the difference between the sales and the costs, Profit = Sales – Costs.

In Activity 12 you will enter a formula.

ACTIVITY 12

1 Choose cell B4.

2 Type =B2-B3 and press the right arrow key.

3 C4 is the active cell. Type =C2-C3 and press the right arrow key.

4 D4 is now the active cell. Type =D2-D3 and press the right arrow key.

What do you see displayed in cells B4, C4, and D4?

You will notice that you have instructed Excel to perform the profit calculations for you. This is very important, you should *never* perform a calculation yourself when using Excel – *always* get Excel to do it for you.

Your completed worksheet should look like this:

	A	B	C	D
1		Jan	Feb	Mar
2	**Sales**	12500	14950	13590
3	**Costs**	7500	7500	7500
4	**Profits**	5000	7450	6090

SAVING YOUR WORK

Saving your worksheet should be familiar to you, as it is the same procedure used by Word, the word processing package. In Activity 12 you will need a formatted disk in drive A with at least 20Kbytes of free space.

ACTIVITY 13

1 Click on File on the menu bar (see Figure 1).

2 Click on Save As.

3 Choose drive A and select an appropriate subdirectory to store your spreadsheet. Change the file name from the current default to first and leave the file extension as .xls.

4 Click on OK.

Note that Excel expects worksheet files to have a file extension of .xls.

If you have previously saved your work then you choose Save in step 2 and not Save As unless you want to save your work with a different name or in a different location.

Summary

In this section you have learned:

- how to start Excel from the Windows Program Manager
- the names given to some parts of the Excel screen, and the essential features of a spreadsheet and its base element – a cell
- about cell addresses and cell contents, including the different data types that a cell may have
- how to enter text and numbers to make a table
- how to copy one cell to another
- how to enter a formula
- how to change the data contained in a cell as well as how to blank a cell
- how to save a worksheet to disk.

SECTION 2

Basic Excel Techniques

Introduction

The techniques in this section will enable you to become more efficient when you design a worksheet.

2.1 Moving around the sheet

To be able to enter anything in a worksheet you need to know how to move about. As you have already seen, the four arrow keys and clicking the mouse when it is positioned over a cell can be used to change the active cell (i.e. the one you want to enter data in or format, etc).

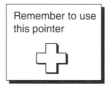

You can use the mouse or the keyboard to move around the worksheet. However, sometimes the active cell does not change. Table 1 summarises the most common methods. Sometimes two keys are used together. For example, where you see CTRL+Home this means depress and do not release the control key, then press the home key and finally release both keys.

Method	Result	Changes active cell?
Page Up Key	Moves up one full screen	Yes
Page Down Key	Moves down one full screen	Yes
Home Key	Moves to leftmost cell in current row	Yes
CTRL+Home Keys	Moves to cell A1	Yes
ALT+Page Up Keys	Moves one full screen to the left	Yes
ALT+Page Down Keys	Moves one full screen to the right	Yes
Horizontal Scroll Bar with mouse	Moves left or right	No
Vertical Scroll Bar	Moves up or down	No
Click mouse pointer in Name Box, type in cell reference and press ENTER	Moves to requested cell	Yes
Function Key F5	Moves to requested cell	Yes

Table 1: Methods of moving around the sheet

The last method in Table1 requires further explanation. When you press F5, you are using the shortcut key for the Edit, Go To command. A dialog box appears as in Figure 2.

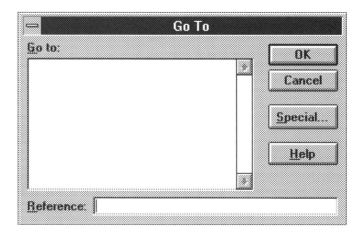

Figure 2: Go To dialog box

Notice that the insertion point is in the Reference text box. You are being invited to type in the cell reference of the cell you want to go to. Once you have typed in a valid cell reference (e.g. Z9) you click the OK command button in the dialog box to carry out the action. In Activities 14 and 15, you experiment with keyboard and mouse movements.

ACTIVITY 14

Make A1 the active cell.

1   Press Page Down

Which is the active cell? _____

2   Press ALT+Page Down

Which is the active cell? _____

3   Press Home

Which is the active cell? _____

4   Press CTRL+Home

Which is the active cell? _____

5   Press F5 and in the cell reference text box type AA100, then click the OK command button

Which is the active cell? _____ _____

6 Press F5 again and notice the contents of the cell reference box (this should be highlighted and be the address of the cell you came from). You can return to this cell by clicking OK. (To go to another cell simply enter its reference in the cell reference box then click OK.)

Which is the active cell? _____

7 Click the mouse pointer in the Name Box (see Figure 1),delete the current contents, type in AA1 and press ENTER.

Which is the active cell? _____

Note your answers to questions 1 and 2 will depend on the number of cells your computer is displaying.

ACTIVITY 15

Ensure that the active cell is A1 (use CTRL+HOME)

1 Click the "down" scroll button.

By how many cells did the worksheet move? _____

Did the active cell change? _____

2 Click the scroll bar in the grey area under the scroll box.

By how many cells did the worksheet move? _____

Did the active cell change? _____

3 Click the scroll bar in the grey area above the scroll box.

Did the active cell change? _____

4 Drag the scroll box downwards.

Did the active cell change? _____

Note your first answer to question 2 will depend on the number of cells your computer is displaying.

You may find it useful to refer to Table 1 to check your answers.

2.2 Selecting cells

In order to carry out many basic Excel operations (e.g., changing the appearance of the cell contents to bold) you must first select the cell or cells on which you want to perform the operation. You can carry out cell selection in many ways, although those we describe here will be sufficient for most of your work.

SELECTING A SINGLE CELL

Selecting a single cell is the same as making that cell the active cell. You have already encountered this in section 2.1 where you entered and edited data in the active (or selected) cell. However, there are a number of operations on cells, other than enter and edit data, where you may want to perform the same operation on a number of cells. You could select each cell and then perform the operation individually, but this would be very time consuming if a large number of cells were involved. For example, you might wish to underline or make bold all of your column headings.

Excel allows you to select multiple cells on which to perform such operations.

SELECTING A RANGE OF ADJACENT CELLS

We use the following convention to define a range of cells:

- identify the address of the cell that forms the top left corner of the cell range

- identify the address of the cell that forms the bottom right corner of the cell range.

In Figure 3 the address of the cell in the top left corner is cell A1 and the address of the cell in the bottom right corner is C6. We will describe this range as A1 to C6, and will use a similar means of describing ranges of cells in Activities 16 and 17.

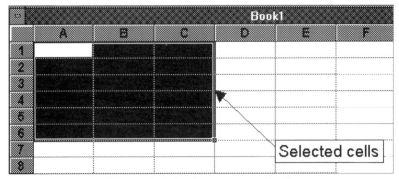

Figure 3: Selecting a range of cells

To cancel ranges already selected simply click on another cell. That cell becomes selected and all others become deselected.

There are two main methods that may be used to select a range of adjacent cells and you will practice these in Activities 16 and 17. The method described in Activity 17 is more useful when part of the range of cells to be selected is not visible on screen at the same time.

ACTIVITY 16

1   Move the mouse pointer so that it is over cell A1.

2   Press the left mouse button and keeping it pressed drag the mouse down and to the right until the mouse pointer is over cell C6. You will notice that as you drag the mouse pointer over cells they appear black as shown in Figure 3.

3   When the mouse pointer is over cell C6 release the mouse button. Your screen should look similar to Figure 3 – if it isn't then click on any cell and then start the activity from step 1.

ACTIVITY 17

Selecting a Range of Adjacent Cells (A3 to M7)

1   Make cell A3 the active cell.

2   Using the scroll bars if necessary, make cell M7 visible on screen.

3   Place the mouse cursor over (BUT DO NOT CLICK) cell M7.

4   Press and hold down the Shift key.

5   Click with the left mouse button and then release the shift key.

6   Check using the scroll bars that the range of cells, A3 to M7, has been selected.

SELECTING AN ENTIRE ROW OR COLUMN

To select a single column, position the mouse pointer on the column letter (see Figure 4) of the column you want to select and click the left mouse button. Selecting a single row is similar except the mouse pointer must be on the row number (see Figure 1) of the row you want to select. Be careful to use the same mouse pointer as for cell selection above. Remember that there are many different mouse pointers in Excel, depending on the mouse position.

ACTIVITY 18

1 Move the mouse pointer until it is over the column letter of column B.

2 Click with the left mouse button.

3 Check that column B has been selected as in Figure 4.

4 Move the mouse pointer to cell A3.

5 Click the left mouse button.

6 Check what has happened. (You should find that column B has been deselected and cell A3 is the active (selected) cell.)

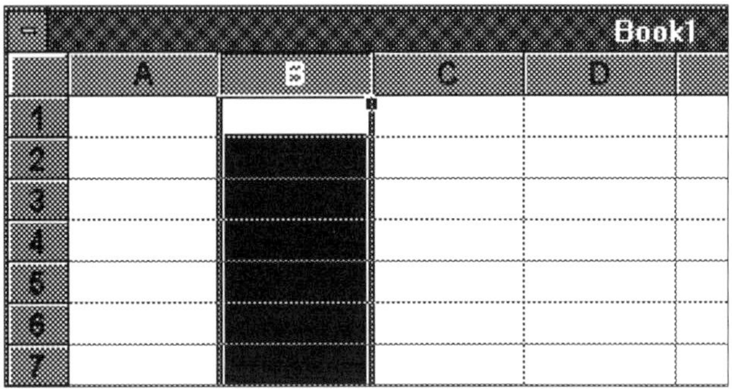

Figure 4: Column B selected

This selection can be extended to select adjacent multiple columns or rows using either of the methods in Activities 17 and 18. You will meet selecting non-adjacent cells shortly.

SELECTING THE ENTIRE WORKSHEET

Above the row headings and to the left of the column headings is an unmarked grey button (Figure 5). Clicking on this will select the entire worksheet. You try this in Activity 19.

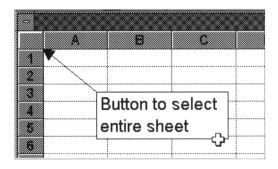

Figure 5: Selecting the entire worksheet

ACTIVITY 19

1 Click on the button shown in Figure 5 to select the entire worksheet.

2 Observe what happens. (The visible portion of the worksheet should now show in black indicating it is selected.)

3 Use the scroll bars to look at other parts of the worksheet. Make sure that you have selected the entire worksheet.

SELECTING NON-ADJACENT CELLS OR RANGES

To select non-adjacent cells or ranges you can use one of two methods.

Method One (as in Activity 16)

Select the first range of cells using the drag method. You may then select additional cell ranges using the drag method but holding down the CTRL key whilst doing it. For example to select cells A1 to C6 and then cells F1 to H7:

- select A1 to C6 as in Activity 16
- hold down the CTRL key and drag from F1 to H7.

Both ranges of cells will then be selected.

Method Two (as in Activity 17)

Select the first range of cells using the Shift key method. To select a second hold down the CTRL key whilst selecting the first (top left corner) cell of an additional range but hold down only the Shift key whilst selecting the second (bottom right corner) of the additional range. For example to select cells A3 to M7 and then cells P1 to T7:

- select A3 to M7 as in Activity 17
- hold down the CTRL key to select cell P1
- hold down the Shift key to select T7.

Both ranges of cells will then be selected.

You can apply this technique to non-adjacent rows and/or columns.

If you accidentally select more cells than you require, you will need to start the selection process again.

In Activity 20 you format text in ranges of cells. Formatting of text in Excel is very similar to the text formatting you met in Unit 5, Word 6. You will meet formatting cells later in the unit; we introduce it here simply to illustrate a use for cell range selection.

ACTIVITY 20

1   Open the worksheet called 'select.xls' on your module disk.

2   Select cells B2 to D2.

3   Press the Bold button on the Formatting Toolbar (see Figure 1).

4   Select cell A1.

5   Change the font size to 14 point using the Font Size button on the Formatting Toolbar.

6   Select cell A8.

7   Make this selection bold.

8   Select cells B2 to D2.

9   Hold down the CTRL key and select A8. (You have selected some non-adjacent cells.)

10 Make this selection italic by pressing the Italic button on the Formatting Toolbar.

11 Save a copy of the worksheet to your own disk in drive A.

12 Close the worksheet.

Your completed worksheet should look like Figure 6.

	A	B	C	D	E
1	Library borrowings, Quarter 1, 1995				
2		January	February	March	
3	Books	2100	1956	2225	
4	Videos	114	100	120	
5	Music Cassettes	567	621	480	
6	CD's	326	322	352	
7	Paintings	89	92	74	
8	*Total*	3196	3091	3251	
9					

Figure 6: Worksheet following selection practice

AUTOFILL

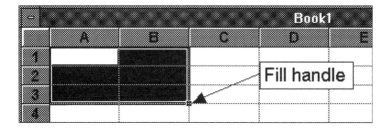

Figure 7: Preparing for AutoFill

AutoFill is a technique which basically saves you typing. It is used to fill a series of adjacent cells with data based on the cell immediately to the left or above the cells. It is easier to explain what it can do with an example, but before starting Activity 21, ensure that you can correctly position the mouse pointer over the Fill Handle on the selection border. You can find it at the bottom right-hand corner of the selection (see Figure 7). When correctly positioned the mouse pointer will change to a +.

	A	B
1	Jan	
2	March	
3	Sat	
4	Monday	
5	Q1	
6	Quarter 1	
7	Qtr 1	
8	1995	
9	1995	

Figure 8: Autofill.xls

ACTIVITY 21

1 Open the worksheet 'autofill.xls'. The worksheet has a series of entries in the first nine cells of column A (see Figure 8). Ensure A1 is the active cell.

2 Position the mouse pointer on the Fill handle of cell A1 and drag to the right. Nothing will happen until you have dragged at least half a cell to the right. Then an outline will appear. Continue dragging until it is in column F. As you are dragging try to see what is showing in the Name Box.

3 Perform the same operation on cells A2, A3, A4, A5, A6, A7 and A8. What happened with A8?

4 Try autofilling from cell A9. What happened this time?

The reason that cells A8 and A9 gave different results is because A8 contains a number and A9 contains text and AutoFill treats these differently.

5 Look carefully at these two cells (make each one active in turn). What differences are there between A8 and A9?

The number in A8 is aligned to the right of the cell and that in A9 is aligned to the left; in addition, the number in cell A9 has a quote mark ' at the front. The quote mark should be typed in if you want to enter a number as text. (You will not often need to do this.)

ACTIVITY 21 Continued

6 Make cell A10 active. Type in your first name and a number, e.g. Susan 1. Now use AutoFill on this cell. What happens?

It creates a series with your name and number so that you get Susan 1, Susan 2, Susan 3, etc.

You can, of course use AutoFill left OR right or up OR down. There is one special use of AutoFill.

ACTIVITY 21 Continued

7 Select cells A1 through F1, position the mouse pointer on the Fill handle and drag LEFT until all the cells are highlighted in GREY. When you take your finger off the mouse button the cells should disappear. In other words you can delete the contents of a cell or a range of cells using AutoFill.

2.3 Deleting the contents of cells

You have already used the simplest method for deleting cell contents – you select the cell and press the delete key. If you select a range or ranges of cells then pressing the delete key will operate on all cells selected. Also, as we have just seen, you can use AutoFill to delete cell contents. It is important that you learn to do this properly; it is not enough to blank out the previous contents with the SPACE BAR, that does not empty the cell. In Activity 22, you delete a range of cells.

ACTIVITY 22

1 Select the range A1 to A9.

2 Press the Delete key.

3 Note what has happened to cells A1 to A9.

Try deleting the contents of the entire worksheet in Activity 23.

ACTIVITY 23

1 Select the entire worksheet

2 Press the Delete key.

Remember when you close the worksheet DO NOT SAVE CHANGES. Close the worksheet now.

Summary

In this section you have learned how to move around within the total worksheet area. You have also learned how to select particular cells, ranges of cells and complete columns or rows. You have been introduced to 'Autofill' as a means of fast data entry in specific instances. Finally you learnt how to delete cell contents.

SECTION 3

Using Formulae and Functions

3.1 Simple formulae

As you saw in Section 1, a cell may contain a formula. To tell Excel that you are about to enter a formula you start by pressing the equals (=) sign. An example of a very simple formula is converting inches to centimetres. To do this you need to multiply the number of inches by 2.54. For example, to find out how many centimetres there are in 11.5 inches you multiply 11.5 by 2.54. You would enter into a cell:

$$=11.5*2.54$$

The cell would then display the result (29.21).

However, this may not be the best way of doing it. If you wanted to do several conversions then you would have to edit the cell each time. In this case it would be better to enter the number of inches in one cell and the formula in a second cell. The formula cell would then contain a reference to the cell containing the number of inches.

In Figure 9, cell A2 contains the number of inches and cell B2 contains a formula (you wouldn't see the formula in cell B2 – you would see the result). The formula says 'multiply the *contents* of cell A2 by 2.54'. The result would be displayed in cell B2.

	A	B	C
1	Inches	cm	
2	11.5	=A1*2.54	

Figure 9: Converting inches to centimetres

Activity 24 will guide you through the steps to construct a conversion table from inches to centimetres to produce the worksheet shown in Figure 9. The range to convert will be from 0.5 inches to 12 inches with an interval of 0.5 inches.

	A	B
1	Inches	Centimetres
2	0.5	1.27
3	1	2.54
4	1.5	3.81
5	2	5.08
6	2.5	6.35
7	3	7.62
8	3.5	8.89
9	4	10.16
10	4.5	11.43
11	5	12.7
12	5.5	13.97
13	6	15.24
14	6.5	16.51
15	7	17.78
16	7.5	19.05
17	8	20.32
18	8.5	21.59
19	9	22.86
20	9.5	24.13
21	10	25.4
22	10.5	26.67
23	11	27.94
24	11.5	29.21
25	12	30.48

Figure 10: Conversion table for inches to centimetres

To create the worksheet in Figure 10, you only need to type in a few figures. All the rest is done by Excel. To get Excel to do the work, you will:

- Use AutoFill to put in the lengths in column A
- Put one formula into cell B2
- Use AutoFill to copy the formula to the other cells in column B.

ACTIVITY 24

1   Use AutoFill to create column A.

2   Type Inches into cell A1.

3   Type 0.5 into cell A2.

4   Type =A2+0.5 into cell A3.

5   Use AutoFill to copy the contents of cell A3 down as far as cell A25.

6   Look at the values that are displayed in column A. (You should find a column of numbers that start at 0.5 in cell A2 and increase by 0.5 in each successive cell until the final value 12 in cell A25.)

7   Use AutoFill to create column B.

8   Type Centimetres in cell B1.

9   Type =A2*2.54 into cell B2.

10 Use AutoFill to copy the formula in cell B2 down as far as cell B25.

11 Look at the displayed value in cell B3 and the contents of B3 in the formula bar. (You must make cell B3 the active cell to see this.)

In step 5 of Activity 24 you should have noticed that the contents of cell A4 was the formula =A3+0.5. But the formula that you copied was =A2+0.5. This illustrates an important feature of Excel:

When you copy a cell that contains a reference to another cell, Excel automatically updates the reference to that cell.

So, in Activity 24 as you copied column A downwards, Excel updated each cell so that it made each cell contents *the value of the cell above plus 0.5.* Look at the formulae in the cells in column A and check that this is so.

Similarly, when you copied the formula in cell B2 (which is =A2*2.54) Excel updated the reference to column A. Make cell B8 the active cell and check its content. (You should find the formula =A8*2.54.) If you check the other cells in column B you will find that each cell has been updated to refer to its adjacent cell in column A.

In Activity 25 you will construct a *horizontal* conversion table that converts feet to centimetres (cm). Your table will look like Figure 11.

	D	E	F	G	H
3	feet	1	2	3	4
4	cm	30.48	60.96	91.44	121.92
5					

Figure 11: Converting feet to centimetres

Again, you will type just a few numbers, AutoFill will do the rest.

ACTIVITY 25

1 Type feet in cell D3 and cm in cell D4.

2 Type 1 in cell E3.

3 Type =E3+1 into cell F3.

4 Use AutoFill to copy the formula in cell F3 to G3 and H3.

5 Type =E3*12*2.54 into cell E4.

6 Use AutoFill to copy the formula in cell E4 to F4, G4 and H4.

7 Note the formulae in cells G3 and H3.

8 Note the formulae in cell F4, G4 and H4.

RELATIVE ADDRESSES

In step 7 of Activity 25 you noted the formula in cell G3 (this should be =F3+1), and in step 8 you noted the formula in cell H4 (this should be =H3*12*2.54). This time the update has been made to columns. If you copy cells *vertically* Excel updates cell references by rows, and if you copy cells *horizontally* Excel updates cell references by columns. Where cell address references can be updated in this way they are called **relative addresses**.

Sometimes relative addressing is inconvenient. The following example will help you to see why this is so.

Suppose that you wished to create a seven times multiplication table as in Figure 12. You can do this using the relative addressing methods which you have already learnt.

	A	B	C
1		7	times table
2			
3	1	7	
4	2	14	
5	3	21	
6	4	28	
7	5	35	
8	6	42	
9	7	49	
10	8	56	
11	9	63	
12	10	70	
13	11	77	
14	12	84	

Figure 12: Seven times table

Open a new worksheet and create the seven times table in Figure 12.

ACTIVITY 26

1 Cell B3 should contain =7*A1

2 Cells B4 to B14 should have been filled by using AutoFill to copy B3.

So far, there is nothing new in Activity 26. But, suppose that you wanted to make a five times table, or a nine times table. How convenient it would be to just change the '7' at the top of the table! If we make cell B3 use the 7 in cell B1, then we could just change cell B3 each time we wanted a new table. In Activity 27 you explore the formulae in more detail.

ACTIVITY 27

Return to your seven times table worksheet and:

1 Change cell B3 to =B1*A3.

2 AutoFill cell B3 down the rest of the B column.

3 Look at the result!

4 Explore the formulae in the cells in column B and try and work out why the table is completely wrong.

Looking at the formulae in column B, you can see that Excel has updated the references for each new row. So the formulae go:

B1*A3, B2*A4, B3*A5, ...

But they should go:

B1*A3, B1*A4, B1*A5, ...

In other words, to get this table to work as we want it to, we want to stop Excel updating the reference to cell B1. We want to say 'update cell A3 but do not update cell B2'.

To tell Excel not to update a reference, we just put $ signs in front of the relevant part of the reference as follows:

B1 means 'update the column reference' and 'update the row reference'

$B1 means 'do not update the column reference, but do update the row reference'

B$1 means 'update the column reference, but do not update the row reference'

$B$1 means 'do not update the column reference and do not update the row reference'.

Returning to Activity 27, we want to tell Excel to use cell B1 for every row in the table. In other words, do not update the 'B' and do not update the '1'. So, we write $B$1 in the formula. Activity 28 shows you how to do this.

ACTIVITY 28

Continue with the same worksheet as you used for the seven times table.

Put in the absolute reference to B1.

1 In cell B3, type =$B$1*A3.

Cell B3 now refers to the 7 in cell B1 using an absolute address. If you AutoFill this formula to another cell, it will still contain $B$1. Only the A3 part will be updated.

2 AutoFill cell B3 to the rest of column B. You should now have a correct seven times table.

3 Explore the new formulae.

Have a look at the cells in column B. Make sure that they all contain an absolute reference to cell B1. For example, cell B6 should contain = $B$1*A8.

> 4 Produce an instant nine times table.
>
> Change the 7 in cell B1 to 9. Your table should instantly become a nine times table.

We could have constructed the table by entering a formula into each cell in column B that contained a reference to B1 instead of $B$1, but that would mean typing the formula 15 times. Copying is much easier but you must remember to use absolute cell references, where appropriate.

3.2 Excel functions

In Excel a function is something that carries out a calculation and puts the answer into a cell in your spreadsheet. There are hundreds of functions in Excel, but we shall look at a few only.

The best way to understand functions is through an example. Figure 13 shows, in rows 1 to 8, a student's record of one week's expenditure. Underneath the data, you can see four pieces of information that have been calculated from the data:

● total for the week

● average expenditure per day

● lowest expenditure of any one day

● highest expenditure of any one day.

Each one of these four pieces of information was obtained by using an Excel function.

	A	B
1	Day	Expenditure £
2	Sunday	3.01
3	Monday	5.67
4	Tuesday	6.22
5	Wednesday	3.89
6	Thursday	8.30
7	Friday	2.25
8	Saturday	8.01
9		37.35
10		
11	Average exp	5.34
12		
13	Lowest exp	2.25
14		
15	Highest exp	8.30

Figure 13: Student's expenditure for one week

FINDING A TOTAL

The total expenditure was found by typing into cell B9:

=SUM(B2,B3,B4,B5,B6,B7,B8).

However, typing long list of cells like this is tedious, so Excel allows you to type:

=SUM(B2:B8)

B2:B8 just means 'all the cells from B2 to B8'.

FINDING AN AVERAGE, A MAXIMUM AND A MINIMUM

The other three calculations were done as follows with three other Excel functions:

Function	Cell	What to type
Average	B11	=AVERAGE(B2:B8)
Lowest	B13	=MIN(B2:B8)
Highest	B15	=MAX(B2:B8)

Figure 14: Finding an average, a maximum and a minimum using Excel functions

Activity 29 enables you to create the table in Figure 13 and to calculate the four pieces of information using Excel's functions.

ACTIVITY 29

Start with a new worksheet.

Type in the data.

1 Type the column headings in.

2 Type Sunday in cell B2. Then use AutoFill to put in Monday to Saturday.

3 Type each day's expenditure in (cells B2 to B8).

   Put in the SUM function.

4 Make cell B9 the active cell and type in =SUM(B2:B8).

   The total of 37.35 should appear.

Put in the other three functions.

5 Type =AVERAGE(B2:B8) in cell B11.

   Type =MIN(B2:B8) in cell B13.

   Type =MAX(B2:B8) in cell B15.

   Check the answers.

6 Make sure that your functions produce the same answers as in Figure 12. If you have any wrong answers, you have probably put the wrong cell range into your function. To correct this, make the relevant cell active and then edit the entry.

   See the power of functions.

7 Try changing the expenditure for some of the days. Notice how all four functions update instantly.

3.3 Different types of functions

When you used the functions in Activity 29 you had to tell each one which numbers it was to work on. For example, for SUM, you had to write:

   =SUM(B2,B3,B4,B5,B6,B7,B8).

The cell references B2, B3, B4, ... are called the arguments of a function.

There are three basic types of functions in Excel. These are:

● functions that have no arguments, e.g. RAND() which produces a random number

● functions with a fixed number of arguments, e.g. ROUND(number, places) which rounds a decimal number. ROUND has *two* arguments: number and place

● functions with a variable number of arguments, e.g. SUM(number1, number2, number3, ...).

Whenever you see a function written down, it will have two parts:

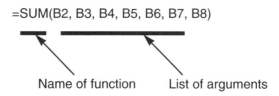

=SUM(B2, B3, B4, B5, B6, B7, B8)

Name of function   List of arguments

MORE ON LISTS OF CELL NUMBERS

You have seen that you can put a list of cell numbers into a function as:

=SUM(B2,B3,B4,B5,B6,B7,B8)

or as:

=SUM(B2:B8).

Sometimes you may wish to have list of non-consecutive cells. You can do this as follows:

SUM(A4:F12,J28:P28)

This would add together the numeric values in the rectangular block A4 to F12 with the values in row 28 between the cells J28 and P28. Any non-numeric cells (e.g. blank or text) are ignored by the function.

Normal usage of the SUM function is with a SINGLE range of cells, for example, =SUM(A4:A10) will add together all the cells between A4 and A10. You should NOT use the SUM function to do anything other than adding a range of cells. The following examples work, but are extremely bad practice:

=SUM(A5*B5)	Here, SUM is not needed since A5*B5 will produce a single number – there is nothing to sum.
	This example can be replaced by =A5*B5.
=SUM(10)	Again, SUM is not needed since there is no calculation to do on the 10.
	This can be replaced by 10.
=SUM(A1+B1+C1+D1)	This one involves unnecessary typing and is better written as =SUM(A1:D1).

ROUND

A particularly useful function is ROUND which rounds a number to a given number of decimal places. It has the format:

ROUND(number, number of decimal places)

ROUND (54.38, 0) produces the number 54 since 54.38 is the number to be rounded and 0 is the number of decimal places to be displayed.

The number can be a cell reference:

ROUND (B4, 3) will round the number in cell B4 to three decimal places.

COMBINING FUNCTIONS

You can make one function act on another. For example:

ROUND (RAND(), 2)

will create a random number (that's what RAND() does) and then round it to two decimal places.

MORE PRACTICE WITH FUNCTIONS

In Activity 30 you will construct a worksheet that calculates the final mark for students studying a particular module. The final result is found by calculating 40% of the coursework mark plus 60% of the examination mark. There are four pieces of coursework that each contribute 25% towards the overall mark. Data is given in Figure 15.

	A	B	C	D	E	F	G
	Name	cw1	cw2	cw3	cw4	Exam	Final
2							
3	Barker L	19	12	9	4	58	52
4	Francis M	22	15	16	10	63	63
5	Grady H	15	17	12	11	45	49
6	Smith P	18	15	9	11	57	55

Figure 15: Data for student's final work

ACTIVITY 30

1 Type all of the data in Figure 15 into a worksheet except for the numbers in column G.

2 Make cell G3 the active cell.

3 Type the formula =(SUM(B3:E3)*0.4)+(F3*0.6)

4 Copy the contents of G3 to the other cells in column G using AutoFill.

5 Modify the formulae in column G so that the final marks are rounded and no decimals are displayed.

PI() AND POWER

These are two useful mathematical functions.

PI() returns the value of π (i.e. 3.142........).

POWER(number, power) raises a number to a power, e.g. POWER(12,2) returns 12 squared (i.e. 144).

In Activity 31 you will practise using PI and POWER by calculating the area of a circle ($2 \times \pi \times$ radius).

ACTIVITY 31

Start with a new worksheet.

1 Type Radius in cell A1.

2 Type Area in cell A2.

3 Type 2.4 in cell B1.

4 Type =2*PI()*POWER(B1,2) in cell B2. (Cell B2 should now show the area a circle of radius^2, i.e. 36.19115).

DATE AND TIME FUNCTIONS

Excel has many useful functions for dates and times. Excel stores every date since 1904 as a serial number. This enables Excel to carry out calculations on dates. For example, Excel can immediately find the date 20 days from now.

To use the date and time system, you first need to know about two basic functions:

TODAY()   This gives today's date.

           For example, =TODAY() gives 5/9/96 on the day of typing this page.

NOW()   This gives today's date and time.

           =NOW() at the time of typing gave 5/9/96 14:38.

You can use these two basic functions to find other date and time functions such as:

Function	Result at the time of typing
Weekday (TODAY())	5 (It's a Thursday)
Year (TODAY())	1996
HOUR(NOW())	14

Figure 16: Date and time function

PERFORMING CALCULATIONS ON DATES

Because Excel stores dates as serial numbers, it is easy to perform arithmetic on a date. For example, you can add a number to a date and the result is a date; you can subtract one date from another and the result is a number (the number of days between the two dates); and you can add a number to a date to give another date.

Activity 32 gives you practice in using dates.

ACTIVITY 32

Use a new worksheet for this activity.

1 Type the text from Figure 17 into the cells indicated.

2 Type the function =TODAY() in cell C1.

3 Type the formula =C1+28 into cell C2.

4 Type the formula =C2-C1 into cell D2.

5 Type the function =WEEKDAY(TODAY()) into cell C4.

	A	B	C
1	Date:	28/04/96	
2	Date in 28 days:	26/05/96	28
3			
4	Today is day:		
5		1	

Figure 17: Using date functions

MATHEMATICAL AND TRIGONOMETRICAL FUNCTIONS

Excel has a wide range of mathematical and trigonometrical functions, most of which are for specialist use only. However there are some functions that have wide application. We deal with a few of these (Figure 18).

Function	Result	Example
EVEN(number)	This gives the next even number above the number you put in.	EVEN(24.0001) gives 26.
INT(number)	This converts a number to the next integer (whole number) below it.	INT(25.6) gives 25.
ODD(number)	This converts a number to the next odd number above it.	ODD(23.0001) gives 25.
PRODUCT (number1, number2, number3, ...)	This multiplies all the numbers together.	PRODUCT(2,3,4) gives 24.
SQRT(number)	This gives the square root of the number.	SQRT(25) gives 5.

Figure 18: Maths and Trig functions

In Activity 33 you will display random numbers, random odd and even numbers, and calculate the product and square root of the numbers.

ACTIVITY 33

Start the activity with a blank worksheet

1   Type Random number in cell A1.

2   Type =RAND()*50 in cell C1 (this will display a random number between 0 and 49.99999.....).

3   Type Even number in cell A3.

4   Type Odd number in cell A4.

5   Type =EVEN(C1) in cell C3.

6   Type =ODD(C1) in cell C4.

7   Type Product in cell A6.

8   Type =PRODUCT(C3,C4) in cell C6.

9   Note the value displayed in cell C6.

10 Type Square root in cell A7.

11 Type =SQRT(C6) in cell C7.

12 Note the values displayed in cells C6 and C7.

AUTOMATIC RECALCULATION

Look at the values for C6 that you noted in steps 9 and 12 in Activity 33. They should be different! This is because each time you enter something into a cell the worksheet is updated. So when you carried out step 11, all of the cells containing =RAND() returned new random numbers (and each one would be different). This is known as **automatic recalculation**.

Sometimes you will want to control when Excel does a recalculation. Also, if you have a very large worksheet with lots of linked calculations, these will slow down your data input. You can switch off the automatic recalculation using Tools Options Calculations on the menu – click on Manual.

Whether or not recalculation is switched off, you can force a recalculation by pressing the function key, F9. Do this now. Notice that every time you press F9 new numbers appear. This is because you have used the RAND() function, otherwise you would not have seen a difference because the recalculated values would be the same as before the recalculation took place.

USING FUNCTIONS IN WORKSHEETS

You can enter functions into a cell in two ways:

- If you know which function you want, then you can type it in. This is the method which you have used so far.

- If you do not know which function you want, then you can call up the Function Wizard which will give you a list to choose from. You can do this by:

  - click Insert, Function, or

  - click the Function Wizard button.

USING THE FUNCTION WIZARD

In Activity 34, you insert the Function SUM(..) using the Function Wizard.

ACTIVITY 34

1 Open select.xls from your module disk.

2 In cell E2 insert Total.

3 Make cell E3 the active cell.

4 Click on the Function Wizard button (fx), or choose from the menu Insert Function. A window appears as in Figure 19.

5 In the left-hand part of the window click on Math & Trig.

6 In the right-hand part of the window click on SUM. A window as in Figure 18 will appear.

7 In the box labelled 'Number 1' insert the cell range B3:D3.

8 Click on Finish.

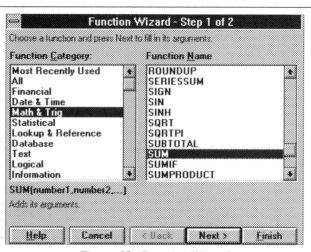

Figure 19: Function Wizard

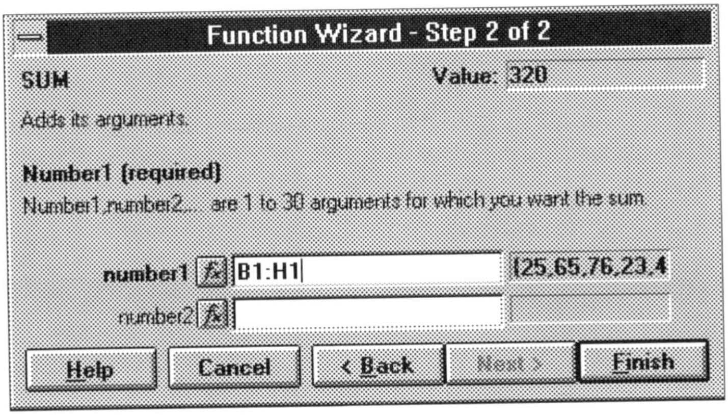

Figure 20: Function Wizard

The value for the total number of books borrowed during January, February, and March should appear in cell E3 (6281). Note that the value and range shown in Figure 20 will not be the same that you will see during Activity 35.

COPYING USING AUTOFILL

Worksheets often contain several columns (or rows) that contain similar data. It may be a column of cells that contain functions and formulae that process data in adjoining cells. In this case copying by AutoFill can work in a fast and efficient way. Supposing we want to construct a worksheet where cells B11 to B20 contain the dates for the next ten days, that is the cells *always* contain the dates of the next ten days. You can do this as shown in Activity 35.

ACTIVITY 35

1 Make cell B11 the active cell.

2 Type the =TODAY().

3 Make cell B12 the active cell.

4 Type the formula =B11+1.

5 Ensure that B12 is the active cell and then click on the AutoFill handle and drag downwards to cell B20. Release the mouse button.

Now the cells will display today's date and the dates of the next nine days. This will always be true. Tomorrow you would see that the date in cell B11 had been updated to show the new date for 'today' and the remaining cells would display the corresponding next nine dates. In Section 4 you will learn how to make Excel display dates in different formats, here, we will accept the default date display.

3.4 Printing worksheets

Using the menu selection File Print opens up a large number of options that can be used to print your spreadsheet space. We will concentrate on a few of these choices.

Choosing File Print opens the dialog box in Figure 21.

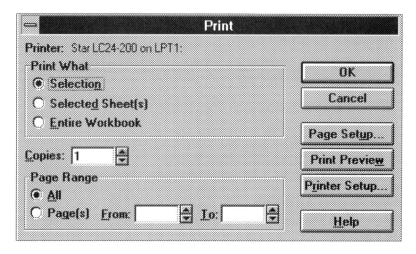

Figure 21: Print dialog box

This dialog box allows you to choose what to print, the number of copies to print, and the number of pages to print. You are also given the opportunity to change printer settings (Printer Set-up button), see what the printed page will look like (Print Preview button), or to fine tune what the printed page will look like.

Choosing the Page Setup button displays a tabbed dialog box (Figure 22) with four tabs: Page, Margins, Header/Footer, and Sheet. You may switch between the sections by clicking on the name on the appropriate tab.

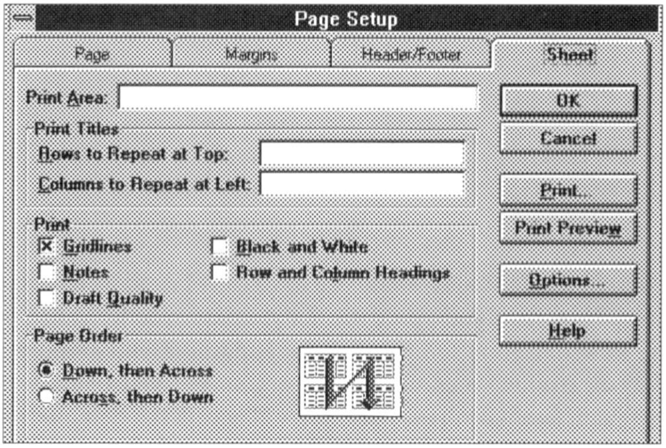

Figure 22: Page Setup dialog box

Note the checkbox 'Gridlines' in the sheet tab of the dialog box. If this checkbox is clear then the gridlines surrounding the cells on the worksheet won't appear on the printed page.

You may also choose specific rows to be repeated at the top of each printed page and columns to be repeated at the left of each printed page. This is particularly useful to repeat row and column headings where the data would otherwise become meaningless if separated from them.

By default, Excel prints the sheet name at the top of each page (header) and the page number at the bottom of each page (footer). These can be changed to a number of settings or customised using the Headers/Footers tab shown in Figure 23.

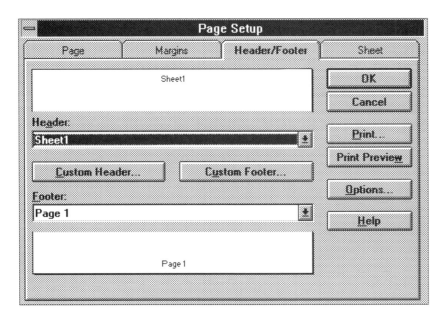

Figure 23: Customising headers and footers

The Margins tab allows you to change page orientation (portrait or landscape) and the top, bottom, left, and right margins sizes as you wish.

Choosing the OK button in any section sends you back to the Print dialog box and choosing OK in this dialogue box sets the printing process in operation.

Before starting Activity 36 close any open worksheets. You need to be connected (directly or via a network) to a printer in order to complete this activity, as you will be printing selected cells from a spreadsheet.

ACTIVITY 36

1 Open the file select.xls that you used in section 2.

2 Select the cells A1 to D8.

3 From the menu choose File Print.

4 Click on OK.

Summary

In this section you have learnt how to use simple formulae in a worksheet. You have also learnt that Excel provides an extensive range of built-in functions and have learnt how to use some of them in a worksheet. Additionally, you have learnt how to copy using AutoFill. Finally, you have learnt how to print a worksheet.

SECTION 4

Formatting: Changing the Appearance of the Worksheet

Introduction

Excel, in common with other Windows applications, gives you a great deal of control over the appearance of your worksheet. For example, you can change:

- all or part of the contents of a cell to bold
- put a border around cells
- and change the fonts.

Formatting is a large subject so we will limit our discussion to the following points:

- worksheet appearance
  - column width
  - row height
- cell appearance
  - numeric display
  - cell alignment
  - cell font
  - cell borders
  - cell background pattern
- inserting rows and columns
- deleting rows and columns.

There are many formatting shortcuts. All formatting options are available from the Format menu. In general, you can get a menu of options which apply only to the currently selected object (e.g. a cell, a drawing object or a chart item.) To get the menu, just click the right-hand mouse button on the object. You will learn this technique in this section.

4.1 Changing worksheet appearance

COLUMN WIDTH
The width of a column can be changed using the mouse or the Format, Column command.

USING THE MOUSE TO CHANGE COLUMN WIDTHS
Activity 37 will show you how to:

- increase or decrease the width of a column
- get Excel to choose the width of a column.

ACTIVITY 37

Start the activity with a new worksheet.

To widen a column.

1 Type into cell A1:

   This is a long piece of text.

   Note that the text is displayed over a wider area than cell A1 on the worksheet.

2   Using the mouse, position the mouse pointer on the right-hand border of the column A heading (see Figure 23).

3   You will see that the mouse pointer changes shape to the symbol shown in the margin.

4   Hold down the left mouse button and drag right to widen the column. When the column is as wide as the text in cell A1 stop dragging.

To narrow a column

5   Now drag column A to the left until it is approximately the same width as the other columns.

To get a best fit.

6   If you double-click the mouse when you have the width-change pointer you will get the best fit width for the column. That is, the column will automatically be widened to fit the widest entry in that column. Do this now for column A and observe what happens.

Coloumn A, right-hand border

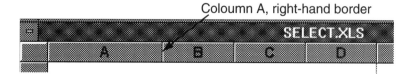

Figure 24: Getting the best fit

Often, we want several columns to be the same width. You could set their widths one at a time, but that is tedious. Also you cannot be certain that the widths are all exactly the same. Excel, though, can make the widths exactly equal. Activity 38 shows you how to make columns A, B and C all the same width. Continue with the worksheet that you used in Activity 37.

ACTIVITY 38

1   Select columns A, B, and C.

2   Position the mouse pointer on the right-hand border of column B.

3   Click and drag the border to the right.

4   Release the mouse button and observe that all columns have the same width.

USING COMMANDS TO CHANGE COLUMN WIDTHS

To change cell widths using the menu you must first select the columns containing those cells. Then choose the Column command from the Format menu. A dialog box appears that enables you to alter the column width in a number of ways:

- **Width** – this allows you to specify the width as a numeric value.

- **AutoFit Selection** – here, Excel selects the 'best fit' width.

- **Hide** – this hides the column, effectively sets the width to zero. You may wish to do this if you have columns with intermediate calculations that you do not want displayed or printed.

- **Unhide** – this makes a hidden column visible.

- **Standard Width** – this resets the width to the Excel standard.

In Activity 39 you will practise hiding a column and then revealing it. You can carry this out on the worksheet you used in Activity 37.

ACTIVITY 39

To hide column C.

1 Make cell C1 the active cell.

2 Choose Format, Column, Hide, from the menu.

3 Observe that column C is no longer visible on screen. Note also that the Name Box shows cell C1 is the active cell (providing you haven't used the arrow keys).

4 Press the right arrow key to make cell D1 the active cell.

5 Watch the Name Box (which currently displays D1) and press the left arrow key twice. (Notice that the Name Box displays B1 then A1, but doesn't display C1.)

To reveal column C.

6 Select cell C2 by clicking on the Name Box and then typing C2, then press the Enter key. C2 should be displayed in the Name Box.

7 Now choose Format, Column, Unhide, from the menu. Note that column C is now visible and has the width that it possessed before it was hidden in step 1 above.

CHANGING THE ROW HEIGHT

Changes to the height of a row or rows can be made in a similar way to changing column width.

USING THE MOUSE TO CHANGE ROW HEIGHT

It is necessary to place the mouse pointer in the row headings on the bottom border of the row (see Figure 25).

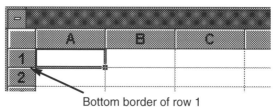

Bottom border of row 1

Figure 25: Changing row height

When the mouse pointer changes to the shape shown below, drag up to reduce the row height and down to increase it.

USING COMMANDS TO CHANGE ROW HEIGHT

The options available from the Format, Row command are:

● **Height** – this allows you to specify as a numeric value.

● **AutoFit** – this resets the row height to the standard height; this depends on the font in use.

● **Hide** – this sets the height to zero and the row is no longer visible.

● **Unhide** – this makes the row visible.

Activity 40 gives you practice in changing the height of a row. You can carry on using the same worksheet as you used in Activity 37.

ACTIVITY 40

1 Set the height of row 12 to 25.

2 Hide row 7. This will make its height equal to zero.

3 Now return both row 7 and row 12 to the standard row height.

4.2 Changing cell appearance

There are a number of ways in which you can change the appearance of a cell, for example, you can display the contents in bold, or use another typeface. The changes are called format changes. They have no effect on the data held in the cells.

THE FORMATTING TOOLBAR

The quickest way to change a cell's appearance is to use the Formatting Toolbar. The position of the formatting toolbar can be seen in Figure 1. Figure 26 shows the Formatting Toolbar in more detail. It is shown here in two parts but in reality it is one long bar.

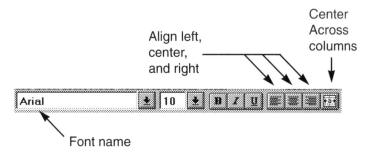

Formatting Toolbar (left side)

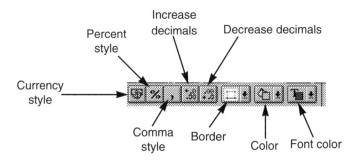

Figure 26: Formatting Toolbar (right side)

ACTIVITY 41

Open Excel and identify the Formatting Toolbar.

The names shown in Figure 26 are those displayed by the 'Tool Tips' (hence the American spelling). A brief explanation of each button follows:

Activity 42 helps you to explore the toolbar. The activity may look long, but it won't take you much time to do.

ACTIVITY 42

You can do this activity on any worksheet. You will need two cells side-by-side, one with text in it and one with a number in it. For example:

Price	18.50

Highlight these two cells and then try out each of the following on them.

1 **Font**. This is used to change the current font to one of the others on your computer. The Excel default font is Arial. You may also find fonts such as Times New Roman, Brush Script MT, and Impact. Always select TrueType fonts, i.e. those which have TT alongside the name in the font list.

Change the font of your two cells.

2 **Font size**. This changes the point size of the characters in the cells. (1pt = 1/72 inch.)

Make the point size of your cells two points larger.

3 **Bold**. This displays the contents of a cell in bold. (The bold button stays pressed whenever you make a cell with the bold attribute active.)

Make your two cells bold.

If you keep the cells highlighted, clicking again on the bold button will return the display to normal.

4 **Italic**. The italic button displays text in italic.

Highlight your two cells and change them to italic.

Then change them back to normal type.

5 **Underline**. This button will underline the contents of a cell. It is not used much as it is easier to use the border command to put a line at the bottom of a cell.

Apply underline to your two cells.

6 **Align left**. This lines up the contents of a cell with the left-hand edge of that cell. Remember that, by default, text entries are aligned to the left and numbers to the right.

Align both your cells to the left.

7   **Center** puts the contents of a cell in the cell's centre.

Centre the contents of each of your two cells.

8   **Align** right lines up the contents of a cell with its right-hand edge. Remember that, by default, numbers are always aligned right.

Align both your cells to the right.

9   **Center across columns**. This centres the contents of a range of cells in the middle of all the selected columns.

To try this one out, you need a longish piece of text to display. Type in a new cell the words:

A nice long column heading to display

Highlight this heading and 2 cells to the right then use the Center across columns button to place the text across a range of columns. Your range must include the cell into which you typed the text.

10 **Currency style**. We do not cover this format in this module, but you need to note that it is *not* the same as Currency format. *Do not* use it.

11 **Percent style**. This displays a number in percentage format. For example, if a cell contains 0.175 it will be displayed as 18%. The default is for *no* decimal places. Note that the cell content is still 0.175 and it is this value which Excel uses in its calculations.

Apply Percent style to 18.50. It should display as 1850%.

If you wish to change this back to 18.50, you have to use Edit, Clear, Formats. The percentage format cannot be removed with the percentage button.

12 **Comma style** displays numbers greater than 999 with a thousands comma separator. For example, 1500 is displayed as 1,500.

Use some new cells to type in numbers of more than three digits. Then use Comma style to display them with commas.

Again, to clear this format you need to use Edit, Clear, Formats.

13 **Increase decimals** is used to increase the number of decimal places displayed. This does *not* affect the number used in Excel's calculations. If a cell contains 1.5, but is being displayed with no decimal places (i.e. 2), 1.5 will still be used in any calculations.

Apply Increase decimals to your cell containing 18.50.

14 **Decrease decimals** is just the opposite of Increase decimals.

Apply decrease decimals to your cell containing 18.50.

15 **Borders**. This enables you to add borders to a range of selected cells. It offers a number of pre-set border styles and you just have to click on the one which you want to use.

Use this button to put a border of your choice around your two cells.

Notice that one of the options has no borders at all. You can use this option to remove all the borders from the selected cells.

16 **Colour change** alters the colour of the background of a cell or range of cells.

Put a light grey background behind your two cells.

17 **Font colour** changes the colour of the contents of the cell or cells.

Change the colour of the text in your two cells to red.

You have tried out many of the formatting options in Activity 42. In Activity 43 you will learn to apply formats to cells in a worksheet.

ACTIVITY 43

1 Open leisure.xls.

2 Select cell B1 and change the font to a TrueType font other than Arial.

3 Change the font size to 16pt.

4 Select cells B1 through E1 and press the Center across columns button. Note the effect. The words Leisure Facility Use are positioned in the middle of the selected columns. Which cell contains the words?

5 Select cells B2 through F2 and A11 and make them bold. Remember you can make selections of non-adjacent cells.

6 Select cell F2 and right align it.

7 Save the worksheet as leisure2.xls.

USING COMMANDS TO FORMAT CELLS

So far you have used the mouse and the toolbar to apply formats. You can also use commands. For, example, having selected a range of cells, use the Format, Cells command to bring up the tabbed dialog box (Figure 27).

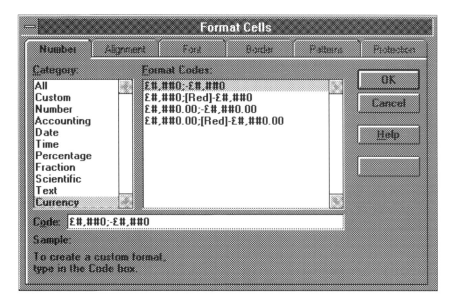

Figure 27: Format Cells dialog box

Each tab covers a different aspect of formatting. In Figure 27, the current tab is that for formatting numbers. To choose another aspect, simply click on the tab required. You will learn about each of the tabs in the sequence they appear.

NUMBER

You should be aware that, when it can, Excel automatically assigns the correct number format to your entry. For example, when you enter a number that contains a pound (£) sign before the number or a percent sign (%) after the number, Excel automatically changes the cell's format from general format to a currency format and a percentage format, respectively. If you enter something which Excel recognises as a date (e.g., 1/1/96, 06/96, 1 Jan) one of the date formats will be applied automatically. You can change the format to one of the built-in number formats, or create your own number format.

Activity 44 introduces you to some of the ways in which Excel can format numbers. Use a new worksheet for this activity.

ACTIVITY 44

1 Type the number 5.569 in cell A1.

2 Make A1 the active cell.

3 From the menu choose Format, Cells.

4 In the left-hand window (Category) choose Number.

---

5 In the right hand window (Format codes) choose 0.00. Click OK.

6 Observe the display for cell A1 (5.57).

7 Click the Increase Decimals button on the Format Toolbar.

8 Repeat step 7.

9 Observe the display for cell A1 (5.5690).

NUMBER FORMAT CODES

The way in which a number is displayed is dependent on a format code. This is made up of a series of letters, numbers and special characters.

It is easier to describe the use of the codes by means of examples, as in Figure 28. The first column contains a number as you enter it into a cell, the second, an example of a format code and the third, the number as it will be displayed:

Number as entered	Format code	Number as displayed
1	0	1
1	0.00	1.00
1000.56	0	1001
1000.56	#,##0.00	1,000.56
27.3	£#,##0.00	£27.30
27.3	£0,000.00	£0,027.30
.3	£#,###.00	£.30
19.548	0.00	19.55
.254	0%	25%
.254	0.00%	25.40%
34857	dd/mm/yy	07/06/95
34857	dd-mmm-yy	07-Jun-95
34857	dd mmmm yyyy	07 June 1995
34857	dddd	Wednesday

Figure 28: Numbers and format codes

The difference between # and 0 in a code is that 0 forces a zero digit if there is not one in that position in the number.

Activity 45 enables you to practise using format codes.

ACTIVITY 45

1 For each of the following format codes write down how the number 12345.64 will be displayed.

	Code	Result
(a)	£#,##0.00	_____
(b)	0	_____
(c)	0.00	_____

2 For each of the following format codes write down how the number 0.8746 will be displayed.

	Code	Result
(a)	0%	_____
(b)	0.00%	_____

3 For each of the following format codes write down how Saturday 10th June 1995 will be displayed.

	Code	Result
(a)	dd/mm/yy	_____
(b)	dddd	_____
(c)	mmmm	_____
(d)	mmm-yyyy	_____

Your results should be as shown in Figure 29.

	Number	Code	Display
1(a)	12345.64	£#,##0.00	£12,345.64
1(b)	12345.64	0	12346
1(c)	12345.64	0.00	12345.64
2(a)	.8746	0%	87%
2(b)	.8746	0.00%	87.46%
3(a)	34860	dd/mm/yy	10/06/95
3(b)	34860	dddd	Saturday
3(c)	34860	mmmm	June
3(d)	34860	mmm-yyy	Jun-1995

Figure 29: Using format codes

STRUCTURE OF NUMBER CODES

You will see from Figure 27 that there is more than one part to some number codes. The first part of the code refers to positive numbers; this is then followed by a semi-colon (;) and the code for negative numbers. When [red] is included in the code negative numbers are displayed in red.

FORMATTING NUMBER CELLS

Activity 46 gives you practice in using several of the number formatting options. Use a new worksheet for this.

ACTIVITY 46

1 Enter the left-hand column of Figure 28 into the worksheet using cells A1 to A12.

2 Select the range A1 to A12 and use AutoFill to copy to B1:B12.

3 Now apply the formatting from column 2 in Figure 28 to column B in the worksheet. Note that you should use Format, Cells, from the menu and then the following Categories from the left-hand list box in Figure 27.

   Cells A1 to A4, and A8: Number Cells A5 to A7: Currency Cells A9 and A10: Percentage Cells A11 and A12: Date.

   The display in column B should resemble column 3 in Figure 28.

If you are unable to follow the above table please see your tutor for further explanation.

CREATING YOUR OWN CODES

Below the two list boxes in Figure 27 you will see that any format code you select is repeated in the Codes text box and if the active cell contains a number it will be shown in that format in the Sample area. The Codes text box is editable to enable you to create your own custom codes. You may wish, for example, to set up a code to format telephone numbers. If you want 1915152000 to display as 0191–515–2000 then the code you would use is 0000–000–0000.

ALIGNMENT FORMATS

Clicking the alignment tab will display the dialog box in Figure 30. You met alignment in Activity 42 where you met those options which are available as buttons:

- horizontal left align
- horizontal centre align
- horizontal right align
- horizontal centre-across-selection.

You will now explore the other alignment options.

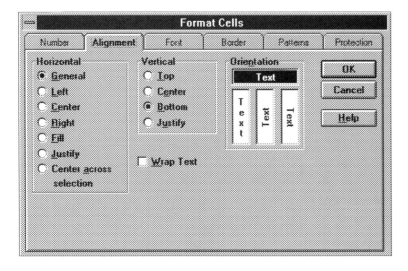

Figure 30: Format Cells dialog box

The other horizontal options are:

● **Horizontal: General**

This resets the alignment to Excel's default (text left, numbers right). When any General alignment cell is active, none of the alignment buttons on the Formatting ToolBar will be depressed.

● **Horizontal: Fill**

This is only present for compatibility with older spreadsheet packages and therefore we do not cover it here.

● **Horizontal: Justify**

This aligns wrapped text (see below) within a cell to the right and left. You must have more than one line of wrapped text to see the effect.

Activity 47 will show you how wrapping works. Use a new worksheet for this.

ACTIVITY 47

1 Enter Current Sales Figures into cell A1. Note that the text is much wider than the column width.

2 Make cell A1 the active cell.

3 From the menu choose Format, Cells, and then choose the Alignment Tab on the dialog box.

4 Near the centre of the box you will see a box labelled Word Wrap. Click on the box so that a cross (x) appears and choose OK.

5 Observe that the text is now 'wrapped' in cell A1 and the height of row 1 has increased.

6 Now click on the Center alignment button on the toolbar and observe the display of cell A1.

Vertical options

The *Vertical* group refers to the vertical alignment of the cell contents:

- **Vertical: Top**

  This aligns the contents at the top of the cell.

- **Vertical: Center**

  This aligns the contents in the middle of the cell.

- **Vertical: Bottom**

  This aligns the contents at the bottom of the cell.

- **Vertical: Justify**

  This justifies the contents of the cell or cells vertically within the height of the cell.

- **Wrap Text**

  This option allows more than one line of text in a cell, enlarging the cell height as appropriate.

- **Orientation**

  This allows you to change the way text appears in the cell.

A useful combination of features is to use Horizontal and Vertical Center with Wrap text. This enables you to achieve the effect in Figure 31. Activity 48 shows you how to do this.

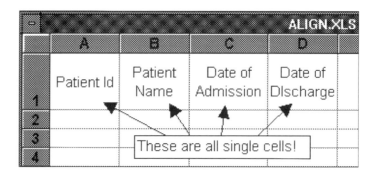

Figure 31: Horizontal and vertical centre with word-wrap

ACTIVITY 48

Use a new worksheet for this activity.

1 Enter the text in Figure 31 into the appropriate cells in your worksheet.

2 Select the cells in the range A1 to D1.

3 From the menu choose Format, Cells, and click the Alignment tab.

4 In the panel choose Horizontal, Center; Vertical, Center; and Wrap Text.

Your spreadsheet should resemble Figure 31.

FONT

Clicking the Font tab displays the formats dialogue box in Figure 32.

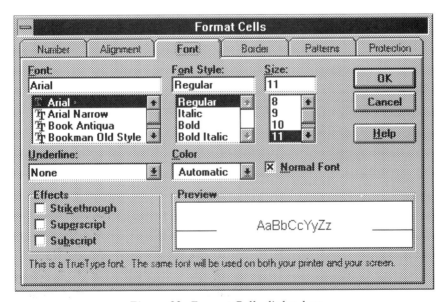

Figure 32: Format Cells dialog box

You will find that many of the facilities in this dialog box are available to you on the Formatting ToolBar. You may have come across some of these facilities in Unit 5, Word 6. The use of these facilities is beyond our scope in this unit. If you wish you can find out more about them by using the Help menu, by doing Activity 49.

ACTIVITY 49

1 Click on Help on the menu.

2 Choose Search for Help on.... in the dialog box.

3 Type font in the upper box.

4 Choose Font tab, Format Object command in the middle box.

5 Click on the Show Topics button.

6 A single topic should appear in the lowest box. Click on the Go To button
to see Help about this topic.

BORDER FORMATS

Activity 50 will give you practice in the use of the next two formatting facilities
Border and Pattern.

Clicking the Border tab gives you the Border dialog box shown in Figure 33.

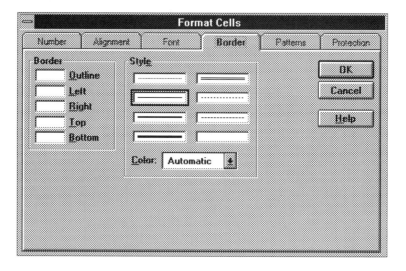

Figure 33: Border dialog box

There are three sets of options available in this dialog box:

● Select the border position (outline, left, right, top, bottom);

● Select the border style, i.e., dotted, single double and various
thicknesses;

● Select the border colour.

Remember that the border you choose will apply to the currently selected cell or cells. If you apply a border to a range of cells, the following rules apply to the border position.

1   Outline refers to the entire range, it takes precedence over left, right, top and bottom;

2   Left puts a border on the left of all cells except the left-hand column if outline has also been chosen;

3   Right puts a border on the right of all cells except the right-hand column if outline has also been chosen;

4   Top puts a border at the top of all cells except the top row if outline has also been selected;

5   Bottom puts a border at the bottom of all cells except the bottom row if outline has been selected.

To achieve the effect in Figure 34, you could use Outline (thick border), Right (thin border), Bottom (thin border).

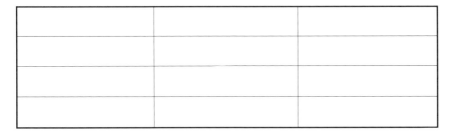

Figure 34: Using the border facility

PATTERNS FORMATS
Clicking the Patterns tab brings up the following dialog box (Figure 35).

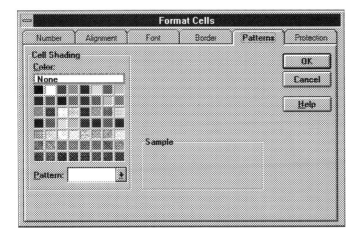

Figure 35: Pattern dialog box

This dialog box allows you to change the colour and shading of the cell background. It is equivalent to using the Color button on the Formatting ToolBar, although the ToolBar button gives you fewer choices of colour and shading.

Activity 50 shows you how to create the borders and patterns in Figure 36.

ACTIVITY 50

In Figure 36 the titles shown in row 2 are formatted for Horizontal Center; Vertical Center; and Wrap Text set to 'on'. There is also a thick, single line, outline border around the range A2:D2. You will also apply a pattern to the cells in this range. This pattern has been omitted from Figure 36 for clarity.

Start this activity with a blank worksheet.

1   Enter the text from Figure 36 into the appropriate cells in your worksheet.

2   Select the range A2:D2.

3   Select the menu Format, Cells and choose the alignment tab.

4   Select Horizontal, Center; Vertical, Center; Wrap Text.

5   Choose the Border tab.

6   Click on Outline and click on the thickest single line style.

7   Choose the Patterns tab.

8   Click on Arrow on the Pattern list box at the bottom of the dialog box (another list box containing patterns appears).

9   Click on the sparse dots pattern (top right in the list box).

10 Click on the OK button. Your spreadsheet should resemble Figure 36 with the addition of a dotted background to the cells A2:D2.

	A	B	C	D	E
1					
2	First Quarter	Second Quarter	Third Quarter	Fourth Quarter	
3					
4					

Figure 36: Using borders and patterns

PROTECTION

This tab dialog box does not form part of this module. If you require further details please refer to the Excel User Guide or search the Help facility for protect. You can protect many things in Excel from possible change, objects, charts, cells, etc.

INSERTING AND DELETING ROWS AND/OR COLUMNS

Whilst not strictly formatting, this is something you will need to do from time to time. There are several methods for doing this, but you will only look at the simplest here.

To insert a new column:

- select the column after the position for your new column
- select Insert Columns.

To insert a row:

- select the row below the position for your new row
- select Insert Rows.

If you want to insert more than one column (row), then select the number of columns (rows) and choose Insert, Columns (Rows). For example, if you want two columns to be inserted to the LEFT of column B, select columns B and C before carrying out the command.

Deleting is the reverse of this. Select the column (row) you want to delete and choose Edit, Delete. For more than one column (row) select as many as you require. Note that this removes the column (row) completely and all columns (rows) to the right (below) will be renumbered.

Activity 51 helps you practice inserting rows and columns.

ACTIVITY 51

Start with a new worksheet.

1 In cell A1, type A; in cell B1, type B; in cell C1, type C.

2 Highlight column B.

3 Insert a column. Your row 1 should now read: A, blank, B, C.

4 Insert two columns so that your row 1 reads: A, blank, B, blank, blank C.

5 Clear the cells which you have been using.

6 In A1, type 1; in A2, type 2; in A3, type 3.

7 Insert a row between rows 1 and 2 so that your column A reads: 1, blank, 2, 3.

8 Insert two rows so that your column A reads: 1, blank, 2, blank, blank 3.

Summary

In this section you have learned how to change the width of columns and height of rows to enhance the presentation of your worksheet appearance. You have aligned data within cells and changed the background pattern and border around cells. You have also applied formatting to numeric data so that cells formatted in this way automatically display: a fixed number of decimal places; a currency (£) symbol in front of a number; a percent (%) symbol.

SECTION 5

Basic Charting

Introduction

Charting in Excel means producing graphs of your spreadsheet data. There are many different types of chart you can produce with Excel, from the simple bar, line, column (vertical bar) and pie charts to sophisticated radar and high-low-open-close charts. You do not, at this stage, need to know anything about the latter.

5.1 Constructing a chart

Before you can attempt to draw a graph from your data, you need to know about the component parts of a chart, and then, where on your spreadsheet data these are located.

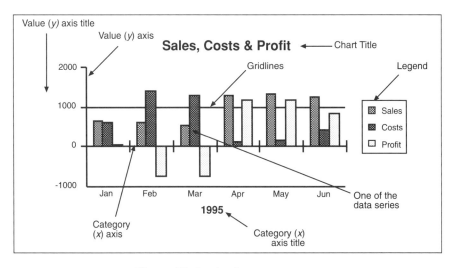

Figure 37: Basic chart components

Figure 37 shows the basic chart components for a column chart. Note the amount of information contained in this chart. For each of the six months between January and June (the *x*-axis), three items of information are given: the Sales figure; the Costs figure; and the Profit figure. Excel automatically assigns the minimum and maximum values to use for the *y*-axis.

Figure 38 shows the worksheet data that was used to construct the chart.

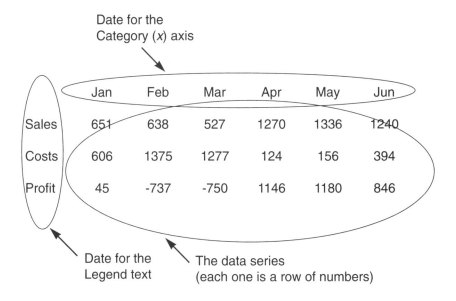

Figure 38: Worksheet data for constructing the chart

All the other items on the chart were added during the production of the chart. The following steps show the various dialog boxes of ChartWizard which were used to create the chart. You will create charts later in this section.

1 The cells making up the chart were selected by highlighting the area from the empty cell to the left of 'Jan' and above 'Sales' to the last value of 'Profit' and then pressing the ChartWizard button.

2 When the ChartWizard button is pressed the mouse pointer changes to a small cross with a graph alongside. This cursor enables you to open a box in which the chart will be presented on the worksheet. Position the pointer where you want the top-left corner of the chart to be, hold down the left mouse button and drag down and right until you have reached the position where you want the bottom-right corner to be. Don't make the box too large or too small.

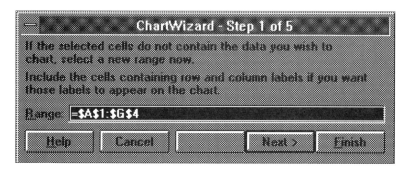

Figure 39: ChartWizard dialogue box

3 The dialogue box in Figure 39 is now presented to enable you to verify that you have selected the correct cells (or change the selection if you wish).

4 If the selection is correct, click the Next > button and the second dialog box will appear to enable you to select the chart type (Figure 40).

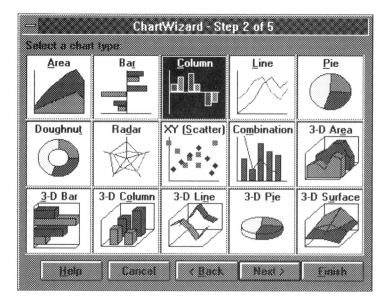

Figure 40: Step 2 in ChartWizard

A default column chart type is already selected and this is the one required to produce the chart (Figure 37). If this is not the one you require just click on any of the others.

When you have chosen the type, click the Next > button to confirm the selection of a style appropriate to the chart type you have chosen. This displays the dialog box shown in Figure 41.

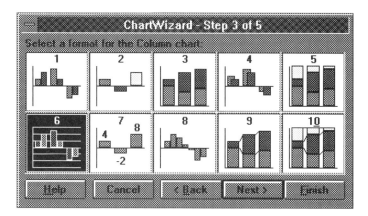

Figure 41:Step 3 in ChartWizard

5   The style required for the chart in Figure 37 is the default, so just click the Next > button. This will display the dialogue box for Step 4 of ChartWizard.

Step 4 enables you to further check some of your settings and gives you a sample of your chart (Figure 42).

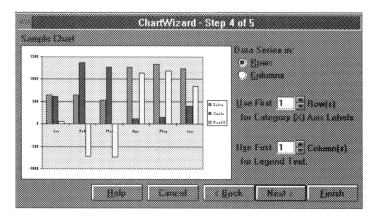

Figure 42: Step 4 in ChartWizard

6   Check that Excel has indeed got it right:

- that the data series are in rows (you would click the columns option if your series were in columns)

- that the first row is the data for the category *(x)* axis (if not change the number of rows)

- that the first column is the data for the legend text (again, if not change the number of columns).

When you have checked this dialog box click Next > for the dialog box for step 5 (the last one) (Figure 43).

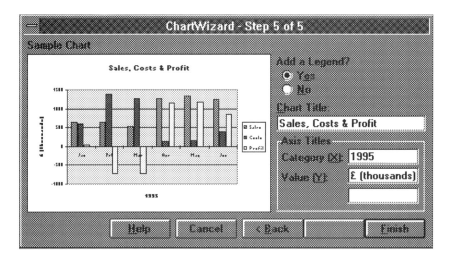

Figure 43: Step 5 in ChartWizard

7   Again, do some checking. Do you need a legend? Here you can also enter the titles you require. (Do not press Enter after entering a title, since doing so effectively selects the Finish button for you; click in each box where you want to type a title instead.) When the sample looks correct, press the Finish button.

5.2 Creating your own chart

You will use the information in Figure 44 in Activity 52. The worksheet represents the sales, in millions of pounds, for each quarter in the years 1990 to 1994.

	A	B	C	D	E	F
1	Year	Qtr 1	Qtr 2	Qtr 3	Qtr 4	Total
2	1990	£17.70	£19.30	£12.40	£18.30	£67.70
3	1991	£19.75	£20.50	£17.90	£23.21	£81.36
4	1992	£18.50	£21.67	£18.20	£24.00	£82.37
5	1993	£20.00	£23.50	£24.50	£26.80	£94.80
6	1994	£20.50	£23.00	£25.60	£29.35	£98.45

Figure 44: Sales for 1990 to 1994

First you need to put the data into a spreadsheet.

Next you will need to decide which sets of data you are going to show, and which sets need to be shown on the same chart.

In Activity 52 you will construct three charts to show:

1   The 'Total' column to illustrate the steady increase over the period 1990-1994.

2   The four quarters for each year to show the relative contribution of each quarter to the total for that year. All years will be the same chart so a comparison can easily be made between the years.

3   The four quarters for each year but displayed so that a comparison can be made with the same quarter in the other years.

THE LINE GRAPH
In Activity 52 you will follow the steps to construct the chart. For the first chart, you will choose a simple line graph with the years on the *x*-axis and the financial totals on the *y*-axis. You will then insert a title for the graph 'Sales (1990 – 1994)'; a title for the *x*-axis 'Years'; and a title for the *y*-axis '£ (millions)'.

ACTIVITY 51

1   Construct the worksheet as in Figure 44 ensuring that you use the same cells as in the figure.

2   Highlight the 'Year' column cells A2 to A6 then move the mouse cursor to cell F2 press and hold down the Ctrl key click on the 'Totals' column drag down to highlight all of the values, F2 to F6. Both columns should now be highlighted.

3   Click on the ChartWizard tool. Move the mouse cursor to a blank part of the worksheet below the data. The mouse cursor will change to a '+'. Click and drag right to form a rectangular box large enough to hold the chart. You can change the size once the chart is complete, so don't worry if your box is too large or too small.

4   The first of five ChartWizard windows should now open, and should show the chart range as:

$A$2:$A$6,$F$2:$F$6.

(If the ranges shown on screen are incorrect, amend them to read as above. Click the 'Next' button.)

5   You are now shown examples of chart types – select 'Line'. Click the 'Next' button.

6   The next step is to choose the chart format. Choose '2'. Click the 'Next' button.

7   In the next window, ensure that the following are selected:
   ● data series in columns
   ● use first 1 columns as *x*-axis labels
   ● use First 0 columns for legend text.

8   Click 'Next' button.

9   Now choose 1 type in:
   ● add a Legend?   No
   ● chart Title: Total Sales
   ● axis Titles:
      Category *x*   Years

      Value y   £ (millions)

10 Click the 'Finish' button.

11 If your chart is the wrong size or shape, adjust it as follows:

12 Click once on the chart – eight handles should appear.

13 Drag on the appropriate handle to produce the shape of your choice.

Your screen should look similar to Figure 45.

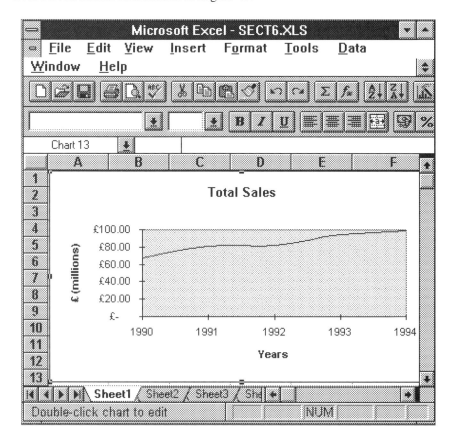

Figure 45: Constructing a line chart

You can edit the chart as in Activity 53.

ACTIVITY 53

Use the worksheet and sales chart from Activity 52.

Look carefully at the graph. Notice that it is crowded into the upper portion of the area. The reason for this is that Excel has chosen the *y*-axis range automatically and it starts at 0.

1 Double-click on the chart, anywhere inside the border that surrounds the chart object.

The border should change to a blue hatched line. This allows you to edit your chart. If your chart is bigger than the screen area a separate window will open. Don't worry about this.

2 Put the tip of the mouse arrow on the *y*-axis line and double-click. The following box in Figure 46 should appear.

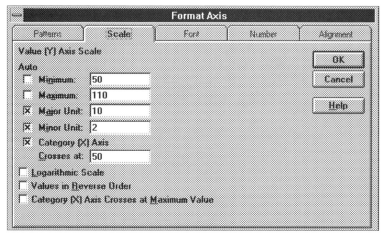

Figure 46: Format Axis dialog box

3 Change the 'Minimum' and 'Maximum' values to 50 and 110 respectively, as shown above, and click the 'OK' button. The chart should now look like Figure 47.

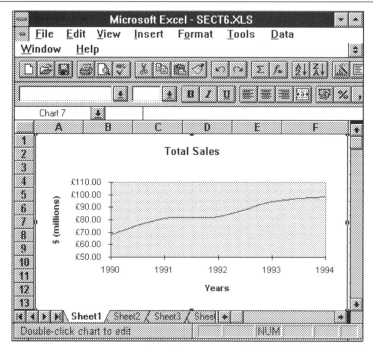

Figure 47: Changing the y-axis

Line charts are particularly good for showing 'trends' in data, particularly where only one or two graphs appear on the same chart.

BAR CHARTS

For the second and third charts you need to show a lot more information: each quarter of every year is twenty pieces of information (4 quarters times 5 years = 20). However the emphasis is different for each of these charts. For the second chart you need to emphasise the relative contribution of each quarter. This needs a 'stacked bar chart'; you create this in Activity 54 using the worksheet from Activity 52.

ACTIVITY 54

1 Select cell range A1 to E6.

2 Click on the ChartWizard button on the toolbar and make a box for the chart (see Activity 52, step 3).

3 Verify that the cell range is correct and click on the 'Next' button.

4 Select the '3D Column' chart type and click on the 'Next' button.

5 Select type 2 and click on the 'Next' button.

6 Verify that that data series is in <u>columns,</u> first column as axis labels, and the first 1 row as legend text have been selected. Then click on the 'Next' button.

7 Choose: Legend Yes; Chart title: Sales by Year; and Axis titles: Category X: Years; Value Z: (millions). Click the 'Finish' button.

Your chart should look like Figure 48.

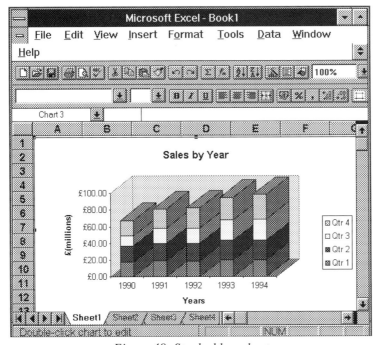

Figure 48: Stacked bar chart

For the third chart there is the same amount of information, but we need to emphasise the comparison of the same quarter within each year. For this, you need the 3D column chart again but use type 2 which shows, for each year, the four quarters grouped side-by-side. You see this in Activity 55.

ACTIVITY 55

1 Select cell range A1 to E6.

2 Click on the ChartWizard on the toolbar.

3 Verify that the cell range is correct and click on the 'Next' button.

4 Select the '3D Column' chart type and click on the 'Next' button.

5 Select type 1 and click on the 'Next' button.

6 Verify that the data series is in <u>columns</u>, first 1 column as axis labels, and the first 1 row as legend text have been selected. Then click on the 'Next' button.

7 Choose: Legend Yes; Chart title: Sales by Quarter; and Axis titles: Category X: Years; Value Z: £ (millions). Click the 'Finish' button.

Your chart should look like Figure 49.

8   Save the completed worksheet on Drive A as charts.xls.

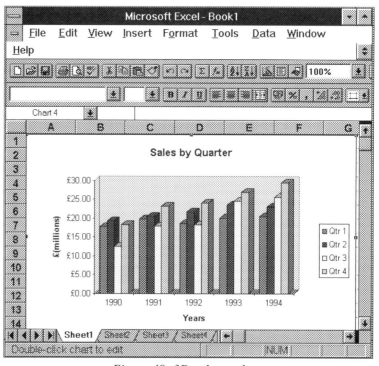

Figure 49: 3D column chart

In Activity 56 you carry out some further charting to create a 3D pie chart.

ACTIVITY 56

1 Open the worksheet leisure2.xls and create a 3-D pie chart to show the annual totals by category. Ensure that your chart is fully labelled with appropriate titles and a legend.

2 Save the worksheet with the chart as leisure3.xls.

Your chart should look something like Figure 50.

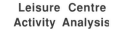

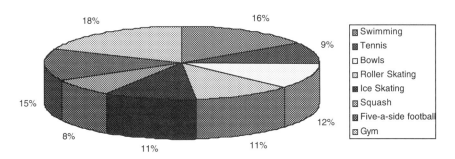

Figure 50: 3D pie chart

CHART TYPES

Excel offers a comprehensive range of charts to display worksheet data in graphic form. Graphic forms of data are extremely useful when presenting numeric data where the underlying trends etc. are not immediately obvious from looking at the numeric values alone.

Excel allows you to choose from a number of chart types. Each chart type has its own limitations, constraints and advantages. Which chart type to choose for a particular presentation will depend very much on the data, comparisons to be made, conclusions to be drawn etc. We give you some guidance to help you decide on which chart type to use later.

Summary

In this section you have created graphical representations of your worksheet data. You have gained a basic understanding of some of the basic graphical chart types and the some of the purposes for which they can be used. These types of graphical representations are extremely useful in written reports and in visual aids for oral presentations. They will help you in communicating your message effectively in some of the activities in Units 3 and 4.

SECTION 6

Advanced Functions

Introduction

In Section 3 you met some functions. Here you will meet some more; they operate in a more advanced way than the functions we discussed in Section 3. You can use them to change numeric displays and to conditionally vary a displayed value. You will also use look-up tables.

6.1 COUNT function

We often need to know how many items there are in range of cells. We might want to know:

- how many cells contain numbers
- how many cells are not empty.

For example, consider Figure 51, which is a simple sales sheet. The summary statistics show that the average line produced an income of £16.89. To get this figure, the total sales income (cell B11) had to be divided by the number of lines (cell B12).

As you know no one typed 6 into cell B12 – that's a job for Excel. So how did the 6 get there? It came from telling Excel to count the number of items in column A. In this section, you will construct the worksheet in Figure 51, but first you will have a chance to explore COUNT.

	A	B	C	D
1	Item	Sales value per item	Number sold	Sales (£)
2	Biros – black	0.25	43	10.75
3	Biros – blue	0.25	57	14.25
4	Folders – A4	0.20	26	5.2
5	Pads – A4	0.45	94	42.3
6	Pencils	0.05	49	2.45
7	Ring binders – A4	1.20	22	26.4
8	6		291	101.35
9				
10	Summary			
11	Total sales (£)	101.35		
12	Lines in stock	6		
13	Sales (£) per line	16.89		
14	Sales (£) per item sold	0.35		

Figure 51: Sales sheet with summary statistics

COUNT AND COUNTA

Figure 52 identifies the car registrations and house numbers of three people. The car registrations are a mixture of numbers and letters; the house numbers are pure numbers. Excel has two functions, one for each of these circumstances:

COUNT which counts up the number of cells containing numbers.

COUNTA which counts the number of non-blank cells.

To count the car registrations we need COUNTA and to count the houses, we need COUNT.

	A	B	C
1	Name	Car registration	House number
2	Paul	ABC999	23
3	Jill	DEF111	41
4	Anna		
5	Number of items		

Figure 52: Car registration and house numbers

Activity 57 enables you to explore COUNT. Start with a new worksheet on your screen.

ACTIVITY 57

1 Set up Figure 52 on your screen.

2 In the car registration total box, type =COUNT(B2:B4). Press Enter.

   Note what number appears in the total box.

3 Now edit =COUNT(B2:B4) to read =COUNTA(B2:B4).

   Note what number appears in the total box.

4 Repeat steps 2 and 3 for the house numbers.

You should have found the following results:

Function	Car registrations	House numbers
COUNT	0	2
COUNTA	2	2

COUNT finds how many cells contain numbers. There are no cells with pure numbers in the car column, but two cells with numbers in the house column.

COUNTA finds how many cells are not blank. Both columns have two non-blank cells.

Now that you know how to use COUNT, you can return to the sales example in Figure 51.

The example in Activity 58 gives you a chance to use COUNT in a realistic setting and to get more practice at some of the functions which you have already met.

ACTIVITY 58

Start with a new worksheet.

1   Type in the data in the shaded cells from Figure 51 or load the data from the file lines.xls. You do not need any functions for this.

2   In cell D2, calculate the value of the stock sold. Use a formula, not a function.

3   Copy D2 down to D7.

4   Use the SUM function in C8 to find the total number of items sold.

5   Copy this function to cell D8 to find the total sales income.

6   Make cell B11 equal to cell D8. This is just to get a copy of cell D8 into the summary table.

Using COUNTA.

So far, you have used functions that you have met already. Now it is time to use COUNTA. We need to know how many lines are on sale so that we can find the sales per line.

7   In cell B12, put =COUNTA(A2:A7).

Make sure that it shows the result 6.

8   In cell B13, put a formula to find sales per line (i.e. cell B11 divided by cell B12).

Make sure your answer starts 16.8...

9   Now edit cell B13 to add in the function ROUND so that cell B13 displays to two decimal places.

10 Finally, put a formula in cell B14 to find the sales per item.

Exploring your worksheet.

Now that you have COUNTA in place (as well as other formulae and functions), try the following to see how powerful your sales sheet is.

11 Put a new row in between Pencils and Ring binders. Type erasers in as the item, but do not put any sales data in.

What has happened to:

Lines in stock cell?

Sales per line cell?

Sales per item cell?

Make sure that these results are what you would expect.

12 Now put in the following sales data for

Erasers:

sales value: 15p

number sold: 26.

You will see that D7 is blank. Put your cursor on it to see why. Correct this.

13 Now that you are selling erasers, what has happened to the sales per item value?

In step 12 you will have found that cell D7 was blank. When you inserted the extra row for the erasers, Excel did not copy the formula being used in column D. **New rows and columns are always blank.** Whenever you insert new rows or columns, you will need to type in any functions and formulae that you need.

6.2 IF function

There are many occasions when what will appear in a cell needs to depend on the result of a calculation. For example, there may be a pass/fail column in a table of course marks. If a student gets enough marks to pass, then 'Pass' will appear; with fewer marks 'Fail' will appear. We need to be able to say to Excel something like:

If the student passes, put 'Pass' in the cell; if the student fails, put 'Fail' in the cell.

We can see how Excel does this by an example.

Figure 53 shows the marks achieved by four students. Column C contains 'Pass' or 'Fail', depending on whether the student reached the pass mark of 40%. The cells in the C column contain the function:

For Smith: =IF(B3>=40, 'Pass', 'Fail')

For Williams: =IF(B5>=40, 'Pass', 'Fail')

Because Smith's mark is more than 40, Excel selects 'Pass' from the function. Because Williams' mark is less than 40, Excel selects 'Fail' from the function.

	A	B	C
1	Name	Score	Pass/Fail
2			
3	Smith	45	Pass
4	Jones	64	Pass
5	Williams	24	Fail
6	Andrews	59	Pass

Figure 53: IF function worksheet

The function is summarised as in Figure 54.

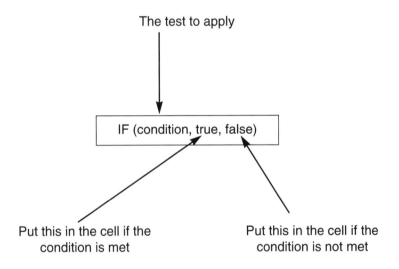

The test to apply

IF (condition, true, false)

Put this in the cell if the condition is met

Put this in the cell if the condition is not met

Figure 54: IF function

Activity 59 asks you to construct the worksheet in Figure 53 and gives you practice in using the IF function.

ACTIVITY 59

Start with a new worksheet.

1 Type in the data in the shaded cells of Figure 53.

2 Then type the IF function into cell C3.

3 Copy this function to the other cells in column C.

4 Make sure that 'Pass' and 'Fail' are appearing correctly in each cell in column C.

5 Try changing some of the marks in column B. Make sure that the correct result is always displayed in column C.

You will find a solution to this activity on your course disk in exam.xls.

6.3 The ABS function

Another useful function is ABS, which gives us the difference between two numbers, ignoring any negative sign. So:

ABS(5 – 3) = 2

and

ABS(3 – 5) = 2.

In the following example you see how this can be useful. A haulage company sets target times for the standard journeys that it makes. Drivers' times are checked to see whether they are within 5% of the targets. (If they get there too quickly, perhaps they are speeding; if they take too long, this costs extra money.) The company needs to find the difference between the target journey time and the actual time, ignoring whether the result is positive or negative. This difference can then be expressed as a percentage of the target time. The company's calculations will look like Figure 55. As usual, the shaded area is the data; the clear cells contain formulae and functions.

In Figure 55, cell D2 contains =ABS(B2-C2). This formula is then copied down column D.

	A	B	C	D	E	F
1	Driver	Target time	Actual time	Difference	% difference	Difference >5%?
2	Jones	240	250	10	4.17%	No
3	Gupta	300	290	10	3.33%	No
4	Strauss	280	320	40	14.29%	Yes
5	McKay	360	365	5	1.39%	No
6	Smith	270	300	30	11.11%	Yes

Figure 55: ABS function worksheet

In Activity 60 you will construct Figure 55.

ACTIVITY 60

Use a new worksheet for this.

1 Type in the data (the shaded cells) from Figure 55.

2 Type =ABS(B2-C2) in cell D2 and copy it down the column.

3 Put a formula in cell E2 to express cell D2 as a percentage of cell B2.

4 Use the IF function in cell F2 to print 'Yes' if the percentage in cell B2 is more than 5% and to print 'No' if it is less than 5%.

5 Make sure that your table displays the correct results in column F. Try changing the times in columns B and C. Does column F adjust appropriately?

6.4 More complex uses of IF

You have seen how the IF function can be used to put one of two values into a cell, e.g. 'Pass' or 'Fail'. Sometimes there are more than two possibilities. How can IF be used then?

Before we show you the answer to this, first try Activity 61 which introduces you to a typical situation with more than two possibilities. This activity involves constructing the worksheet shown in Figure 56. It gives you more practice in using advanced functions, including ABS, and introduces you to a situation with more than two outcomes.

ACTIVITY 61

Start this activity with a blank worksheet.

1 Enter the data shown in Figure 56 into the cells indicated in the figure or load the data from the file times.xls.

2 In column E use the ABS() function to display the difference between columns C and D.

3 Use the IF() function in column F to display either Overspent or Underspent. Note the condition for overspent is: is column D value greater than column C?

4 Make sure that column F is showing the correct outcome.

5 Try changing some of the figures in columns C and D, again checking that column F still shows the correct outcome.

6 What happens to column F when the actual expenditure is equal to the budgeted expenditure?

Save this worksheet for use in Activity 62.

	A	B	C	D	E	F
1	Budget		Budgeted	Actual		
2	Item		Expenditure	Expenditure	Difference	
3						
4	Holiday		£950.00	£1200.00		
5	Car Insurance		£450.00	£430.00		
6	Mortgage		£1200.00	£1000.00		
7	House Insurance		£250.00	£275.00		
8						

Figure 56: Worksheet with more than two outcomes

At the end of Activity 61 you should have found that column F shows 'Underspent' when the actual and budgeted figures are the same. This is because the IF statement you used can only choose between:

● actual less than budget – prints 'Underspent'

● actual more than budget – prints 'Overspent'.

There is no provision here for budget and actual being equal.

To cope with this situation you would need to be able to display three different text values, for example:

Condition	Displayed Text
D4>C4	Overspent
D4<C4	Underspent
D4=C4	Balanced

How can we achieve this when the IF() function allows only two outcomes? The answer is to use the IF() function twice! We describe the second use of the IF()

function as a nested function. The syntax would look like this:

IF(*condition1*, *True1*, IF(*condition2*, *True2*, *False2*))

Figure 57 shows how this works:

The first IF test can produce one of two results: True or False:

- if the result is True, then the True action of the first test is carried out and the second test is not used
- if the first test produces the result False, then the second test is carried out.

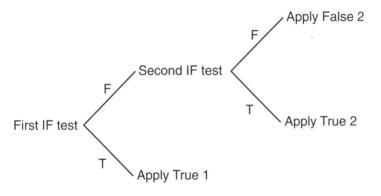

Figure 57: Using IF function twice

In Activity 62, you try out nested IF function.

ACTIVITY 62

Use your worksheet from Activity 61.

1 In cell F4 type the formula:

    =IF(D4=C4, 'Balanced', IF(D4>C4, 'Overspent', 'Underspent'))

    This must all be typed on one line.

2 Use Autofill to copy the function in F4 down to F5 to F7.

3 Change the value in cell D5 to be 430.

    The value in cell F5 should now be 'Balanced'.

6.5 Ceiling functions

These functions are like the rounding functions, but with a much wider application. Suppose that you are cooking chicken quarters and you have bought four – one for each person. Then a friend rings up and you invite her to join you. Now you need five chicken quarters, so you will have to buy another … But, the local shop only sells them in twos, so you will have to buy two. You have just applied the Ceiling function to your shopping by saying: I need to buy one chicken piece when they come in twos. So I will have to buy two.

Excel would write this as follows:

=Ceiling (1, 2)

This finds the next number above 1 which is a multiple of 2.

Activity 63 enables you to find out how Ceiling works.

ACTIVITY 63

Start with a new worksheet.

1 Type in the shaded parts of Figure 58.

2 Use the Ceiling function in column D to find out how many items you need to buy.

You should get the answers 2, 40, 10 and 3.

3 Put some more examples of your own into the table. Make sure that you understand the answer that Ceiling gives.

Save this worksheet for use in the next Activity 64.

	A	B	C	D
1	Item	You need	Sold in	Have to buy
2	Chicken pieces	1	2	
3	Cigarettes	25	20	
4	Discount bus tickets	8	10	
5	Cheap soap	2	3	

Figure 58: Ceiling function worksheet

Ceiling can also be used when the second number is less than one, in which case it behaves a bit like rounding (but it is not exactly the same).

Examples

Ceiling (1.42, 0.5) returns 1.5

Ceiling (1.421, 0.01) returns 1.43

The Ceiling function is summarised in Figure 59.

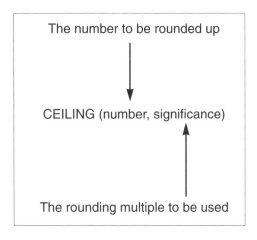

Figure 59: The Ceiling function

FLOOR

When you went to buy the extra two chicken pieces, we did not ask whether you can afford them. You bought what you needed. Often, we buy what we can afford, that is where Floor comes in.

Suppose that, although chicken pieces are sold in twos, you can only afford one piece. How many twos do you buy? None.

Excel's Floor finds the next multiple below your number. If you can't afford one pack of two chicken pieces, then you can afford no packs. Excel would write this as:

    = Floor (1, 2)

and would give the answer zero.

Activity 64 enables you to explore what you can afford with Floor using the same data as you did in Activity 63. Use the worksheet you made in Activity 63 or load the file items.xls.

ACTIVITY 64

1 Copy your table to an empty part of the worksheet. Then change the cells which are shaded in Figure 60.

2 Type the = FLOOR (B2, C2) into cell D2.

You should get the answers 0, 20, 0 and 0.

Make sure you understand what FLOOR has done. For example, if you have only enough money for two bars of soap and soap is sold in packs of three bars, then you cannot afford to buy soap.

	A	B	C	D
1	Item	You need	Sold in	Have to buy
2	Chicken pieces	1	2	
3	Cigarettes	25	20	
4	Discount bus tickets	8	10	
5	Cheap soap	2	3	

Figure 60: Floor worksheet

Floor can also be used when the second number is less than one, in which case it behaves a bit like rounding (but it is not exactly the same).

Examples
FLOOR(2.676, 0.01) returns 2.67

FLOOR(6.89, 1.5) returns 6.0

The FLOOR function is summarised in Figure 61.

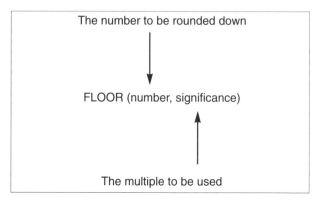

Figure 61: The Floor function

6.6 Look-up tables

We often look things up in tables. For example, we look up lecture times, prices and bus times. Excel can also look things up in tables. An example is the best way to see how Excel does this.

Suppose that an insurance company offers the no-claims discount rates shown in Figure 62. A salesperson could carry a copy of this around and consult it as needed. However, if the salesperson were using Excel to help make quotes and record business, then Excel can keep a copy of the table and look up the discount for each new customer.

Years	Discount
0	0%
3	30%
4	40%
5	50%
6	60%

Figure 62: No-claims discount rates

The function which Excel uses to look-up something in a table like this is quite complex. It needs to know four things:

- the cell which holds the value to be looked up
- the range of cells which make up the look-up table
- the column number in which Excel is to find the value
- whether the look-up table is sorted or not.

Look now at Figure 63 which shows the look-up table within a spreadsheet.

We want to find the discount for the number of years typed into cell C11. So, we need to tell Excel:

- The reference value, i.e. the cell which holds the value to be looked up – C11.
- The range of cells which make up the look-up table – B5:C9.
- The column number in which Excel is to find the value, i.e. 2. This is called the offset.
- Whether the look-up table is sorted or not, i.e., TRUE.

We put all this information into the function:

VLOOKUP(reference value, range, offset, sorted)

and it then reads:

VLOOKUP(C11, B5:C9, 2, TRUE).

	A	B	C
1		Discount	Table
2			
3		Years	Discount
4			
5		0	0%
6		3	30%
7		4	40%
8		5	50%
9		6	60%
10			
11	Customer claims (years)		4
12	Discount given		40%

Figure 63: Look-up table within a spreadsheet

You try this in Activity 65.

ACTIVITY 65

Use a new worksheet for this.

1 Construct a worksheet using the data in Figure 63.

2 Try lots of values in cell C11 and make sure that cell C12 always gives the right discount.

You will find a solution to this activity on your module disk in distable.xls.

HLOOKUP

Sometimes you will want to look up a value in a horizontal table. In that case you use HLOOKUP(...) instead of VLOOKUP(...).

6.7 Joining up text

The final function that we will look at in this section is one which enables you to join together the contents of different cells.

Look back at Figure 58. In column D you have the quantities to buy. This would look better if it read like column E of Figure 64. To achieve this effect for cell E2 we need to join together the 2 in cell D2 with the word 'packs'. 'Join together' is called **concatenate** in Excel, so cell E2 contains:

=CONCATENATE(D2, ' packs')

Notice that we have put a space in front of 'packs' so that we get '2 packs' and not '2packs'.

A	B	C	D	E
1 Item	You need	Sold in	Have to buy	
2 Chicken pieces	1	2	2	2 packs
3 Cigarettes	25	20	40	40 cartons
4 Discount bus tickets	8	10	10	10 books
5 Cheap soap	2	3	3	3 bars

Figure 64: Joining together or concatenate

You use concatenate in Activity 66.

ACTIVITY 66

Recall your worksheet from Activity 66 for this.

1. In cell E2, type:

=CONCATENATE(D2, ' packs')

2. Copy to cells E3 to E5.

3. Edit cells E3 to E5, changing 'packs' to the appropriate description.

CONCATENATE can be used to join several items. For example you could change cell E2 to:

CONCATENATE(Need to buy, D2, packs)

Summary

In this section you have used Excel functions that have multiple parameters and functions that operate conditionally upon the data. Also you have used functions to provide some advanced formatting of numeric data and used nested functions in a cell.

Section 7

Using a Worksheet for 'Database' Activities

Introduction

Excel can be used to perform many 'database' style operations such as sorting, filtering, external database access and cross-tabulation. Excel is NOT a database program like Access that you will meet in Unit 8, and should not be used as such. However, the database functions can be very useful as part of worksheet operations. We cover sorting and filtering of data, which are the two simplest techniques available within Excel.

7.1 A simple list

Figure 65 illustrates a simple list, or table as it is sometimes called. It is part of a company's staff telephone list. The cells in row 1 contain 'labels' for the data in the columns beneath them. So we can easily see that column A contains names, column B office room numbers and column C telephone numbers. Each of the rows contains a 'record' of the data associated with a single staff member. Each record contains (in this case) three 'fields' or cells. The set of all records is the list.

	A	B	C	D
1	Name	Office	Telephone	
2	Jenkins R	103	2475	
3	Jones M	115	2612	
4	Kelly P	103	2849	
5	Knight K	113	2344	

Figure 65: Simple list of telephone numbers

In Excel, you don't need to do anything special to a list to make it into a database. When you perform database tasks, such as finding or sorting data, Excel automatically recognises the list as a database. Excel assumes that:

- the columns in the list are the fields in the database

- the column labels in the list are the field names in the database

- each row in the list is a record in the database.

An Excel list is defined as being surrounded by the edge of the worksheet and/or blank rows or columns. For this reason, your list should contain NO blank rows or columns. Excel can automatically determine the extent of your list by using the above rule.

To carry out any of the processing described in this section you merely need to ensure that the active cell is somewhere inside your list.

SORTING

Figure 66 shows a typical list in fairly random order. Note that the list is surrounded on two sides by the edges of the worksheet and on the other two sides by a blank row (11) and a blank column (E).

	A	B	C	D	E
1	Last Name	First Name	Course	Average Grade Point	
2	Baggins	Bilbo	BABC	12	
3	Baggins	Frodo	BScIT	13	
4	Oakenshie	Thorin	BABC	6	
5	Meredith	Jack	BScC	7	
6	Mantel	Samuel	BScC	9	
7	Champagr	Tom	BScIT	5	
8	Karelias	George	BABC	14	
9	Alexander	Sylvia	BScC	10	
10	Grindley	Kit	BScIT	11	
11					
12					

Figure 66: Student list

The active cell is currently D10 which is inside the list (or table). If you wish to sort this list into Average Grade Point Order (Descending) all that is required is to choose Data, Sort from the menu and ensure that the dialog box looks like that in Figure 67.

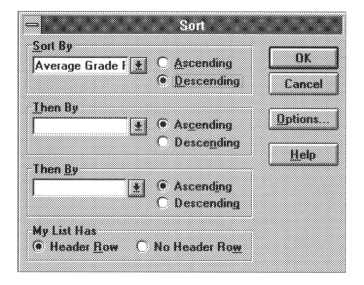

Figure 67: Sort dialog box

The dialog box allows you to sort on up to three columns each in ascending or descending sequence. If you have correctly set up your list as described above, the My list option should always be set to Header Row.

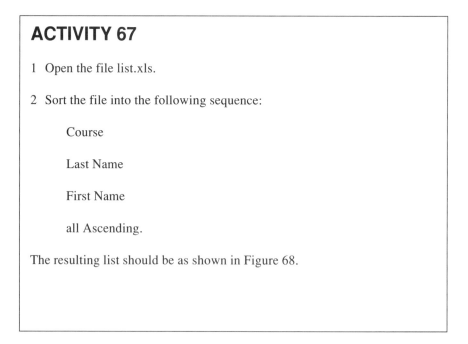

ACTIVITY 67

1 Open the file list.xls.

2 Sort the file into the following sequence:

   Course

   Last Name

   First Name

   all Ascending.

The resulting list should be as shown in Figure 68.

	Last Name	First Name	Course	Average Grade Point
2	Baggins	Bilbo	BABC	12
3	Baggins	Frodo	BABC	13
4	Karelias	George	BABC	14
5	Oakenshield	Thorin	BABC	6
6	Alexander	Sylvia	BScC	10
7	Mantel	Samuel	BScC	9
8	Meredith	Jack	BScC	7
9	Champagne	Tom	BScIT	5
10	Grindley	Kit	BScIT	11
11				

Figure 68: Sorted list

Note that the original sequence of the data is lost. What would you need to do if it was important?

FILTERING

Filtering enables you to see just the rows that match criteria chosen by you. For example, you might wish to list the students on the BABC course. Activity 68 shows you how to do this.

ACTIVITY 68

Continue using the spreadsheet from Activity 67.

1 Ensure that the active cell is within your table.

2 Choose Data, Filter, AutoFilter from the menu.

   This produces drop-down arrows at the top of each column as in Figure 69.

3 Click on the arrow for the Course column.

   This shows you the options in Figure 70. These include each of the values in the Course column. (There is also a Custom option that we can look at later.)

4 You want BABC students, so click on that option.

   Your screen should now show just the four rows corresponding to BABC students, as in Figure 71.

Notice the shading. This shows you:

● which drop down arrow has been applied

● which row numbers have been selected.

The other rows are still there. To see them, just click All in the drop-down menu.

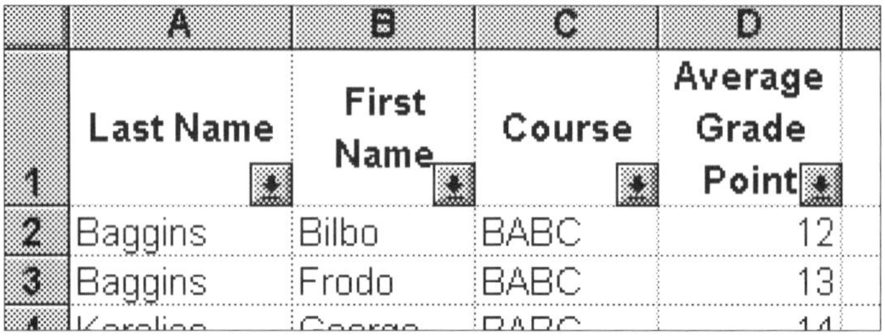

	A	B	C	D
1	Last Name	First Name	Course	Average Grade Point
2	Baggins	Bilbo	BABC	12
3	Baggins	Frodo	BABC	13
4	Karelias	George	BABC	14

Figure 69: Drop-down arrows at top of each column

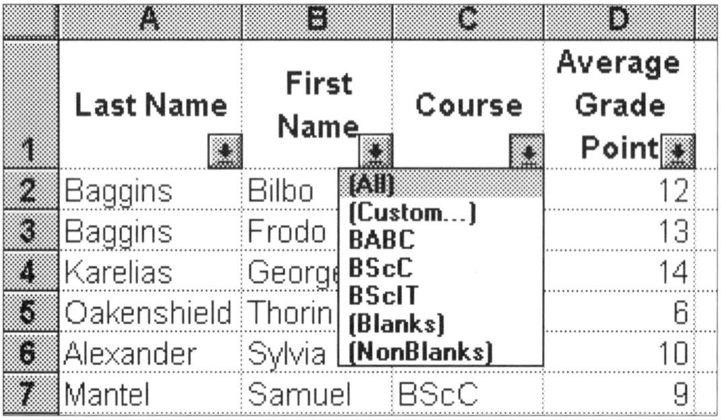

	A	B	C	D
1	Last Name	First Name	Course	Average Grade Point
2	Baggins	Bilbo	[All]	12
3	Baggins	Frodo	[Custom...] BABC	13
4	Karelias	George	BScC	14
5	Oakenshield	Thorin	BScIT [Blanks]	6
6	Alexander	Sylvia	[NonBlanks]	10
7	Mantel	Samuel	BScC	9

Figure 70: Course options

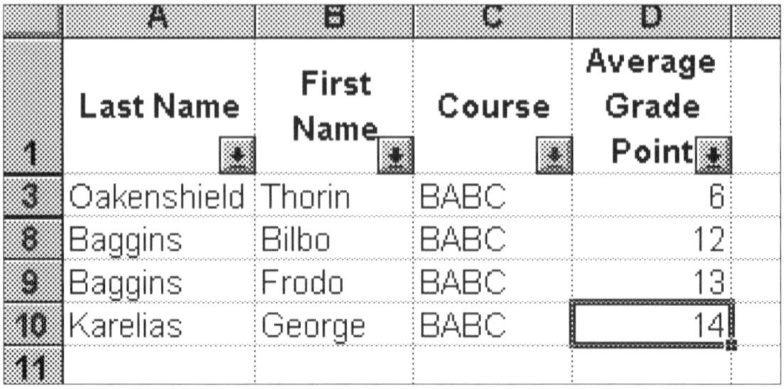

	A	B	C	D
1	Last Name	First Name	Course	Average Grade Point
3	Oakenshield	Thorin	BABC	6
8	Baggins	Bilbo	BABC	12
9	Baggins	Frodo	BABC	13
10	Karelias	George	BABC	14
11				

Figure 71:Four rows showing BABC students

ACTIVITY 69

Continue using the spreadsheet from Activity 68 with the BABC filter applied.

1 Click the drop-down arrow for the 'Average Grade Point' column and choose the Custom option.

A dialog box should appear (Figure 72).

2 Click the drop-down next to the '=' sign and change '=' to '>='.

Type 13 in the text box alongside '>='.

3 Click OK.

The new filter takes effect as in Figure 73.

Notice that the combined effect is cumulative.

4 In step 2, you could use a more complicated condition such as '>=6 and <=10'.

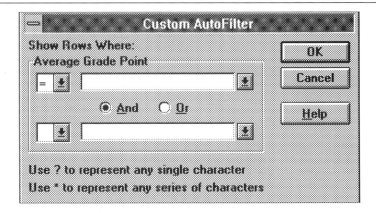

Figure 72: Customer AutoFilter dialog box

	A	B	C	D	
1	Last Name	First Name	Course	Average Grade Point	
9	Baggins	Frodo	BABC	13	
10	Karelias	George	BABC	14	
11					

Figure 73: Custom AutoFilter

REMOVING FILTERS

To remove filters, just choose Data, Filter, AutoFilter again and the drop-down arrows disappear and all the data is shown (see Activity 70).

ACTIVITY 70

1 Open the file called orders.xls

2 By using the AutoFilter feature, view only those orders to customers in Greece.

   How many records are displayed?

   The answer should be 13 (out of 87)

3 Reset the filter on Country to All.

4 Set the filter on Country to Eire and on Item to Camcorder

   How many records are displayed now?

   The answer should be 5.

5 How many records are there where the Revenue is between £40,000 and £50,000?

   The answer is 7.

For more about filtering or using more complex criteria, use the Help facility and search for Advanced filter commands.

Summary

You now understand what a simple list is, and how to apply database operations such as sorting and filtering. You have also learned some simple database terminology and understand what is meant by: a list or table; a record; and a field.

SECTION 8
Worksheet Construction

Introduction

The primary purpose of using a spreadsheet is to simplify the handling of numeric data. As you have seen during this module in Excel, 'handling' can mean:

- entering 'raw' numbers
- entering a formula
- entering functions into cells.

You have also seen how this numeric data can be integrated and combined to form calculations which can be simple or very complex. Text can be added to enhance the meaning of the numeric data and you can format the numbers and text to present information in an organised and meaningful way. Few, if any, worksheets exhibit all of the possible features. In the following example, you will use a number of the worksheet features that you have encountered in the other sections of the module in a small, but complete, worksheet application.

8.1 Worksheet organisation

Before starting to construct a worksheet for some purpose, you need to think about its layout. You may wish to display certain results in one or more of the following ways:

- on screen
- printed in a company report
- on a transparency slide for a presentation.

The aim of displaying results is usually to bring some point to the attention of an audience. If the display includes irrelevant data or information then the point may be lost. The point may also be hidden if your display contains *too much* information at once. In other words, the *quality* of the display can be as important as its *content*. Data is only irrelevant to the aim of the display. This data may be essential to the calculation and someone in your audience may be interested in how the calculation was made, but that is another matter. Cells which are only necessary for calculation are best clustered together into a working area out of normal view.

Figure 74 shows a possible layout for a worksheet that requires four distinct functional areas. Each would be a multiple of the screen area in size. In this way you could move from the Input Area to the Output Area by pressing the Page Down key (perhaps more than once).

Input Area	Process Area
Output Area	Chart Area

Figure 74: Worksheet layout

Also you could move from the Input Area to the Process Area by pressing ALT+Page Down. (See Section 2.1, Moving Around the Sheet.)

For other worksheets it may be more appropriate to combine the Input and Output Areas. It may also be more appropriate to lay out the areas horizontally so that the functional areas can expand downwards, see Figure 75.

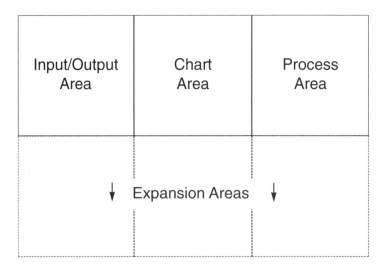

Figure 75: Alternative worksheet layout

The appropriate layout for a worksheet will depend on a number of factors including:

● Will the worksheet grow significantly in size over a period of time? If so, allow for expansion.

● If the output data is only meaningful when compared with the input data, then combine (at least part) of the Input and Output Areas.

● Will your Process area contain lookup tables and intermediate calculations? If so, subdivide the Process Area.

Although the Process Area is normally only seen by the worksheet constructor (you!), it is worthwhile placing text labels adjacent to tables etc that explain their function. You may need to alter the worksheet in one or two years time and your original ideas about how the worksheet functions may not be clear any more. Labels help explain why you decided to implement certain features.

AN EXAMPLE WORKSHEET

The worksheet that you are going to look at holds assessment data for a group of students. The data is used to calculate and analyse course results.

The general layout of the worksheet is shown in Figure 76.

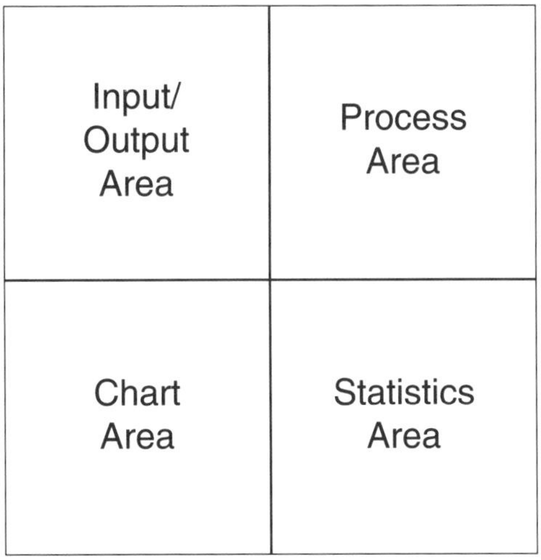

Figure 76: Worksheet layout

We shall now take you on a tour of each of these areas.

INPUT/OUTPUT AREA

This area holds the raw data (marks) and presents the final output (grade-point). The columns are used as follows:

Column	Contents	Contents type
A and B	Student details	Data
C, D and E	Coursework marks	Data
F	Coursework total, i.e. 25% x CW1 + 35% x CW2 + 45% x CW3	Formula
G	Exam mark	Data
H	Module percentage, i.e. 40% x Coursework total + 60% x Exam mark	Formula
I	Module grade-point, found from a look-up table	Output

In addition to the column use shown above, each of the cells C1 to G1 holds a weight used in the marks calculations.

	A	B	C	D	E	F	G	H	I	J
1	Student		Weight 25%	Weight 35%	Weight 40%	Weight 40%	Weight 60%	%	GP	
2	Name	Initials	CW1	CW2	CW3	CW Total	Exam	Module	Module	
3	Greensitt	HC	47	54	48	50	45	47	7	
4	Hawkins	P	59	48	64	57	46	50	8	
5	Robson	L	54	39	38	42	26	32	2	
6	Smith	P	56	45	75	60	52	55	9	
7	Armstrong	T	33	43	45	41	32	35	3	
8	Smith	KL	41	53	36	43	39	40	4	
9	Sculley	D	45	40	60	49	37	41	5	
10	King	O	56	48	74	60	30	42	5	
11	Peacock	H	50	35	73	54	40	45	6	
12	Marsh	J	38	44	40	41	31	35	3	
13	Cooke	R	50	35	43	42	51	47	7	
14	Hepburn	W	44	47	63	53	54	53	8	
15	Burns	Q	26	43	40	38	31	33	2	
16	Fraser	D	49	38	61	50	51	50	8	
17	Walton	R	59	69	62	64	72	68	13	
18	Patel	J	28	49	69	52	53	52	8	
19	Mattocks	C	45	50	54	50	57	54	9	
20	Pemberton	L	73	75	71	73	68	70	14	
21	Banoub	KH	63	57	69	63	64	63	11	
22	Ashton	V	65	67	60	64	65	64	12	
23	James	P	49	46	30	40	28	32	2	
24	Heath	M	47	52	57	53	50	51	8	
25										

Figure 77: Input/Output Area

CHART AREA

A graph has been constructed to show Total Coursework mark and Exam mark and this is displayed in the Chart Area (see Figure 78).

The Chart Area occupies cells A26 to J50.

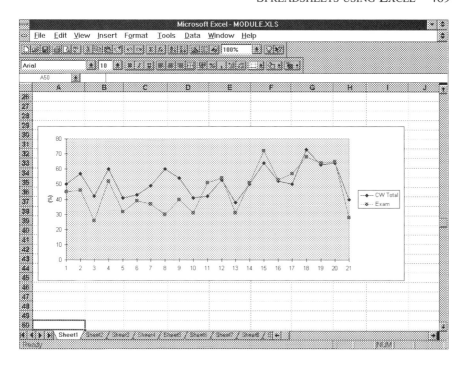

Figure 78: Chart Area

PROCESS AREA

The Process Area is immediately to the right of the Input/Output Area and is shown in Figure 79. It contains the look-up table that converts percentages to grade points.

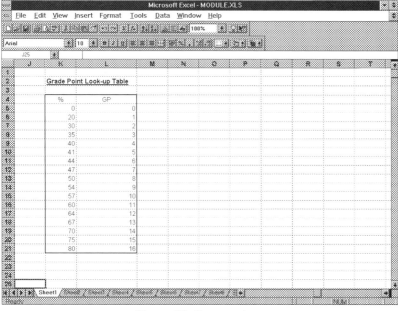

Figure 79: Process Area

The Process Area occupies cells J1 to U25. Note that column J is displayed in both the Input/Output Area and the Process Area.

This is because ALT+Page Down has been used to move from the Input/Output Area to the right and this displays column J for both areas. It is for this reason that column J has been left blank.

STATISTICAL AREA

Some statistical information about the results is also required and, since it is intended to print this off separately, it is displayed in its own area immediately below the Process Area. This is shown in Figure 80.

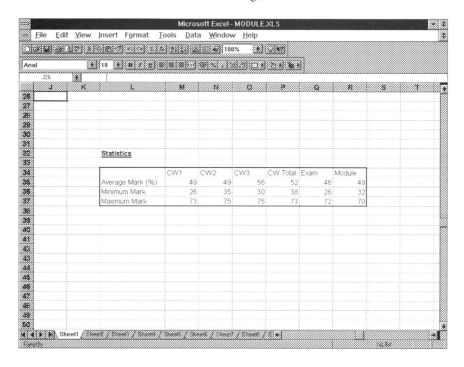

Figure 80: Statistics Area

In Activity 71, you identify these screen areas.

ACTIVITY 71

The worksheet described here is on your module disk as module.xls.

1 Open module.xls and use Alt, Page up and Page down to check that you can now move from one area to another.

2 When you are happy that you can see how different screen areas work in a spreadsheet, close the file.

CREATING YOUR OWN SPREADSHEET AREAS

Now that you have seen how spreadsheets are organised, you can use these ideas to re-organise some of your own worksheets.

In the following activities, you can use any layout that you think makes your spreadsheet easy to use and to understand. However, we shall suggest layouts based on the format in Figure 81.

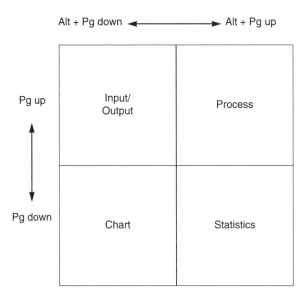

Figure 81: Layout format

Activity 72 uses the profit table and its chart that you looked at earlier.

ACTIVITY 72

1   Open the file profit.xls containing the table and chart.

2   Choose one of the four areas in Figure 81 for your worksheet and one for your chart.

3   Move either or both of the worksheet and chart to their chosen areas. You can do this by selecting the area you wish to move and then using cut and paste.

4   Use Alt, Page up and Page down to check that you can now move from one area to another.

5   Check that, at any one time, only the chart or the worksheet is on the screen.

Activity 73 uses the discount table that you created earlier.

ACTIVITY 73

1 Open the worksheet.

2 Decide on two areas for your worksheet:

- one for input/output
- one for the look-up table.

3 Move either or both parts of the worksheet as necessary.

4 Use Alt, Page up and Page down to check that you can now move from one area to another.

5 Check that, at any one time, only the chart or the worksheet is on the screen.

Summary

A worksheet can be physically organised into a number of different areas. You have consolidated your knowledge of Excel by working through an example worksheet which contains a number of the features. You have also had an opportunity to construct a worksheet from a specification.

Unit Review Activity

The Technical Support Group have decided to monitor the rate at which computer faults are reported and fixed on a day-by-day basis. You have been asked to help them by designing a spreadsheet which can be used to analyse the pattern of faults over a one week period. A typical set of data (including old faults 'brought forward' from the previous week and unfixed faults 'carried forward' to the next) might be as follows:

Old Faults	10	
Day	**New Faults Reported**	**Faults Fixed**
Monday	4	5
Tuesday	11	4
Wednesday	9	13
Thursday	2	6
Friday	8	4
Continuing Faults		

Carry out the following tasks:

Create a worksheet to represent the above data except for 'Continuing Faults'. You should include an appropriate Main Title (bold and enlarged) and column headings (bold). Put borders around appropriate parts of the data.

Add a new row immediately under the figures for Friday. Label this row 'Total' and use the SUM function to calculate the whole week totals for each of the 'New Faults Reported' and 'Faults Fixed' columns.

Add a fourth column entitled 'Faults at the End of Day'. This should use an appropriate formula to calculate the faults remaining at the end of each day.

Add a new row under the totals row. Label it 'Average' and use appropriate functions to calculate the average for each of the 'New Faults Reported', 'Faults Fixed' and 'Faults at End of Day' columns.

Add a cell to the right of 'Continuing Faults' that displays the number of faults that should be carried forward to the next week.

Create a Column Chart showing the three figures in the table for each day of the week. Add a Title, Labels and a Legend.

	Task	Mark
1		10
2		8
3		5
4		2
5		2
6		10

UNIT 8
DATABASES USING ACCESS

Introduction

This unit introduces you to the world of databases and will help you to create and use your own databases as well as to make better use of existing database software. Database software has been around for a long time. Although computers were originally devised to perform calculations very rapidly, it was soon realised that they could also be used to store and manipulate vast quantities of information. In order to do this, programs were written to handle the data. Originally, these database programs were designed to run on large mainframe computers, which were the only machines then available. Very few people had access to these computers, and most people only saw the end products, such as computerised bills and junk mail.

The arrival of PCs at the end of the 1970s changed all that. Suddenly it was possible to store data on a small desktop computer, and software was speedily developed to use with the new machines.

Early database software for PCs was primitive by today's standards, but advanced features were continually added. By the late 1980s, small but capable PCs could handle the volume and complexity of work that had required a whole roomful of equipment just 10 years earlier.

Over the same period in which computers were being improved and developed, many people began to use them. The machines were found useful mostly in business, but also in education and research, manufacturing and at home. Most users input or retrieve data using software specially designed by experts. They have little or no understanding of how to program databases themselves.The unit will concentrate on building your skills so that you can work easily and confidently with databases. In this unit, you will use the module disk Unit_8.MDB.

Objectives

By the end of the unit, you will be able to:

- identify your own uses for a database
- create and modify a database design
- load and save files
- add to and amend data
- create forms and reports for entering and viewing data
- sort your data
- print reports and labels
- use relational databases and create queries to extract information from them.

TERMINOLOGY

The study of databases is an academic subject in its own right, taught as an essential component of degrees in Computer Science. Fortunately, you do not need to know much theory to use PC software. This unit, based on the popular Microsoft Access package, introduces you to the basics of databases. It uses enough theory to enable you to follow the module, even when you are using other database software packages. The terminology used is as standard as possible. However, note that software suppliers use different words for the same ideas.

DATA PROTECTION ACT

All of the databases and examples used in this unit are either fictional or based on non-copyright material. If you intend to use your database software to store information about real people, you may need to register with the Data Protection Registrar under the terms of the UK Data Protection Act 1984. With some exceptions, it is illegal to store such information without being registered. Under this law, too, you must supply any person who asks to check the information with a copy of the data you hold on that individual.

Further information about the Data Protection Act and registration may be obtained from: Data Protection Registrar, Wycliffe House, Water Lane, Wilmslow SK9 5AF Tel: 01625 535777.

TOOLBARS AND ICONS

We refer to icons for selecting options and controlling views etc. These icons appear on toolbars which are usually displayed at the top of the screen. In Access the user can choose which toolbars are displayed and these preferences are stored for future sessions. If someone has used Access on your machine they may have altered the toolbars on display. You should ensure that the toolbars you need are displayed before you start a set of activities.

TURNING TOOLBARS ON AND OFF

This operation is performed by selecting View and then Toolbars from the main menu. This will display a list of toolbars. Those which will be displayed will have a small tick ✔ at the side. To switch a toolbar on highlight it with the cursor and click on Show. To turn a toolbar off highlight it with the cursor and click on Hide. When your choices have been set click on Close.

SUGGESTED SETTINGS

For Tables:	Table Design
	Table Datasheet
For Forms:	Form Design
	Form View
For Reports:	Report Design
	Print Preview
For Queries:	Query Design
	Query Datasheet

SECTION 1

Database Basics

Introduction

Databases are one of the most common software applications: almost every organisation makes use of them in some way. Whenever information needs to be stored for subsequent retrieval or analysis, a database is a good approach.

This section takes you through the basics of using an existing database to find information, edit it and add to it. We deal essentially with the maintenance aspects of database work. Then we deal with the creation of new databases and the extraction of information in various forms.

1.1 What is a database?

A database is a way of storing information so that you can retrieve it quickly in a useful form. You can use a database to store almost any kind of information that a computer is capable of handling: words, numbers, financial transactions, stock lists, exam results and so on. You can then view or print any or all of the information in a variety of ways. The information can be sorted and grouped as you wish. The obvious advantage of this computerised approach is the time saved when compared with dealing with the information manually.

To define what a database is in more detail, you'll find it helpful to think about some of the specific things that you might use a database for, and in particular what kinds of data are best stored in a database. Spreadsheets and word processors are also very powerful ways of manipulating information, and in some cases may be more appropriate tools. For instance, if you have a large amount of text to organise, a wordprocessor is much more flexible than a database, while if you have a lot of statistics requiring extensive calculations a spreadsheet will be of more use. Databases are at their best when dealing with large amounts of information of various types, especially when the data you wish to store is clearly defined and when several different people need to use the information in different ways.

For example, a large quantity of financial information would probably be best handled in a spreadsheet, because of the need to perform many calculations quickly. A database, on the other hand, would be more suitable for storing names and addresses, because of its ability to print the information in a variety of ways.

ACTIVITY 1

Make a list of six situations in which a database would be a good way of dealing with information. If you need help, consider the ways in which you make use of information from day to day.

You might have listed some of the following ideas:

- name and address list
- club membership list
- a stock catalogue
- library catalogue
- ticket booking system
- details of a collection (video tapes, records, stamps)
- list of sports results.

There are many more possible situations.

We can identify a database as: **a structured set of data held in a computer, which is accessible in various ways.**

Notice how each of your examples might fit the first part of this definition: they all have a structure. For example, suppose you wanted to catalogue your own personal collection of video tapes in a database.

You could structure the information for each tape according to:

- title
- the type of material (e.g., film or TV programme)
- length
- names of the principal actors or presenters.

What you store depends on what you want to use the data for. The owner of a video rental store might also want to include information about who is currently hiring the tape, when it was hired, the film censor's classification (PG, 18 etc.) and so on.

ACTIVITY 2

Take one of the situations you listed in Activity 1 and list the separate items that define the structure of the information.

Using the example of a list of names and addresses, one possible structure could be:

- First name
- Last name
- Street
- Town
- County
- Postcode

For most instances, you would probably also want to add:

- Telephone number

This information could then be tabulated so that each person occupies one row in the table:

First name	Last name	Street	Town	County	Postcode	Phone no.

Each row (in database terminology) is called a **record**, and each column is called a **field**. This is the basic structure of all databases.

By seeing how your information is structured, you can see how a database fits the second part of the definition: the information is accessible. You can search the database for a certain last name, and then find out the telephone number of that person. The last name is like the titles of books on a library shelf: all the personal names and titles are different, but they are all of the same kind. Another example would be to use the postcode to find all the people living in a certain area in order to carry out a survey for test marketing a new product.

DATABASE CONCEPTS AND ACCESS

The purposes of a database are to:

- enable the storage and maintenance (input/amend/delete) of data

- provide information by retrieving and analysing the stored data.

Microsoft Access is a Relational Database Management System (RDBMS) which enables users to create and use databases on a PC.

Earlier RDBMS software, such as Ashton Tate's dBase 3, stored the various elements of a database as separate files on disk, each with its 8 character DOS filename. Looking at a list of files on a disk, it is not always obvious which files belong to which database unless the designer has made good use of directories and filenames. This problem has been overcome in Access as all the **elements** of one database are stored as one file on disk. This file must have a name which conforms with DOS naming conventions (e.g. 8 characters or less) and should have a file extension of .MDB. For example: **GOLF.MDB** could contain a database for managing a golf club.

Earlier we referred to **elements** of a database, what is meant by this? Access has six different types of element:

Table   Access stores data in tables. A table is a collection of data about a particular subject. In a table, this data is presented in columns (called fields) and rows (or records). Data can be input and viewed directly in the table but in a very basic and unfriendly way. A database can have more than one related table.

Forms   These are screen layouts that enable the user to maintain (add records, amend records etc.) and view the data in tables and queries in a sophisticated way, and enable the user to create menus (in conjunction with macros, see below). The layout can be made to match the actual paper forms used in a system, and can control the update of fields, add calculations, display data from other tables etc. The database stores the format for displaying the data NOT the data itself.

Reports   A report is used to give your data its best presentation and it enables you to print data from tables and queries. Reports contain facilities to produce report headers and footers, page headers and footers, group data into blocks, perform calculations, produce label formats etc. A report can be previewed on the screen before printing. The database stores the format for setting up the report NOT the data itself.

Queries   These enable the data to be analysed. Related tables can be joined to appear as one large table; columns (fields) and rows (records) can be selected to produce just the required data. The data can be totalled. This data can then be viewed using Forms and Reports. Other types of queries can be used to update or delete records in a table which match given criteria. The database stores the 'rules' for extracting or updating the data NOT the data itself.

Macros   This topic is beyond our scope here. They are a simple way of automating defined sets of actions.

Modules   This topic is beyond our scope here. They provide sophisticated programming facilities to automate a database system.

Each of these elements can be accessed by selecting the appropriate **tab** when an Access database is first opened and the database directory window is displayed.

1.2 Running the database software

The second part of the definition of a database was that it is accessible. Once you know how, gaining access to your data is simple. You can examine the data in your database by means of your database software.

ACTIVITY 3

Start your database software (consult your database software manual if necessary). The actual method you use to do this will depend on your computer's set-up.

To run Access you would probably do something like this:

1 Start Windows if necessary.

2 In Program Manager, find the Microsoft Access program group and open it.

3 Double-click on the Microsoft Access icon.

You can use a similar method to run any Windows program.

If you succeeded in running your program you will now be looking at the program's window as shown in Figure 1.

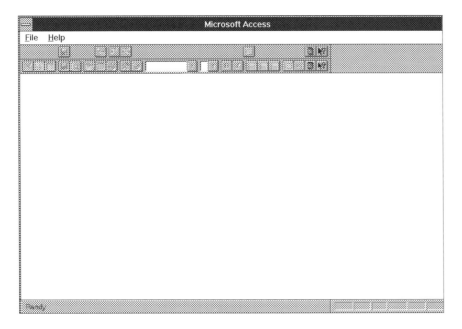

Figure 1: The Access window

This is a fairly typical program window. It might seem a little sparse (there are only two menus – File and Help – in the menu bar, for instance), but that is because you have not yet opened a database. At the foot of the screen is the status bar, containing the message 'Ready' on the left. The boxes on the right indicate whether certain keys (such as Num Lock or Scroll Lock) are pressed.

ACTIVITY 4

Click on the File menu to display it, but don't choose any options. Use the up and down arrow keys to move up and down the menu.

Write down what you can see on the screen.

You should have noticed various messages appearing in the status bar at the foot of the window. For each option in the menu, this message gives a fuller description of what that option does. You can see the same messages if you click on a menu item but don't release the mouse button.

Two of the options in the File menu appear in light grey, and if you click on them they have no effect. This is because you cannot use them until you have opened or created a database. Access makes available only those menu options that you can use in a given situation. Most other software also behaves like this.

The other item of interest is the up arrow/question mark icon to the right of the screen. Clicking on this icon starts up the help facility, which you will meet later on in this unit.

MOVING AROUND THE DATABASE

The next step is to open a database and have a look at what it contains. Access uses the standard Windows file selector for this purpose. As you are familiar with Windows you should have no difficulty with the next activity. You use your module disc, Unit_8.MDB for this unit.

ACTIVITY 5

Click on Open database.... and open the file A:UNIT_8.MDB. (Don't forget to put your floppy disk into the drive first!)

Note any changes that appear on the screen.

In Access, clicking on Open database brings up the file selector, shown in Figure 2. UNIT_8.MDB will be stored on your floppy disk for this unit. In the latter case, you will probably need to click on the Drives list box to select the disk drive on which UNIT_8.MDB is stored and then use the file selector to find it.

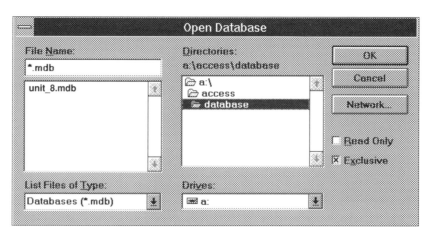

Figure 2: The file selector

Using the floppy disk to work on this unit will make Access quite slow. To speed up your work rate you could copy the database files to the hard disk instead. If you decide to do this, copy all the files with the extension .MDB to any suitable directory on your hard disk or to your personal directory area.

What you see after opening a database is shown in Figure 3.

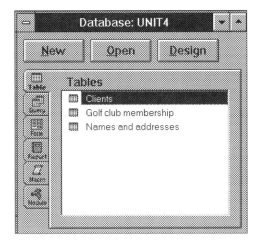

Figure 3: The database window

The database window has a row of buttons across the top (New, Open and Design) and a row of tabs down the side (labelled Table, Query, Form, Report, Macro and Module). You will find out how to use all of these (except for Macro and Module) in this unit. In the main part of the window there is a list, one item of which is highlighted.

You should also have noticed that there are now several more menus in the toolbar: Edit, View, Security and Window. Like the menus, the Toolbar changes according to what the program allows you to do. All of the buttons in the Toolbar represent short cuts to menu options, and initially you will find it easier to use the menus, rather than trying to remember what the buttons do. We will not use the Toolbar in this unit.

ACTIVITY 6

Make sure that the Table icon is depressed (so that the word 'Tables' appears below the top row of buttons).

Highlight the entry 'Names and addresses' and click the Open button.

What can you see?

You should see the window shown in Figure 4. We describe a table later, but for now just think of it as a basic view of your database.

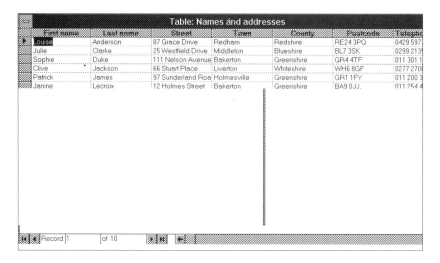

Figure 4: The Names and addresses table open in a window

The window has a title, 'Table: Names and addresses', telling you what is in the window. Just below the title is a row of column headings: 'First name', 'Last name', 'Street', 'Town', 'County', 'Postcode' and 'Telephone number' (you may not be able to see the last of these). Each of these columns is a field. Below the field names are 10 rows of names and addresses, arranged in a kind of grid. An empty file would be indicated by a blank row in the grid. Each row in the grid is a record. Notice how this is almost identical to the tabular arrangement shown earlier in this section when we defined fields and records.

The small triangle beside Louise Anderson's name indicates which record is currently selected. At the bottom of the window are 'forward' and 'reverse' symbols similar to those on video or CD player controls, separated by the text 'Record: 1', which indicates that you are looking at the first record in the database.

MANIPULATING THE TABLE WINDOW

In most respects, the table window is like any other window: you can resize it, minimise it to an icon or move it around using standard Windows techniques. However, you can also modify the appearance of the table within the window in order to improve your view of the data. For example, in the Names and addresses table the column holding the Street name data is too narrow for the information stored in that field. In Activity 7 you change the column width.

ACTIVITY 7

Move the mouse pointer to the dark line separating the column headings Street and Town. When the pointer turns into a double-headed arrow with a thick bar in the middle, click and hold the left mouse button and drag it a short distance to the right. What happens?

You probably found that the Street column grew wider, and that the information to the right of it moved further to the right. Your screen should look something like Figure 5.

First name	Last name	Street	Town	County	Postcode
Louise	Anderson	87 Grace Drive	Redham	Redshire	RE24 3PQ
Julie	Clarke	25 Westfield Drive	Middleton	Blueshire	BL7 3SK
Sophie	Duke	111 Nelson Avenue	Bakerton	Greenshire	GR4 4TF
Clive	Jackson	66 Stuart Place	Liverton	Whiteshire	WH6 8GF
Patrick	James	97 Sunderland Road	Holmesville	Greenshire	GR1 1FY
Janine	Lecroix	12 Holmes Street	Bakerton	Greenshire	BA9 0JJ
Sunil	Patel	11 Albert Road	Redham	Redshire	RE24 2ZY
William	Tennant	12 Beaumont Walk	Liverton	Whiteshire	WH7 6DD
Andrew	Watson	Flat 3, North Court	Lightville	Blueshire	BL26 3TT
Alison	Zajac	16 Tudor Road	Middleton	Blueshire	BL7 6GH

Table: Names and addresses

Record: 4   of 10

Figure 5: Re-sizing columns

If the table is wider or deeper than the window, scroll bars will appear at the right and bottom of the window. These allow you to see different parts of the table.

1.3 Viewing the database

You can use the table window to find data or to edit it, although there are simpler and better methods which you will see later on. However, it is useful to know how to move around the table and edit information in this form.

To move around within the table in Access use the mouse to click on the item you want to move to and the cursor will automatically move there. Alternatively, you can use the cursor keys on your keyboard.

ACTIVITY 8

1 Move the cursor to the name of the county in which Andrew Watson lives using the mouse.

2 Now using the keyboard instead move the cursor to Sophie Duke's telephone number.

Are there any differences between the two methods?

Clicking on an item places the cursor within that item, whereas using the keyboard highlights the entire item. You will see the difference that this makes shortly. If you want to highlight an item, move the mouse pointer to the very left-hand edge of that item until it becomes a right-pointing arrow and then click once.

To move from record to record you can use the video-style control buttons (Figure 6). The left-most button moves you to the first record in the table, the next one moves you to the record preceding the current one, the third moves you to the record following the current one, and the last moves you to the final record in the table.

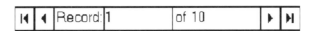

Figure 6: The 'video' buttons

ACTIVITY 9

Use the 'video' buttons to move to Janine LeCroix's record.

Now move directly to the first record and then to the last record.

If you did this successfully you will have seen the black triangle at the left of the window move from record to record.

Finally, you need to know how to find a specific piece of information in the table. To find information in a specific field, the cursor must be in the required field before starting Activity 10. Note that the Find option allows you to search in a specific field as already discussed, however it also allows you to search across all fields. Obviously, in a big table, searching all fields can be very time consuming.

ACTIVITY 10

1 Put the cursor somewhere in the Town column and choose Find from the Edit menu. This brings up the Find dialog box (Figure 7).

2 This dialog box contains a lot of options. In the Find What box, type the information you want to find (for example a town name).

3 In the Where box there are three options.

Choose:

a) **Any Part of Field.** This will find the text that you type in the Find What box regardless of where it appears in the piece of data.

Type 'ton' in the Find What box.

Access will find any piece of data that contains the letters 'ton' in it. In the Names and addresses table, it would find all the records with town names ending in 'ton' i.e. Middleton, Liverton and Bakerton. It would also find (if they were in the table) Folkestone and Weston-super-Mare.

Now choose:

b) **Match Whole Field.** This finds the text in the Find What box only if that text exactly matches the text in the piece of data. Type 'Bakerton' in the Find What box. This will find records whose town is Bakerton, but would not find Bakerfield.

Now choose:

c) **Start of Field.** This finds the text in the Find What box if it matches the start of the piece of data. Using this option with 'Baker' would find any town name that starts with Baker, for example Bakerton, Bakerfield etc.

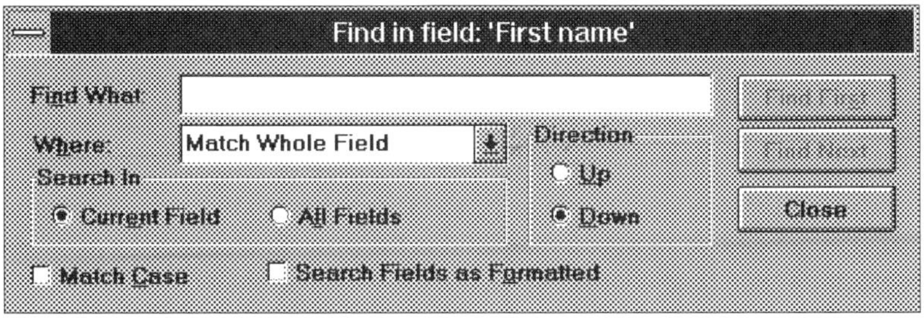

Figure 7: The Find dialog box

The Search In options (Current Field and All Fields) allow you to search only in a particular field (in which case you must click in that field before choosing Find) or in all fields. Using the 'Baker' example above, if Start of Field and Current Field were selected then 'Baker' would find anyone named Baker if the current field was Last name, or anyone in Bakerton if the current field was Town. If any other field was selected it would find any entries in that field beginning with Baker. If you select All Fields instead, then the program will search all the data in the table.

ACTIVITY 11

When do you think you should use Current Field? When should you use All Fields?

Current Fields is much faster than All Fields, especially in large databases. It will also stop you from finding irrelevant information (such as people who live in Bakerton when you only want people whose last name is Baker). All Fields is useful if you are not sure which field contains the data you are looking for, which is possible in more complex databases.

Continuing with the Find dialog box, if there is a cross in the Match Case box then the program will consider 'Baker', 'BAKER', 'baker' and 'BAker' all to be different. If there is no cross, then it does not matter how you type the information as long as you spell it correctly. Usually, it is easiest not to match the case of the text.

Search Fields as Formatted is an advanced option and is not usually available and we do not discuss it here.

The Direction options, Up and Down, determine the direction in which the search proceeds. Up searches from the last record to the first, while Down searches from the first record to the last.

There are three buttons: Find First, Find Next and Close.

- **Find First** finds the first record in the table that matches the text that you typed.
- **Find Next** finds the next matching record before or after the one that the cursor is currently in (the one with the triangle beside it). If you selected Up as your search direction then it finds the previous record; if you selected Down then it finds the record after the current one.
- **Close** closes the Find dialog box and returns you to the table.

When finding records in this way you may need to drag the Find dialog box away from the data that you are interested in so that you can see it. You now know all that you need to know to do the next activity.

ACTIVITY 12

Use the Find dialog box to find the entry for William Tennant.

Which options did you choose?

What did you type in the Find What box?

Click on Find Next before you close the dialog box. What message appeared?

The simplest way to find William Tennant's record is to click in the Last name column before selecting Find from the Edit menu and then to use the options shown in Figure 8. Notice that you can only search for either 'William' or 'Tennant' using this method. If you typed 'William Tennant' in the Find What box, you will not have succeeded in your search.

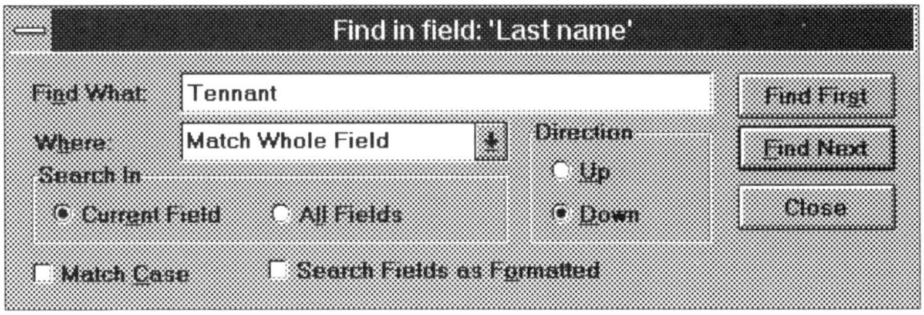

Figure 8: Searching for William Tennant

When you clicked on Find Next, you should have seen a message similar to Figure 9. Click Yes if you want to continue searching or No if you have finished.

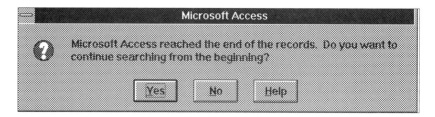

Figure 9: The message displayed when there are no more records to be found

1.4 Editing data

There was a good reason for locating William Tennant's record: he has just moved, and you want to alter the database to hold the new information. His new address is 26 Howard Close, Middleton, Blueshire BL7 6FS, and his new telephone number is 0299 616116.

ACTIVITY 13

1 Modify William Tennant's details. To edit a record in Access, first find it, as described above.

2 Move the cursor to the first field to be changed. It is easiest if you use the cursor keys, for reasons that we explain shortly.

3 Edit the record to replace his old address and telephone number with the new information by typing in the new data. Notice how the previous data simply disappears. You do this until you have changed everything you need to change. Notice that you didn't have to change the data in the First name or Last name fields.

4 Write down what happens to the triangle at the left of the window.

5 Alison Zajac has also moved house. Change her details. Her new address etc. is: 37 Lower Road, Lightville, Blueshire BL26 3QT (Telephone 0299 213312).

The moment you start typing, Access places a small pencil beside the record. This indicates that the record is being edited but that the changes have not been saved by the program. Any changes that you make are saved the moment you move to another record.

You can undo changes very easily. If you change your mind about any changes before you move to a new record, choose Undo Current Field from the Edit menu. If you have saved the changes by moving to another record, simply move back to the record whose changes you want to undo and select Undo Saved Record from the Edit menu.

If you only wanted to edit a small misspelling of a piece of data, you would not want to have to retype the entire entry. In this case, use the mouse (not the keyboard) to select the item to be changed by clicking somewhere away from the left-hand edge so that the text is not highlighted. Then you can edit the text in the normal way, using the left and right cursor keys, the Delete and Backspace keys and so on.

ADDING DATA

To add data to a record move to the blank row at the end of the table and type in the details.

ACTIVITY 14

William Tennant has moved because he and his girlfriend, Juliet Dawes, have just married and bought a house. Juliet isn't in the database. Add her name, address and telephone number to the database.

The table should now look like Figure 10, in which Juliet Dawes is now added to the end of the table.

First name	Last name	Street	Town	County	Postco
Louise	Anderson	87 Grace Drive	Redham	Redshire	RE24 3PQ
Julie	Clarke	25 Westfield Drive	Middleton	Blueshire	BL7 3SK
Sophie	Duke	111 Nelson Avenue	Bakerton	Greenshire	GR4 4TF
Clive	Jackson	66 Stuart Place	Liverton	Whiteshire	WH6 8GF
Patrick	James	97 Sunderland Roa	Holmesville	Greenshire	GR1 1FY
Janine	Lecroix	12 Holmes Street	Bakerton	Greenshire	BA9 0JJ
Sunil	Patel	11 Albert Road	Redham	Redshire	RE24 2ZY
William	Tennant	26 Howard Close	Middleton	Blueshire	BL7 6FS
Andrew	Watson	Flat 3, North Court	Lightville	Blueshire	BL26 3TT
Alison	Zajac	37 Lower Road	Lightville	Blueshire	BL26 3QT
Juliet	Dawes	26 Howard Close	Middleton	Blueshire	BL7 6FS

Table: Names and addresses

Record: 11   of 11

Figure 10: A record added to the table

DELETING DATA

Suppose now that you want to delete a record from the database. To do this, simply click on the grey rectangle to the left of the record that you want to delete and either press the Delete key or choose Delete from the Edit menu. Access gives you the chance to change your mind by displaying the message in Figure 11. Click on OK to delete the record or Cancel to leave it in the table.

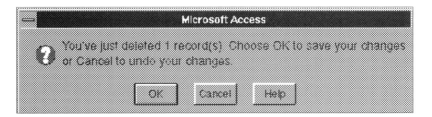

Figure 11: Deleting a record

ACTIVITY 14 Continued

Julie Clarke has set off around the world on a year-long working holiday. She won't be coming back to her present address and cannot be contacted while she's away. You decide to delete her record from the database.

Find her record and carry out the deletion.

Your Names and addresses table should now look like Figure 12.

First name	Last name	Street	Town	County	Postco
Louise	Anderson	87 Grace Drive	Redham	Redshire	RE24 3PQ
Sophie	Duke	111 Nelson Avenue	Bakerton	Greenshire	GR4 4TF
Clive	Jackson	66 Stuart Place	Liverton	Whiteshire	WH6 8GF
Patrick	James	97 Sunderland Roa	Holmesville	Greenshire	GR1 1FY
Janine	Lecroix	12 Holmes Street	Bakerton	Greenshire	BA9 0JJ
Sunil	Patel	11 Albert Road	Redham	Redshire	RE24 2ZY
William	Tennant	26 Howard Close	Middleton	Blueshire	BL7 6FS
Andrew	Watson	Flat 3, North Court	Lightville	Blueshire	BL26 3TT
Alison	Zajac	37 Lower Road	Lightville	Blueshire	BL26 3QT
Juliet	Dawes	26 Howard Close	Middleton	Blueshire	BL7 6FS

Table: Names and addresses

Record: 2   of 10

Figure 12: Final Names and addresses table

You now know the basic skills for manipulating data in a database. Later on in this unit you will see more sophisticated ways of handling data.

1.5 Help

Help is always available in Windows database programs, simply by using the Help menu and navigating your way around the help system. Access uses the standard

Windows methods of providing help, so you will not study it specifically in this unit. A few important points are dealt with below. If you are not familiar with the way that Help works in Windows, choose How to Use Help from Program Manager's Help menu.

Most programs provide context-sensitive help, that is, help specific to what you are trying to do. Whenever a message appears on screen with a button labelled Help, or a dialog box has a Help button, clicking on that button will give you context-sensitive help.

In addition, most windows within Access also supply help in the form of explanatory text (see, for example, the 'wizards' that we introduce in Section 2). It is always worth looking around the screen to see if your software is providing some sort of help that you have not noticed.

Access also has a special addition to its help facility: cue cards. You can use these by choosing Cue Cards from the Help menu. Cue cards take you step by step through various processes involved in using Access, including much of the material in this unit. You will find it useful to use the cue cards either to refresh your memory or to learn more about Access.

1.6 Exiting from your database program

When you have finished working with your database program you should exit safely from it by choosing Exit from the File menu. You must exit in this way and not simply switch off your computer, since otherwise your data could be damaged or lost.

Summary

In this section we described what databases are and some typical situations in which they are used. You have learned the fundamental skills of maintaining an existing database. You should be able to take any database file, open it, edit any particular records and save the data safely. You have also seen how to start the Help facility and how to leave your database program safely.

SECTION 2

Creating a Table and Using Forms

Introduction

In Section 1 you used a database that had already been set up for you. What happens when somebody says 'I think it would be a good idea if we put all of our club members and financial records into a database'? How do you set up a new database?

In this section we take you through the steps needed to create a new database in addition to showing you how to alter the definition of an existing database so that it can hold new fields of data. You will also learn how to create a form which provides a better way of entering data.

2.1 Planning the database

In this unit we have used the words 'database' and 'table' interchangeably. But we need to make an important distinction. A database can, and usually does, include more than one table. Later in this unit you will see an example of a database containing more than one table. However, you will concentrate on creating databases with only one table and we use the word 'table' in its strict sense.

The first thing to do when setting up a completely new table is to think carefully about what data you want to include in each record. You should also think about how you are going to use the table. This means deciding:

- what kind of information should go into each field
- what type of field is needed
- what the width of the field should be
- which fields should be indexed.

This process is common to all database programs.

You have decided to catalogue your compact disc collection by creating a database.

ACTIVITY 15

Write down a list of the information that you will need to keep about each track on your CDs. Do not worry about field names, field types or widths.

Here are some possible ideas: disc name; artist's name; song title; track number.

If you know about creating catalogues and their workings you might also have added items such as song identifier and disc identifier. Remember that several artists will record the same song and that a disc name may also be used by different artists. Hence, it is wise to include an extra field that can uniquely identify a particular recording of a song.

The next stage is to break this information down into items that will make suitable fields. You have already seen (in Section 2) how names and addresses are normally split into fields: look at the Names and addresses tables if you need to refresh your memory. Notice how names are broken into two fields and addresses into several fields (street, town, county, postcode and, if necessary, country).

ACTIVITY 16

For each of the kinds of information required for the discs catalogue table, split the information into suitable fields where you think it necessary.

Here is one way of separating the information into fields.

Disc title   some discs have subtitles so it may be a good idea to break this into two fields for the main title and the subtitle. However, for this example we'll just have a single field for disc title.

Artist   this could be one or two fields but since singers and groups are almost always known by their complete name we only need to use one field.

Song title   like discs, songs sometimes have subtitles. But again, to keep things simple, we will ignore this possibility and use only one field.

This analysis gives a list of six fields:

- Disc Identifier
- Disc Title
- Artist
- Song Identifier
- Song Title
- Track Number

Next we turn these into field names that your software understands. Access allows field names to contain a maximum of 64 characters comprising of letters, digits, spaces and most other characters that you can type on your keyboard except for full stops (.), exclamation marks (!) and square brackets ([]). The only other restriction is that you can't begin a field name with a space. You can use upper case and lower case letters.

ACTIVITY 17

Which of the following proposed field names would Access allow?

	Not allowed	Allowed

1 FRED

2 Fred.

3 Videotape_(Title)

4 Videotape [Classification]

5   2nd name

6 1994's Sales Figures:

For those that are not allowed, why not?

In this list, only field names 1, 3 and 6 would be allowed. The rest are not allowed for the following reasons:

2   Fred. is not allowed because it contains a full stop.

4   Videotape [Classification] is not allowed because it contains square brackets.

5   2nd name is not allowed because it starts with a space.

You do not need to worry too much about whether your field names are acceptable as Access will not accept names that do not obey the rules.

ACTIVITY 18

For each of your six identified fields choose a suitable field name.

Disc Identifier

Disc Title

Artist

Song Identifier

Song Title

Track Number

Your names might be:

Disc Identifier	Disc Id
Disc Title	Disc Title
Artist	Artist
Song Identifier	Song Id
Song Title	Song Title
Track Number	Track Number

Notice that in most cases the field name matches the category of information on the left exactly. The two exceptions have been made just to show that you can give the field any name you like. The names are as informative as possible without being too long. As you will see later, Access allows you to add longer descriptions to your fields.

The next task is to determine what type of field each one should be. First you need to know what is meant by 'field type'; this is called 'data type' by Access.

In the Names and addresses table all the fields were of one type – text. This meant that you could type anything into the field, letters or numbers or any combination of letters and numbers.

You can, however, restrict what may be entered in a field. If you want to store prices, for example, you would not want to type in anything that was not a number. For storing dates, it would be convenient to have a field type that only allowed valid dates to be stored and which would reject dates like 30 February 1995 or 25/13/95.

Here are some of the data types that Access uses:

Text   may contain any character on a normal keyboard. The maximum number of characters (called the maximum size or width) is 255.

Memo   fields can contain any character and can be of any size up to 32,000 characters. Usually you would only want to store a few sentences. They are useful for storing unstructured information of varying width. In the case of the CD catalogue you might use the memo field to store a brief description of each disc.

Number   may contain digits, plus or minus signs and a decimal point. The maximum number of characters depends on what sort of number you want to store. You will see how to choose this later on.

Counter   contains an integer number, in LongInteger format, generated automatically by the DBMS. The DBMS remembers the number allocated to the field when the last record was created and automatically adds one to that number. This ensures that a field of type counter will contain a unique value.

Date/time must contain a valid date or time. Access allows you to choose from among several different date and time formats.

Currency   stores monetary values in one of several formats.

Yes/No   must contain values such as Yes or No, True or False, or On or Off. You could use such a field to record whether a club member has paid his or her subscription this year.

For example, in the Disc table the second field Disc Title can contain any characters and will certainly be far less than 255 characters in size. Hence, you should make Disc Title a text field.

ACTIVITY 19

For each of the remaining fields chosen for our disc table, write down the type of field that it would be best to use.

Field	Type
Disc Id	
Artist	
Song Id	
Song Title	
Track Number	

Does your choice agree with these?

Field	Type
Disc Id	text or number
Disc Title	text
Artist	text
Song Id	counter
Song Title	text
Track Number	text or number

Disc ID and Track Number have all been shown as being either text or number. To some extent the choice is up to you.

However, here are some simple guidelines:

- If you will need to do arithmetic with the contents then choose number.
- If you will not need to do arithmetic with the contents and the contents have a definite shape, for example, a year will always have four digits, then text should be used as text is easier to manipulate.

In our case Track Number should be number and Disc Id could be either. We will go for number.

In this database there is no need for Yes/No, Date/Time or Memo fields. Song Id is a counter field because there will have to be one record for every song in the table and hence this field needs to be unique. However, Disc Id will not be unique because most discs contain more than one song.

The structure of the database is now taking shape. The next step is to choose the field size (the number of characters to be used) for each field where it is necessary.

Disc title is likely to be quite a long field. Some discs have very short titles (e.g. So) others, like Dark Side Of The Moon – 21 characters, are a lot longer. A reasonable estimate would be to allow 30 characters, but if you can think of a longer title then you could allow for even more.

In a **Text** field, the field size parameter sets the maximum length for a field. If you set it as 25, Access will not allow more than 25 characters to be input. However,

Access only stores the characters which are entered, for example, if you enter Fred, only 4 characters will be stored, that is Access optimises the amount of storage used. It is still good practice to set the maximum field size as it is used by some **wizards** when setting up Forms etc.

For **Number** fields you need to specify the field size (which is the type of number that you want to use) and the number of decimal places. The field size options will not be dealt with in detail here. For simplicity, this unit will only deal with Integer, LongInteger (for storing whole numbers) and Double (for large numbers and/or fractions) sizes.

The number of decimal places is useful for ensuring that all the data in the field are stored to the same level of precision.

You don't need to specify a field size for Memo fields, Yes/No fields, Counter fields or Date/Time fields. Access allocates as much space as is needed for memo fields, and it fixes the sizes of the other types.

ACTIVITY 20

Choose suitable field sizes, formats and numbers of decimal places (where appropriate) for each of the fields in the disc table.

Field	Type	Size
Disc Id	number	
Disc Title	text	
Artist	text	
Song Id	counter	
Song Title	text	
Track Number	number	

Here are some possible choices:

Field	Type	Size
Disc Id number	LongInteger	0 d.p.
Disc Title	text	30
Artist	text	25
Song Id	counter	(predetermined)
Song Title	text	40
Track Number	number	integer, 0 d.p.

In the suggestions above we have used both Integer and LongInteger to give you the opportunity to examine the difference between the two.

2.2 Creating the table

So far, the table structure exists only on paper. The time has now come to transfer it to our software. Start Access before continuing.

Creating a table in Access is very simple. First you need to decide whether the table is to be part of an existing database or will form part of a new one. Unlike most other programs Access stores all the tables and other related files for a single database in just one file. Other programs store each table as a separate file, relying on you to keep track of which files belong to which database. Later on in this unit, when you meet databases with more than one table, you will find out when you should create a new database and when you should simply add a table to an existing database. In this section, each new table will be placed in its own database file.

First you will need to create a new database if you are using Access. The steps to take to create a database are:

1   From the File menu, choose New Database.

2   Choose the drive and directory in which you want to store your database (we assume that your files will be stored on A:).

3   In the File Name box type the name of your database file. This must obey the usual MS-DOS rules for filenames. You only need to type the first 8 characters as Access adds the '.MDB' for you.

4   Click OK.

Access then creates the new database and displays its database window.

ACTIVITY 21

Create a new database called DISCS.MDB.

If you have done this successfully, you will now have an empty database window as in Figure 13.

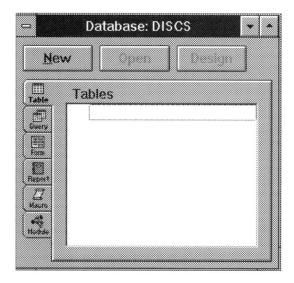

Figure 13: The empty DISCS database

You are now ready to create a table. In Access, the process is:

1   Check that the word 'Tables' appears in the line below the New, Open, Design
    buttons line. If it doesn't, click on the Table button on the left hand side of the
    database window.

2   Click the New button in the database window. Then click on the New Table
    button in the New Table window. (In this module, we will not be using the
    Table Wizard.)

3   In the table design window that then opens (Figure 14) type the field names.
    Choose the data types and add a description if you wish.

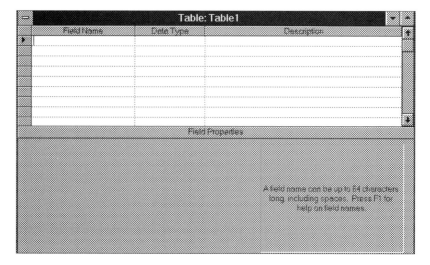

Figure 14: The table design window

4   Enter the field properties (size, format etc.) for each field in the Field Properties section of the table design window.

5   Choose a primary key for the table. We explain this below.

6   Save the table by choosing Save As from the File menu.

Typing field names and descriptions is very similar to entering information into a table, as described in Section 1.

To choose a data type, you can either type it into the Data Type column or choose it from a list. To see the list, click anywhere in the Data Type entry that you wish to set. To select an item from the list, click on it (see Figure 15). This kind of drop-down list occurs throughout Access.

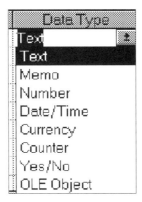

Figure 15: The Data Type drop-down list

The field properties that you can set depend on the data type chosen. In this unit we mention only a few of these properties.

For Text fields, you should first enter the Field Size. To do this click on the Field Size box and type the number of characters that you want.

You should also decide whether the field is to be indexed. Indexing a field speeds up searching and sorting in the database, but can slow down any changes that you make. You can compare the searching of a database with looking through a book to find all the pages on which a particular subject is mentioned. You would use the book's index to go straight to those pages, whereas without the index you would have to read the whole book. Database indexes work in much the same way.

You can have as many indexes as you want in a table, but you should only index those fields that you definitely want to use when searching for data. For example, you would very rarely search for records by telephone number, so there is little point in indexing such a field. Adding an index that you never use wastes disk space and slows down the operation of your database.

As a general rule always create at least one index which should be based on the field you search most often. Whenever people are the main subject of a database the field containing the last name is an excellent choice for indexing. Access constantly updates the indexes for you, so you do not have to pay any further attention to them.

In Access, you have the following choices when creating an index, which you choose from a drop-down box in the same way as choosing a data type:

No	No index for that field
Yes (Duplicates OK)	The field is indexed and you can have the same text or numbers appearing in that field more than once. Use this option for fields such as a person's last name, where you are likely to have several people with the same names.
Yes (No Duplicates)	The field is indexed but the text or number in the field must be unique. If you have a table of customers each of which you have given a unique identity code you can use this option to ensure that you never give two customers the same code.

You do not need to set any field properties for Memo fields.

For Number fields you should set the field size, the number of decimal places, and whether or not it is indexed.

You can choose the field size from a drop-down list as we described above. You can also choose the number of decimal places in the same way although the default option Auto (i.e. automatic) is usually sufficient.

You do not need to set any field properties for Date/Time fields, although you may find it helpful to choose a format from the drop down-list. The three most useful formats for dates (with examples) are:

Long Date	25 December 1997
Medium Date	25-Dec-97
Short Date	25/12/97

The primary key consists of one or more fields that uniquely define each record in the table and which acts as the main index for the table.

A primary key is essential if the table is to be a parent of other tables. For example, if you have a Department table which describes each department in a company, and you have a related Employees table which describes each employee and which department they work for, this is a one to many relationship with one department having many employees and Department is therefore the parent table. Each department must have a unique identifier that can be referenced in the Employee table. If two departments both had the department code 123, and an employee works for department 123, how do you know which department they work for? The code must be unique for each department.

Understanding what constitutes a good primary key is important. The primary key must identify each record uniquely. A person's last name is a bad choice. You would only be allowed to have one person called 'Smith' in your table. Adding the person's first name to the primary key would help but there are still many John Smith's so this is probably not a good choice.

If you now added the telephone number to the primary key you would be on much safer ground since people who share the same name are unlikely to have the same telephone number and people who share a telephone number tend not to have the same name.

Even this is not a perfect primary key since it is, in principle, possible for there to be two or more people with identical names and telephone numbers. If you want to be absolutely certain of having a good primary key you can either allocate each record its own code or number yourself (by creating a new field for that code) or you can let Access do it for you.

To set a primary key click on the grey box to the left of the field name in the table design window. Then hold down the Control (Ctrl) key and do the same for any other fields in the primary key. Finally, choose Set Primary Key from the Edit menu. Small key symbols appear next to the fields in the primary key.

If you don't set a primary key then when you save the table, Access will ask you if you want it to create one for you. If you choose Yes, then Access adds a new field called ID with data type Counter. As you add records, Access gives each one a different number in the counter field. You can use this method if there is no obvious primary key. (However Access tables do not have to have a Primary Key set so in this case you would reply No.)

In our table we already have a counter field, Song Id, so this could be used as the Primary Key. Without this field we would have to combine at least Disc Title and Song Title and would probably need to add Artist as well to be sure of a unique key.

ACTIVITY 22

Enter the table design for the disc table. Remember to set the field properties for each field. Give it a suitable primary key and save the table with the name 'Discs'.

If you have done this correctly, your table design window should look similar to Figure 16. Notice that some fields have descriptions that give a little more information about the field.

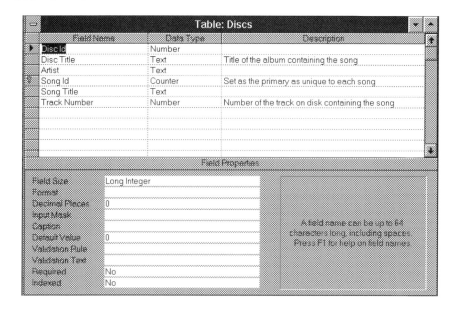

Figure 16: The Discs table design

The primary key chosen here includes just one field, Song Id. This is sufficient. The table design also assumes that there is only one copy of each disc. This assumption is unrealistic, and if the table design took account of these factors the primary key and possibly the table data fields would need to be changed. Altogether, this table design is rather clumsy as much of the data is repeated from one record to the next. Disc Title, Artist and Year all appear for each song title. This is very wasteful of disk space. We look at the solution to this problem in Section 4.

Now that you have defined the table you can start entering data. To do this you could choose Datasheet from the View menu and add data in the same way that you did in Section 1. There is a better way to do this which you will learn about. Before you move on carry out Activity 23, which closes the table design window.

ACTIVITY 23

Close the table design window by choosing Close from the File menu or by double-clicking its control box (top left-hand corner of the table design window).

If you did this correctly you should now be able to see the database window with the disks table added to the window and highlighted.

2.3 Forms

A form is a way of entering data to one or more tables in a simpler way than editing the tables directly. Using a form is rather like filling in details on a piece of paper.

ACTIVITY 24

To create a form in Access:

1 Open the database that contains the tables you want to work with. Choose the Record Discs table as the basis for your form.

2 In the database window, click the Form button.

3 Click the New button and then use the drop-down list in the dialog box that appears to choose the table or query for which you want to create a form. (We deal with queries later in this unit.)

4 Click on the Form Wizards button to create your form. A Wizard is a part of the program that takes you step by step through a complicated process making it much easier and quicker to do. (The Blank Form button is also given as an option here. Until you are expert in the use of Access it is much easier to choose the Wizards button. If you start with a blank form you will have to do much more work which is beyond the scope of this unit.) On clicking the Form Wizards button you will see the window in Figure 17. This asks you to choose which Form Wizard you want to use. As you can see there are several to choose from.

5 Choose Single-column type and then click on OK. This tells Access to use the Single-column Form Wizard. The first step is shown in Figure 18. For simple data entry this is the best type of form to use. We do not discuss the other types in this unit.

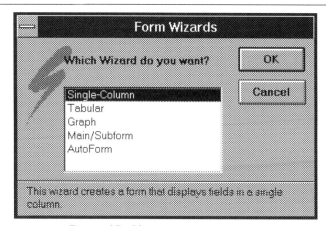

Figure 17: Choosing a Form Wizard

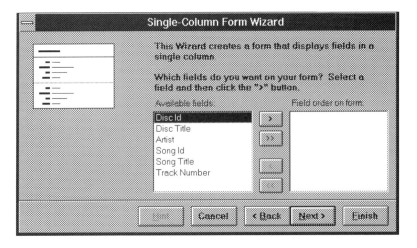

Figure 18: Using a Form Wizard – step 1

Using a wizard involves making a set of choices one by one and after each choice, moving on to the next step in the wizard. In the Single-column form wizard Access asks you to choose:

1   Which fields to include in the form.

2   What kind of appearance your form should have.

3   What title the form should have.

At any stage you can press Cancel to abandon creating the form or use the other buttons to move backwards and forwards in the wizard. Back takes you back one step and Next takes you forward one step.

In step 1 of the Single-column type wizard Access asks which fields you want to include in your form. The Available fields list initially contains all of the fields in the table design.

Click on the button with two right-facing chevrons ('>>') to add all of the fields to the Field order on form list in the same order as they appear in the table definition.

To add fields singly highlight each one by clicking on it and then click on the single right-facing chevron (>).The fields will appear on the form in the same order in which you choose them. As you select fields they are removed from the Available fields list. You do not have to include every field in the table form.

If you change your mind about including a field on the form use the left-facing chevron buttons in the same way as you used the right-facing ones.When you are satisfied that you have all the fields that you want and that they are in the right order click Next.

ACTIVITY 25

Use the wizard to add all the necessary fields in the Disc table to the form, and then click Next. Remember that this form is to be used for data entry!

Because a counter field value is generated automatically by Access the Song Id field does not need to be included on a data entry form!

The next step in the wizard is to choose a style for the form (see Figure 19). If you click in each option (Standard, Chiselled, Shadowed, Boxed or Embossed) Access displays a mini-preview of the look of the form on the left-hand side of the wizard. Which you choose depends on your own personal preferences.

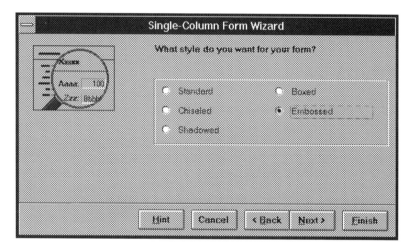

Figure 19: Choosing the style of your form

ACTIVITY 26

Click on each of the different styles to see what the preview looks like. Then choose the Standard style and click Next.

Access now asks you what title to give the form suggesting 'Discs' as being suitable (Figure 20). When you have chosen the title you can then choose to open the form for data entry or for further design. In this unit you will not study any further aspects of form design. For most purposes, the design produced by the wizard is sufficient.

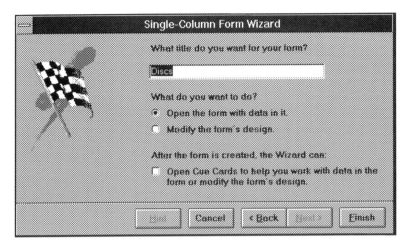

Figure 20: Giving your form a title

ACTIVITY 27

Edit the form title to read 'Discs in the Collection' and then click the Finish button.

You should now be looking at your form, which will look something like Figure 21.

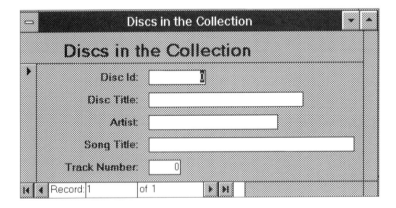

Figure 21: The finished form

How much of the form you can see depends on your monitor's display resolution and the size of the form window. To work with the form you should maximise the window so that you can see as much of it as possible.

Before entering any data you should save the form.

ACTIVITY 28

Save the form by choosing Save Form As from the File menu. Use the same name as the form title ('Discs in the Collection').

The form is now ready for data entry. As you can see the field names appear on the left of the form with an empty box to the right. To enter data in a field, click in the empty box with the mouse and then type in the data. To move to the next field, press the TAB key. To move to the previous field, press SHIFT+TAB. If the next field is not visible, the window will scroll to display it.

ACTIVITY 29

Enter the following data:

Disc Id   1

Disc Title   The Red Shoes

Artist   Kate Bush

Song Id   (generated by Access)

Song Title   Rubberband Girl

Track Number   1

What happens when you press TAB when you are in the last field ?

The completed form for this set of data is shown in Figure 22.

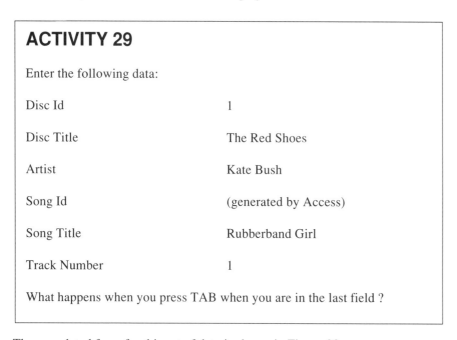

Figure 22: Data entered in a form

When you press TAB in the last field, all the data seems to disappear. In fact, Access has saved the information and is now showing you a new blank record. If you click the left-facing 'video' button at the foot of the window, you will see the data you just entered.

Whenever you want to add a new record you must move to the blank record at the end of the table. If you type data into an existing record you will lose the previous data in that record.

ACTIVITY 30

Enter the following data. Remember that YOU do not need to enter the Song Id this is why it is not in the table below.

Disc Id	Disc Title	Artist	Song Title	Track No.
3	Dark Side of the Moon	Pink Floyd	Speak to me / Breathe in the air	1
4	Debut	Bjork	Human Behaviour	1
5	Dreamland	Aztec Camera	Birds	1
10	So	Peter Gabriel	Red rain	1
1	The Red Shoes	Kate Bush	And so is love	2
3	Dark Side of the Moon	Pink Floyd	On the run	2
4	Debut	Bjork	Crying	2
5	Dreamland	Aztec Camera	Safe in sorrow	2
10	So	Peter Gabriel	Sledgehammer	2
1	The Red Shoes	Kate Bush	Eat the music	3
3	Dark Side of the Moon	Pink Floyd	Time	3
4	Debut	Bjork	Venus as a boy	3
5	Dreamland	Aztec Camera	Black Lucia	3
10	So	Peter Gabriel	Don't give up	3
1	The Red Shoes	Kate Bush	Moments of pleasure	4
3	Dark Side of the Moon	Pink Floyd	Great gig in the sky	4
4	Debut	Bjork	There's more to life than this	4
5	Dreamland	Aztec Camera	Let your love decide	4
10	So	Peter Gabriel	That voice again	4
1	The Red Shoes	Kate Bush	Song of Solomon	5
3	Dark Side of the Moon	Pink Floyd	Money	5
4	Debut	Bjork	Like someone in love	5
5	Dreamland	Aztec Camera	Spanish horses	5
10	So	Peter Gabriel	In your eyes	5

When you have finished check each record to make sure that you have entered all the data correctly. The data for Song of Solomon should appear as in Figure 23.

What happened when you entered the song title 'Speak to me / Breathe in the air'?

Before continuing close the form window.

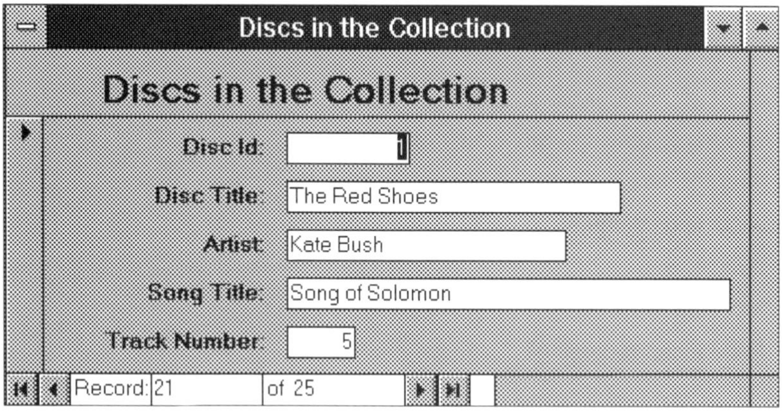

Figure 23: Data entered for Song of Solomon

You may have found that 'Speak to me / Breathe in the air' did not fit in the space allocated to it. Instead Access allows you to type the whole title but only displays part of it at any time. You could change this by modifying the form but this is beyond our scope in this unit.

There are a few more important points to note about forms in Access:

- You can leave any fields blank (such as the track number field) except for fields that are indexed or which are part of the primary key.

- Next, you can create a form for a table that already has data in it you do not have to create the form immediately after designing the table.

- Finally, in Access, you can switch from the form to the table itself very quickly by choosing Datasheet from the View menu. To return to the form, choose Form from the View menu.

2.4 Modifying the database

When we first analysed the data for the Songs table we did not consider the year in which a particular disc was issued. You have now decided that this piece of information is required. In fact there is a lot of extra data that could usefully be held.

We should go through the same sort of analysis for modifying the database as we did for defining it in the first place.

ACTIVITY 31

Decide what new fields could be added and give a reason for each.

Write down definitions for the new field(s).

You may have come up with some of the following:

- year of issue
- recording company
- number one hit?
- first album?
- live concert recording?

For our example we will only add in the Year of Issue field. A suitable name could be Year and the field type could be either text or number. If we look back at how to decide between the two it is likely that the choice should be text.

Summarising you should have the following new field:

Field	Type	Size/format
Year	Text	4

ACTIVITY 32

1. To modify the table design click the Table button in the database window, click on the table you want to modify, and then click the Design button.

2. Add the extra field to the end of the table design. Having already defined the table you should find this a straightforward task.

3. Save the new definition.

The new field in your table definition should look like Figure 24.

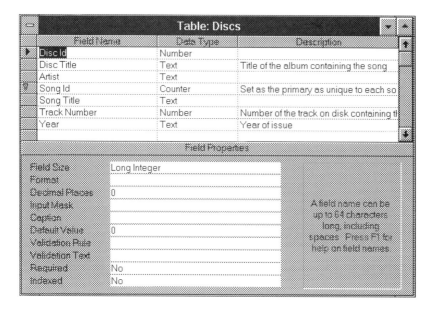

Figure 24: Modified design of the Discs table

The only problem is that the form you created earlier does not contain this field. You have the following options:

● Enter the data directly into the table

● Modify the form

● Create a new form.

The first of these is clearly not a good idea. It is not sensible to enter most of the data using a form but better to enter an odd field directly into the table.

Modifying the form is the best choice if you know how to do it.

The quick and easy solution is to create a new form using the form wizard. However, this is a very lazy solution and you should not get into the habit of doing this. It is beyond our scope in this unit to describe how to design forms without using a wizard.

ACTIVITY 33

Create a new form which includes the new field. Save it using the name 'Discs in the Collection' and answer Yes when Access asks you if you want to overwrite the existing form.

Use your new form to enter the issue date for the five discs currently stored in the table:

The Red Shoes	1993
Dark Side of the Moon	1973
Debut	1993
Dreamland	1993
So	1986

If you have done this correctly, the record for Song of Solomon will look like Figure 25.

Figure 25: Amended record for Song of Solomon

Did you find it irritating to enter the same piece of data five times for each disc, once for each track? This should emphasise the clumsiness of the table design we have developed and its wastefulness. We will revisit this problem in Section 4 to find a solution.

Close the form before continuing with this unit.

Summary

This section has shown you how databases are planned and defined. You have seen several of the different types of data that Access provides (Text, Memo, Number, Counter, Date/Time, Yes/No, and Currency) and have learned some of the different properties and uses of these fields. You have seen how to create a form for easy data entry and have also learned how to modify the definition of a database that already exists.

SECTION 3

Reports

Introduction

Databases would be of limited use if there was no way of producing a printed analysis of the data. There is not much point, for instance, in keeping a list of names and addresses in a database if you cannot then print address labels using that information. Or suppose, as part of a market survey, that you have sent out a questionnaire to local people concerning the use of recreation facilities in their neighbourhood. You can easily store the information in a database but it would take a long time to go through the data by looking at individual records especially if you had to write down the information as it appeared on the screen.

Database software provides a solution to this problem in the form of reports. A report can be any set of data extracted from the database, arranged in a suitable manner and either displayed on the screen or printed out on paper. Address labels, membership renewal forms, invoices, summaries of experimental data and marketing survey results are all examples of possible reports that might be produced from particular databases. Note that this is a different kind of report than the report writing you did in Unit 3.

3.1 Creating a report

Simple reports are easy to create in Access using the Report Wizard. This is similar to the Form Wizard you met in Section 2. In this section you will create some simple reports that show you how to sort and group your data. You will also see how to modify a report to include a calculation.

The report that you will create is based on the Clients table in the UNIT_4 database. This contains details of the clients of a small printing company, Redham Printers Ltd, summarising how many jobs each client has used the company for and how much money each client has paid in total.

There are a lot of options available in the Report Wizard, most are not explained as you do these activities. For different types of report you will need to experiment for yourself.

ACTIVITY 34

Open the UNIT_4 database and then open the form called 'Redham Printers' clients'. Examine the data stored in the file.

Suppose that you wanted to find out which are the company's best clients. Which data from the Clients table would you use to find this out?

With the data available, one way of determining the best customer would be to see who had spent the most money with Redham Printers. Another way would be to see which company had used the company most often and a third would be to see which company paid the highest average amount for each job. Which of these methods is best would depend on what criteria the management of Redham Printers wanted to apply.

To begin with you will create a report that shows which company spent the most money with Redham Printers.

ACTIVITY 35

Which fields from the Clients table should you include in this report?

This shows one of the main differences between reports and forms. Forms, which are used for data input or general viewing of the data, tend to contain many fields. Reports, which concentrate on extracting useful information from the database, generally only contain a few fields. In the present case only two fields are really necessary: Company name and Total amount spent. For various reasons you might want to include other information (such as the Account number) but this report will be as simple as possible.

Creating a report is very similar to creating a form.

ACTIVITY 36

1 In the database window, click the Report button and then click New.

2 When the New Report dialog box opens, choose Clients from the drop-down list and then click on the Report Wizards button.

3 When asked which wizard you want, click on Groups/Totals and then click on OK.

If you have done this successfully you will be at the first step of the Report Wizard (Figure 26). Notice how similar this was to the way you started to create a form in Section 2.

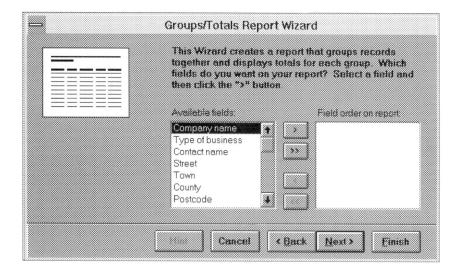

Figure 26: First step in the Report Wizard

The next step is to tell Access which fields you want to include in the report. The process is the same as for adding fields to a form.

ACTIVITY 37

Add the fields Company name and Total amount spent to the report by clicking on the name and then clicking the right-facing chevron for each field. Then click Next to move to the next stage of the wizard.

You should now see the next step of the wizard (Figure 27).

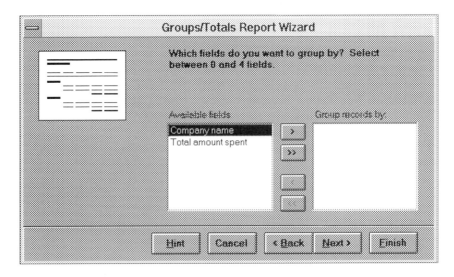

Figure 27: Second step in the Report Wizard

This step asks you how you want to group your data. Grouping data is useful when you have a field that contains the same entry in many different records, and in a later activity you will see how to do it. This report, which contains each client's name only once, does not need to be grouped. Access allows you to skip this step.

ACTIVITY 38

Click Next to move to the next step in the Report Wizard without adding any fields to the list of fields to group by.

You have now reached the third step of the wizard where you are asked which fields you want the data to be sorted by (Figure 28).

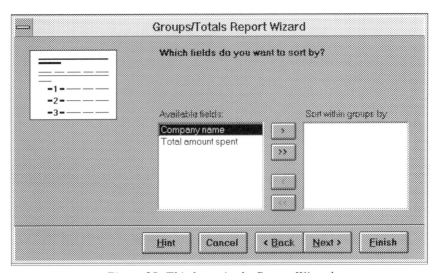

Figure 28: Third step in the Report Wizard

There are two fields in the report. If you sort the data by company name, which is a Text field, the data will be sorted alphabetically. If you sort the report by Total amount spent, which is a Currency field, the data will be sorted numerically with the smallest number first. In this report you are interested in finding out which company has spent the most money so you should sort by the Total amount spent field.

ACTIVITY 39

Add Total amount spent to the list of fields to be sorted by clicking on it and then clicking on the right-facing chevron. Click Next to move to the next step.

You should now be at the fourth step in the wizard (Figure 29).

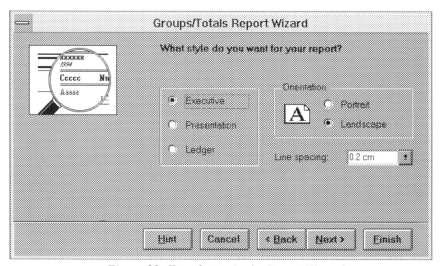

Figure 29: Fourth step in the Report Wizard

This step asks you what the appearance of the report should be: Executive, Presentation or Ledger. It also asks which orientation and what line spacing are required.

ACTIVITY 40

Choose Presentation for the appearance of your report and landscape. Then click Next.

You have now reached the last step of the Report Wizard (Figure 30), which is very similar to the last step of the Form Wizard.

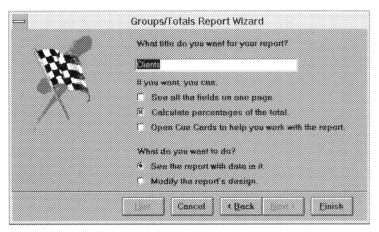

Figure 30: Last step in the Report Wizard

ACTIVITY 41

1 Enter the title 'Redham Printers' best clients' for the report title.

2 De-select 'calculate percentages of the total'.

3 Select 'See the report with data in it'.

4 Click on the Finish button. Save the report as 'Best clients 1' by choosing Save As from the File menu but DO NOT close it.

Your report should now be visible on screen looking something like Figure 31. Maximise the window if necessary to see the report more clearly.

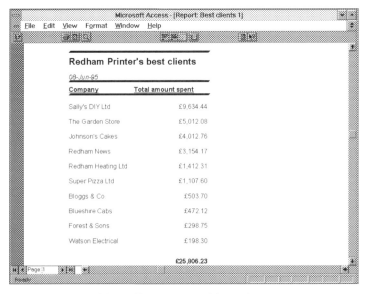

Figure 31: Redham Printers' best clients report

You should see that the current date is included in the heading of the report. The amounts in the second column are laid out in ascending order and the amounts spent have been totalled at the foot of the column. Access has done all of these things automatically for you.

However, there are two small problems with this report. The first is that it would be better if the client who had spent the most was at the top of the list. The second is that one of company names has been cut short. To fix these problems you need to edit the report.

ACTIVITY 42

Click the Close Window icon on the print preview toolbar.

Describe what you see.

When you clicked the Close Window icon, your view of the report should have changed to the report design window shown in Figure 32. (This only applies if you have not yet closed the report after creating it via the wizard. If you have closed it, you will need to open the report in design mode to display Figure 32.)

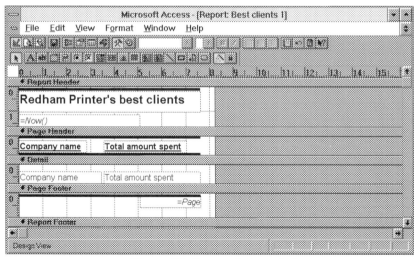

Figure 32: Report design window

To understand this window first of all notice that it is split into five separate sections. These are:

Report Header Anything in this section is printed only once on the first page of the report. In this case there is a thick black line at the very top, the title of the report (which you entered in the Report Wizard) and a box that includes the text '=Now()'. This is a command that Access understands. It means 'Put the current date here'.

Page Header Anything in this band appears at the top of every page of the report. You cannot really see the effect of this in the print preview window as your report only occupies one page. In this report, you have thick black lines at the top and bottom of the page header and the column headings for the two fields of data included in your report. You could, if you wanted to, edit these so that they contained different text.

Detail This is the actual heart of the report. The two boxes contain field names, although as you will see later, they could also contain calculations based on fields (among other things).

Page Footer Anything in this band appears at the bottom of every page in the report. In this report there is a thick black line and the text '=Page'. This is another command which tells Access to put the page number at that position on every page of the report.

Report Footer This appears only at the very end of the report. In this report the command '=Sum([Total amount spent])' appears although you cannot see all of the command. It tells Access to add up all of the values in the Total amount spent field and print the total at the end of the report.

You can change anything in your report. The next activity shows you how to change the text at the top of the column containing the Company name field.

ACTIVITY 43

1 Click once on the box containing the text 'Company name' in the Page Header section (not the Detail section).

2 What do you see happen?

3 Now click on it again. What happens now?

4 Use the keyboard to delete the word 'name' from the box and then choose Print Preview from the File menu to see the effect this has on the report.

When you clicked the box for the first time it should have changed so that it looked like Figure 33. The small black squares (called 'handles') indicate that the box is 'selected'. This means that you can now perform various operations on it. Later in this section you will see some examples of things that you can do when an item is selected. Anything that can be selected in this way in a report design is called a 'control' by Access.

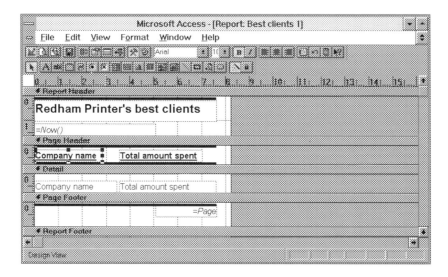

Figure 33: A selected box

When you clicked in the box again the handles disappeared and a text cursor appeared inside the box allowing you to edit the text. Choosing the Print Preview option will have confirmed that the change really did have an effect.

Note that although the text 'Company name' appeared in the Page Header section and in the Detail section, and they can both be edited in the same way. The effects of editing the two are very different because Access treats the two sections differently. The Page Header is just considered to be text, so you could add anything you want to it (even complete rubbish) and Access would simply put it into the report. In the Detail section Access actually uses the information you type so it must be meaningful to Access. In this instance, if you were to edit 'Company name' to read 'Company' in the Detail section Access would not print a meaningful report. Always be very careful when editing the Detail section.

Before doing Activity 44 save your report.

The next step is to tackle the problems with the report noted earlier. First, you will change the order in which the report is sorted.

ACTIVITY 44

1 Make sure that you are in the report design window. Then choose Sorting and Grouping from the View menu.

2 In the window that appears click where the word 'Ascending' appears and then use the drop-down list to its right to change 'Ascending' to 'Descending'.

3 Close this window and then check that the sort order has changed by choosing Print Preview.

The Sorting and Grouping window (Figure 34) allows you to change which field (or fields) the report is sorted by and the order in which the sort occurs.

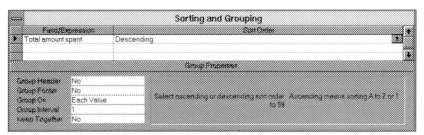

Figure 34: Sorting and Grouping window

In your report the field that is used for sorting was chosen when you used the Report Wizard to create the report. The wizard did not ask you to choose the sort order so this is where you do it. 'Ascending' order means from smallest number to largest for Number or Currency fields, or in alphabetical order (A to Z) for Text fields. 'Descending' order is the reverse of these.

Finally, you need to increase the space allowed for the company names.

ACTIVITY 45

Select the Company name Text box in the Detail section and make it slightly larger by dragging the bottom-right handle to the right. Save and preview your report.

Your report should now be finished. If it still does not look quite right, go back and alter the design until it does.

The report you just created was very simple. It contained just two fields and Access did almost all of the work for you. The next report you create will include another field from the Clients table and Number of jobs done. It will also form the basis of a third report which will include a calculation. Before you continue close the report you just created.

ACTIVITY 46

1. Use the Groups/Totals Report Wizard to create a form containing the three fields Company name, Total amount spent and Number of jobs done, in that order.

2. Do not group the records. Sort them by the number of jobs done.

3. Choose the Presentation look and give the report the title 'Jobs per client'.

4. Preview the report and save it as 'Best clients 2'.

If you have done this successfully, your report will look like Figure 35.

Microsoft Access - [Report: Best clients 2]

File   Edit   View   Format   Window   Help

Jobs per client

08-Jun-95

Company name	Total amount spent	Number of jobs done
Blueshire Cabs	£472.12	1
Forest & Sons	£298.75	1
Watson Electrical	£198.30	2
Bloggs & Co.	£503.70	3
Redham Heating Ltd	£1,412.31	5
Super Pizza Ltd	£1,107.60	5
Redham News	£3,154.17	8
The Garden Store	£5,012.08	11
Johnson's Cakes	£4,012.76	12
Sally's DIY Ltd	£9,634.44	21
	£25,806.23	69

Page 1

Figure 35: A new report

This report suffers from similar flaws to the previous one. Although sorted by the correct field, it is sorted in the wrong order.

ACTIVITY 47

Change the sort order so that clients with the most jobs appear first.

Your report should now look like Figure 36. Save it before you carry on.

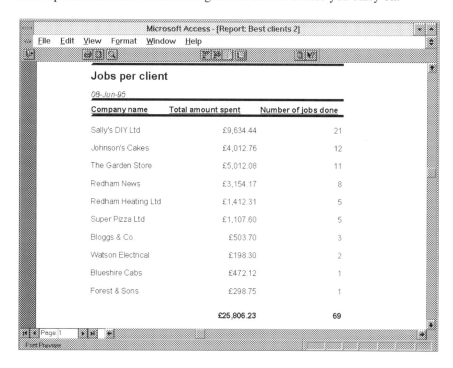

Figure 36: The modified report

You are now going to use this report to create a new report that calculates the average price per job for each client and then sorts it in order of highest average price.

ACTIVITY 48

Choose Save As and give the new report the name 'Best clients 3'. Next make sure you have the report design window open.

These first steps ensure that you will always have the basic version of the report to go back to if you make a mistake that you cannot undo. It is a good idea to save different versions of your report with different names as you make changes. When you have finished you can delete the intermediate steps using the database window.

First of all, you need to create some space in which to put the column that contains the calculated averages.

ACTIVITY 49

1 In the report design window move the mouse pointer to the right-hand edge of the white area of the report.

2 When it turns into a double-headed arrow click and drag the mouse to the right so that you have enough space for your new column.

3 Next select the thick line in the Report Header section and click and drag the handle at its right so that the line extends to the edge of the form.

4 Repeat this for the other black lines.

You may have found it a little tricky to keep the lines straight, but this will come with practice. Your report design should now look like Figure 37.

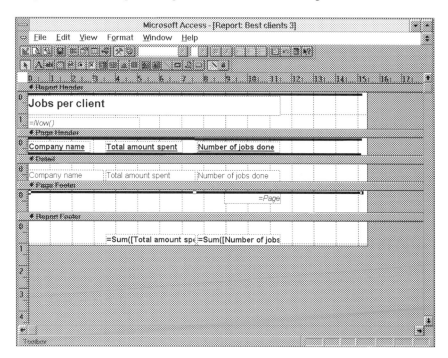

Figure 37: Making the report wider

The next step is to add the column heading in the Page Header section and the box which will contain our calculation in the Detail section. As the column will contain the average amount spent for each job a suitable column heading might be 'Average per job'.

ACTIVITY 50

1 Choose Toolbox from the View menu.

2 Near the top of this window (Figure 38) you should see a button containing the letter 'A'. This is the label tool. Use it to draw a label box in the Page Header section by clicking the mouse and dragging the mouse down and to the right. Do not worry if the box is the wrong shape or in the wrong place at first.

3 Type in the column heading: 'Average per job'.

Figure 38: Toolbox window

ACTIVITY 50 Continued

1 When you have drawn the box you can use the large handle at the top left to move the box around by clicking on the handle and dragging the mouse.

2 Use the other handles to alter its shape until you are happy that it is about the same size as the other boxes in the Page header.

3 Click on the button labelled 'ab' in the Toolbox. This is the Text Box tool.

4   Use it to draw a text box in the Detail section in a similar way to that in which you drew the label box. Do not attempt to type anything in this box yet.

When you have done this your report should look like Figure 39.

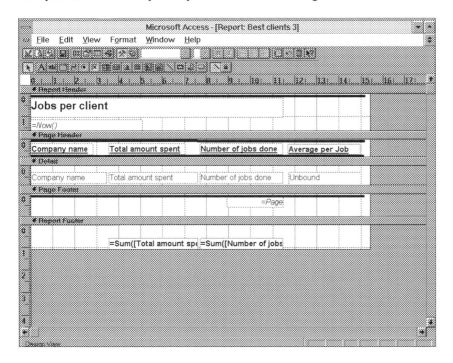

Figure 39: Adding label and text boxes to the report

Notice how Access automatically chose the correct appearance for the text in your label box. The word 'Unbound' in the text box simply means that you have not yet told Access what to put in the text box.

The final step is to add the calculation that you want to perform in the Detail section. Clearly, to calculate the average amount per job for each client, you need to divide the total amount spent by each client by the number of jobs done for that client. In other words, you should divide the field Total amount spent by the field Number of jobs done.

In order to tell Access how to do this you need to type the formula for dividing these two fields into the text box in the Detail section. Access has various rules for calculations some of which are important here. First, all calculations must begin with an '=' sign. This simply tells Access to treat what follows as a calculation. Second, all field names must be enclosed in square brackets. Finally, you can use the standard arithmetic symbols to perform the calculations: '+' for addition, '-' for subtraction, '/' for division and '*' (not 'x') for multiplication.

ACTIVITY 51

Based on the description of formulae above write down the formula that you should use in your report.

The formula that you should type is:

=[Total amount spent]/[Number of jobs done]

ACTIVITY 52

Click on the text box to select it and then click on it again. Type in the formula above and save your report. Then preview it to see how it looks.

Print Preview will display the report shown in Figure 40. If you made a mistake (such as mis-typing one of the field names) Access will ask you for a parameter value. Since this is not what you want click Cancel to return to the design window and edit the formula to correct it.

Microsoft Access - [Report: Best clients 3]

File   Edit   View   Format   Window   Help

Jobs per client

08-Jun-95

Company name	Total amount spent	Number of jobs done	Average per Job
Sally's DIY Ltd	£9,634.44	21	458.782857142857
Johnson's Cakes	£4,012.76	12	334.396666666667
The Garden Store	£5,012.08	11	455.643636363636
Redham News	£3,154.17	8	394.27125
Redham Heating Ltd	£1,412.31	5	282.462
Super Pizza Ltd	£1,107.60	5	221.52
Bloggs & Co.	£503.70	3	167.9
Watson Electrical	£198.30	2	99.15
Blueshire Cabs	£472.12	1	472.12
Forest & Sons	£298.75	1	298.75
	£25,806.23	69	

Page 1

Figure 40: A report with a calculation

Now you need to tell Access to sort the report according to the results of your calculation. The wizard did not know about the calculation so the report is still sorted by Number of jobs done.

ACTIVITY 53

1 Choose Sorting and Grouping from the View menu.

2 Edit the top line of the Field/Expression column so that it includes exactly the formula that you added to the Detail section.

3 Make sure that the sort order is still Descending. Preview the report and save it.

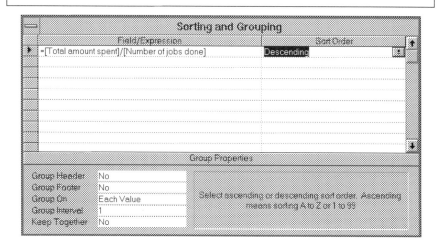

The report should now look like Figure 41.

The report is nearly complete. Only one problem remains, that of setting the properties of the calculation text box so that it displays the averages in a sensible format. At present Access is displaying all of the decimal places created by the calculation which is clearly nonsense. Monetary quantities only need two decimal places. It would also be sensible to include a '£' symbol before the averages.

```
┌─────────────────────────────────────────────────────────────────────┐
│            Microsoft Access - [Report: Best clients 3]                │
│  File  Edit  View  Format  Window  Help                               │
└─────────────────────────────────────────────────────────────────────┘
```

Jobs per client

08-Jun-95

Company name	Total amount spent	Number of jobs done	Average per Job
Blueshire Cabs	£472.12	1	472.12
Sally's DIY Ltd	£9,634.44	21	458.782857142857
The Garden Store	£5,012.08	11	455.643636363636
Redham News	£3,154.17	8	394.27125
Johnson's Cakes	£4,012.76	12	334.396666666667
Forest & Sons	£298.75	1	298.75
Redham Heating Ltd	£1,412.31	5	282.462
Super Pizza Ltd	£1,107.60	5	221.52
Bloggs & Co.	£503.70	3	167.9
Watson Electrical	£198.30	2	99.15
	£25,806.23	69	

Page: 1

Figure 41: The correctly sorted report

ACTIVITY 54

1 Return to the design window and select the calculation text box.

2 In the properties window, click on the Format option and choose Currency from the drop-down list.

Preview your report again and save it.

Your report (Figure 42) is now complete. You can print it out if you wish by clicking the Print icon or by choosing Print from the File menu. Access uses the standard Windows printing techniques.

From the report you can now see that Sally's DIY is probably Redham Printers' best client even though it does not have the highest average. You can also see that it would be well worth the company trying to build up its relationship with Blueshire Cabs. They have just had one job done so far but for a relatively large amount.

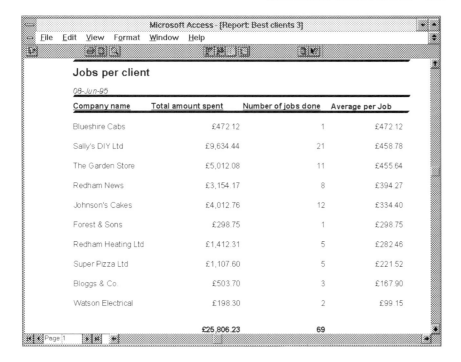

Figure 42: The completed report

There are some cosmetic changes which could be made to your report such as aligning the column headings differently or using different fonts. You can experiment by choosing different options in the properties window.

3.2 Grouping records

The next report that you will create is a simple example of grouping records. Suppose that Redham Printers Ltd wanted to find out which towns its clients come from. The next activity shows how you would do this.

ACTIVITY 55

1 First close any reports that you already have open.

2 Make sure that the UNIT_8.MDB database window is open.

3 Click the Report button and then click the New button.

4 Choose the Clients table.

5 Use the Groups/Totals Report Wizard to create the new report.

6 Include just the Company name and Town fields in your report. When asked which field you want to group by, choose the Town field and click Next.

This brings up a step in the wizard that you have not seen before (Figure 43). It asks you how you want to group the data. Usually the Normal option is best.

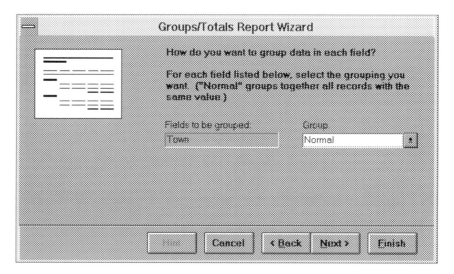

Figure 43: Choosing how to group data

ACTIVITY 56

1 Click on Normal and then click Next.

2 Sort the records by Company name.

3 Choose the Presentation look and give the report the title 'Location of clients'.

4 Preview the report and save it as 'Location of clients'.

Your report should look like Figure 44.

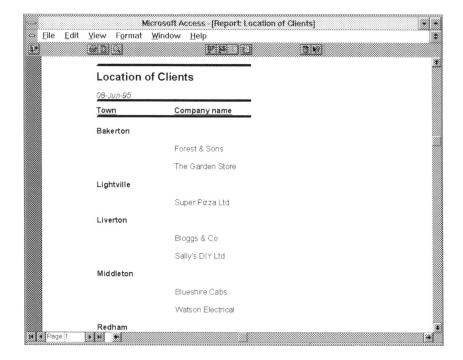

Figure 44: A grouped report

As you can see, the report lists each client according to which town it is in. You can edit the report in the design window in the usual way if you want to.

Summary

In this section, you have learned how to design and modify reports using the Report Wizard. You have learned how records can be grouped in a report. You have seen how using the Report Wizard includes totals at the end of your report, where appropriate. You have also learned how to include calculations in a report.

SECTION 4

Relational Databases and Queries

Introduction

So far in this unit we have assumed that all databases contain just one table. In reality this is not the case and it is often very inefficient to try to contain everything in one table. In this section we explain why and will introduce the idea of databases with more than one table. These are called **relational databases**.

The reports and forms you met earlier in this unit were useful ways of looking at data when you were interested in all of the records in the database. They are not so useful if you only want to look at the records that mean particular criteria such as 'all sales made after 1 June'. **Queries** provide a way of doing this.

4.1 Relational databases

Look back at the Song Titles table you created in Section 2. The table attempts to do two things: record the information about a song; and the details of the disc on which the song appears. To achieve this you had to repeat the data for Disc Id, Disc Title, Artist and Year for each song on a Disc. This can lead to errors (entering different data where it should be the same) and is time consuming both when entering the data and amending it. Databases with a single table only are called 'flatfile' databases and, as you can see, they are very inefficient. It would be much better to store the information about songs and discs in two separate tables (Songs and Discs).

The Songs table contains data relating to each song. This could be:

- Song Id   To uniquely identify each song
- Song Title   To uniquely identify each song
- Disc Number   To identify which disc the song appears on
- Track Number   To identify the track on the given disc.

The Discs table contains data relating to each disc. This could be:

- Disc Id
- Disc Title
- Artist
- Year

Each of which uniquely identify each disc.

ACTIVITY 57

This activity will destroy your original Discs table. In order to be able to repeat this exercise you must take a back up of your database now. Use File Manager as this cannot be done in Access.

1 Open the database which contains your Discs Table from Section 2.

2 Rename the Discs table by highlighting it in the table section of the Directory Window, selecting File and Rename, entering the new name as Songs and clicking on OK.

3 Open the Songs table in Design mode and delete the Disc Title, Artist and Year fields.

4 Change the name of the Disc Id field to Disc Number.

5 Save and close the table.

6 Create a new table with the following definition.

Field name	Data type	Size/format
Disc Id	Number	LongInteger
Disc Title	Text	30
Artist	Text	25
Year	Text	4

7 Make Disc Id the primary key, save the table as Discs and close it.

8 Enter the following data into the Discs table.

Disc Id	Disc Title	Artist	Year
1	The Red Shoes	Kate Bush	1993
3	Dark Side of the Moon	Pink Floyd	1973
4	Debut	Bjork	1993
5	Dreamland	Aztec Camera	1993
10	So	Peter Gabriel	1986

9 The Songs table contains the titles of all the songs on the discs in the Discs table. Examine the structure of these two tables.

10 Which field in Songs contains information about the Discs table?

11 Which field in Discs does it refer to?

12 Why is it a good idea to store the information in two tables?

The field Disc Number in Songs contains a number that corresponds to the Disc Id in the Discs table. For example, according to the Song titles table, the song 'On the run' appears on disc 3. Looking up this number in the Disc Id field of the Discs table tells you that the song appears on 'Dark Side of the Moon', by Pink Floyd.

Now, apart from the Disc Id/number which has to appear in both tables in order to show the connection, each piece of data now only appears once.

4.2 Queries

Arranging your data in multiple tables would be of little use if you had to look up all the relationships yourself as above. Not surprisingly, Access and most other database software have facilities for combining data from relational databases. It also has facilities for ensuring that it is easy to add the data to the different tables easily. This section is just a brief overview of relational databases and we cannot cover all of this topic in the space available, instead, we look at just one aspect of relational databases, extracting information.

The first query that you create will be based on one table, the Discs table.

ACTIVITY 58

1 Make sure that the database containing Discs and Songs Tables is open.

2 Click on the Query button and click on New.

3 Click on New Query (We are not going to look at Query Wizards here).

4 In the Add Table dialog box that opens, click on Discs and then click Add followed by Close. This creates a new query.

You should now be looking at the query window (Figure 45).

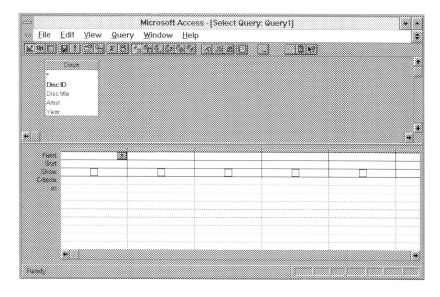

Figure 45: The query window

The top half of the window contains one or more smaller windows that contain lists of fields in the tables that are to be used in the query. In this case, there is just one table, Discs. The bottom half is where you tell Access: what fields to include in the query (the Field line); how to sort them (Sort); whether they should be displayed in the result of the query (Show); and what specific records should be included in the query (Criteria).

The query that you are going to create will find all the discs in the Discs table that were released after 1990, sorted by Artist.

To add a field to the query, click on its name in the list of fields and drag it to the Field row.

ACTIVITY 59

Add the fields Disc title, Artist and Year to the query by dragging them from the list of fields.

Your query should now look like Figure 46.

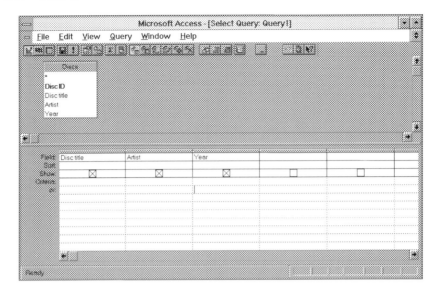

Figure 46: Creating a query

You now have a query (of sorts). It would result in a table containing all of the data in the original Discs table, except for the Disc Id field. This is not particularly useful as it stands. You put this right in the next activities.

The first step is to decide which fields should be shown in the result of the query. In the query window, a cross in the box in the Show line means that that field will appear in the result of the query. Clicking on this box deletes the cross and removes the field from the result of the query. Clicking again on the box restores the field. Note that even if the field is not shown it is still used by the query.

ACTIVITY 60

Which fields should be displayed in the result of the query?

You probably want to show all three fields in this query so that you could see the year in which the discs were released. If you were not concerned with the release dates you might decide not to show the Year field.

The next step is to tell Access that you want to include only those discs released after 1990. You do this by typing instructions in the Criteria lines.

For example, if you wanted to find all the discs released by Kate Bush, you would type 'Kate Bush' (including the quotation marks) on the first Criteria line. If you were interested in discs made by either Kate Bush or Peter Gabriel, you would type

'Kate Bush' on the first criteria line and 'Peter Gabriel' on the second criteria line. You need to include the quotation marks only in Text fields.

In our example you need to find a way of telling Access to include only those records for which the Year field contains a value greater than 1990. To do this Access uses expressions containing mathematical symbols:

> (Greater than)

Selects those records that are numerically bigger or alphabetically later than a certain value. Thus in a field containing prices, >10.99 would find all records containing prices higher than 10.99, but not those lower than 10.99 or equal to it. In a field containing names, >'Smith' would find any names occurring after Smith in alphabetical order (e.g. Smithson, Smythe or Young), but not Smith itself or any name earlier in the alphabet.

>= (Greater than or equal to)

Is exactly the same as '>', except that the value specified is also included in the selection. Thus in the example above >=10.99 would include records containing 10.99 in the price field in addition to the records with higher price values. In the name example, >='Smith' would include Smith in the records selected.

< (Less than)

This is the opposite of '>'. Using the same examples <10.99 would find all the records with prices below 10.99 but not 10.99 itself. <'Smith' would find names appearing before Smith in the alphabet but not records containing Smith itself.

<= (Less than or equal to)

This is the opposite of '>='. <=10.99 would find all the prices below 10.99 and all those that are exactly 10.99. <='Smith' would similarly find Smith as well as all the names preceding it in the alphabet.

If you want to find a single specific value then you would simply type that value in the Criteria line.

If you wanted to find all the records that did not contain a particular value, you would precede the value with the word 'Not' (without quotation marks). Thus:

Not 1992

in the criteria for the Year field would find all the discs not released in 1992, while

Not 'Pink Floyd'

in the criteria for the Artist field would find all the discs except those made by Pink Floyd.

You now know enough to complete your query.

ACTIVITY 61

1 Make sure that all three fields are marked to be shown.

2 Type in a criterion for the Year field that will select all the discs released after 1990.

3 In the Sort line for Artist choose Ascending from the drop-down list.

4 Finally, save your query as Post-1990 by choosing Save As from the File menu.

Your query should now look like Figure 47.

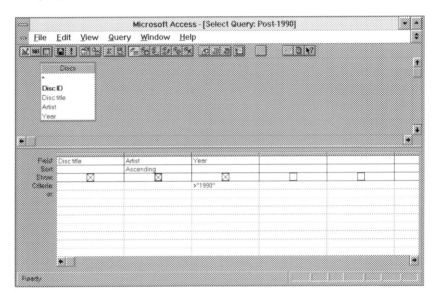

Figure 47: The completed query

All you have to do now is run your query.

ACTIVITY 62

Choose Run from the Query menu to run your query. What form does the result of your query take?

The result of your query is the table shown accurately in Figure 48.

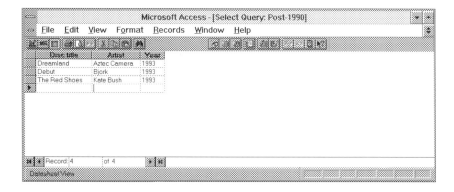

Figure 48: Result of the Post-1990 query

Although this looks like a new table it is actually what Access calls a 'dynaset'. A dynaset takes the form of a table, but actually represents a particular view of the data in one or more tables. Any changes you make to the dynaset will also be made in the original table(s).

This is not the case in all database software. The result of a query in the program Paradox for Windows, for example, is a new table and changes made to that table do not affect the original table. You need to be certain of the effects of changing data in the results of a query in your software.

Queries based on single tables are of limited interest. In the following activities you will create a query that lists all of the songs that appear on a particular disc.

ACTIVITY 63

1 Close the Post-1990 query.

2 Click the Query button and choose New to create a new query.

3 Click on New Query. Add the Discs and Song titles tables to the query window and then close the Add Tables dialog box.

You should now have two tables in your query window, as in Figure 49.

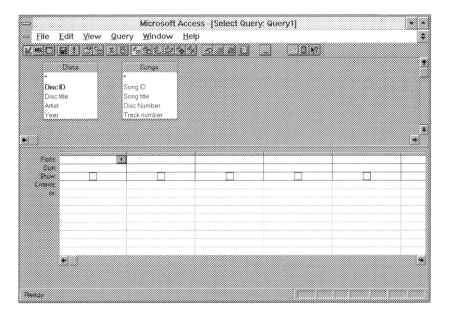

Figure 49: Creating a query with two tables

Before you proceed, you need to tell Access which fields in the two tables contain the same information, that is, how the two tables are linked to one another. As you know, the fields are Disc Id in the Discs table and Disc Number in the Songs table.

To tell Access how to link the two tables click on the field to be linked in the first table and then drag it to the field to be linked in the second table.

ACTIVITY 64

Link the Disc Id field in the Discs table to the Disc Number field in the Songs table. What happens on the screen?

To indicate that a link has been made Access draws a line between the two fields, as in Figure 50.

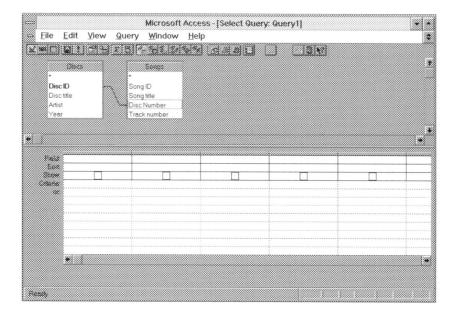

Figure 50: Linking fields in the query window

Notice that the two linked fields do not have the same name. It would be perfectly possible to have left the design of the Songs table so that the Disc Number field was called Disc Id. In general, two fields with the same name might not contain the same data so be wary. Different field names have been chosen in this example to emphasise that it is the data that you should concentrate on not the field names.

To create the query all you have to do now is decide which fields to include and in what order. Since the aim is to produce a disc by disc song listing, you clearly need to include the Disc title field from the Discs table and the Song title field from the Song titles table. In addition, the Artist field should be included from the Discs table. This is so that you know who recorded the disc together with the Track number from the Song titles table so you can sort the songs into the right order.

ACTIVITY 65

Add the four fields identified above to the query. Make sure that they will all show in the resulting dynaset, and sort the Disc Title field and the Track number field in ascending order.

Save your query as 'Disc listing' and then run it.

If you have defined your query correctly, the query window will look like Figure 51.

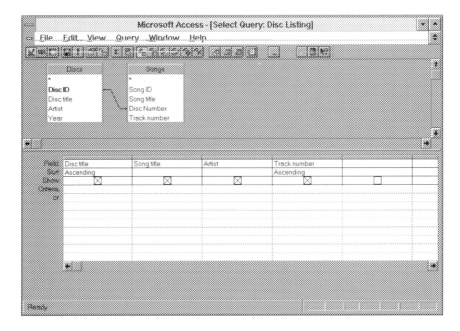

Figure 51: The Disc listing query design

The result of the query is shown in part in Figure 52.

Disc title	Song title	Artist	Track number
Dark Side of the Moon	Speak to me/Breathe in the air	Pink Floyd	1
Dark Side of the Moon	On the run	Pink Floyd	2
Dark Side of the Moon	Time	Pink Floyd	3
Dark Side of the Moon	Great gig in the sky, the	Pink Floyd	4
Dark Side of the Moon	Money	Pink Floyd	5
Debut	Human behaviour	Bjork	1
Debut	Crying	Bjork	2
Debut	Venus as a boy	Bjork	3
Debut	There's more to life than this	Bjork	4
Debut	Like someone in love	Bjork	5
Dreamland	Birds	Aztec Camera	1
Dreamland	Safe in sorrow	Aztec Camera	2
Dreamland	Black Lucia	Aztec Camera	3
Dreamland	Let your love decide	Aztec Camera	4
Dreamland	Spanish horses	Aztec Camera	5
So	Red rain	Peter Gabriel	1
So	Sledgehammer	Peter Gabriel	2
So	Don't give up	Peter Gabriel	3
So	That voice again	Peter Gabriel	4
So	In your eyes	Peter Gabriel	5
The Red Shoes	Rubberband girl	Kate Bush	1
The Red Shoes	And so is love	Kate Bush	2
The Red Shoes	Eat the music	Kate Bush	3
The Red Shoes	Moments of pleasure	Kate Bush	4
The Red Shoes	Song of Solomon, the	Kate Bush	5

Record 11 of 25

Figure 52: Result of the Disc listing query

The resulting dynaset has 25 records. You should be able to see that, if you stored all your data in one table like this, it would have wasted a lot of space (just as in Section 2). Both the disc titles and the artists' names are repeated in every record.

4.3 Creating a report from a query

The usefulness of a query lies not in the query itself but in what you can do with it. The Disc listing query that you created above contains all the information you want but not in a very useful form. To get a proper view of your data, you can create a report based on this query.

ACTIVITY 66

1 Use the Groups/Totals Report Wizard to create a report based on the Disc listing query.

2 Place all the fields except Artist in the query on the report and choose the Disc title field as the field to be grouped by.

3 Choose the Normal grouping method and then choose Track number for the sort order.

4 Choose the Presentation look and accept the name 'Disc listing' as the report title.

5 Save your report as 'Disc listing' and preview it.

Your report should look like Figure 53.

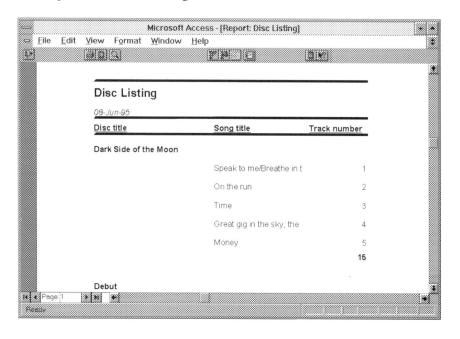

Figure 53: Report based on the Disc listing query

There are still some things to do to this report. The artist's names need to be added, the space allowed for the song titles increased, and the totals of the track numbers need to be removed. Finally, it would be nice to give each disk its own page in the report. To do all of these things open the design window and carry out Activity 67.

ACTIVITY 67

1   Make the Disc title Header section deeper by moving the mouse pointer to its bottom edge and then clicking and dragging the mouse downwards when the pointer changes to a double-headed arrow. Make enough space for an extra text box.

2   Use the Toolbox to draw a new text box immediately below the Disc title text box.

3   Click in the new text box to remove the 'Unbound' text and then type in 'Artist' to indicate that you want Access to include the Artist field there.

4   In the Page Header edit the Track number label to read simply 'Track' and then drag the bottom-left handle of the label to the right to make the label smaller. (You will need to click outside the label and then click on it to select it in order to do this.)

5   In the Detail section click on the Track number text box to select it. Do not edit the contents of the box but drag its bottom-left handle to the right so that it is the same size as the Track text box in the Page Header.

6   Also in the Detail section click on the Song title text box to select it and then drag its bottom-right handle to make it wider.

7   In addition open the properties window and select 'Yes' in the Can Grow line. This allows long titles to spill over onto a second line, if necessary.

8   Click on the box in the disk title footer and then press the DELETE key to delete it. (This removes the total of the track numbers.)

9   Delete the two boxes in the Report Footer in the same way so that the total of all the track numbers is deleted.

10 Finally click the grey bar labelled Disc title Footer and set the Force New Page option in the properties window to After Section.

11 Save the report and view it.

The design window of your report should look like Figure 54 and a single page of the finished report should look like Figure 55.

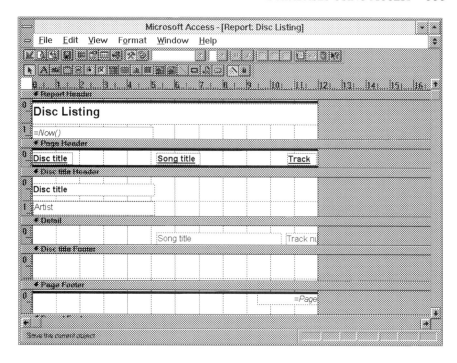

Figure 54: Design of the finished report

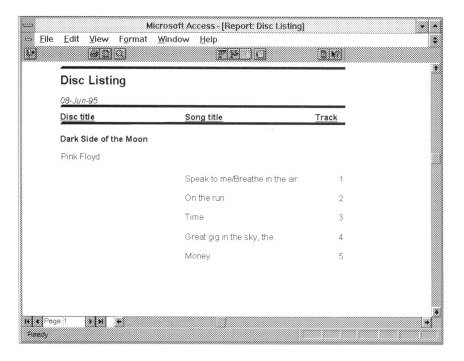

Figure 55: Result of the finished report

You can move from page to page using the 'video' keys at the bottom of the window. If there is anything still not quite right you can go back to the design window to correct it.

4.4 Many to many relations

In the previous example, we looked at a situation where one disc had many songs/tracks. This was implemented as a one to many relationship using two tables. Each record in the table at the many end of the relationship (Songs in this example) has a field which contains the primary key value of the record in the other table to which it belongs (Disc Number).

Consider the following change to our example. What would happen if a song could appear on more than one disc? (As in the case of songs being re-released on a 'Greatest Hits' Disc, for example.) We could repeat the Disc Number field in the Songs table to have one for each disc. But how many repeats should there be, how often is the same song re-released? This is an example of a many to many relationship where one disc has many songs, and one song can appear on many discs. When this occurs it is usual to define a new table which links the two original tables as follows:

The original tables would be re-defined as:

Songs

    Song Id

    Song Title

Discs

    Disc Id

    Disc Title

    Artist

    Year of Release

A third table is required to define the occurrences of songs on discs as follows:

Disc Contents

    Disc Id

    Song Id

    Track Number

What is the primary key for this new table? It cannot be the Disc Id as there will be several records for each disc (one per song). Similarly, it cannot be the Song Id as again there will be several records for each song (one for each disc on which it appears). There are two main solutions. The first is to introduce a new counter field in order to just give each record a unique identifier. Another solution (which we will use here) is to use the Disc Id and the Song Id together as a Compound Primary Key.

ACTIVITY 68

1 Create three new tables named 'Discs 2', 'Songs 2', and 'Discs with Songs' using the definitions described above.

2 Set the primary key of Discs 2 as Disc Id, the primary key of Songs 2 as Song Id, and the primary key of Discs with Songs as a compound key of Disc Id and Song Id.

Note: to set a compound key, select the first key field (Disc Id), hold down the CTRL key and select the second key field (Song Id). Both fields should now be highlighted so you can now set them as a primary key.

The design window of your three tables should now look like Figures 56, 57, and 58.

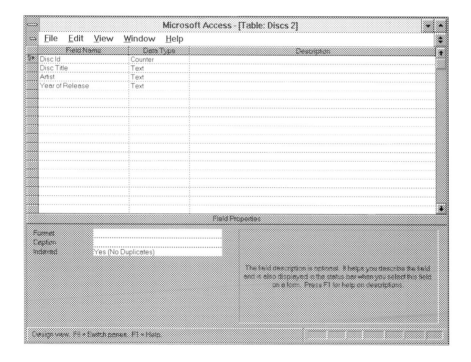

Figure 56: Design for Table Discs 2

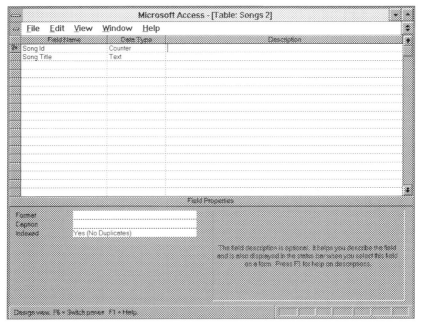

Figure 57: Design for Table Songs 2

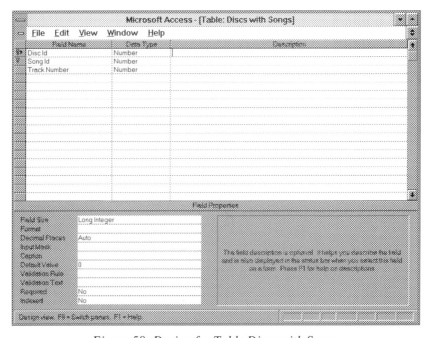

Figure 58: Design for Table Discs with Songs

ACTIVITY 69

Enter the following data into the three tables.

Discs 2

Disc Id	Disc Title	Artist	Year of Release
1	Queen's Greatest Hits	Queen	1994
2	Jazz	Queen	1994
3	Foreign Affair	Tina Turner	1989
4	Simply the Best	Tina Turner	1991

Songs 2

Song Id	Song Title
1	Steamy Windows
2	The Best
3	You Know Who (is doing you know what)
4	Undercover Agent For The Blues
5	Look Me In The Heart
6	Be Tender With Me Baby
7	What's Love Got To Do With It
8	I Can't Stand The Rain
9	I Don't Wanna Lose You
10	Nut Bush City Limits
11	Let's Stay Together
12	Private Dancer
13	We Don't Need Another Hero
14	Better Be Good To Me
15	River Deep – Mountain High
16	Bohemian Rhapsody
17	Another One Bites The Dust
18	Killer Queen
19	Fat Bottomed Girls
20	Bicycle Race
21	Mustapha
22	Jealousy
23	If You Can't Beat Them

Discs with Songs

Disc Id	Song Id	Track Number
1	16	1
1	17	2
1	18	3
1	19	4
1	20	5
2	19	2
2	20	4
2	21	1
2	22	3
2	23	5
3	1	1
3	2	2
3	3	3
3	4	4
3	5	5
3	6	6
4	1	11
4	2	1
4	7	2
4	8	3
4	9	4
4	10	5
4	11	6
4	12	7
4	13	8
4	14	9
4	15	10

At this stage, it is not easy to see which song titles are on each disc. A simple solution is to create a query to join all three tables, and to inspect the results.

ACTIVITY 70

1 Create a new query which is based on all three tables.

2 Join Discs 2 to Discs with Songs using the Disc Id fields.

3 Join Songs 2 to Discs with Songs using the Song Id fields.

4 Sort the data into Disc Title and Track Number order.

5 Run the query.

You should now have results similar to those in Figure 59.

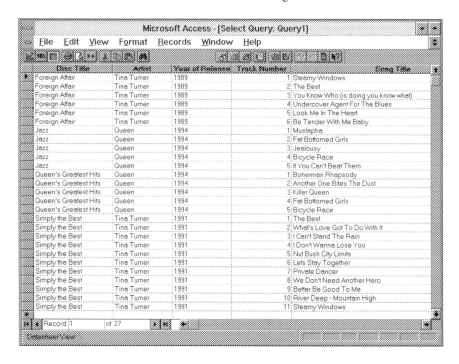

Figure 59: Query output from all three tables

You can see from this that 'The Best' and 'Steamy Windows' by Tina Turner appear on both Discs but there is only one occurrence of each in the Songs 2 table. Similarly, 'Fat Bottomed Girls' and 'Bicycle Race' by Queen appear on both of the Queen discs.

Finally, would this system accommodate Compilation Discs where a number of artists have songs on the same disc? No, as we have said that one attribute of Discs 2 is Artist. If we want to allow Compilation Discs we would have to review our table definitions and delete the Artist field from Discs 2 and add it to Songs 2. (This would also require the Artist data to be re-entered against Song.)

4.5 Organising your tables

In Access you should keep all of the tables of a particular database in a single database file (one with a .MDB extension). No other tables should appear in that database file. The file UNIT_8.MDB breaks this rule but only for the purposes of making it easy to distribute the module software. You should never mix tables from different databases.

Summary

In this section, you have learned what a relational database is and what their advantages are over flatfile (single table) databases. You have learned how to create a query for both flatfile and relational databases and have also seen how to use that query to create a report on more than one table.

There is much more to be learned about relational databases and queries. This section is merely a brief introduction.

SECTION 5
Field Validation

Introduction

In this session you will determine appropriate validation rules and apply them to tables.

5.1 What is validation?

Validation is the process of checking the value of a field when data is entered or amended to ensure that the 'business rules' are not being broken. Validation can be carried out in various ways such as:

- In isolation, to ensure that the value is sensible, for example, a date field only contains a date.

- By reference, to ensure that the value is compatible with that in another field or table, such as the date you join a club must be later than the date you were born.

By defining these rules in the database system we reduce the risk of users entering invalid data and we can signal when they attempt to do this by the use of meaningful error messages.

The first type of validation can be defined for each field in a table in design mode. When in data entry mode the value of the data is validated at the point when the user moves to the following field. If the entry is invalid, Access will display the error message and return the user to the field in error.

Look at Figure 60 which shows the table design screen from the Golf Club Membership table.

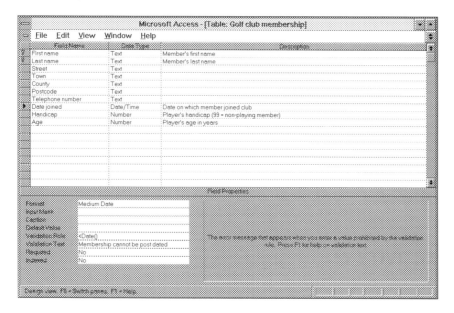

Figure 60: Field validation

For each field in a table, you can define a validation rule, and the associated error message. In this example we have entered a validation rule for the Date Joined which says that this date must be before today (i.e. no post-dated membership). It uses the Date function which returns today's date as set in the computer's clock. The rule is:

<Date()

If we want to validate a field based on the contents of another field then, in Access 2.0, this has to be defined at the table level in design mode and is validated during data entry when the record is added or replaced in the table (i.e. when closing the table or moving to another record). The validation rule is entered by selecting View and Table Properties when the table is open in design mode. This will result in the window in Figure 61 being displayed.

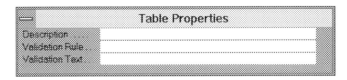

Figure 61: Blank table validation window

In this example we want to add a rule which checks that the Year of the Date of Joining is later than the Year of the member's birth. The table does not hold the date of birth but does hold the current age of the member in years. We have therefore entered the following rule:

Year([Date Joined]) > Year(Date()) – [Age]

This says 'to be valid, the year of the date of joining must be greater than the current year minus the member's current age'.

This has been entered together with a suitable message as in Figure 62 below.

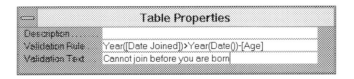

Figure 62: Completed table validation window

ACTIVITY 71

1 Open the Golf Club Membership table in Design mode.

2 Enter the validation rules described above and save the table.

3 Enter new records or amend existing records which have joining dates in the future and in the past to check whether the first rule works.

4 Enter new records or amend existing records which have ages and/or dates of joining which result in the members joining before and after they were born.

5 Check whether the second rule works correctly. Make notes of the point at which the error messages occur.

Summary

In this section you have been introduced to the idea of automatically checking the value of data items and features which enable the data to be validated as it is amended or entered.

SECTION 6

Labels

Introduction

Printing labels is such a common task that Access gives it its own wizard. In this section, you will see how to use the wizard to create a set of mailing labels using the Golf Club members table in the UNIT_8 database.

The Golf Club members table contains information about some of the members of West Redshire Golf Club. (Open the table if you want to see the information.) As the club secretary you want to mail the club newsletter to the members, using the information in the table.

6.1 Creating mailing labels

To create mailing labels, use the Mailing Label Report Wizard.

ACTIVITY 72

1 Open UNIT_8.MDB if necessary and click on the Report button.

2 Click on New, choose the Golf Club members table.

3 Click the Report Wizards button.

4 Choose Mailing Label and then click Next.

You should now see the first step of the Mailing Label Wizard (Figure 63).
Although it may appear familiar to you will see that it contains a number of extra
items.

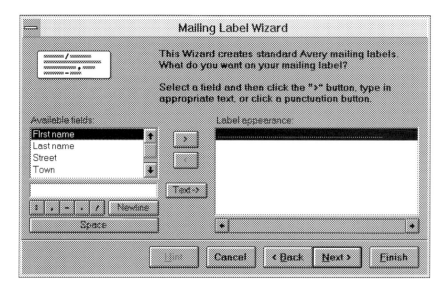

Figure 63: First step in the Mailing Label Wizard

Immediately below the list of available fields is the edit box. If you type text in this
box (e.g. the name of the golf club) and then click on the Text button this text will
be added to every label.

The next row of buttons adds punctuation to the label: from left to right a colon (:),
comma (,), hyphen (-), full stop (.) or a solidus (/). The button below them adds a
space to the label and the new line button starts a new line in the label. Activity 73
will show you how to use these.

ACTIVITY 73

The label will include a member's first name and last name (separated by a
space) on one line, followed, on separate lines, by the Street, Town, County
and Postcode fields. There will then be a blank line followed by 'W.R.G.C.',
the initials of the golf club.

1 Click on the First name field and then click on the right-facing chevron.

2 Click on the Space button (do not click the chevron button). Now, click on
   the Last name field and then on the chevron button. To start the next line,
   click on the new line button.

3 Now add the remaining fields line by line. Remember to press the new line
   button to put each field on a new line. If you make a mistake, such as
   putting two fields on one line when you did not want to, press the left-facing
   chevron to delete the mistake.

4 When you have added the Postcode field click the new line button twice to
   add a blank line. Then type 'W.R.G.C.' in the edit box below the available
   fields and click Text to add this to the report.

The Wizard should now look like Figure 64.

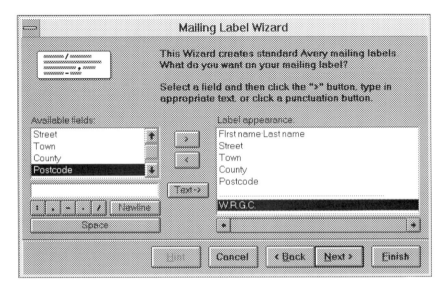

Figure 64: Designing a mailing label

You can now go on to complete your label report.

ACTIVITY 74

1 Click Next.

2 When asked how you want to sort the labels, choose Last name followed by
   First name, and click Next again.

3 The wizard now asks you for the type of label you want to use. This
   depends on what label stationery you have available, as well as what your
   printer will accept. For the purposes of illustration, choose Unit of Measure
   English, Label Type sheet feed, and Label Size 5095, at the top of the list,
   which prints two labels side by side on your label stationery.

4 Click Next and the wizard now asks you for the font style, size, weight and colour. Leave as the default settings and click Next.

5 Select to view the labels and click Finish to preview your labels.

6 Save the label report as 'Golf Club labels'.

Your label preview should look like Figure 65.

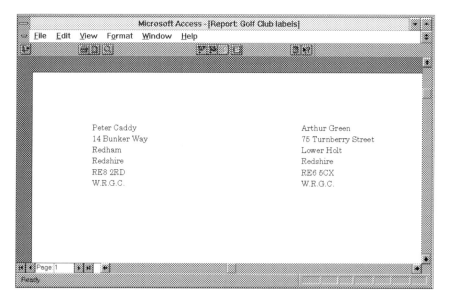

Figure 65: Previewing labels

Access has not yet included the blank line you asked for. It would also be nice to move 'W.R.G.C.' over to the right-hand side of the label, away from the address.

ACTIVITY 75

1 Click Close Window to display the design window.

2 Click twice on the text box that says 'Unbound' so that the word 'Unbound' disappears and then type = " " (i.e. an equals sign followed by a space between two double quotation marks). Access will now know that you want that line to be blank.

3 Next select the 'W.R.G.C.' text box and open the properties window.

4 Click the Text Align option and choose Right from the drop-down list.

5 Save your report and preview it.

Your labels should now look like Figure 66.

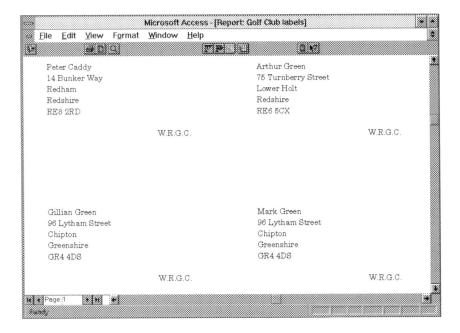

Figure 66: The finished labels

As with any other report you can edit your labels until you are happy with the way they look. Printing the labels depends on your printer (e.g. dot matrix or laser) and you may have to take care if you have a dot matrix printer to ensure that your label stationery is correctly positioned in the printer. If you do not you might find that your labels are printed across the gaps between the labels thus making them useless and wasting the labels. If you can, use ordinary paper to check that the labels print correctly.

Unit Review Activity

The following activity is intended to help you find out how much expertise you have acquired with databases and to help you decide whether you should look again at any of the sections you have studied. Do not spend any time trying to work out something if you cannot do it. Instead go back and redo the relevant section. The test assumes that Access is already installed on your computer and should not take you more than 50 minutes to complete.

This test is based upon the following scenario:

The requirement is to manage data related to departments and the employees in those departments.

The data attributes for each department are:

Department Number

Department Name

Telephone Number

Budget

The data attributes for each employee are:

Employee Number

Surname

Forenames

Date of Birth

Date of Employment

Salary

Department Code

1   Create a database with two tables, one for department and one for employee. Fields must have appropriate data types and lengths/formats.

2   Create a form suitable for data entry for each table and enter correctly, the following data.

Department Number	Department Name	Telephone Number	Budget
1	Finance	323 1234	$3,000,000.00
2	Human Resources	323 5432	$3,500,000.00
4	Computer Services	323 0101	$11,000,000.00
7	Sales	323 0567	$14,000,000.00
9	Marketing	356 0012	$11,250,000.00
11	Purchasing	311 0978	$9,750,000.00
20	Production	522 1076	$25,000,000.00

Emp No	Surname	Forenames	DOB	DOEmp	Salary	DC
9001	Smith	Geoff	21/03/54	01/09/74	$14,000.00	1
9002	Williams	Sarah	01/08/72	02/03/90	$8,500.00	2
9003	Jones	John William	20/11/46	01/02/64	$12,000.00	1
9012	Appleby	Michael	16/04/55	04/04/79	$16,685.00	1
9032	Goldberg	Aaron	25/11/65	01/09/88	$18,500.00	4
9034	O'Brien	James	22/12/70	01/04/94	$18,000.00	2

3   Create and save a query which joins the two tables.

4   Create and save a report based on the query which lists the departments and the corresponding employees and salaries.

Ensure the report prints each department's name once only and that the Departments and their Employees are listed in alphabetical order.

5   Modify your query to list only those employees in the Finance Department. Save the query with a different name.

Solution

A sample solution is provided on disk as:

INITIAL.MDB

Spend some time checking your answer and the sample and determine if there are any differences and their significance.

If you need help ask your tutor.

RESOURCES

RESOURCE 1.1

Learning Styles

In this session you will consider:

- Your preferred learning style
- The benefit of this and other learning styles
- How to learn more effectively by adopting a style which takes account of experiential learning.

Introduction

Most people have a preferred learning style – in other words, ways of going about learning - which has developed over years in school or college. As one of education's successes you may feel that this approach has served you well in the past and you might as well carry on as before.

This session aims to provide you with an introduction to a number of theories of learning style with which to understand better your own approach and adapt your style to be most effective during your time as a student.

How to go about it

The first step is to identify your own learning style preferences.

Learning styles questionnaire

This questionnaire (Table 1.1) is designed to find your preferred learning style(s).

Over the years you have developed learning 'habits' that help you benefit more from some experiences than from others. Since you are probably unaware of this, the questionnaire will help you pinpoint your learning preferences so that you are in a better position to select learning experiences that suit your style.

Complete the questionnaire, trying to be as honest as you can. There is no time limit, but it will probably take you 20 to 25 minutes. The accuracy of the results depends on how honest you are. There are no right or wrong answers. If you agree more than you disagree with a statement, put a tick by it ($\checkmark$). If you disagree more than you agree, put a cross by it (x). Be sure to mark each item with either a tick or a cross.

Scoring the learning styles questionnaire

Enter your results on the scoring sheet given in Table 1.2. You score 1 point for each item you ticked ($\checkmark$). There are no points for items you crossed (x). Simply circle the item you ticked.

2	7	1	5
4	13	3	9
6	15	8	11
10	16	12	19
17	25	14	21
23	28	18	27
24	29	20	35
32	31	22	37
34	33	26	44
38	36	30	49
40	39	42	50
43	41	47	53
45	46	51	54
48	52	57	56
58	55	61	59
64	60	63	65
71	62	68	69
72	66	75	70
74	67	77	73
79	76	78	80
Totals			
Activist	Reflector	Theorist	Pragmatist

Table 1.2 Learning Styles Score Sheet

☐ 1 I have strong beliefs about what is right and wrong, good and bad.

☐ 2 I often 'throw caution to the wind'.

☐ 3 I tend to solve problems using a step-by-step approach, avoiding any 'flights of fancy'.

☐ 4 I believe that formal procedures and policies cramp people's style.

☐ 5 I have a reputation for having a no-nonsense, 'call a spade a spade' style.

☐ 6 I often find that actions based on 'gut feel' are as sound as those based on careful thought and analysis.

☐ 7 I like to do the sort of work where I have time to 'leave no stone unturned'.

☐ 8 I regularly question people about their basic assumptions.

☐ 9 What matters most is whether something works in practice.

☐ 10 I actively seek out new experiences.

☐ 11 When I hear about a new idea or approach I immediately start working out how to apply it in practice.

☐ 12 I am keen on self-discipline, such as watching my diet, taking regular exercise, sticking to a fixed routine etc.

☐ 13 I take pride in doing a thorough job.

☐ 14 I get on best with logical, analytical people and less well with spontaneous, 'irrational' people.

☐ 15 I take care over the interpretation of data available to me and avoid jumping to conclusions.

☐ 16 I like to reach a decision carefully after weighing up many alternatives.

☐ 17 I'm attracted more to novel, unusual ideas than to practical ones.

☐ 18 I don't like 'loose ends' and prefer to fit things into a coherent pattern.

☐ 19 I accept and stick to laid-down procedures and policies so long as I regard them as an efficient way of getting the job done.

☐ 20 I like to relate my actions to a general principal.

☐ 21 In discussions I like to get straight to the point.

☐ 22 I tend to have distant, rather formal relationships with people at work.

☐ 23 I thrive on the challenge of tackling something new and different.

☐ 24 I enjoy fun-loving, spontaneous people.

☐ 25 I pay meticulous attention to detail before coming to a conclusion.

☐ 26 I find it difficult to come up with wild, off-the-top-of-the-head ideas.

☐ 27 I don't believe in wasting time by 'beating around the bush'.

☐ 28 I am careful not to jump to conclusions too quickly.

☐ 29 I prefer to have as many sources of information as possible - the more data to mull over the better.

☐ 30 Flippant people who don't take things seriously enough usually irritate me.

☐ 31 I listen to other people's point of view before putting forward my own.

☐ 32 I tend to be open about how I'm feeling.

☐ 33 In discussions I enjoy watching the manoeuvring of the other participants.

☐ 34 I prefer to respond to events on a spontaneous, flexible basis rather than plan things out in advance.

☐ 35 I tend to be attracted to techniques such as network analysis, flow charts, branching programmes, contingency planning etc.

☐ 36 It worries me if I have to rush out a piece of work to meet a tight deadline.

☐ 37. I tend to judge people's ideas on their practical merits.

☐ 38. Quiet, thoughtful people tend to make me feel uneasy.

☐ 39 I often get irritated by people who want to rush headlong into things.

☐ 40 It is more important to enjoy the present moment than to think about the past or future.

☐ 41 I think that decisions based on a thorough analysis of all the information are sounder than those based on intuition.

☐ 42 I tend to be a perfectionist.

☐ 43 In discussions I usually pitch in

with lots of off-the-top-of-the-head ideas.

44 In meetings I put forward practical, realistic ideas.

45 More often than not, rules are there to be broken.

46 I prefer to stand back from a situation and consider all the perspectives.

47 I can often see inconsistencies and weaknesses in other people's arguments.

48 On balance I talk more than I listen.

49 I can often see better, more practical ways to get things done.

50 I think written reports should be short, punchy and to the point.

51 I believe that rational, logical thinking should win the day.

52 I tend to discuss specific things with people rather than engaging in 'small talk'.

53 I like people who have both feet firmly on the ground.

54 In discussions I get impatient with irrelevances and 'red herrings'.

55 If you have a report to write I tend to produce lots of drafts before settling on the final version.

56 I am keen to try things out to see if they work in practice.

57 I am keen to reach answers via a logical approach.

58 I enjoy being the one that talks a lot.

59 In discussions I often find that I am the realist, keeping people to the point and avoiding 'cloud nine' speculations.

60 I like to ponder many alternatives before making up my mind.

61 In discussions with people I often find I am the most dispassionate and objective.

62 In discussions I'm more likely to adopt a 'low profile' than to take the lead and do most of the talking.

63 I like to be able to relate current actions to a long-term bigger picture.

64 When things go wrong I am happy to shrug it off and 'put it down to experience'.

65 I tend to reject wild, off-the-top-of-the-head ideas as being impractical.

66 It's best to 'look before you leap'.

67 On balance I do the listening rather than the talking.

68 I tend to be tough on people who find it difficult to adopt a logical approach.

69 Most times I believe the end justifies the means.

70 I don't mind hurting other people's feeling so long as the job gets done.

71 I find the formality of having specific objectives and plans stifling.

72 I'm usually the 'life and soul' of the party.

73 I do whatever is expedient to get the job done.

74 I quickly get bored with methodical, detailed work.

75 I am keen on exploring the basic assumptions, principles and theories underpinning things and events.

76 I'm always interested to find out what other people think.

77 I like meetings to be run on methodical lines, sticking to laid-down agenda. etc.

78 I steer clear of subjective or ambiguous topics.

79 I enjoy the drama and excitement of a crisis situation.

80 People often find me insensitive to their feelings.

Table 1.1 Learning Styles Questionnaire

Total your score of points in each of the four columns. You should now have a score against four styles of learning: Activist; Reflector; Theorist; Pragmatist. Check the strength of your preference for each style by using the checklist in Table 1.3.

The following pages describe each style in detail. You should be able to identify your own preferences from this.

Typically, you may have a very strong preference for one style, but you may find that you have preferences for more than one style. As we shall see in a moment, this is healthy and reflects a rounded approach to study and learning.

Description of Learning Styles

This model is based on the work of Honey and Mumford and you should read their *Manual of Learning Styles* (London, BBC Books, 1986) for more detailed information. Essentially their view is that students need to identify the style(s) which they most prefer and then arrange learning experiences which match their preferences. In other words, activists learn through active experiences; reflectors learn through observation; theorist learn through intellectual analysis; and pragmatists learn through examples of practical experiences.

Activists involve themselves fully and without bias in new experiences. They enjoy the here and now and are happy to be dominated by immediate experiences. They are open-minded, not sceptical, and this tends to make them enthusiastic about anything new. Their philosophy is 'I'll try anything once'. They tend to act first and consider the consequences afterwards. Their days are filled with activity. They tackle problems by brainstorming. As soon as the excitement from one activity has died down they are busy looking for the next. They tend to thrive on the challenge of new experiences but are bored with implementation and longer-term consolidation, They are gregarious people, constantly involving themselves with others, but in doing so they seek to centre all activities around themselves.

Activists learn best from activities where:

Activist	Reflector	Theorist	Pragmatist	
20	20	20	20	
19	19	19	19	
18	18	18	18	
17		17	17	Very strong preference
16		16		
15				
14				
13				
12	17	15	16	
	16			Strong preference
11	15	14	15	
10	14	13	14	
9	13	12	13	Moderate preference
8	12	11	12	
7				
6	11	10	11	
5	10	9	10	Low preference
4	9	8	9	
	8		8	
	7	7	7	
	6	6	6	
	5	5	5	
	4	4	4	Very low preference
3	3	3	3	
2	2	2	2	
1	1	1	1	
0	0	0	0	

Source: P. Honey and A. Mumford, *Manual of Learning Styles* (London: BBC Books, 1986)

Table 1.3 Learning Styles Profile Based on General Norms

- There are new experiences /problems /opportunities from which to learn.
- They can engross themselves in short 'here and now' activities such as business games, competitive teamwork tasks and role-playing exercises.
- They have a lot of the limelight, they lead discussions, give presentations.
- They are allowed to generate ideas without restrictions of policy.
- They are thrown in at the deep end with a task they think difficult.
- They are involved with other people; solving problems as a team.
- It is appropriate to 'have a go'.

Reflectors like to stand back to ponder experiences and observe them from different perspectives. They collect data, both first hand and from others, and prefer to think about it thoroughly before coming to any conclusion. Because the thorough collection and analysis of data about experiences and events is what counts, they tend to postpone reaching definitive conclusions for as long as possible. Their philosophy is to be cautious. They are thoughtful people who like to consider all possible angles and implications before making a move. They enjoy observing other people in action. They listen to others and get the drift of the discussion before making their own points. They tend to adopt a low profile and have a slightly distant, tolerant, unruffled air about them. When they act it is part of a wide picture which includes the past as well as the present and others' observations as well as their own.

Reflectors learn best from activities where:
- They are allowed to watch/think/chew over activities.
- They are able to stand back and observe; observing a group at work, watch films/videos etc.
- They are allowed to think before acting and have time to prepare.
- They can carry out painstaking research, investigation and probing.
- They have time to review what has happened, what they have learnt.
- They are required to produce carefully considered analyses and reports.
- They are helped to exchange views within a structured learning experience.
- They can reach a decision without pressure within their own time.

Theorists adapt and integrate observations into complex but logically sound theories. They think problems through in a vertical, step-by-step, logical way. They assimilate disparate facts into coherent theories. They tend to be perfectionists who won't rest easy until things are tidy and fit into a rational scheme. They like to analyse and synthesise. They are keen on basic assumptions, principles, theories, models and system thinking. Their philosophy prizes rationality and logic: 'If it's logical it's good'. Questions they frequently ask are: 'Does it make sense?' 'How does it fit with that?' 'What are the basic assumptions?'. They tend to be detached, analytical and dedicated to rational objectivity rather than anything subjective or ambiguous. Their approach to problems is consistently logical. This is their 'mental set'. They rigidly reject anything that doesn't fit with it. They prefer to maximise certainty and feel uncomfortable with subjective judgements, lateral thinking and flippant remarks.

Theorists learn best from activities where:
- The learning material is part of a system, model concept or theory.
- They have time to explore the associations and relationship between ideas, events and situations.
- They have the chance to question and probe the basic methodology, assumptions and logic behind something.
- They are intellectually stretched, i.e. analysing a complex problem, being tested in a tutorial session, being asked searching questions.
- They are in structured situations with a clear purpose.
- They can read or listen to ideas and concepts that are rational and logical.
- They can analyse and then generalise problems.
- They are offered interesting ideas and concepts even if they are not relevant.

Pragmatists are keen on trying out ideas, theories and techniques to see if they work in practice. They positively search out new ideas and take the first opportunity to experiment with applications. They are the sort of people who return from courses brimming with new ideas that they want to try out in practise. They like to get on with things and act quickly and confidently on ideas that attract them. They tend to be impatient with ruminating and open-ended discussions. They are essentially practical, down-to-earth people who like making practical decisions and solving problems. They respond to problems and opportunities 'as a challenge'. Their philosophy is 'There is always a better way' and 'If it works its good'.

Pragmatists learn best from activities where:
- There is an obvious link between the subject and a practical problem.

RESOURCE 1.1

- They are shown techniques that have obvious practical advantages.
- They have the chance to try out and practice techniques with an expert who can provide feedback.
- They are shown a model they can copy, a successful person, a film showing how something is done etc.
- They are given immediate opportunities to try out what they have learnt.
- They are given good simulations and real problems to solve.
- They can concentrate on practical situations.

Look at Table 1.4 and compare the advantages of your preferred style which those of the others styles. When you have done this, look at the disadvantages of each style given in Table 1.5.

Activist	Reflector
You:	You:
• get totally involved in something that interests you	• see new ways of doing things
• work well with other people, ask for help, and talk through problems with others	• come up with creative solutions
	• see long-term implications of things
	• can see the total picture
• enjoy writing freely – as it comes	• are unhurried, don't get in a flap
• will try any new idea or technique	• listen to others and share ideas
• like taking risks generally	• see connections between different subjects being studied
• work quickly and get others involved and enthusiastic too	• present work in novel and artistically appealing ways
• like variety and excitement	• are good at coming up with new alternatives
• are not concerned about making a fool of yourself by asking questions or volunteering for something new	• pinpoint important new questions
• learn by talking with other people	
• skip-read books	

Pragmatist	Theorist
You:	You:
• work well alone	• organize facts and materials well
• are good at setting goals and making plans of action	• see links between ideas
• know how to find information	• like to understand everything you are working on
• see the applications of a theory	• are curious, and enjoy problems
• get things done on time	• work things out well on paper
• don't get distracted	• work well alone with minimum help from teachers and friends
• have revision timetables and work plans	• are precise and thorough
• organize time well and have time for other things	• plan well in advance for essays and exams
• read instructions carefully	• set clear goals, know why you are doing something, and which topic is of the highest priority
• research examination papers thoroughly	• rework essays and notes
• have notes classified and filed	• are a good critic

Table 1.4 Advantages of Each Learning Style

Activist	*Reflector*
You: • don't plan work in advance • rush into examination questions and essays without thinking them through • tend to neglect subjects you're not interested in • are not good at organizing time • try to do too many things at once • are not good at working out priorities • leave things until the last minute • can be demanding of friends • can't be bothered with details • don't read through or check work • don't rework notes or classify material	You: • can't see the 'trees for the wood' – forget important details • wait too long before getting started • can be uncritical of ideas • don't organize work well • don't like work or revision timetables • only work in bursts of energy • forget to bring key books, etc. for homework • are easily distracted from the job in hand • don't rework notes or classify material • are too easy-going, not assertive enough with friends or teachers
Pragmatist	*Theorist*
You: • are impatient with others' viewpoints • think there is only one way of doing something – your way! • fail to use friends and teachers as resources • 'can't see the wood for the trees' • get preoccupied with details • lack imagination • are poor at coming up with new questions • often don't work well with others • are more concerned with getting the job done than with making sure it's really a good job • cut corners • are not very interested in presentation of your work	You: • need too much information before getting down to work and allowing yourself an opinion • fail to use friends and teachers as resources • are reluctant to try new approaches • can get bogged down in theory • like to do things in a set way – uncreative • don't trust feelings – your own or others' • don't function very well in group discussions • keep problems to yourself • only trust logic • are overcautious, don't like taking risks

Table 1.5 Disadvantages of Each Learning Style

Managerial Communication: A Finger on the Pulse

Meetings and Conferences

The fifty salesmen from all over the county arrived the night before: but it's nine-thirty a.m. when the nine o'clock sales meeting begins. The welcome message from the president was naturally delayed until he arrived. But waiting for the president is not only polite, its smart, and what's a half hour? Actually, for fifty salesmen its only 25 hours or three full days of selling time.

"Gentlemen", says the president, "good morning and welcome to home base. I don't want to take any of your valuable time, but I asked Artie if I could say a few words before you get down to work. I know it will be a fruitful and busy day for you men who are, in my opinion, the most important asset this company has. Welcome! I'm sorry I can't spend time with each of you, but I've got to catch a plane." And the president leaves, smiling to the applause of the salesmen who give him a standing ovation, principally because the chairs haven't arrived yet.

"Men" says Artie the sales manager, "you've heard from our president: now let's get down to business. But to use the time until the tables and chairs arrive, I have a few housekeeping announcements. The coffee break will be at 10:30 instead of 10:00, so make a note of that on your agenda."

"I didn't get an agenda," one of the salesmen says.

"Those of you who got an agenda can share it", says Artie and continues.

"Although our president has already set the tone of this meeting. I want to add a few words before we get down to the nitty-gritty. You men represent the finest sales organisation in our industry. Why? Because your company demands, and gets, selling skills and performance above and beyond the call of duty. That's why at this year's meeting there are so many new faces."

"Artie , a question please?" comes a plea from one of the salesmen.

"Sure, Joe, fire away. But before you do, for the benefit of the new men, let me tell them who you are. Men, Joe is our man in the Midwest who is doing one helluva job. Really knows the market, his customers and the product. How long have you been knocking 'em dead for the company, Joe? Four years? Five?'

"Eight months" says Joe.

"Oh, yeah, right. Now, what's the question?"

"Are we going to talk about the competition today?"

"What the competition is doing right now, you worried about it?"

"What they're doing now," says Joe.

"You tell me. What is the competition doing now?" Artie is smirking.

"What the competition is doing right now," says Joe, "is calling on our customers while we're in this sales meeting."

You're Probably Wondering Why I Called You Here Today

Try asking someone in your organisation "Been to any good meetings lately?" and you're likely to hear "You've got to be kidding!"

Many of us spend too much time in meetings. A lot of organisations have too many meetings and /or ineffective meetings. The frustration or cynicism of those who have too long suffered through overuse or misuse of the 'group methods' is reflected in statements like: "A meeting brings together a group of the unfit, appointed by the unwilling, to do the unnecessary." Or, "When all was said and done, a lot was said but nothing was done." Meeting is something we do instead of making decisions.

Why is it that for many managers,

RESOURCE 4.1

meetings lead to feelings of restlessness, disgruntlement, and raw boredom? Do meetings have to be a burden for the manager? What can be done to make the group process live up to its potential to produce high quality outcomes? To get at these questions, let's first look at qualities of small group communication as used in organisations. Meetings have some very significant potential advantages as well as some serious limitations.

Advantages of Meetings

One characteristic of organisations as social systems is called the principle of *equifinality*. In the language of systems theory this means that "a system can reach the same final state from differing initial conditions and by a variety of paths."[1] In the language of clichés it means there is more than one way to skin a cat. The problems or issues facing the organisation could have come about by a number of different sequences of events and they can be solved by an equally diverse number of remedies.

Since our range of experiences as individuals is limited, it follows that several individuals working on the same problem, issue, or decision can bring more relevant information to light. Each participant represents a unique frame of reference - an individual way of looking at the world - that may provide the key to a better solution. The usefulness of these multiple inputs is, of course, limited by the extent to which the group can assimilate the different viewpoints. To be successful the group must develop procedures for (1) sharing ideas and perspectives so that members may build upon one another's insights, and (2) resolving differences among group members which, if left unattended, would prevent eventual consensus. In short, groups must work under conditions which foster the creation of understanding. When successful, the group process creates a synergistic effect with the end product being greater than the sum of its parts; a better decision will be reached than if the same people worked individually on the problem.

The nature of the group's task seems to affect the degree to which a group's decision or solution is likely to be superior to an individual's. Research by behavioural scientists suggest that there are certain kinds of problems groups handle best. For example, studies show that groups are better at solving problems that require the making of relative rather than absolute judgements. That is, groups can better solve problems for which there is no single correct solution and for which solutions are difficult to verify objectively. This finding suggests that groups are not much better than individuals at handling certain kinds of clerical tasks (such as adding up columns of figures) or at solving logical "brain teasers" which require purely rational answers.[2]

In addition, groups tend to be more successful than individuals working alone when the task problem is complex, having many parts and requiring a number of steps to solve. Groups also seem better at dealing with controversial or emotionally charged problems.

When the problem is relatively simple or noncontroversial, or involves routine logical tasks, group discussion does not seem to offer significant advantages. Many organisational problems, however, are clearly candidates for the group process.

There is a second significant advantage to the discussion method which, in many cases, may be even more important than the quality-of-the-solution advantage discussed above. There is likely to be a *higher degree of commitment to a group decision and* a concomitant reduction of hostility or resistance to it (at least among those who participated). Similarly, if those who participated are commissioned to execute the decision, they will do so more faithfully because they understand why and how the decision was reached. In one well-known study conducted more than thirty years ago, Coch and French [3] compared workers' resistance to technological changes in their jobs. It was found that when workers participated in discussions regarding the implementation of the changes there was significantly less resistance than among workers who were excluded from such participation. Since this important study in 1948, other research has shown similar results among American workers in industrial settings.

The significant advantages of meetings and conferences, then, are (1) potentially better quality decisions and (2) less resistance to implementation. There are, however, situations under which these advantages can be completely negated by inept or unqualified participants and leaders as well as by some other factors we'll discuss later.

Disadvantages of Meetings

Important disadvantages to the use of meetings can be categorised into three general types. First, meetings in many organisations have become *substitutes for action.*

Some managers use meetings as an alternative to making the tough decision. They confuse the appearance of such activity with the hard reality that nothing substantive is happening. Consciously or unconsciously the hope that by "talking it out" they can avoid the unpleasant necessity of acting. For some, it's hard to face up to the fact that filibusters are seldom a useful management technique.

Either the participants or the leader who initiates a meeting or committee can create a problem by not really wanting to take action. By definition, an operating meeting calls for participation, involvement, and commitment of each member. To gain commitment from members of a group, management has to inspire some motivation to participate. It makes little sense to assign a person to a committee without regard to his or her values or interests. Don't assume that because we recognise a problem which should be handled by a committee others recognise and feel the same need for resolution. Too often, I've seen people drafted for committees that cope with issues that participants couldn't care less about. They have nothing personally vested in the issue. The likelihood of such people being productive participants is low. They may go through the motions but their only motivation for reaching a conclusion will be to simply get it over with.

A second general disadvantage of meetings is that they *cost a lot of money.* A group decision inevitably takes more time

than an executive action. And the costs of such time can really add up. Example:

RESOURCE 4.1

Meeting Cost:
Estimated salary of meeting participants
(@$20,000 year) hourly $10
Number of participants   12
Hourly meeting cost $120

A four-hour meeting can easily cost $480 in labour costs alone. And this figure doesn't include the added "burden" costs for each employee fringe benefits, social security, medical coverage etc. This is only the *direct* labour cost. There is also a ripple of psychological costs to the individual and the organisation which can be staggering. Work done by employees subordinates is often tied up while the boss is in conference. Talented employees engage in monotonous busywork while waiting for direction from the absent leader. Customers are annoyed that they cannot talk with the conferring manager. The manager's work piles up, so that she is faced with a stack of phone messages to respond to, a pile of papers in her inbasket, and a half dozen people who just have to talk about some pressing matter when the conference ends. Each of these kinds of things saps psychic energy from people who are paid to use their minds. And each of these things adds to the aggravation of the manager's job. For some, it is likely to end in turnover, depression or worse. The question is one of opportunity cost: what could the meeting-goer do with that time if he or she weren't tied up in the meeting? The manager must ask, "Is this meeting worth it?"

In addition to these disadvantages of meetings - their use as substitutes for action and their potentially enormous cost - the group process can result in *low quality decisions.* I said earlier that one advantage of conferences *may be* higher quality decisions, but there are some situations where the group process may backfire and negate that potential advantage. There are two general situations where this can occur: (1) when the group members lack sufficient expertise to deal with the problems, and (2) when pressures censor the free flow of

▷ RESOURCE 4.1

information. In the former case, the solution will reflect pooled ignorance. In the latter situation, the quality of the group's decision is distorted by either *groupthink* or *individual dominance* of the process.

The term *groupthink* was coined by Irving Janis to describe a condition of likemindedness which tends to arise in groups that are particularly cohesive. While cohesiveness is normally a desirable condition in groups, it can be carried so far that it becomes counterproductive. This is especially likely when the group has a high esprit de corps and where members desire for consensus or harmony becomes stronger than their desire for accuracy. Under such conditions critical thinking and the independent and objective analysis of ideas are foregone in defence to a smooth running group. The likelihood of groupthink increases if the group becomes insulated from outside influence and the fresh flow of information. Based on Janis's concept, VonBergen and Kirk describe eight symptoms of groupthink:[4]

1   Illusion of unanimity regarding the viewpoint held by the majority in the group and an emphasis on team play.
2   A view of the "opposition" as generally inept, incompetent, and incapable of countering effectively any action by the group, no matter how risky the decision or how high the odds are against the plan of action succeeding.
3   Self-censorship of group members in which overt disagreements are avoided, facts that might reduce support for the emerging majority view are suppressed, faulty assumptions are not questioned, and personal doubts are suppressed in the form of group harmony.
4   Collective rationalization to comfort one another in order to discount warnings that the agreed-upon plan is either unworkable or highly unlikely to succeed.
5   Self-appointed mindguards within the group that function to prevent anyone from undermining its apparent unanimity and to protect its members from unwelcome ideas and adverse information that may threaten consensus.
6. Reinforcement of consensus and direct pressure on any dissenting group member who expresses strong reservations or challenges, or argues against the apparent unanimity of the group.
7   An expression of self-righteousness that leads members to believe their actions are moral and ethical, thus inclining them to disregard any ethical or moral objections to their behaviour.
8   A shared feeling of unassailability marked by a high degree of esprit de corps, by implicit faith in the wisdom of the group, and by an inordinate optimism that disposes members to take excessive risks.

It is apparent that each of these symptoms of groupthink damages realistic thinking and effective decisions. A combination of several or all of these can be devastating to group effectiveness.

A second type of pressure which censors the free flow of information is *individual dominance*. In many groups, certain individuals become excessively dominant by virtue of their personality, organisational position, or personal status. Other participants become reluctant to interact freely, perhaps feeling that their contributions are of lesser value.

While individual dominance can speed up the decision process, it does so at the cost of a potential reduction in decision quality.

Managers need to be sensitive to how differences in status and expertise as well as communication styles can put a damper on free discussion. And one of the committee leader's chief concerns must be with drawing out the participant who may feel suppressed by other dominating members. I'll talk more about leader responsibilities later.

The point is that hindrances to group decision quality can be caused by lack of group expertise, by groupthink, and by individual dominance.

Still another problem which has been identified by social scientists can affect the quality of group decision. Cartwright and

Zender[5] two researchers well-known for their studies in group dynamics, pointed out what they called the *risky shift phenomenon.* A series of widely replicated experiments showed that groups tend to make more daring or more risky decisions than individuals working alone. Again, social pressures from within the group result in potentially counterproductive behaviour. Risk taking is viewed as a positive personality characteristic which we demonstrate to others as we work in groups.

The potential danger in this is that some groups adopt a "safety in numbers" position and recommend extreme solutions that they wouldn't dream of taking responsibility for as individuals. You end up with a lynch mob mentality.

One final disadvantage of group decision making is simply that it is sometimes inappropriate because of time constraints imposed by the problem. A battle group in combat cannot use participative decision making while the enemy awaits their solution. Similarly, in business, some decisions must be made quickly. To delay a decision may squander a potential competitive advantage or organisational opportunity.

Although advantages and disadvantages must be carefully considered in decisions about conferences or meetings, many such decisions are still likely to come down on the side of continued and even expanded use. Most of the disadvantages can be overcome; they are not inevitable. As Richard Dunsing said:

> "When you accept poor meetings as a fact of life, you are in collusion with many others doing the same thing. In effect, you are aiding and abetting them on clogging the system and in eroding the quality of working life. Managing means changing things that aren't what they need to be. Surprisingly often, it is merely the management of the obvious."[6]

While griping about the overuse or misuse of "those miserable meetings" has certain cathartic value, the real issue is how to maximise the value of needed committees.

Let's first look at the types of committees typically used in an organisation and then focus on variables that determine effectiveness of this potentially powerful communication activity.

RESOURCE 4.1 ◁

Types of Committees

There are three general types of committees frequently used in organisations: the *standing* committee, the special committee, and the *ad hoc* committee.

Standing committees serve to relieve the manager of administrative burdens and substitute collective judgement for his individual judgement in certain recurrent, noncritical situations.[7] Since standing committees act as a form of work delegation, it would be self-defeating for the manager to act as chairman. The committee membership should be representative of the organisation and should be chaired by a ranking member who can comfortably allocate work to others. The work of standing committees is ongoing so long as there is organisational need.

Special committees may be assembled to deal with a single specific issue which cannot be realistically handled via ordinary organisational procedures. Often these situations are too controversial, too complex, or deal with issues of symbolic or highly emotional significance which are simply too important do be handled in a routine manner. When the work of a special committe is done, it should disband. Problems arise when special committees don't disband but become self-appointed standing committees. The manager should ensure that this does not happen unless there is a clear need to 'upgrade' to standing status.

Ideally, the organisational leader should assemble the special committee, give it its "charge" in clear unequivocal detail, and step back to let it work. Its membership should include representatives from all factions who stand to be affected by the decision or outcome. This often means a larger than usual number of participants which, in turn, calls for a chairperson who is skilled in parliamentary procedures, is

▷ RESOURCE 4.1

reasonably high in seniority or rank, and as one writer says, has grey hair. The key to the special committee's effectiveness lies in the degree of clarification provided by the manager who calls it together. His or her instructions should describe the task in detail, indicate clearly what the end product (usually a written report) should be like, and explain what resources are available from the organisation. Deadlines and instructions about conditions of secrecy or publicity under which the group should work should also be spelled out. Equally important, once this information is presented to the group, the manager should remove himself from the process except for occasional briefings or further clarification.

Ad hoc committees, like special committees, deal with nonrecurrent, special tasks. They differ, however, in that ad hoc committees typically handle relatively noncontroversial tasks, are smaller in number of participants and do not necessarily represent the views of all organisation members. Members should be selected on the basis of interest in and/or competence with regard to the committee's assignment. The group may consist of as few as two members and seldom more than five. Like the special committee, their work should be temporary and they should not develop into standing committees unless the needs of the organisation clearly demand this. Typically their work is somewhat less complex than the special committee. Examples of ad hoc committee assignments may be inspecting an item for sale, developing a one-time analysis of office equipment needs, or arranging facilities for a convention or training session. The manager who assembles the ad hoc committee should have no regular involvement in its deliberations.

Five Major Elements of the Effective Meeting

The effective manager needs to build some flexibility into his or her approaches to meetings and conferences, for there is no one best way to run all types of meetings. There are, however, five major elements upon which effective meetings are built:
● The goals of the meeting

● The climate of the meeting
● Leadership and the internal workings of the meeting
● The decision strategy
● Post-meeting evaluation and follow-up.

Group Goals:

Everyone Knows Why We're Here, Right?
More often than not, wrong! Although the person who called the meeting probably has a pretty good idea of why it's been called, others are seldom so clear. If you don't believe this, try asking everyone in the group to write down specifically why the meeting is being held and compare answers. As we try to work down the ladder of abstraction from general expression of the topic (solving our morale problem) to more concrete objectives (reducing high absenteeism rate among keypunch operators), we introduce a clearer focus to the meeting. It's not necessary to predetermine exactly what all possible goals are before meeting, but it should be the priority activity in the early part of the discussions. Otherwise, how will you know when the job is done? That may be the key question to be answered before setting out to discover solutions.

Although we may come to agree on the discussion topic, committee meetings seldom have just one goal. There are other, subsidiary objectives even when the task seems clear. Sometimes these "hidden agenda" items, real though they may be, are implied but never stated. For individual participants they may include such things as
● "getting some exposure" (i.e. to favourably impress others)
● providing a status arena in which we can assert our power or abilities
● filling some perceived quota for having meetings
● providing a chance to socialise with others
● providing a chance to assert dominance of one group or department over others (or a chance to break that dominance)
● working on leader and participant communication skills
● diffusing decision responsibility so one person won't have to take all the heat if a decision fails

	General Purpose of Committee	*Examples of Such Committees*	*Ideal Type of Membership*
Standing	relieves manager of administrative burden substitutes collective judgment for individual judgment on recurrent non-critical situations	Safety committee Professional school admissions committee Loan committee of a bank Computerization committee Personnel committee	Widely representative of all departments that may be affected by decisions reached Wide range of organizational rank, personal characteristics
Special	Considers particularly knotty poblems too complex, too controversial, or too important to be handled in a regular way Appointed to defer or avoid an otherwise pressing decision To deflect the onus of an unpopular decision or to allay suspicions that have arisen in connection with a particular issue To cope with problems that are intrinsically unimportant but have acquired symbolic significance	Committees to iron out conflicts between organizational factions Disciplinary action committees Decision appeals or policy review committees	Representative of all relevant shades of opinion and every important faction of the organization which is likely to be affected by the decision
Ad Hoc	Deals with some nonrecurrent, noncontroversial task	Drafting a statement Inspecting an item for sale Arranging convention facilities Surveying organization needs	Compatible with each other Competent with respect to the committee assignment Do *not* need to be representative of organization members

Figure 6.1 summarises key points about consulted committees.

		Number of Members	*Qualifications of Chairperson*	*Manager's Participation*
Standing		5 to 9	Senior to most other members (so can comfortably allocate work to others) Not holding extreme position with respect to committee's task Not someone new to organisation who does not understand its informal norms	As ex officio member
Special		10 to 30 (limited only by size of organisation's largest conference table)	Manager of considerable seniority Good command of parliamentary procedures Organizational maturity	Should start the committee off with unequivocal charge; describe the group's task in detail; indicate clearly what type of report should be produced; state time interval, resources available, and conditions of publicity or secrecy under which group should work Is kept posted of progress via informants
Ad Hoc		2 to 5	Interested in the assignment	None after group's assignment is given

Figure 6.1 (continued) summarises key points about consulted committees.

- getting away from unpleasant work duties.

By fulfilling such personal objectives as these, the conference can be a genuinely satisfying experience which may motivate additional participation. A good group work experience will go a long way torward reducing employee reluctance to work on future committees.

The three key questions that must be answered early in a discussion are:

- what exactly are we here for?
- what exactly will we have when we've completed our job?
- how will we go about accomplishing our task?

Agreeing on the answers to these three questions is crucial to the effective meeting. If the primary task objective and procedures are never clearly established, participants will never know when they are finished. Then the likelihood of time-wasting, extended meetings increases sharply.

The Meeting Climate

Clarity of goals is a legitimate part of the climate of an organisation or group. But several other equally important climate characteristics affect the communication of participants. These are *physical* factors and *interactional* characteristics.

Physical dimensions of climate include such things as room temperature and lighting, presence or absence of distracting noises, odours or interruptions, the arrangement of furniture, and the availability of tools such as chalkboard, paper and pencils, flip charts, and the like. Seating arrangement allowing participants to comfortably talk to each other and to have unobstructed view of others and of visual aids is a must. Often the impressive, large wooden table of the board room is not the best for working meetings. People should feel free to get up, move around, and not be chained to their chairs. Avoid meeting in rooms with auditorium style seating where all participants see is the back of others heads. Do not seat some people at "power positions" while others are placed in clearly subordinate places. Planning for good physical climate is a preconference responsibility of the leader.

Leadership and the Internal Workings of the Meeting

For many years social scientists attempted to define specific personal traits or characteristics inherent in individuals that seem to make them effective leaders. This research approach predominated in the studies of leadership for the first half of this century. The underlying assumption was that leaders are somehow different from other people in the population. If we could but identify what makes them different we would be able to "scientifically" select the best leaders. One of the earliest studies, for example, indicated a positive correlation between a person's height and his or her organisational position. Other studies looked at such attributes as "general intelligence", "self-confidence", "persuasiveness", or "institution", as these relate to leadership.

Several problems arose from this avenue of study. For one thing, some of the labels for the traits being studied were pretty ambiguous. A more important criticism is that the findings were largely inconclusive when applied to different task situations. An effective sales manager may not be successful as a railroad crew foreman, for example.

Social scientists who come to recognise the importance of the situational variable began to regard the search for universal leadership traits as virtually worthless. But before we write off more than fifty years of research, it may be well to consider a massive review of such leadership literature prepared by Ralph Stogdill. His analysis of almost 300 studies did conclude that leaders, when compared to nonleaders, tended to be more goal-directed, venturesome, self-confident, responsible, tolerant of interpersonal stress and frustration, and capable of influencing behaviours of others. He also concludes, however, that these "characteristics, considered singly, hold little diagnostic or predictive significance. In combination, it would appear that they interact to generate personality dynamics advantageous to the person seeking the responsibilities of leadership."[8]

Perhaps one reason some totally discredit the traits approach to leadership studies is that it seems to imply that either a leader has the desired characteristic or he/she doesn't – an implication that questions the value of leadership training. If you've got it, you don't need the training; if you don't, the training probably won't help.

Clearly there have been methodological and theoretical problems with trait studies. But, as Hampton, Summer, and Webber say, "the complete denial of any (leadership) traits could be an overcorrection."[9]

Before we conclude this discussion, let's consider an interesting variation of the traits approach that is potentially useful to our understanding of leadership dynamics. John Geier[10] applied what was later referred to as a "method of residues" to conclude that certain personality characteristics consistently *eliminate* an individual from leadership consideration in almost all situations. The individual who is seen as (1) uninformed about issues important to the group, (2) a very low participator, or (3) very rigid in thinking will be passed over when groups select leaders.

In view of the serious limitations of many of the traits studies, how can we predict leadership success? What should we consider when diagnosing and responding

RESOURCE 4.1 ◁

to leadership opportunities? Researchers today would contend that there is a complex network of factors at work in any leadership situation. From the situational perspective, three classes of variables predominate in accounting for leader effectiveness:

1. the nature of the task to be accomplished by the leader's group
2. the leader's personality compared to the predominant personality characteristics of the group's members
3. the leader's power.

The first two variables arise from the way people interact in groups. To understand such interactions we must recall the two classes of activities at work in every meeting: *task activities* and *maintenance activities*. Task has to do with *what* the group is doing: *maintenance* is concerned with *how* they do it. The process of goal clarification is primarily a task activity while the establishment of climate is mostly a maintenance activities. Most leaders understand their task roles - they see a job to be done and know they're responsible to see that it is accomplished - some, however, underestimate the importance of maintenance. Although one can go too far with either activity, the degree of emphasis is an important management judgement. While it is the task activities that get the job done, neglect of maintenance can lead to serious dissatisfaction which could undermine the entire process. The manager who rams through his solution may find himself facing group resentment that eventually will more than offset his "victory". And there are cases where the maintenance activities are, legitimately, the most important outcome of the meeting, making participants just plain feel good about the opportunities for affiliation and participation in the group work. The manager's sensitivity to an appropriate balance between task accomplishment and interpersonal need satisfaction will be reflected in her or his personality. The degree which group members view such personality characteristics as appropriate will affect their willingness to go along with the leadership efforts.

The third variable which affects the leadership situation is power. People bring two types of power to the group: *personal* power and *position* power. Personal power is that which is given to a individual based on how others perceive him or her. It usually arises when one is seen as possessing expertise, skills, ability, and other characteristics the viewer deems important. There is a natural attraction toward people with high personal power. Position power, on the other hand, is conferred upon an individual by someone in a higher level of authority. It is made known by rank, position, status, and the capability of providing others with rewards and/or punishment. Most leaders exhibit some combination of both types of power.

The newly announced political candidate may run initially on his or her personal power (personality, appearance, experience etc.) until position power in the form of endorsements and party nomination is granted.

After being elected, the office holder has position power (having been legitimately selected by the voters), which adds significantly to his or her potential for leadership effectiveness.

Fred E. Fiedler has developed a leadership contingency model which focuses on the three variables I have mentioned. He refers to these as *leader-member relations*, *task structure*, and *position power*. His research has suggested that emphasis on *task* or *maintenance* leadership efforts should be determined by the "*favourableness of a situation*" which he defines as "the degree to which the situation enables the leader to exert his influence over his group"[11]. "The most favourable situation would be one where the leader is well liked by the participants, is directing a clearly defined task, and has recognised status or position power. An unfavourable situation would be the negatives of these. Some mixture of positive and negatives would put the leader in an intermediate situation.

Fiedler's research concludes that when the situation is either very favourable or very unfavourable to the leader, he or she would do well to stress task activities and not be overly concerned with maintenance activities. When the favourable of the

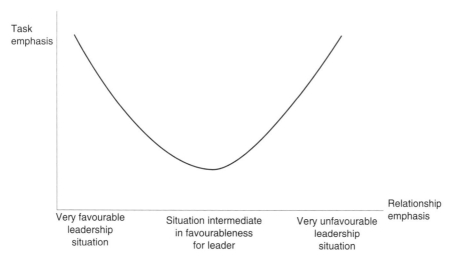

Task
emphasis

Relationship
emphasis

Very favourable
leadership
situation

Situation intermediate
in favourableness
for leader

Very unfavourable
leadership
situation

situation is intermediate, the leader needs to be more concerned with maintenance activities and should emphasise the building of good relationships. Figure 6.2 illustrates shifts in leadership emphasis.

A skillful leader should be aware of these two channels of activity and be capable of switching emphasis as needed. As changes appear in, say, task clarity and relationships with group participants, a marked increase in situational favourableness may call for a shift in emphasis from maintenance (building support etc.) to getting down to tasks.

Management theorists Paul Hersy and Kenneth H. Blanchard have synthesised the ideas of Fiedler and a number of others to develop their "situational leadership theory". According to their approach, a leader can determine an appropriate mixture of relationship building and task directing behaviour to increase the probability of effectiveness. "To determine what leadership style is appropriate in a given situation, a leader must first determine the maturity level of the individual or group in relation to a specific task that the leader is attempting to accomplish through their efforts".[12]

What is this "maturity level"? According to Hersey and Blanchard, the *task-relevant maturity* of a person or group can be diagnosed by considering four characteristics of the group *in relation to the specific job the group is called upon to accomplish*. These characteristics are:

1   the capacity to set high but attainable goals
2   the willingness and ability to take responsibility
3   education and/or experience (or a combination of both) relevant to the task
4   personal maturity on the job in combination with a psychological maturity or self-confidence and self-respect.

Let's look at an example. You have been asked to lead a committee to recommend a marketing strategy for a new product line. In gathering information about those who will work on the committee you determine that

1   The participants have a good record for setting ambitious yet realistic targets for themselves.
2   The participants have shown an eagerness to work on the committee and to take responsibility for marketing this new product line in a vigorous manner. If it goes over well, they expect to get credit; if it flops, they expect to shoulder the blame.

3   Each participant has been in on the new product development from the ground floor. They know how it's made, why it's built the way it is, and, based on past experience, they have a good idea of potential markets.

4   The participants are seasoned professionals in their field. They are success-oriented people with a proven track record.

Obviously in such a scenario, we have a committee with very high task-relevant maturity. But what if our team consists of quite another group?

1   They tend to take excessive risks (they have a record of "biting off more than they can chew").

2   They want credit if their plan works but won't accept blame if it fails.

3   They have never worked on a committee like this one before.

4   They are "rookies" in this business.

Under these circumstances, the leader's job is likely to be quite different. Hersey and Blanchard would classify the first group as high in task-relevant maturity and the second example as very low. Figure 6.3 indicates how the effective leadership style would be determined.

As shown in Figure 6.3, once the maturity level of the participants is identified (or realistically guessed at), " the appropriate leadership style can be determined by constructing a right (90⁰) angle from the point on the continuum that represents the maturity level of the follower(s) to a point where it intersects the (curve) in the style-of-leader portion of the model. The quadrant in which that intersection takes place suggests the appropriate style to be used by the leader in that situation with follower(s) of that maturity level."[13]

Or we could say that the leader's predominant communication behaviour changes in relation to the group's maturity:

Telling, selling, participating, and delegating all call for a different mix of communication skills to establish understanding. In moving from behaviours appropriate for the immature worker toward those for the more highly mature, communication skills become more important to effective leadership because of the increased complexity of communication inter-action between the leader and follower(s). For example, the high task, low relationship quadrant of the model is characterised by one-way communications where the leader simply gives directive – tells the follower(s) what to do and when to do it. The leadership attempt is successful to the extent that the follower does the desired thing. As workers become more mature, communication is more interactive; there is more emphasis on sharing information for mutual benefit rather than simply getting compliance.

The leadership style appropriate for highly mature employees calls for a substantial reduction in communication interaction, since the follower(s) start to run their own operation. The leader steps into the background, and the leader's function moves away from what we've viewed as traditional leadership toward less involvement and more "group-centred" leadership.

Current thinking on leadership seems to be that the mature group can function effectively with very little intervention from the designated leader. The leadership *process* of guiding and directing the group's activity is likely to move from person to person within the mature group rather than be centred in one individual. Leland Bradford[14] contrasts individual-centred, traditional conceptions of leadership with such group-centred leadership.

Traditional Leadership

1   The leader directs, controls, polices the members, and leads them to the proper decision. Basically it is his group, and the leader's authority and responsibility are acknowledged by members.

2   The leader focuses his attention on the task to be accomplished. He brings the group back from any diverse wandering. He performs all the functions needed to arrive at the proper decision.

3   The leader sets limits and uses rules of order to keep the discussion within strict limits set by the agenda. He controls the time spent on each item lest the group wander fruitlessly.

Group Task-Relevant Maturity Level Behaviour		Leader's Predominant Communica
Low	– – – – –	Telling
Moderately low	– – – – –	Selling
Moderately high	– – – – –	Participating
High	– – – – –	Delegating

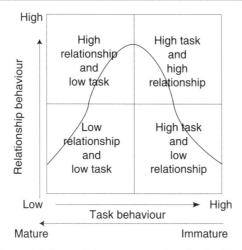

Figure 6.3 Determining an appropriate leadership style

4   The leader believes that emotions are disruptive to objective, logical thinking, and should be discouraged or suppressed. He assumes it is his task to make clear to all members the disruptive effect of emotions.

5   The leader believes that he should handle a member's disruptive behaviour by talking to him away from the group; it is his task to do so.

6   Because the need to arrive at a task decision is all important in the eyes of the leader, needs of individual members are considered less important.

Group Centred Leadership

1   The group, or meeting, is *owned* by the members, including the leader. All members, with the leader's assistance, contribute to its effectiveness.

2   The group is responsible, with occasional and appropriate help from the leader, for reaching a decision that includes the participation of all and is the product of all. The leader is a servant and helper to the group.

3   Members of the group should be encouraged and helped to take responsibility for its task productivity, its methods of working, its assignment of tasks, its plans for the use of the time available.

4   Feelings, emotions, conflict are recognised by the members and the leader as legitimate facts and situations demanding as serious attention as the task agenda.

5   The leader believes that any problem in the group must be faced and solved within the group and by the group. As trust develops among members, it is much easier for an individual to discover ways in which his behaviour is bothering the group.

6   With help and encouragement from the leader, the members come to realise that the needs, feelings and purposes of all members should be met so that an awareness of being a group forms. Then the group can continue to grow.

As the group evolves toward higher levels of task-relevant maturity over time, the leader must be ready to adjust his or her behaviours accordingly. As communications scholar Franklin Haiman said almost thirty years ago, "The man officially called *leader* performs only those tasks which the group itself is not yet mature enough, intellectually or emotionally, to handle for itself. The leader's goal is to work himself out of a job."[15]

The Decision Strategy

Problem solving is the most frequent use of the group discussion process.

Most educated people readily understand the process of problem solving: i.e., they easily learn and can talk or write about the steps involved. Yet many people seem incapable of or unwilling to apply them in actual discussion. Understanding the decision process does little good until this knowledge affects our behaviour.

There are two phases in the development of a decision strategy: *problem description* and *problem solution*. The description phase seeks to crystallise the nature of a disquieting situation which has come to the attention of group members. Such a situation may be attributed to an inability to achieve desired objectives, a dissatisfaction with the speed at which goals are reached, an uncertain sense of morality or ethical standards, or just a general condition of wondering whether or not the very best is being achieved. Removal of such feelings of dissatisfaction presupposes a clear problem description. There are three phases of problem description:

(1) *Problem Definition.* What exactly is exerting pressure on us? Participants, in the initial stage of discussion, should attempt to identify, in specific terms, the elements of the problem This process of defining contributing factors usually involves defining critical terms.

The group called together to "do something about employee morale" should define what they mean by *morale*. How do they know when morale is good or bad? Often, an *operational definition* – one that defines in terms of something clearly measurable – works well. In this case we might say that bad morale is what

we have when absenteeism, number of grievances filed, and employee turnover reaches some specific level.

It is crucial to get on the same wavelength by clarifying all relevant terms. And be sure group members use the terms only in the agreed upon way.

(2) *Problem Analysis.* Once the problem is defined, there should be a general discussion of objectives, where we stand now vis-à-vis the objectives, and what obstacles we face. The objectives or ideal solution should be described in terms of criteria. That is, we might say, an ideal solution to our perceived morale problem would:

● reduce absenteeism to less than 2 percent per day
● reduce grievances filed to one per month
● reduce turnover to .5 percent per month

This operationally defines the objective. We should also develop additional qualifying criteria. An ideal solution would:

● not undermine the authority of the supervisor in any way
● not cost additional money for wage or benefit incentives
● be easily implemented
● serve as a prototype for future employee motivation programs
● be based in sound management theory

These criteria should be listed on a chalkboard or chart so that everyone can refer to them as possible solutions are evaluated. You may not get full agreement on each criterion but strive for a general consensus that the criterion does reflect a highly desirable condition.

Once criteria are established, solution ideas generated in the discussion can be weighed against them. Evaluating any potential solution is extremely difficult if the requirements of the solution are hazy.

(3) *Problem Reformulation.* At times discussion of the "obvious" problem breaks down and people get frustrated

by a seeming inability to come up with workable ideas. If the problem definition and analysis processes have been carried out, and still we have no luck, the problem may be due to underlying assumptions we may be holding. The effective problem solver recognises that even the best groups sometimes "bark up the wrong tree." Here's an example:

.....an automobile manufacturing company .... was concerned because they were running out of drying sheds in which to store their cars while the paint dried. At first the problem seemed to be simply the need to build more sheds. Land was expensive; building were expensive; and construction was time-consuming. But one person had an idea: If the paint dried faster, more cars could be accommodated in the existing sheds. This problem reformulation led to the discovery of faster drying paint (which solved the problem).[16]

In my earlier examples of an employee morale problem resulting in absenteeism, grievance, and turnover, a problem reformulation might be useful. The group's predominant and perhaps unspoken assumption may be that supervisor-subordinate relations are at fault. In reality, some physical environmental condition such as the presence of a harmful chemical may become suspect at the root cause of much absenteeism. Evidence pointing to previously unsuspected problem variables can require new ways of viewing the problem. Reformulation means taking a new tack, and often it can lead to more productive results in the group.

Once problem description has been satisfactorily achieved, the solution stage begins. This may involve four more steps.

(4) *Solution Proposal*. There is a general tendency among participants to jump to this step before the problem description phase is complete. What may emerge could be an excellent solution - but to a different problem! Depending on the

nature of the problem, it may be desirable to collect as many potential solutions as possible, especially where the task calls for creativity.

One popular way of generating lots of solutions is by using the *brainstorming* techniques. This approach requires a communication climate in which free expression of all kinds of ideas is valued and encouraged – no matter how offbeat or bizarre they may seem.

Brainstorming was developed by Alex Osborn, an advertising executive, to stimulate creative and imaginative problem solving. There are four basic rules:

a. don't criticise any ideas
b. no idea is too wild
c. quantity of ideas generated is important
d. seize opportunities to improve or add to ideas suggested by others.[17]

The rules of brainstorming are easier to state than to obey – especially rule (b). Unless great care is taken, nonverbal cues can be interpreted as evaluation of ideas which can discourage additional "wild ideas". When using brainstorming, the participants should prominently post the rules as a constant reminder.

(5) *Solution Testing*. Once ideas have been generated, they may be tested against the criteria established back in the problem description phase. Which ideas, alone or in combination with others, would be most likely to solve the problem? It is possible that no proposal will meet all criteria fully. You must then predict which is most likely to rectify most of the problems, most of the time.

(6) *Action Testing*. Now comes the acid test. When the chosen solution is implemented, we have the final step in the decision process. Since solutions are seldom perfect, or everlasting, rechecking over time is important.

Problems have ways of recurring in a cyclical pattern or reemerging in different variations. Seldom can a solution settle the matter once and for all. Action testing checks on implementation and should be re-administered periodically.

Post-Meeting Evaluation and Follow-Up
Evaluation and adjustment should be ongoing processes for leadership during any meeting. In addition, taking a retrospective look at the meeting can be very useful in overcoming problematic areas in future meetings. Let's discuss for a moment some of the elements that should be observed.

Think about a recent meeting you attended. How would you answer these questions about task activities? Did the meeting participants:
● State exactly what the meeting was to accomplish? Set goals and objectives, list priorities, identify clearly the problem areas to be dealt with?
● Apply a systematic, logical, decision-making strategy?
● Combine useful ideas while sorting through possible solutions? Was background information gathered when needed? Were more details called for when appropriate?
● Examine potential solutions in terms of their impact on others, their costs and benefits, and the need for support from others in order to be effective?
● Seek creative and innovative approaches? See new relationships by linking other issues into the problems that were being evaluated?
● Delegate assignments and agree on such things as time limits and resources to be used? Determine times for follow-up sessions when necessary?
● Process the final decision into a usable form, usually a written report?
Now recall the group maintenance activities. These included the ways participants thought, acted, and felt while they were immersed in the task. Did the meeting participants:
● Clearly understand the reasons for the meeting? Did they share a common view of its urgency?
● Interact in constructive ways through supportive word choice, body language, "strokes" and a sense of caring?
● Avoid patterns of excessive dominance

and passivity?
● Share in commitment to cooperate? Avoid factionalism or the "hard sell" of personal viewpoints?
● Freely express feelings as well as information?
● Manage disagreement and conflicting ideas in constructive ways?
● Mix seriousness with playfulness?
● Seem to enjoy the work and feel good about being together?
The degree to which these kinds of things are happening determines the likelihood of meeting effectiveness. Before we leave this topic, there is one other area which should be addressed – the role of conflict in meetings.

Coping with Conflict
I said earlier that interactional characteristics which affect meeting climate include the effective use of conflict. This deserves clarification.

Traditionally, it has been assumed that conflict should be avoided in meetings. The term conjures up images of fistfights or people screaming at each other. In reality, conflict is simply a state of incompatibility, and incompatibility itself is neither good nor bad. What makes that incompatibility either desirable or undesirable is the participants' reaction to it. Communication professor Elliott Pood [18] suggests several responses to conflict:

(1) We can attempt to avoid conflict by not expressing opposing views and by withholding even nonverbal feedback which indicates disagreement. Here we keep from rocking the boat and minimise the possibility of being subjected to rejection or reprisals from others. By so doing, however, we also preclude a full sharing of ideas and feelings within the group. And without a free sharing of information, the group cannot maximise its potential for producing superior solutions.

(2) A second response to conflict reflects the opposite view. We can engage in *unregulated confrontation*, which is traditionally characterised by a win-lose orientation, leading to a no-holds-

barred, open warfare among participants. The goal here is to win over others at any cost. Unregulated conflict becomes very personal rather than group task-oriented and results in the elimination of some group members, usually by their psychological withdrawal from participation. The result again is the reduction of information sharing and lower quality group decisions.

(3) A third and most beneficial response to group confrontation is what Pood calls *conflict management*. The effective management of conflict seeks to regulate but not eliminate confrontation. Recognising that the abrasive actions of opposing views polish the final product, the skillful leader seeks free exchange of information but without the win-lose destructiveness of unregulated conflict. Accomplishing this calls for effective communication skills which encourage the generation of information without inhibiting or turning off participants. These skills are essentially those which I've discussed throughout this book: establishing and maintaining a supportive constructive climate, avoiding defensiveness, and freely exchanging feelings as well as data to create mutual understanding.

So, What's Good Morning Like?

If your committee meetings could be described as polite, orderly and carefully led, with each participant taking his or her turn to address the group or the leader, your meetings are probably a flop. Good, effective meetings, where people wrestle with tough problems, are likely to bear little resemblance to parliamentary discussions in hushed conference rooms among polite and scrupulously "reasonable" people. Some good meetings are more likely to resemble cattle auctions.

Good meetings are often noisy, with hard-thinking, challenging people talking straight and bouncing ideas off each other. Under effective leadership, which often rotates from person to person as the need arises, participants debate, discuss, and even argue about the problems before them. The

meeting often looks disorderly and, in fact, the phrase "wrestling with problems" conjures up a rather accurate picture of an effective meeting. Before we get too carried away with this rough-and-tumble metaphor, be reminded that there remains method to the madness of a good meeting.

The key to success is that participants never lose track of what they are doing. The objective of the meeting remains clear and commitment to accomplishing the goal is unwavering. Sure, there will be momentary sidetracks to explore possibilities that ultimately may not prove productive, but the focus remains on the issues. When the job is done, the meeting ends, period. Even if it is way before scheduled quitting time.

These are the kinds of goings-on you'll find at a good, productive conference. Many managers have never been to such a thing. Perhaps this is because we've come to expect something different. Let's look at some expectations of how meetings "should be" that are actually counterproductive to effectiveness.

Misconception 1: Meetings should be orderly, with the leader managing the flow of information

If your meetings are characterised by the raise-your-hand-and-be-recognised syndrome, participation is being stifled and you're not getting the maximum benefit from the process: *Robert's Rules of Order* are fine for large group and formal proceedings but not for most business conferences. If you need such tight structuring to avoid total chaos, your group probably has too many members.

The designated leader need not function like a traffic cop. Tight leader control on the group's activities, according to Dunsing, results in

> ...a lot of "reporting." Each member
> is choreographed to give his or her
> view of things in one blurt: "Here's
> how we see it down in the
> laboratory." No one is permitted to
> interrupt. Dialogue is cut off. There
> is no free flow. Participants need
> not pay close attention because they
> can't respond naturally to ideas as
> they are presented – so they cast off

RESOURCE 4.1

into dreamland or start rehearsing their big moment.

...a bizarre kind of human interaction results: People don't talk to each other directly – they talk to each other through the leader.[19]

Such tight control destroys the vibrant, free-flowing *interaction* that makes meetings work.

Misconception 2: Conflict Should Be Avoided in Committee Meetings; We Should Seek Co-operation at All Cost

If there is a free exchange of ideas, there is bound to be some conflict.

One reason for the group process is to subject ideas to the abrasive action of other ideas. That's the way we smooth out the rough edges. Conflict should be managed, not discouraged. Managed confrontations remain issue-oriented, not people-oriented. The use of appropriate communication skills allows all the benefits of assertive information exchange without the destructiveness of unregulated, win-lose warfare.

The real apprehension people associate with verbal conflict arises from a fear of hurt feelings - our own or others - from such interaction. If, however, the conflict remains on the adult level, where issues, positions, evidence, and reasoning are attacked without the advocate's *self-worth* being questioned, conflict can be useful. This, of course, is easier said than done. We have skin of varying thickness that at some point is penetrated when our pet idea is put down or unfairly (we think) criticised.

If we go into the committee meeting knowing that such useful confrontations will take place as a normal course of events, we puncture this misconception and improve the quality of the meetings. Maybe we should all shake hands before we come out swinging.

Misconception 3: The Leader is Totally Responsible for the Success of the Meeting

Effective communication can never be assured by one participant in the interaction. Communication means the creation of common meanings – understanding –

among two or more parties. If a conference or meeting is to work, it will require efforts from several participants. A designated leader does have some special responsibilities, however. He or she can (1) set the tone and establish patterns of interaction, (2) clarify the task to be accomplished and guide participants back on track when they stray too far, (3) mediate conflicts to be sure they remain productive, (4) arrange pre-session agenda and post-session follow-up, and (5) make assignments as appropriate. While these responsibilities are considerable, they do not constitute control over the outcome of the committee's deliberations.

The effective leader will share responsibility with participants in an adult-to-adult relationship. Participants need to accept responsibility for the group's success and not permit a child-parent relationship with the leader to permeate the committee.

An effective committee meting is one in which these popular misconceptions are not assumed. Over emphasis on orderliness, "correct" procedures, and elimination of conflict can only detract from the usefulness of the group process. When the leader and the led share a mutual sense of responsibility for getting the job done, your group will succeed.

Diagnosing Your Meetings and Conferences

There are many ways we can diagnose the quality of conferences held in our organisation. Some very simple procedures will produce feedback from participants immediately after the completion of a conference assignment. To assess the effectiveness of the designated leader, we might simply ask participants to complete a ballot such as the one in Figure 6.4.

In addition to such a simple balloting procedure, it is also easy to ask participants to complete a group performance index such as the one shown in Figure 6.5. This easy-to-complete questionnaire provides useful feedback to the manager. These should be completed anonymously and tallied by a disinterested third party. A total score may be useful to easily compare different meetings.

'If you were called to participate on a committee dealing with the topic that you have just completed, who would you designate to be the official conference leader?'

Why did you feel the leader was effective or ineffective?

Figure 6.4 Post-meeting response ballot

Listed below are seven statements relating to group competence. Please circle the number on the scales which best describe the performance of the group you have just participated in as you see it.

1 There was a high degree of involvement among participants.

agree   disagree
strongly   5   4   3   2   1   strongly

2 Commitment to group decisions by most members was:

high   5   4   3   2   1   low

3 Leadership (i.e., responsibility for moving the group along toward task accomplishment) moved from person to person as the meeting went on.

agree   disagree
strongly   5   4   3   2   1   strongly

4 Feelings were openly dealt with.

agree   disagree
strongly   5   4   3   2   1   strongly

5 A systematic approach was used to clarify the problem (issues), establish criteria before solutions were considered.

agree   disagree
strongly   5   4   3   2   1   strongly

6 Confrontation and conflicting ideas were managed to improve quality of the group's decision.

agree   disagree
strongly   5   4   3   2   1   strongly

7 The overall success of the group's performance should be evaluated as

high   5   4   3   2   1   low

Total score _____
(sum of scales)

Figure 6.5 Group performance rating form

▷ RESOURCE 4.1

Name of committee or meeting: _____

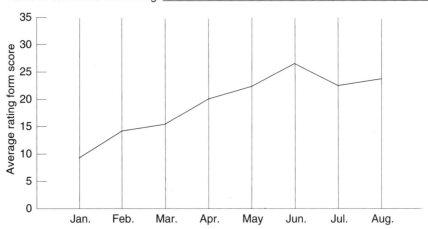

Figure 6.6 Meeting effectiveness trend sheet

Like other diagnostic instruments, these will provide more indicators which can help you as a manager to make decisions about leadership assignments and the general effectiveness of the group process in your organisation. Although I would caution against using this raw data at face value, it can be used very effectively in developing trends. For example, the data obtained from each meeting of a particular committee could indicate deterioration or growth in the potential of that particular committee.

Similarly, data obtained for the same leader in different situations may provide interesting information as to where that individual can be most effective. A simple trend form could be constructed by plotting rating form scales over time as illustrated in Figure 6.6.

Notes

1 Daniel Katz and Robert L. Kahn, *The Social Psychology of Organizations,* 2nd ed. (New York: John Wiley & Sons, 1978), p.30.

2 Corwin P. King, 'Decisions by Discussion: The Uses and Abuses of Team Problem Solving,' *S.A.M. Advanced Management Journal,* Autumn 1976, p. 33.

3 Lester Coch and John P. French, Jr., 'Overcoming Resistance to Change,' *Human Relations,* 1 (1948), pp. 512–532.

4 Reprinted from Van Bergen, Clarence W. and Kirk, Raymond J. 'Groupthink: When Too Many Heads Spoil the Decision,' *Management Review,* March 1978 (New York: AMACOM, a division of American Management Associations) p. 46.

5 Dorwin Cartwright and Alvin Zander, eds., *Group Dynamics: Theory and Research,* 3rd ed. (New York: Harper & Row, 1968).

6 Richard J. Dunsing, 'You and I Have Simply Got to Stop Meeting This Way' (Part 1), *Supervisory Management,* September 1976, p. 9.

7 Theodore Caplow, *How to Run Any Organization* (Hinsdale, Ill.: Dryden Press, 1976), p. 59.

8 Ralph M. Stogdill, *Handbook of Leadership* (New York: Free Press, 1974), pp. 81–82.

9 David R. Hampton, Charles E. Summer, and Ross A. Webber, *Organizational Behavior and the Practice of Management,* 3rd ed. (Glenview, Ill.: Scott, Foresman 1978), p.597.

10 John Geier, 'A Trait Approach to the Study of Leadership,' *Journal of Communication,* 17 (1967), pp. 316–323.

11 Fred E. Fiedler, *A Theory of Leadership Effectiveness* (New York: McGraw-Hill, 1967), p. 13.

12 Paul Hersey and Kenneth H. Blanchard, *Management of Organizational Behavior*, 3rd ed. (Englewood Cliffs, N.J.: Prentice-Hall, 1977), p. 165.

13 *Ibid.*

14 Leland Bradford, *Making Meetings Work* (La Jolla, Calif.: University Associates, 1976), pp. 11–12.

15 Franklin S. Haiman, *Group Leadership and Democratic Action* (Boston: Houghton Mifflin, 1951), pp. 38–39.

16 R. Victor Harnack and Thorrel B. Fest, *Group Discussion: Theory and Technique* (New York: Appleton-Century-Crofts, 1964), pp. 66–67.

17 Alex F. Osborn, *Applied Imagination: Principles and Procedures of Creative Thinking* (New York: Scribner's, 1953), pp. 300–301.

18 Elliott A. Pood, Assistant Professor of Communication at the University of North Carolina at Greensboro. Interview, March, 1979.

19 Dunsing, 'You and I Have Simply Got to Stop Meeting This Way' (Part 2) *Supervisory Management,* October 1976, p. 12.

Recommended Reading

Although there is a wealth of printed material available dealing with small group communication, the items listed below are those I have found to be particularly useful to the practicing manager. Each of them has a very practical orientation. Each can provide some tips on making meetings more effective.

Bradford, Leland P., *Making Meetings Work,* La Jolla, Calif.: University Associates, 1976. Bradford combines his extensive experience in educational psychology and training to produce a very useful, readable guide for leaders and group members. The book elaborates on many of the points covered in this chapter; in addition, it shows the reader how to be effective in larger meetings. His chapters on giving a large assembly the qualities of small group meetings, and planning the work group conference give additional insights that may be useful to the manager. Several appendices at the end of the book provide alternatives to the diagnostic techniques I have suggested.

Dunsing, Richard J., 'You and I Have Simply Got to Stop Meeting This Way,' *Supervisory Management,* September 1976-February 1977. This six-part series by Professor Dunsing is especially enjoyable to read and full of good information on meetings. The first three sections discuss problems that typically arise with the meeting format. In Part 4 he details analyses and diagnoses of your meetings. In Parts 5 and 6, he identifies changes that leaders can make in organisations as well as changes that individual participants can make. These are some of the most interesting and well-written articles I've seen on the topic of effective meetings. I highly recommend you looking at this material.

Caplow, Theodore, *How to Run Any Organisation: Manual of Practical Sociology,* Hinsdale Ill.: Dryden Press, 1976. As Caplow's title implies, this is a very practical orientation to being effective in leading organisations. One chapter of this book deals specifically with communication.

Jay, Anthony, 'How to Run a Meeting,' *Harvard Business Review,* 54, (March-April 1976), pp. 43-57. This excellent article illustrates the kinds of things that can go wrong in meetings and how to put them right.

RESOURCE 4.1

▷ RESOURCE 4.2
Paul Bray, *The Daily Telegraph*, 7 May 1996

The Long and the Short of the CV

We British go terribly coy when it comes to selling ourselves to a prospective employer. Paul Bray tells you how to get it right.

Your curriculum vitae may be the most important document you ever write.

Competition is stiff, and your CV may have just 30 seconds to impress a harassed personnel officer before being passed over.

Being modest to a fault, the British find CV-writing a trial. 'It isn't easy to write a CV. It's a sales document, and the thing it's selling is you', says Rob Reason, director of recruitment specialists, Reason International.

A CV has one function – to get you an interview – so keep it short. Not everyone does. 'We get CVs where people put their weight, height, the names of their children and append their swimming certificates,' says Robbie Cowling, a director of Jobserve, another firm of recruitment specialists. 'We once received a 46-page CV.'

Three pages is the optimum. Anything longer will not be read; anything shorter and you look inexperienced.

Customise your CV for each job application. Begin with a summary page, giving name, address, phone number, qualifications, a one-paragraph summary of yourself, your achievements and aspirations, and a list of half a dozen relevant skills.

Pages two and three should list your career history, in reverse chronological order. Give most space to your most recent or most relevant experience. Jobs more than 10 years ago can be summarised in one line. Focus on your achievements and managerial experience as well as technical skills.

Education details can be brief: the number of O-levels passed, A levels with subjects and grades, and the subject and class of degrees or equivalent. Only include training courses if relevant. There is no need to supply referees or salary details.

Presentation is as *important* as content.; 'If you get 4,000 CVs, you tend to look at the most appealing' says Ted Giles, a director of The Agency Partnership. 'The best person for the job may end up in the reject pile because their CV wasn't well enough presented.'

Handwritten CVs are out, as are old CVs with handwritten updates. At the other extreme, multimedia CVs featuring sound and video clips are over the top for most jobs. A word processor is best, but a typewriter is acceptable. Either way, grammar, spelling and good layout are most important.

The trickiest issue is those things we would rather a potential employer did not know: being sacked; unemployment; a criminal conviction; advanced age or lack of experience.

'You mustn't lie, but you can polish the truth', says Giles. 'Don't give them reason to reject you. If you don't have to say it, just leave it out.'

A few months' unemployment can be fudged by giving dates only in years, not months.

It is unwise to write that you were sacked or have a criminal record, but failure to reveal this might cost you the job later on. Best to volunteer the information at the end of the interview.

Age is difficult to hide. If your career history extends back to 1996, no one will assume you are 28. However, some over-40's have found that fudging their age at least gets them an interview. But do not claim experience you do not have.

Finally, include a line or two on your interests and hobbies, especially if they demonstrate achievement. One woman listed under 'successes' the fact that she had once saved a man from drowning. She got the job.